CHRIST AMONG US

CHRIST AMONG US

A Modern Presentation
of the
Catholic Faith

(Third Revised Edition)

by
ANTHONY J. WILHELM

PAULIST PRESS
New York/Ramsey

Nihil Obstat:
Rev. Charles W. Gusmer
Censor Librorum

Imprimatur:
Most Rev. Peter L. Gerety, D.D.
Archbishop of Newark

July 27, 1981

Library of Congress
Catalog Card Number: 72-86595

ISBN: 0-8091-2410-6

Published by Paulist Press
545 Island Road, Ramsey, N.J. 07446

Printed and bound in the
United States of America

Contents

Preface 1

1. Our Life and God 5
    Something to Live For, 5—How People Come to Know
    God, 7—What Is Necessary to Know God, 8—What Can
    We Say about God?, 12—Daily Living: Prayer—Our Con-
    tact with God, 15

2. God's Plan for Us Begins with Creation 19
    The Source of Our Story, 19—Human Beginnings, 22—
    What Are We?, 23—Other Worlds, Angels and Devils, 26
    —Daily Living: Worshipping Our Creator, 28

3. God's Gift of Himself and Our Rejection of Him 33
    God's Great Gift and His Desire for Man, 33—Man's Re-
    jection of God's Love, 35—Facing Our Sins, 39—God's
    Plan of Greater Love, 40—Daily Living: God's Constant
    Helps, 41

4. God's Plan Unfolds in the Old Testament 44
    The Great People of the Covenant, 44—The Making of the
    Old Covenant, 48—Daily Living: Meeting God, 53

5. Priests, Kings and Prophets Prepare the Way 56
    Sacrifices, Priests and Kings, 56—The Prophets, 59—Daily
    Living: Our Faith Expressed by Reverence and Worship, 64

6. Christ Comes Among Us 67
    The Coming of Jesus Christ, 67—The Kingdom of God Is
    Here!, 73—The Promised Messiah—and His Rejection, 75
    —Daily Living: The Life of His Kingdom Is Love, 78

7. **Christ Reveals to Us the Father, the Spirit and Himself ....** **82**
Our Father, 82—The Human Son, One of Us, 83—The Divine Son, 85—The Holy Spirit, 93—Daily Living: Our Dignity as Bearers of the Trinity and Brothers and Sisters of Christ, 98

8. **Christ Saves Us by His Death and Resurrection** **102**
In Christ We Died and Rose Again, 102—Through Christ's Perfect Worship We Can Now Reach God, 105—The New and Unending Covenant of Love, 106—What This Cost and Why, 108—Christ Is in Glory Among Us, 112—Daily Living: Our Attitude toward Sin and Suffering, 117

9. **Christ Sends the Holy Spirit to Form His Church** **122**
The Spirit Forms God's New People, 122—The Community of the Spirit, 124—A Unified, Universal Community, 125—Union with Christ Among Us, 129—Daily Living: Loving Our Fellow Members of Christ and All Men, 133

10. **Those Who Serve as Our Guides** **136**
Christ Chooses the Apostles and Peter, 136—The College of Bishops, 140—The Papacy, 143—The Gifts of All to Serve All, 147—The Gift of Infallibility, 149—Daily Living: Our Attitude toward Authority, 154

11. **The Great Book in Which We Meet God** **158**
The Bible, God's Word and Man's Too, 158—The Bible's Origin and Development, 162—The Church's Tradition Interprets the Bible, 168—An Outline of the Bible, 171—Daily Living: The Bible in Our Life, 175

12. **The Great Signs in Which We Meet God** **179**
The Sacred Liturgy, Christ's Signs of Love, 179—The Sacramentals—Reaching Out for Christ, 183—Christ's Seven Sacraments—Our Great, Intimate Contacts with Him, 185 —Word and Sacrament, 191—Daily Living: Signs of God's Presence, 191

13. Christ Unites Us to Himself By Baptism 194
What Christ Does for Us in Baptism, 194—Who Can Be Baptized?, 198 —Conversion, 202—The Christian Initiation of Adults, 204—The Majority Who Are Not Baptized, 209—Daily Living: Renewing Our Baptismal Conversion, 212

14. Our Worship Together: The Mass 215
Why We Gather Together to Worship, 215—Christ Gathers Us to Share in His Greatest Action, 216—This Is Our Covenant Meal, 219— . . . And Our Perfect Sacrifice, 221 —The Mass Is God's Word, Our Gift, And His Gift, 223 —Daily Living: The Mass And Our Daily Life, 230

15. The Eucharist in Christ's Church Today 232
How the Mass Developed, 232—The Mass and Christian Unity, 237—Christ Among Us at Mass, 239—The Christian People at Mass, 241—Reliving Christ's Life through the Liturgical Year, 244—Christ Among Us in the Eucharist, 248—Daily Living: One Bread Makes Us One Body, 253

16. The Inner Life of a Christian 256
Faith—Acceptance and Commitment, 256—How One Comes to Faith, 259—Doubting, Growing, Returning to Faith, 262—Hope—A Confident Expectation, 264—Love—The One Thing Necessary, 265—Christian Prayer, 269—Daily Living: Love in Our Life, 274

17. Our Christian Presence in the World 278
Our Christian Presence of Service, 278—The Dignity and Sacredness of Each Human Life, 279—Our Christian Commitment to Justice, 282—Our Christian Commitment to Peace, 286—Christ Sends Us the Holy Spirit in Confirmation, 289—Daily Living: Being Open to the Spirit, Peaceful and Prodding, 295

18. Sin and What It Can Do to Us 299
Sin in Our Life, 299—Judging the Seriousness of Sin, 301—

The Concept of Hell, 305—Making Up for Sin, 307—Daily Living: Overcoming Sin, 309

19. **The Christian's Continuing Conversion** 314
Our Need of Continual Conversion, 314—God Wants to Forgive Our Sins, 314—Christ Forgives and Reconciles through His Church, 316—Sorrow, the One Thing Necessary, 319—The Rite of Reconciliation, 321—Daily Living: Doing Penance for Our Sins, 325

20. **When Illness Comes to a Christian** 328
The Power of Sickness over Us, 328—Christ's Power over Sickness, 329—The Anointing of the Sick, 329—Daily Living: Our Attitude toward Sickness, 333

21. **Christ Joins a Man and Woman in Marriage** 336
Why Marriage?, 336—What Is Christian Marriage?, 337—Before Marriage, 343—How to Get Married, 347—Creative, Responsible Married Love, 349—Christian Family Life Day by Day, 357—What of Interfaith Marriages?, 360

22. **The Family That Is the Church** 367
God's Gifted People, 367—Priests, God's Instruments at the Service of Men, 369—The Role of Religious, 378—Our Bishop and Our Diocese, 380—The Emerging Role of Women in the Church, 384—Daily Living: The Matter of Vocation, 386

23. **The Greater Family to Which We Belong** 389
The Saints: Our Models and Intercessors, 389—God's Mother and Ours, 392—Mary, First Among Christians, 394—Daily Living: The Spur of Sanctity, 397

24. **Christ's Church in the World Today** 400
Christ's Church Is Divine, 400—Catholic Christian Education—Sharing the Good News and a Way of Life, 405—Whether or Not to Join the Church, 406—Christ's Church Is Human, 408—Reconciling the Divided Church and a Divided World, 413 —The Church's Mission of Loving Ser-

vice in Today's World, 424—Daily Living: The Compassionate Church, 427

25. Living Daily the Christian Life..**431**
How Do We Know How to Live?, 431—Our Home Life,
433—Our Work or School Life, 436—Our Social Life,
437—Our Religious Life, 439

26. Fulfillment Forever **443**
Our Meeting with Christ at Death, 443—Purgatory: The
Idea of Accountability, 445—At the End, 449—The New
Universe toward Which We Work, 451—Heaven, Our Destiny, 452—Daily Living: The Difference in Being a Christian, 456

Index **460**

Preface

In the history of mankind there have been a few truly unique moments and special places—occasions when men of stature claimed an encounter with one who is beyond, a divine, transcendent reality.

On these occasions great movements have started that have affected billions of human lives and have changed our world. They have given men hope, courage, compassion, and led them to dream of life beyond.

This is the story of the farthest-reaching claim to contact with divinity in human history. It is a story of real men and actual events—some of the most striking men and most moving events of all time. It is particularly the story of the one who has been called history's outstanding personality, Jesus Christ.

We offer here that to which countless billions, like St. Paul, have dedicated their lives:

> To announce the secret hidden for long ages and through many generations, but now disclosed to God's people . . . to make known how rich and glorious it is among all nations. The secret is this: *Christ in you—among you the hope of glory to come* (Colossians 1, 26–27).

This story of Christ among us is a study of Catholic faith. Catholicism had a Council several years ago, as almost everyone knows, and the Church today is different. We hope that the image and personality of Christ will now begin to shine more clearly through us poor humans who are the Church.

Today while many feel that God is a dead issue in their lives, others believe that this story can—and has—changed their lives. Many of these feel that the Church is now in its most unsettling but promising period since the beginning of institutional Christianity. Perhaps the reader (particularly one who has heard the story before) will find in this contemporary presentation a new hope and a new purpose.

For one who comes to this book seeking something, only two things are necessary: an open mind and a willingness to take a risk.

An open mind, because unless one is open and true to oneself, life is a waste. A willingness to take a risk because one may come to believe. The believer becomes changed. Many things may have to be renounced and life itself staked upon something unseen. Friends, even loved ones, often do not understand. This can be deeply upsetting. But unless it is tried, one will never know the fulfillment it can bring.

The sensation of a swim in cool water cannot be explained to someone who is unwilling to plunge in. A beautiful house cannot be appreciated by looking at it only from a distance. The experience of love can never be had by one who is unwilling to risk loving. So, too, the deep joys of belief and divine love come only to one who is willing to try—to read, to persevere, to practice as best he can.

Some Words about Using This Book. . . .
(especially for those who will use it as a guide in teaching others)
We have tried to make this book . . .

Useful for different types of people: The sentences in bold print give a summary of the paragraph following. One who wants merely to skim can read these. The paragraphs in small print are for those who want to go more deeply into a particular subject; these may be referred to later, for instance during a catechumenate, when more detailed information is desired. If this book is used as the source for a class presentation, chapters can be combined as one presentation.

Progressive: One thing builds on another, and important themes are repeated so their meaning will be grasped more fully. The DISCUSSION at the end of each chapter is meant not only to help one grasp the point of the chapter, but to stimulate to further insights. The sections entitled FURTHER READING and FURTHER VIEWING/LISTENING give suggestions for current books, movies and cassettes pertaining to the subject matter of the particular chapter; the titles given are not meant to be an exhaustive list but only representative ones that have come to the author's attention. The asterisks marking book titles mean: * good general treatment for anyone; ** for those who want to go a bit deeper.

Relevant to daily life: Each chapter has a section called DAILY LIVING. This contains practical applications of the preceding teaching. The moral teaching of the Church is integrated into these sections, instead of being left to the end of the book. The PERSONAL REFLECTION which ends each chapter gives the reader a chance to do something about what he has read.

Post-Conciliar: This is a presentation of Catholic Christianity as it has emerged from Vatican Council II, the great event in the Church of our century. The teachings of the Council form the basis of what is presented here, but we have also included many theological and pastoral developments since the Council.

Scriptural: The bible is the great legacy of all Christianity; there is no better way to learn Christ's teaching than through its words. Whenever possible, therefore, this book teaches from the bible. The use of a bible with this book is necessary. The Revised Standard Version, with the Apocrypha, has been used for most of the quotations herein.

Liturgical: The liturgy of the Church sums up its purpose on earth; it is the great way we make contact with God in the Church. Sections called IN THE LITURGY are incorporated throughout the book, so the reader can see how our worship expresses our belief.

Ecumenical: Among the greatest achievements of our time is that of Christian groups coming to appreciate one another, and a growing mutual respect among all men of good will. This book has tried whenever possible to present our common Christian teaching, and to give what is specifically Catholic as positively as possible while showing an appreciation of other viewpoints, non-Christian as well as Christian.

Transitional and Tentative: We ask those who use this book to bear in mind that this is an interim effort. It might well be an overly audacious, even foolhardy attempt to speak about God and his revelation at a time when Christianity is undergoing a universal questioning and its theology a massive reconstruction.

Not long ago we could confidently set down volumes of precise information about God and his wishes for us. Today nothing is more apparent than that we know very little indeed. No one is more aware of this than the author. But many people have expressed the need for a book like this—a one-volume, adult-level presentation of our beliefs and practices at this moment in our post-conciliar, pilgrim Church. The author would be grateful for any comments and suggestions for improvement.

A work of many: In this age when we are again discovering ourselves as one Christian family, when collegiality and dialogue have been flourishing, the author has had the help and guidance of many wonderful people. He is particularly indebted to priest friends and colleagues in the Christian ministry, especially the many Paulist Fathers, and to the priests, religious, and lay people of Minneapolis-St. Paul, San Francisco, Oakland, Berkeley, and Nevada who have been so helpful. A special acknowledgement must be given for the generous, unstinting help of so many associated with Berkeley's Graduate Theological Union.

The patient insightfulness of those at the Paulist Center in San Francisco, the San Ysidro Shop in Oakland, and Berkeley's Newman Hall is also acknowledged. Special gratitude is due to the Camaldolese hermits of Immaculate Heart Monastery for their prayerful guidance, to Rev. Clifford and Ethel Elizabeth Crummey for always being there, and to Fr. Kevin Lynch and the Paulist Press editorial board for valor beyond the call of duty.

1
Our Life and God

What is life all about? Is there a God? If there is a God, does he care about us? Can I make contact with God? To answer these questions, we begin with something all men seek . . .

SOMETHING TO LIVE FOR

If there is one thing that men seek from life, it is fulfillment. We need a purpose, something to live for, a goal that will truly fulfill us and bring us happiness.

Many live for a successful marriage and a good home; some want a pleasant job with financial security; some seek power, some a life of pleasure and leisure, or friends and social position.

Many today, including many younger people, find their purpose in the service of others. In this age of great social change and consequent confusion these highly motivated individuals are bringing about great good in our world.

Yet we must acknowledge that none of these things can completely satisfy our aspirations. No matter what we have, there is always something else we want. We also realize that these things cannot give us lasting and secure happiness, nor a lasting sense of accomplishment, for human weakness, tragedy or death can destroy what we have. "Man is like a breath; his days like a passing shadow" (Psalm 144, 4).

The conviction of the Christian believer is that two thousand years ago Jesus Christ revealed to us an ultimate purpose to our life: to live forever with God after death. We know that our greatest happiness in this life comes from love. From childhood everyone has an insatiable desire to love and be loved. Our happiness in human love, Christ tells us, is but a dim reflection of the immense, unending joy of loving God and being loved by him forever.

Jesus told us that this unending life of happiness after death is such as we could not even begin to dream of. It is as if someone lived his life in a closed room, never seeing or hearing anything outside. Then one day someone opened the door to the outside and showed him the world with its marvels. Christ did this for us, but he revealed that our destiny is infinitely more wonderful—so staggering that we can grasp it only bit by bit.

Jesus told us that we begin our life of love and happiness with God while still here on earth. But this happiness is different from what many people think. It does not come from satisfying our desire for pleasure or material things or social achievement. It comes from truly loving, and often involves suffering and sacrifice. It is realistic. It brings, not freedom from pain, but a deep peace and sense of fulfillment even in the midst of pain.

Jesus showed us how to get along with others and how to bear sufferings and frustration. He told us and showed us what we can do about our loneliness and fears, our guilt and uneasiness, and how to have true peace and security.

Jesus revealed that God has a plan by which we are to share in his love and happiness, in other words, that there is a meaning to human history. He told us not only that we have a place in God's plan, but that (as is becoming more apparent today) the working out of this plan depends on us, on our free cooperation with God as co-authors of history. Jesus' great follower, St. Paul, put it this way:

> To me, though I am the very least of all the saints, this grace was given, to preach to the Gentiles the unsearchable riches of Christ, and to make all men see what is the plan of the mystery hidden for ages in God who created all things; that through the Church the manifold wisdom of God might now be made known. . . . This was according to the eternal purpose which he has realized in Christ Jesus our Lord (Ephesians 3, 8–11).

The unique claim that Jesus made for his teaching was that he has a special knowledge of God and his plan for us, and that he alone can lead us to God. He said that he was sent by God, and is, in fact, God's only Son: "I am the way, and the truth, and the life. No one comes to the Father but through me" (John 14, 5).

Therefore the story of Jesus' teaching and God's plan begins with God himself . . .

HOW PEOPLE COME TO KNOW GOD

People come to a realization of God in countless ways. These are some of them:

Some have grown from childhood with a knowledge of God, are accustomed to pray and to make God a part of their thoughts and decisions.

Some reflect on the course of their life, and have an unshakable conviction of God's providence watching over them. Particularly in times of crisis, they realize, someone was there who heard and understood.

Some find God's presence in nature—in hills and mountains, a peaceful lake, an expanse of sky, there comes the conviction of someone. A few might come closest while caught up in a moving piece of music, in the contemplation of an art masterpiece, or something similar.

Some are convinced that they have had an experience of God—shattering, unforgettable, overwhelmingly joyous and unifying, giving great peace and absolute certainty, profoundly affecting their lives yet unexplainable to others. Many who testify to this—and it is rarely and with great reluctance that they do so—are balanced, successful, and credible people.

Some come to God through their desire for perfect love. We know that everyone from childhood has a strong need of understanding affection, perhaps accentuated by suffering or continual frustration. Yet we know that every human love has weaknesses and will eventually disappoint us. We then look to someone, beyond this life, who will never fail us, who can perfectly understand us and fulfill our aspirations and our desire for love.

Some are helped by demonstrations from reason for God's reality. For example, an enormously complicated space satellite cannot make itself and launch itself into orbit. It has to be designed, built, and launched by intelligent human beings. Our world and the countless stars act according to amazingly consistent laws in a universe that is far more complicated than any satellite. The vast universe must, therefore, have been planned and made by one of supreme intelligence and power. This one we call God.

Reasoning like this, "circumstantial evidence," might show some the need for a limitless, timeless force sustaining the universe. But God himself must give us an insight into himself if we are ever to know him as close, personal, interested, loving.

Some are helped by those they love who are lovers of God. The example of the deep faith of their friend or beloved, its effect on that one's life, and the generous love it seems to produce may gradually open the seekers to the divine lover.

Many cannot express why they believe in God or what he is to them. They are instinctively dumb before this unfathomable mystery. Even a master of language like Cardinal Newman said of this: ". . . words are such poor vehicles for what my mind holds and my heart believes." Perhaps the greatest obstacle a believer encounters in expressing his belief to an unbeliever—or even to himself—is the inability to communicate in understandable concepts.

> Seeking God is for many like peering through a fog to see if there is a house at a particular spot; often all we catch is a glimpse, confused, uncertain. We never see God. But most of us reach certainty about him by a "cumulation of converging probabilities" which can give not just an opinion, but the deepest conviction. Some never attain this deepest conviction but seem permitted by God to remain in a state of constant quest. In the search for truth it is perhaps not important how many fragments of the staggering whole a man manages to perceive during his lifetime, but the courage and openness with which he continues his search.
>
> *As one moves toward truth he may come to realize that he is as much being sought as seeking,* that the truth he seeks, the God he would love, is already deeply within him, soliciting his love. He comes to realize his conviction of this all along: one who becomes convinced of God could never recognize him unless he had somehow known him before.

WHAT IS NECESSARY TO KNOW GOD

As in any honest pursuit, we must be open to truth, not only the truth of absolute values but also the truth about ourselves, who we are and what we want ultimately from the experience of life. This requires courage, a willingness to be threatened by often unpleasant truth. The man who is self-assertive, self-satisfied, will have no reason to push out beyond himself in search of a higher good.

We must be willing to take time to question, observe, reflect. In our achievement-oriented society, particularly, it is hard for one to devote time to reflecting on ultimate values. Even when the satisfaction of achievement fails one and all one's striving seems useless, the consideration of a possible God behind it all is usually rejected as a demeaning crutch.

We must be open to our fellow men and treat them as our conscience demands, with dignity and justice. The mature person sees that in each man there is a spark, however dim, of enduring goodness. This spark is the divine within each man, and if one is ever to find God he must recognize and respect this spark in others. The one who is fundamentally turned in on himself, who seeks only his own good, will inevitably find only himself.

Christians believe that God has revealed—and is revealing—himself to men and that one must investigate this claim of revelation if one is to find God as he has shown himself to us. This seems logical to the Christian; if there is an infinite one, we who are finite cannot grasp him unless he reveals himself to us. Thus, although not all men will find God's revelation, it is the highest logic to search for it.

However, to meet God as he has revealed himself—to realize he is there—he must give us faith, the power to recognize him, the intuitive grasp of his reality. Ultimately whether one is a believer or an unbeliever depends on God. This explains why some find God, while others of equal intelligence and good will do not.

Today particularly many feel that God is missing from our world. Caught up by scientific advances and a technology by which man seems able to solve his own problems, a search for God seems to many irrelevant and meaningless. Unbelief is for many the accepted position today. Even some who consider themselves Christians say that we must live as if "God is dead."

> Unlike former days, the denial of God or of religion, or the abandonment of them, is no longer an unusual and individual occurrence. Today it is not rare for such things to be presented as requirements of scientific progress or of a certain new humanism (*Pastoral Constitution on the Church in the Modern World,* no. 7).

Why does not God make himself unmistakably known to all men? Today God is certainly not showing himself to us in any tangible way; he is not at all apparent to the great majority of men. One can only speculate about the meaning of this, but a reason might lie in the true Christian view of God—that far from being a Supreme One who demands that we acknowledge him and give him our obeisance, God is one who is truly among us loving us with great and intimate tenderness, soliciting our free response of love.

Why are many people unable to find God? Some seem unable to detach themselves from the pursuit of modern false gods: money, social status, power, pleasure. As long as one primarily seeks these, he will never find the living and true God.

Even the person of great good will who is continually occupied with material things—for example, the world of science or business—must expect difficulty in coming to realize spiritual reality, however noble his daily pursuits may be. To come to realize God takes time and persevering effort.

Some project a distorted image of God which pictures him as a disinterested power, perhaps capricious, even vengeful. These usually have not had the proper kind of love in their lives, may have experienced much seemingly meaningless suffering, and so cannot accept a loving God. They have never experienced the love they have been told God is—and perhaps they have experienced the unlovingness of those who claim to be friends of God.

The Vatican Council says of this:

Some . . . seem more inclined to affirm man than to deny God. Again, some form for themselves such a fallacious idea of God that when they repudiate this figment, they are by no means rejecting the God of the Gospel. . . . Moreover, atheism results not rarely from a violent protest against the evil in this world. . . . Believers can have more than a little to do with the birth of atheism. To the extent that they neglect their own training in the faith, or teach erroneous doctrine, or are deficient in their religious, moral or social life, they . . . conceal rather than reveal the authentic face of God and religion (Vatican Council II, *The Church in the Modern World,* no. 19).

One perceptive modern author writes:

One of the greatest obstacles to belief in God is the complacency of believers. It is not the adulterers, the takers of bribes, the licentious, whose conduct induces disbelief. It is the righteous, the solid citizens, the people of good reputation in the community. Such believers show few signs of ever having encountered the terrifying God; nor do they appear to live in that cold night of belief in which he is most truly found. Their god seems to be an idol, the idol of habit, routine, sentiment, and self-congratulation. By their words and actions, they treat God as a vague guarantor of the good order which makes them secure. He is the projection of that superego which keeps them conscientious when no one is looking. In his name, they dare to preach mere law and order, rather than also the freedom and inquiry through which the living God is found. Their god is the dead god of the middle classes (Novak, *Belief and Unbelief,* p. 182).

It seems that after a certain point in life one does not change one's basic position from belief to unbelief, or from unbelief to belief. This point seems to be the late teens or early twenties, or it may be even earlier, by the time of adolescence. Some believers may doubt after this, even consider themselves unbelievers, but this is usually a temporary state.

Many young people must go through a rejection—or better, a testing— of the authority structures of their life: their home, their religion, their belief in God, etc. This experience seems necessary for most thinking young people, and some older ones as well, that they might arrive at a more mature faith and one to which they are personally committed.

It is the believer's conviction that many seek God—and find him in the depths of their being—without realizing it: some through their unrelenting pursuit of truth, justice, the good of the community, or another humanitarian ideal—and many through their insatiable thirst for love. They are never satisfied. Through their total commitment to a transcendent idea they are, to the believer, reaching the absolute we call God.

Some have a radical dissatisfaction with any human accomplishment, are unfulfilled by any human love. Nothing any longer impresses them. Even the wonderful interchange and intimacy of human love at its deepest level only elicits in them a further desire, one that cannot be satisfied.

Sometimes, perceiving no end to their quest, they lapse into a seeming cynicism, take refuge in flippancy or strike out against the believer—but to the discerning believer their reaction is only the measure of their unknowing love, a love that might be far greater than his. The believer must always pray, "O God, some know and serve you as truth, honor, integrity, service . . . as well as I, and perhaps better. . . ."

It seems, too, that the unbeliever has a providential role toward the believer, one of challenging him to consider aspects of God that he might otherwise forget: God is truly inaccessible and incomprehensible; we are totally dependent on his revelation of himself and can never take for granted that we know much at all about him and his will for us.

The committed believer and unbeliever then have much in common. Both are dedicated seekers of truth. Both seek in darkness—to both God is an absence, one who is not there, for he is not an object to be found. Yet he is there, for both believer and unbeliever have an objective in their lifelong striving—though called different names, conceptualized differently, by each. To both, then, God is a presence and an absence, one who is there and one who is not there.

The constant temptation of the believer is to fabricate for himself a God with whom he will be comfortable, who will not too much upset his life, with whom he can come to terms once and for all. When doubts come, or new and unsettling views about God, this type of believer becomes confused, perhaps resentful that his faith should be a struggle instead of a secure refuge. Some of these who consider themselves believers, it is evident, have simply never known the living God.

> We cannot believe in God once-for-all any more than we can exist once-for-all. Faith must always realize itself, and yet must always remain unrealized. If so, it must *beware* of seeking rest if it should feel the fatigue of self-exertion, as must he who, tired of existence, imagined he could find repose outside it (Dewart, *The Future of Belief,* p. 65).

Doubts about God, then, must be expected even by believers who try to know and love him faithfully. Faith must grow, and growth is often uncertain, painful. Those who tell us of overwhelming, rapturous experiences of God also testify to states of "darkness" and terrible doubt during which God is no longer a reality. God is utterly silent—and such a state may last for years.

The believer must try to deepen his faith, learn more, live his faith more fully—or else he might lose his ability to experience belief. He cannot consider himself superior to his unbelieving friend, as if his own faith could never slip away into obscurity. He must recognize that his faith is a free gift of God to which he must continually and freely commit himself. Humbly he must say daily, "Lord, I do believe—help my unbelief!"

WHAT CAN WE SAY ABOUT GOD?

We can learn something about God from examining the universe about us. As we learn of the skill of an artist or builder by examining his work, so we can learn about God through the universe he has made. We can come to grasp something of his power, vastness, beauty. "Ever since the creation of the world his invisible nature, namely, his eternal power and deity, has been clearly perceived in the things that have been made" (Romans 1, 20).

The Judaeo-Christian belief is that God has himself told us some-

thing about himself, revealed himself to us. He has done this in many ways, but particularly to the Israelites of the Old Testament. For example, over three thousand years ago he revealed himself to Moses as the living, all-pervading God: **Read Exodus 3, 2–6 and 13–14.**

God is "wholly other," transcendent, infinitely holy. Those to whom he has revealed himself have often testified to a feeling of utter awe, wonderment, profound abasement, a sort of "holy terror" in his presence. Thus the Jewish prophet Isaiah tried to describe his experience of God: **Read Isaiah 6, 1–7.** Moses' experience is also primitive but striking: **Read Exodus 33, 18–23.**

God has revealed that he is a loving, personal God, concerned with each of us. He loves each of us, believer and unbeliever, in a way that he loves nothing else in creation. We will see how he shows himself to be good, kind, patient and faithful. As the Jews of the Old Testament came to realize this, they compared God to a shepherd who carefully guides his helpless sheep, to a good king, a loving father, a mother: "Can a woman forget her sucking child, that she should have no compassion on the son of her womb? Even these may forget, yet I will not forget you" (Isaiah 49, 15).

God's ultimate revelation of himself was through his own Son, Jesus Christ. This is the uniquely Christian view of God—that he has a Son, Jesus Christ, and that this Son has come among us as a man. "In many and various ways God spoke of old to our fathers by the prophets, but in these last days he has spoken to us by a Son. . . ." (Hebrews 1, 1–2).

Jesus teaches us what God is by calling him our Father. He is a Father who has not only given us life but who loves each of us with a limitless love, cares for us each day, and wants us to live happily with him forever. He is a merciful Father, always ready with his forgiveness for us—as long as we are willing to forgive others. The Lord's Prayer, taught us by Jesus, beautifully expresses this:

> Our Father, who art in heaven, hallowed be thy name. Thy kingdom come, thy will be done on earth as it is in heaven. Give us this day our daily bread, and forgive us our trespasses as we forgive those who trespass against us. And lead us not into temptation, but deliver us from evil. Amen.

God reveals himself, we shall see later, as a loving "family" of three Persons who draw us to themselves, to share their happiness. God is not just Father but also Son and Holy Spirit, to each of whom we have a special relationship of love. This paradox of one God who is yet three Persons is the mystery of the Trinity, discussed in chapter 7.

God respects each of us—our freedom, our dignity, our person—because he loves each of us. Though many are not yet aware of this, God enters into a most intimate "I-Thou" relationship with each of us. He calls each of us by our own name. Rather than absorbing us into himself, the God of our Judaeo-Christian revelation enables each of us to develop to our utmost as a person—even as he unites us most intimately with himself. To this paradox the greatest mystics testify.

God has revealed that even the sufferings of innocent people are somehow working out for the eventual happiness of us all. Though we cannot yet understand how, the wars, crimes, and terrible injustices of human history are somehow a part of his plan of sharing with us his love and happiness. Our vision is finite, it sees only the moment of this life—nothing, really, in comparison with an eternity of happiness (though we must be expected to cry out for an explanation while we are here below). We shall see, later, when we consider Jesus and his great work for us, more about the meaning of suffering.

A mind-boggling view of God is presented to us today by process theology which says, briefly, that God is so involved in our human situation that he actually suffers and rejoices with us, in other words, he experiences with us the daily working out of our destiny, with all its hopes and fears, joys and sorrows. God need not have done this, but he loves us so much that he wills to become this involved in the human process.

Ultimately, while we can know that God is—that we are in contact with him, that he is present to us—we cannot know what he is. We seek him, and try to apply to him our poor human categories, but he is "totally other," and all our speculations must ultimately end in awesome ignorance. He is always a hidden God.

Therefore we must expect to find mysteries in our study of God and religion—things about which we can know very little, or which make little sense to us. When we think that we understand him, or when we confidently predict his actions, then we are in trouble.

O the depth of the riches and wisdom and knowledge of God! How un-searchable are his judgments and how inscrutable his ways! For who has known the mind of the Lord. . . . (Romans 11, 33–34)?

DAILY LIVING: PRAYER—OUR CONTACT WITH GOD

To come to know God as he really is, and to experience his love for us, it is absolutely necessary to try to contact him. This is prayer . . .

It is necessary for each person to try to pray. Others might testify about their knowledge of God, what he is like, but each person must form his own acquaintance with God. We might hear much about a wonderful person from those who have met him, but we will never really know that person until we have met him and communicated with him ourselves.

Just as every genuine human love relationship is unique and can be fully experienced only by the lovers themselves, so each person's love relationship with God is unique, can be achieved by him alone, and cannot be communicated adequately to anyone else. If one remains aloof, waiting for God to come to him without trying to reach God, he will never know God any more than he could know another person whom he treated in this way.

The few whose persistent prayer has led them to experience a love affair with the living God know that it can be a terrifying, totally demanding, unbelievably fulfilling, fantastically wonderful thing. Most of us will not—perhaps cannot—bring ourselves to risk such an experience. But if we are wise we will not reject what these lovers of the divine have to say. We will listen to their insights, for they might be of immense help to us all as we struggle enmeshed in our human condition. They are unanimous in telling us that our moments of prayer are the most alive moments of all, that when we pray we are on the threshold of life and beauty and joy that are utterly unimaginable.

Prayer is simply talking with God, trying to put ourselves in touch with him, contact him, become aware of him. By prayer, "something out there" becomes someone personal, close, concerned. We can never be sure there is a God, nor come to know what he is like, unless we pray. When one refuses to try to pray, "the world becomes his jail."

God loves us and respects our freedom. He wants our mature love. He will never force himself upon us. We must try to reach out to him, freely, by prayer.

The reason we pray is not to tell God something he does not know, nor to change his mind. Rather, prayer makes us aware of God, opens us to perceive his love and his desires for us. Prayer gradually makes us realize our complete dependence on God, our radical need of him. It makes us appreciate, bit by bit, how we are utterly bound to him by love. It also makes us realize the great power we have to better our human condition. When one prays the happenings of life, the joys as well as the agonies, begin to take on a meaning.

God always answers a sincere prayer, but not always in the way we expect. We tend to complain of unanswered prayers, but we may have prayed for something that would ultimately be harmful, or we might be expecting God to do what is within our own power to bring about. God always responds, though, by giving his love in a far better way then we envisioned. Jesus said of this:

> What father among you, if his son asks for a fish, will instead of a fish give him a serpent; or if he asks for an egg, will give him a scorpion? If you then who are evil, know how to give good gifts to your children, how much more will the heavenly Father give the Holy Spirit to those who ask him? (Luke 11, 11–13).

We should pray for ourselves and for others, including our enemies. Prayer for ourselves need not be selfish—on the contrary, it is usually an acknowledgment of our total human inadequacy. Prayer for others helps them to be open to God's love and our love and helps us to be open to them. We shall see more later about the power of prayer.

Some suggestions about how to pray: We can simply talk to God as to our best and most understanding friend, our loving Father. The best prayer is from our heart, in our own words. If we wish, we can use words someone else has composed, or we might say nothing, content just to be in God's presence, thinking about him, about ourselves, our loved ones, our life.

We can pray anywhere, anytime. But it is good to set aside a special time—perhaps in the morning and evening—and a special place,

away from distractions. We read about Christ: "And in the morning, a great while before day, he rose and went out to a lonely place, and there he prayed. . . . And after he had taken leave of them, he went into the hills to pray" (Mark 1, 35; 6, 46).

We need not say much. Christ warns us against imitating those who "think that by talking much they will be heard" (Matthew 6, 8). Reading, especially the bible, is food for prayer; people often cannot pray because they know so little about God, his actions and teachings.

Prayer can be difficult. But to try to pray, is to pray. One can feel utterly helpless when trying it for the first time, or returning to it as an adult. He wonders: How should I go about it? Will I be heard? Isn't there a danger of self-hypnosis? It can be like talking into a phone with no one on the other end of the line. One should expect these problems in trying to reach for an Infinite One. But we must be willing to risk, to try.

If we persevere, gradually, perhaps very slowly and painfully, the conviction grows that there is Someone. Things begin to fall into place. We long for more contact, to know more, to have more help, to give ourselves to him. Mysteriously, the bond of love is growing.

SOME SUGGESTIONS FOR . . .

DISCUSSION

If you are a believer, what do you personally conceive God to be like?

What, for you, best makes God real in your life?

If you are an unbeliever—or a believer—can you appreciate the opposite point of view?

FURTHER READING

* *Dreams, A Way to Listen to God,* Kelsey (Paulist Press, 1978)—Some have found this a rewarding book, dealing with "letting God in" through our dreams.
* *God and Evil,* Galligan (Paulist Press, 1976)—A brief but "packed" book on the most basic problem people have with believing in the loving God

of Christianity. Requires some concentration, but very rewarding for one willing to try.

* *Man's Search for Meaning,* Frankl (Pocket Books, 1977)—A powerfully-written study of how those who survived the Nazi death camps had a transcendent purpose in their life. The author, himself a survivor, has written several other books about "logotherapy," i.e., how a meaning to one's life helps one survive today.

** *Does God Exist? An Answer for Today,* Küng (Doubleday, 1980)—Over against nihilistic denial of an ultimate meaning to life, and against those who would only argue logically to God's existence, Fr. Küng says we must say "Yes," commit ourselves most basically (but not in naive optimism) to trust this fundamental Reality, and change the social conditions that shake our trust; then, as we are courageously faithful to our commitment, it becomes a tried and tested belief in God.

* *Beginning to Pray,* Bloom (Paulist Press, 1970)—A beautifully helpful book on prayer by a Russian Orthodox Archbishop, once a French resistance fighter.

* *He Touched Me,* Powell (Argus Communications, 1974)—An immensely popular author, Jesuit priest-professor John Powell tells here of his own "pilgrimage of prayer." Easy to read and incisively moving.

* *I Can Pray, You Can Pray,* Chilson (Winston, 1981)—How can one pray if one may not even believe in God? This is an imaginatively different book on simple techniques of meditation and expanding one's consciousness, especially for those who consider themselves more this-worldly than spiritual.

FURTHER VIEWING/LISTENING

The Man Who Mugged God (Paulist Productions)—28 minutes—An award-winning, moving story of God in the guise of a blind beggar whose limitless love begins a most unlikely chain reaction.

PERSONAL REFLECTION

I am always in the presence of God, my loving Father. Each morning and evening I will offer this simple, expressive prayer:

> "O God, help me to know what to do,
>   and give me the courage to do it."

2
God's Plan for Us
Begins with Creation

How did the human race begin? Is there a conflict between science and the bible? What is man's place in the universe? Will we survive after death? What of other worlds, angels, devils?

THE SOURCE OF OUR STORY

To answer the basic questions of our origin, we look to God's own record of his unfolding plan, history's all-time best-seller, the bible . . .

The bible is a collection of books inspired by God, revealing himself and his plan for our salvation. God is considered the principal author of the bible in that he influenced the men who wrote the books—even though they wrote freely and may not have been aware of his guidance—and so we say it was inspired by God. It expresses his revelation of himself to men and is therefore called his written "Word."

The bible is a religious book whose purpose is to tell of God and his plan for us, especially his great deeds on our behalf and his teaching about how to live and attain heaven. Since its authors were writing religious history, they related historical events only as a means of instructing and inspiring their readers. Sometimes they embellish their accounts with imaginative details, illustrate a point by a fictitious story, or omit things that would detract from their religious purpose.

The bible is a miniature library containing all sorts of writing. It contains poetry, prayers, hymns, love songs, riddles, fables, allegories, various kinds of historical narratives, folklore, biographies, prophecies, letters, etc. Each biblical author used the type of literature, or literary form, that best suited his purpose. Each literary form must be interpreted properly if the author is to be understood, as we today interpret poetry differently than we do a newspaper editorial, and a fairy tale still differently. These ancient oriental literary forms are often hard for us to understand, since they were the expression of the people of ancient times.

For example, a visitor to earth from another planet, understanding our language but nothing more about us, might read a newspaper and consider everything in it equally true—news columns, ads, comics, letters to the editor, etc.—whereas we know that each style of writing must be interpreted differently.

Thus the biblical authors often used myths to convey what they were trying to say. It is important to understand what is meant here by "myth." To most people "myth" means something not real, something that was once believed but is now seen to be untrue, not scientifically or historically verifiable. Actually an historical myth is a story (told in ancient man's symbolic language) whose structure and details were not literally true, but which had a central point that was true. Myths were—and are—ways of expressing real events or facts of our human experiences, especially our universal, worldwide, or "archetypal" experiences.

An example of a myth in which most of us find meaning is the Santa Claus story. This has its origin in a real individual, an early Christian bishop, St. Nicholas, who secretly gave money to poor girls as a dowry for a husband. There are other versions of the secret gift-giver in almost every culture of the world. Thus, the Santa Claus story we tell our children today has a real truth behind it: loving parents everywhere delight in surprising their children with gifts. And its most basic meaning is that God—our almighty and ceaselessly loving Parent—takes care of us with his gifts, ever surprising us with his help, if we are open, humble, and trustful enough to recognize his Presence.

Especially in ancient times, the myth-story expressed humanity's deepest experiences, particularly religious ones. Later, as mankind became more accustomed to abstract thinking, the Church tried to set down in understandable terms (to the extent it could) the God-experiences of Judaism and of the Christian community. Since this experiencing involved God, there was always much more to it than they could ever express.

So when people's religious experiencing is recorded, as in the bible, we expect them to use symbolic language to express what they have experienced as profoundly real and true. Symbols or symbolic "language"—as we shall see—always "stands for something more than is immediately apparent." Religious language or terminology, because it tries to express our experiences of the limitless "beyond," of God himself, is especially symbolic; there is always much more to it than the words convey at first sight.

Just as people's backgrounds, their learning, insights, prejudices, etc., affect what they report as real, just as scientists' reports of their experiments and deductions are affected by their prior theories, their personal paradigms and their own involvement in the experimental process, and just as our personal "bias," acknowledged or not, affects what we report as true, and how we relate it, so with the biblical stories of the God-experiences of Judaism and of Christianity. The more we can "enter into" what is set down and the more we openly and seekingly read with our intuitions and imaginativeness as well as with our reasoning, the more we will get out of the bible. The more we try to grasp the meaning behind what is set down in the bible, and relate it to our own experiences, the more it will "come alive" for us in our life.

The bible is the story of how God enters the lives of those open to him. We believe that God today will communicate, in some way, with anyone who reads the bible story with an open, seeking mind. The bible was written by and about people like us whose lives were changed by their experiences with God. They are the great, "foundational" religious experiences of our Western civilization—and the deeds and experiences related in the bible can have as much of an effect on us today as they did upon the people to whom they originally happened. It is the conviction of the Christian believer that these experiences were meant to help all men and women throughout history. If we truly try to "enter into" these great experiences and deeds and try to relate them to the situations of our life with an open and seeking mind, God can use this story to bring us to himself.

The bible is divided into the Old Testament, the story of God's revelation of himself and his plan up to the coming of Christ; and the New Testament, an outline of Christ's life and teachings. We begin our story with the Old Testament, usually classified as forty-five books, written by many authors over three millennia. The Middle Eastern traditions found in the first five books go back to the time of Moses (13th century B.C.) and beyond, and were first woven together on a major scale about the 10th century B.C. The last book of the Old Testament, Wisdom, was written about 50 B.C.

The first book of the Old Testament, Genesis, begins with the story of the origin of the world and of man ...

HUMAN BEGINNINGS

The story came to us in this way: Over 3,000 years ago, a band of ex-slaves found themselves wandering in the Sinai desert after a dramatic escape from pagan Egypt. In this remote place, God spoke to Moses, their leader, and made these tribes his chosen people, promising them great blessings. But the people, conscious of their vague past and uncertain future and aware of their weaknesses, began to ask Moses questions: How did it all start?—what was this God of theirs like?—was he really an all-powerful God?—if so, why did he choose them?—where did they come from, who were their ancestors?

The answer Moses and others gave—the story of the beginning of God's plan for our world—was elaborated over the centuries. Eventually it was written down as Genesis, the first book of the bible: **Read Genesis 1, 1–2, 24.**

This story of creation is meant to teach us that God made everything that exists and that everything he has made is good. Genesis speaks of creation in six days to help its primitive audience better understand that God made everything, even the things worshipped by other peoples; the picture of God creating for six days and resting on the seventh is meant to teach a Jewish audience that they should rest on the sabbath.

Man is at the peak of creation, in some way like God himself, and is given everything in the world for his use. "... what is man that you are mindful of him, or the son of man that you care for him? Yet you have made him little less than God, and crown him with glory and honor" (Psalm 8, 4–5).

The bible's account of creation can fit in perfectly with science's teaching on the evolution of the universe, even though, as we said, the bible is not meant to be a scientific text. God brings the world to realization, not by continual interventions—stepping in to "make" this or that—but in such a way that the higher emerges from the lower, by evolution. He is continually creating as he activates the whole, gigantic, unfolding process.

By his description of the creation of woman, the biblical author is emphasizing woman's dignity, that she too is a human being. This stands in sharp contrast to the common ancient view of woman as merely something to be used by man. This description also tells us of the origin of marriage—a wonderfully intimate union begun by God himself as a part of his unfolding plan for man.

The biblical story of human origins has been interpreted until relatively recently as meaning one original couple (monogenism). Many current biblical scholars take a broader view and point out that monogenism is not necessarily part of God's revelation. One says, ". . . the question about a monogenetic or polygenetic origin of man remains as obscure for the philosopher as for the paleontologist" (Schoonenberg, *God's World in the Making,* p. 50). Another says, "Studies in exegesis and conciliar history lead us to ask whether the intention of the author of Genesis, of St. Paul, and of the Fathers of the Council of Trent was really directed at the strict unity of origin of the human race and not rather at the universality of 'sin'" (Dubarle, *The Biblical Doctrine of Original Sin,* p. 228).

WHAT ARE WE?

"**What is man?** About himself he has expressed and continues to express many divergent and even contradictory opinions. In these he often exalts himself to the point of despair. The result is doubt and anxiety" (Vatican Council II, *The Church in the Modern World,* no. 12). Christianity, building on God's revelation to us, has reached certain conclusions about man:

Each of us is composed of soul, or spirit, and materiality. With the help of God's further revelation we can see this in the story of man made "in the image of God" and of "the dust of the earth." These are the two "aspects" of man, two "powers," two ways in which we can act.

By our soul, or spiritual aspect, we are "like God," persons, free, immortal, able to reflect on ourselves and realize ourselves. "By his interior qualities man outstrips the whole sum of mere things . . . surpasses the material universe . . . and shares in the light of the divine mind" *(Church in the Modern World,* no. 14).

By our materiality, or material aspect, we are connected with and dependent upon other things, limited, mortal, but capable of perfecting our universe. "Through his bodily composition man gathers to himself the elements of the material world . . . they reach their crown through him, and through him raise their voice in free praise of the Creator" *(Church in the Modern World,* no. 14).

Each of us is a single, unified person. Our soul and materiality are not two "parts," but rather two aspects of the one person who does everything. Our spirit depends upon our materiality—upon our brain, senses, etc.—that we might think and act. Whether we have the loftiest "spiritual" thoughts or engage in the most basic "animal" actions, it is we ourselves, single persons, who do these things.

Our soul, or spiritual power, is just as real as our materiality which we can see and feel. It is the core of our being, our conscious self, our innermost "me." It infuses every part of us that is alive. It enables us to think and make free choices and love. When we think, we call this power our intellect or mind; when we make free choices and love, we call it our free will.

We can be sure that we have this spiritual aspect, or soul, even aside from God's teaching about it. We have non-material or spiritual ideas such as truth, love, etc. We can conceive and carry out plans for the future, and can reflect on our past actions. We make abstract judgments; we produce culture, art and poetry, study philosophy and religion—all having little or nothing to do with our material survival.

> The existence of the human spirit is often best shown by man's triumphs over inhumanity, suffering and death. The diary of Anne Frank, a Jewish teenager's writings discovered in her Amsterdam hideout after her cruel death at the hands of the Nazis, is a striking modern testimony to the power of the spirit.

> *Each person's soul, or spiritual power, comes specially from God,* but not by God's intervening and putting something in us from the outside. Our soul does not exist before we do as a person. Each person's soul is a special "aspect" of God's continuing creation of the universe—an individual spiritual power that comes about by the evolutionary process which God began, working itself out in each of us. In the thinking of the great priest-paleontologist, Teilhard de Chardin, and others, the human soul first came about at the critical point of evolution when a primate became able to reflect on himself—and hence became human, a man, free and immortal, able to think and choose, however primitively, and to relate to others and to God.

By our soul each of us is specially related to God in a unique way. We might sometimes wonder, "How can the infinite God be concerned about me?" And yet he is, in a relationship with each one of us that is most intimate and will never be duplicated. The mystics say that God calls each of us by a secret name, lovingly, constantly, intimately.

Christ's great teaching is that because of our soul, we will go on living forever after death. Before Christ came, men could not be certain of this immortality. He stated emphatically, "Truly, truly, I say to you, if anyone keeps my word he will never see death" (John 8, 51).

> *Mankind generally has believed in some sort of survival after death.* Man's instincts and desires lead him to yearn for this perfection of happiness. "Unless man is immortal the universe is a stairway leading nowhere." If death completely destroys the human personality, then the peak of creation is left unfinished. God would be like a half-witted artist, amusing himself with things that have no ultimate meaning, creating men and wiping them out. But his whole revelation of himself is that he is good, just, and loving.
>
> Historian Arnold Toynbee sums up human belief in a personal immortality in the face of modern unbelievers: "For human beings who have once tasted the hope of personal immortality, the loss of this hope takes much of the light out of life, and the post-Christian racial survival ideologies offer no satisfactory substitute. If I have lost a dearly beloved wife or husband or child or parent, what consolation is it to me that the sacred rights of the community have been vindicated, or that a spaceman has landed on the moon? . . . Collective human triumphs are very fine, but they do not bring the dead back to life, and do not console me for my human losses. . . ."

Each of us is responsible for what happens to us after death. We are free, in God's image, and God will never interfere with our freedom. At the end of our life we will have to give an account of it—of the good we have done and the evil as well—in perfect honesty, before God, without any deception or delusion. Christ reminds us pointedly, "What does it profit a man to gain the whole world and forfeit his life?" (Mark 8, 36).

Each year on Ash Wednesday it is a Catholic custom to have our foreheads marked with ashes by a priest who says, "Remember, man, that you are dust and to dust you shall return." It is a striking reminder at the beginning of the forty days' Lenten penance that our material body is perishable and we should live for immortality.

In God's plan all men are brothers, one human family, working and sharing together. The story of our common first parents makes clear that we are all essentially the same and all have a right to share in the world's goods. Discrimination and prejudice among races insert themselves into mankind later, as a result of sin.

God is continually creating. Rather than considering creation as something over and done with, we should think of it as a process that is continually developing, something like a magnificent painting that is gradually taking form and will be complete only at the end of time.

God's plan is for us to be "co-creators" with him, to develop our world in partnership with him. Thus God said, ". . . let them have dominion over the fish of the sea. . . . Be fruitful and multiply and fill the earth and subdue it. . . ." It is becoming more and more apparent today that God loves us so much that he associates us most intimately and powerfully with himself and his works. We, by our achievements in making a better world, work "in the presence of God" to carry out the plan for the perfection of all things that he has left us to develop.

> This is developed further in chapter 24 and in Vatican Council II's *Pastoral Constitution on the Church in the Modern World,* nos. 36, 57, 67. Some today (following particularly the thought of Teilhard de Chardin) believe that man is made to conquer and perfect the whole universe, that he is truly the center of God's creation.

Love is the whole reason for creation, for us and for everything that exists. God is so loving that he wants to share his happiness, the happiness of loving, at a fantastic, unimaginable level with us, his creatures.

God need not have created anything. He is infinitely happy within himself and needed nothing outside himself—he need not have involved himself with us. But he loves—limitlessly. The universe gives us a tiny glimpse of his beauty, and the heights of human love a mere taste of the divine love he wishes to share with us.

OTHER WORLDS, ANGELS AND DEVILS

In our space age, man has become aware that he is only a part of a vast universe. Other creatures, angels, are mentioned numerous times in scripture.

Angels have traditionally been considered good spirits who worship God, act as his messengers, and guard and pray for us. Intermediaries or messengers between God and us, they were conceived of as moving with the swiftness of thought and are therefore often pictured as winged (Cf. Revelation 12, 11–12; Psalm 103, 20).

The story of the angels, as traditionally conceived, is that God created them and gave them great happiness; he offered them an opportunity to show their gratitude to him, and in return he would give them even greater happiness in heaven. But some of them, led by Lucifer, or the devil, ungratefully refused to love God, and in fact wanted to take over God's position in heaven. Fixed forever on evil, they were relegated to hell, the state of eternal suffering and separation from God (Cf. Revelation 12, 7–9; Isaiah 14, 12ff).

Today, theology is restudying the whole question of angels and devils. Perhaps scripture simply presupposes angels and devils as part of the biblical milieu, rather than directly affirming their actual existence as part of God's revelation. Nor does the existence of angels and devils seem to be a part of the strictly dogmatic teaching of the Church. The numbers and varieties which are mentioned may well be mythological exaggerations.

Also, in a time of simpler religious belief, the devil became for some a convenient, excusing cause of their own sins. And yet it is hard to dismiss totally the reality of an evil, superhuman intelligence, so firmly rooted is it in the long tradition and liturgy of the Church, and in the experience and literature of many cultures.

"Possession" is the supposed taking over of a person's body by the devil or evil spirits, "obsession" the inhabiting of a place or objects by them. Many such cases can be explained naturally, as parapsychology particularly is showing us more and more today. For many theologians today, possession can be simply the coalescing of the very real evil that proceeds from men, concentrated in a certain person or place, and the ritual of exorcism ("driving out the evil spirit[s]") opposes this with the power of God's all-powerful love.

In any event, the portrayal of angelic creatures has served to bridge the gap between God and man and to remind man of unseen spiritual realities, of the dangers of sin and God's ever-present help.

Today, when we face the almost limitless possibilities of life in space, references to angels should remind us how little we really know of God's creation.

Obviously then, there could be other rational creatures in the universe. They, too, would have been created by God and be loved and cared for by him. They would show forth other aspects of his infinite wisdom and love, perhaps some that man cannot. If there are such, it would surely be good for us to reach out lovingly toward them, for the same loving God would have made us all in some sense "brothers."

Contemplating the possibility of man one day standing face to face with other rational creatures should make us realize how ridiculous are our petty human divisions, our wars and other conflicts. Much of the science fiction of our time attempts to tell us this. At any rate, our concern in this book is with what we know of God's revelation to us in this world, staggering and limitless in itself.

DAILY LIVING: WORSHIPPING OUR CREATOR

When we realize that God is our Creator and that we are completely dependent on him, our most natural feeling is one of awe and reverence, and awareness of our nothingness before him. From ancient times man has always felt this way before the vast mystery of God. We want to know more about God, to pay him homage, and yet we know how very limited we are.

Worship is the way we honor God and try to be united with him. Just as a child naturally expresses his dependence on his human father, and desires to be with him, so it is natural for us to do this toward our almighty Father. Worship comes from "worthship"— showing what God is worth to us, how we revere and need him.

God has no need of our worship. But as it is unnatural for a son to ignore a good parent, so it is unnatural for us to ignore God who gives us all we have. Such ultimate selfishness brings only deep unhappiness.

We have the great privilege of being able to respond to God's love. The rest of creation—to the extent we know it—is irrational and cannot experience this love with the Almighty. We are free to accept his love and to love in return.

God loves each of us infinitely, intimately, personally, with all-powerful love and he wants our personal love in return. He has an intimate, loving interest in each of us. Christ says, "Why even the hairs of your head are all numbered" (Luke 12, 7).

Instead of an infinite number of possible people, God created you and me, and guides us through life to an endless eternity with himself. Each of us is loved uniquely and each of us has a unique contribution: we can love God and we can give love to the universe in a way no one else can. Worship gradually makes us aware of God's incredible, tender, personal love.

We can worship God by ourselves, silently honoring him in our thoughts. Worship must be interior and sincere, or else it is a mockery: "... they who worship must worship in spirit and truth," says Christ.

It is also natural to express our worship with others, as anyone in love will show openly how he feels about his beloved. We are members of one human family, and it is as natural to join with others in worship as in any meaningful experience.

We worship, then, as full human beings when we read, speak, sing, stand, sit, kneel in reverence, etc. And we join with all God's creation in worship, and so we use things such as water, oil, fire, stone, bread and wine, branches of trees, ashes, etc. "And God saw everything that he had made and behold, it was very good" (Genesis 1, 31).

Ceremonies of worship are "signs" that express our spiritual feelings. A handshake is a simple ceremony; a person seeing it knows from this sign that two men are friends. A kiss between husband and wife is a sign of their love. So, too, religious ceremonies are the Church's "sign language" expressing our beliefs in a living way. Each time we take part in them we deepen our beliefs.

> Some will feel closer to God while alone, perhaps when out amid nature's wonders, when listening to music, etc. God is infinite beauty, and when we enter into things of beauty we are being drawn to him. Some feel God's presence more in these moments than in church, in man's organized religious assembly. They may find formal worship difficult, meaningless. These should then seek God where they can find him—but they should also try to appreciate the meaning of religious worship, because one's personal contacts with God can remain vague and meaningless unless he seeks God in union with others. Conversely, a formal worship might become a delusion unless it is interior and sincere.

We must remember that if we are to approach the infinite God (even if we are not sure an infinite one is there) we must do so in a reverent setting. We would certainly prepare well for an interview with a president or other important person. Yet we often casually, sporadically approach the infinite God—and then are surprised when nothing comes of it. Worship must be something regular, consistent, given a special time and place in our life.

Christians believe that God has shown us a way to join together and worship him. As people in love want to show their love in the best possible way, so men have always wanted to worship God adequately. Our conviction is that God has come to our aid and told us how. Catholics believe that the Mass, given us by Christ himself, is a special way God has given us to worship him.

Worship, then, is an integral part of the study of Catholic Christianity. The official public worship of the Catholic Church is called the sacred liturgy. To aid this presentation from now on, appropriate ceremonies of the liturgy will be noted in sections called **IN THE LITURGY.**

SOME SUGGESTIONS FOR . . .

DISCUSSION

What is the most meaningful thing for you in the bible's account of creation?

What do you think of the Christian notion of man's exalted, eternal place in the universe?

Can you understand why worship is natural and necessary for the believer?

FURTHER READING

* *On Genesis: A New Reading.* Vawter (Doubleday, 1977)—A fresh interpretation of this first book of the bible, by an outstanding biblical scholar and excellent writer.
* *The Way of Wisdom in the Old Testament,* Scott (Macmillan, 1971)—

Written for the average person, this is an important book for those wishing to understand the Old Testament.

* *The Divine Milieu* and **The Hymn of the Universe,* De Chardin (Harper and Row, 1967)—For an open, intuiting mind these books can be true experiences, sharing a great vision with an outstanding Christian and scientist.

** *Myth, History and Faith,* Kelsey (Paulist Press, 1974)—An insightful clergyman-psychologist shows the necessity, and the wonderful possibilities, of understanding and using our basic myths and symbols. A "must" book for anyone who equates "myth" with "unreal," or who thinks that our religious symbols are out of touch with reality. * *Myths, Dreams and Mysteries,* Eliade (Fontana Library, 1977) is a new edition of a classic that also is guaranteed to expand one's view of what myths, dreams, and mystical experiences have been telling us since man's origin.

* *Fully Human, Fully Alive,* Powell (Argus Communications, 1976)—Clearly, insightfully written, this book by a widely-read priest/teacher/counselor uses some modern psychological insights to show us what a believer in God can and should be: fully human and fully alive!

** *What Are They Saying About Creation?* Hayes (Paulist Press, 1980)—A good discussion of changes in contemporary theology on creation and sin.

FURTHER VIEWING/LISTENING

Understanding Genesis (Thomas Klise)—Two filmstrips on the first book of the Old Testament, including the creation story.

A Song of Beauty (Paulist Productions)—12 minutes, color—A poetic masterpiece in which a group of young students encounter God's beauty in creation.

PERSONAL REFLECTION

I might make some private, sincere act of worship each day.

This Sunday, the Lord's day, I might join with others in worshipping God.

Each Sunday Catholics worship by taking part in the Mass, and everyone is welcome to come and take part. When one first attends, it is natural to be somewhat confused by the ceremonies, the priest's clothing, etc. These will be explained later.

Since the Mass is so central to Catholicism, and since it takes time to familiarize oneself with it, we recommend that those seriously studying Catholicism begin to attend Mass.

If you wish to attend, you might ask a Catholic friend to accompany you. You might stand, sit or kneel when everyone else does. Or, if you wish, just sit and watch—or read and sing along from the booklets or program sheets usually provided.

3

God's Gift of Himself and
Our Rejection of Him

What is God's plan for us? How do we usually respond to God? Why are we drawn to sinful things and actions of which we are ashamed? How does God help us overcome our weaknesses?

GOD'S GREAT GIFT AND HIS DESIRE FOR MAN

A person in love wants to share his happiness with the one he loves. A boy in love with a girl wants to be with her to make her happy. God loves us. He made us to be happy with him in heaven forever.

But we could not exist for a moment in God's presence, much less speak with him and love him. We would be annihilated by even a glimpse of him. So God does something for us, to enable us to live with and love him forever. He gives us a great gift: **Read Matthew 13, 44–46.**

Christ was trying to describe something wonderful when he spoke of this "hidden treasure," the "pearl of great value" for which a man sells all he has. It is the greatest gift which God can give us, sanctifying grace.

Sanctifying grace is God's life and love within us, God's presence loving each of us. It is the way God lives within us and possesses us—the intimate, personal relationship of God to me. It is God himself giving me his friendship, his love, his very life—so we call it God's grace-presence within us.

"Sanctifying" means to make holy or like God. This new life truly makes us like God. "Grace" means a gift—we have no right whatever to it.

To understand this, consider the various personal relationships we have with others: Some we know slightly, as mere acquaintances; with others our mutual appreciation is growing, and with yet others we have a deep love, perhaps the love of friendship, or that of a man and woman, sharing love, strength, and inspiration on a profound level. There is also the relationship of parents to their children—a mother, for instance, communicating life to the child within her. Writers today speak of relationships as "I-it," and "I-thou," according to their meaningfulness. By grace we are most profoundly a "thou" in the eyes of the infinite God.

Sanctifying grace is the closest possible relationship between God and his human creatures. It is God's gift of himself in love to us—the closest possible love. It is also a love that gives us life itself, not just human life but the fullest possible sharing in the limitless life of God.

An orphan's adoption by a millionaire happens only rarely in our world; but by sanctifying grace the infinite God "adopts" us to live with him and share his wealth and his very life forever. "See what love the Father has given us, that we should be called children of God; and so we are" (1 John 3, 1; cf. Galatians 4, 7). We are "born again" into this new life (John 3, 5), and have a completely new relationship with God, that of a son to his Father (Romans 8, 14–17); we are a "new creation" (2 Corinthians 5, 17).

This presence has been called "supernatural" life, i.e., greater than our ordinary natural life, a sharing in God's own life, beyond this life in heaven. Through sanctifying grace we actually begin the life of heaven here on earth; we can begin to know and love God person-to-person and be loved by him.

This is a living love, a relationship that grows and develops as any love must—or else it dies. God's love continually presses us. We either grow in it, or we fall back. We shall see that this love, constantly increasing, never ceases but grows for eternity.

We cannot normally "feel" grace within us. But we shall see that Christ gave us ways to be sure of having this life-presence.

This most personal love of God for each of us has many wonderful aspects: his condescension, continually open to me, and indeed desirous of my constant communication with him; his mercy, continually forgiving me; his protection, unceasingly doing good things, somehow arranging the plan of the universe for me; his unending faithfulness to me, no matter how I treat him—unless I reject him entirely, and even then he wants to return to me.

We know how even a human love relationship can transform a person. Often a person's life is made or broken by whether or not he has someone who truly loves him. As love develops, one is raised beyond himself, taking on more and more the characteristics of his friend or beloved.

If human love can so change one, we can imagine what God's continual look of love must be doing to us. Unfortunately we are hardly ever aware of this, because it is so staggering, so beyond human comprehension. An unshielded look into an atomic pile could blind or kill, such is its power of radiation; one in grace has such interior beauty that if God ever permitted a glimpse of him as he really is, the beholder would be torn apart in ecstasy.

God's grace-presence gives us the power to transform everything we do into eternal happiness for ourselves and others. It expands us, giving us the possibility of life beyond our wildest dreams, and enabling us to share this with others. It is as if everything we touched turned into gold—except that by grace we can turn our every contact into unending unimaginable happiness for all.

God's plan was that man would develop so that he could have his grace-presence, grow in it, and be with him forever in heaven. He would send his Son, Jesus Christ, to earth when men were ready, to fill us with a superabundance of his grace-presence. But man is weak, and God's plan now had to take account of man's hesitancy, his inability to trust himself to this infinite love.

MAN'S REJECTION OF GOD'S LOVE

Everyone who honestly faces himself is aware of his failings. We are all drawn to do things we later regret. We hurt ourselves and others, even those we love. This is sin, a dreary and inevitable fact over which men have puzzled for centuries.

The ancient Hebrews also pondered the fact that all men are sinners. But unlike their pagan contemporaries—who often thought of the gods as cruel, arbitrary, jealous of man—they could not believe that God had originally formed man in such a state of wretchedness and sin. It would be unreconcilable with God's whole revelation of himself as good and loving.

The biblical author looked back to the beginning of the human race and set down the story of how man had sinned from his origin. The background of the story we recall from chapter 2 of Genesis. The first humans are pictured in a luxurious garden, with power over the rest of creation; man and woman are intimately united, of "one flesh." "The man and his wife were both naked and were not ashamed," i.e., they had complete confidence, openness, esteem for one another. Above all man is the intimate friend of God who speaks to him with love and concern. Then comes tragedy: **Read Genesis, chapter 3.**

The first man chose his own way over God's. He had to make a choice like everyone who was to follow him: to give himself to God, or to rely on his own human power. He chose his own way and rejected God's proffered love. "In one man all have sinned," says St. Paul. We all sin as this first man did.

This story is symbolic, so its precise details are unimportant. We do not know what the precise sinful action of the first humans actually was. The serpent is a symbol of evil, some malevolent power outside of man; eating the forbidden fruit signifies man choosing his own way over God's. The effects of their sin are attested by the experience of anyone who has ever done serious wrong.

> Is God revealing that Adam and Eve were perfect specimens of mankind? No, we need only believe that they had true human liberty. Is God saying that they were created in a state of happiness which they lost? This has been the traditional view, but today a number of contemporary theologians also view the biblical imagery as referring to a future fulfillment in Christ.

The worst effect of their sin is that man and woman no longer have confident access to God's friendship. They are pictured as hiding from him and are finally put out of the garden. They also notice they are naked. Man has lost confidence and trust in his fellow humans, has difficulty communicating with them, is subject to social conventions and shame. Man's labor and woman's motherhood—their typical roles—are made difficult and full of anxieties. Woman's help to man becomes servitude. Man no longer has access to the tree of life, i.e., death now becomes a brutal and painful experience. Man's struggle against the serpent, against evil, becomes continual, difficult.

Work has become more burdensome because of this sin; but work itself is natural, necessary, and our privilege, fashioning the universe as "co-creators" with God himself. After the first sin we read, ". . . cursed is the ground because of you; in toil shall you eat of it all the days of your life . . . in the sweat of your face you shall eat bread." But from the beginning man was to work with God, to ". . . fill the earth and subdue it. . . ." It is our attitude toward work that sin changes.

The whole physical world has somehow become involved in man's original sin. Man's work to subdue it is now burdensome and painful. But the universe is still good and, as we shall see, redeemed man can work powerfully with God's grace to bring it to perfection.

This description of sin is a masterful presentation of the way in which we all encounter evil: the temptation, first rejected, then dallied with—then the fall. Our sin, too, is basically one of pride, trying to "be like God," putting our judgment over his. Afterwards we are ashamed, but God seeks us out through our unrelenting conscience. We must face the consequences of our sin. Yet God is always willing to give us a fresh start, promising that we can overcome the serpent of evil with his help.

Why did God let man sin? Why did he not make us so we could not sin? We have no complete answer but perhaps, analogously to human love, we could not enjoy the reward of God's love unless we knew that we had done our part to freely earn it. This means there must be the possibility of not earning it, of not loving, of sinning, and this is what man used his freedom to do.

Further, consider what sin costs God. What is more incredible than that God should subject himself to continual refusals, possibly an eternal refusal, by his creatures? To tolerate such a rebuff God must infinitely love and desire man just as he is. Sin thus proves God's great love, respect and solicitude for each of us.

This is the heart of the matter: God's incredible love wishes to exalt us to himself. But we must freely respond to his love and cooperate in his plan for us. He allows our disobedience because it proves how he respects our freedom, our dignity as a person, our true lovableness. No matter how we strike out at him he still respects us. Even when we do not respect ourselves, the infinite God does.

The evil of sin must also be seen in perspective. God puts us on earth so we can freely choose his love, and this is such a brief moment of choice when compared to eternity! It is like asking a child to spend a few minutes alone in a dark room, and in return giving him a lifetime of tremendous joy—except that for our brief trust God gives us eternal joy.

As mankind developed, we continued to sin, and each generation was affected by the faults of its predecessors. The story of Cain and Abel ("sons" of Adam and Eve in the sense that any of us are) shows how evil men could become: **Read Genesis 4, 1–81.** In this story we see the basic sin in all human relationships: selfish individualism. "Am I my brother's keeper?" should sound familiar to all of us.

The story of the flood and Noah's Ark (Genesis, chapters 6–9) is another symbolic story showing the widespread evil of man, and how God continued to bless the few who served him. After the flood, the ages of men decrease, an ancient literary device to show man's gradual moral deterioration. Then comes the incident of the tower of Babel (Genesis 11, 1–9), another symbolic story showing how men tried to defy God, ended in confusion, and brought disastrous effects upon future generations. As time passed, Adam's sin went on snowballing.

This, then, is original sin: the effect of the sin of the first humans plus the accumulated sin of mankind. We all inherit this accumulation of mankind's defects, its lack of love, its ignorance and corruption. Each of us adds to this common burden of sin by his own sinful acts. Because of it we have a proneness to sin ("concupiscence") passed on from parents to children.

Just as physical heredity and environment transmit certain defects to an infant, so everyone from the womb grows in a sinful moral environment. We experience not only love but what it is to be unloved and therefore we will be unloving in return. We unconsciously adopt the unloving attitudes and values of our society—for example, the pervading notion that money and material success are the important goals of one's life.

This "sin" is "original," then, because it afflicts all of us at our origin, as well as having its inception at the origin of the human race. It is "sin" for us only in an analogous sense, because we have not willed it. But it is real: by it we are alienated from God and others and are prone to willful sins of our own.

From the sin begun by Adam and Eve we should learn particularly

the necessity of humility—to know ourselves as we really are, to acknowledge our weakness and limitations. Pride is its opposite, an unrealistic love of ourselves. The first sin and every sin is basically pride, succumbing to the temptation, "You will be like God. . . ." It is, for all of us, the greatest obstacle to God's love.

FACING OUR SINS

From this story of sin we see that our sins are rejections of God's love and of our fellow man. They are refusals to respond, to let ourselves be loved by God. Adam's sin is typical: God's love surrounds us in countless ways, and to sin we must hide from him, turn away from his loving care. In doing this we also turn away from our fellow man. We turn in on ourselves, choosing our way over God's and our neighbor's.

Everyone has a conscience which he must follow, by which he knows right and wrong. His mind judges that some actions are good, and therefore should be done, and other things are wrong and must be avoided. If one is not true to these judgments, he is untrue to himself, and can never expect real happiness.

> *Conscience is really one's center of awareness, the innermost "place" within me where God leads me to awareness of himself and of others.* It is where God opens my awareness to look honestly at myself in relation to others—the needs of others, my effect on others, my duty to others in love. The more I allow God to "come through," and the more I am in touch with this core of myself, the more sensitive I will be to others, to their dignity, needs and hopes. Then, hopefully, I will follow my conscience-awareness and be more loving toward them, and toward God.

Our conscience must be guided by God, because only he is infinitely wise and sees what is truly right and wrong. Just as we make mistakes in other things, so we sometimes form a mistaken sense of morality. We must investigate, to make sure that our conscience agrees with God's loving plan for us. We shall see that he has given us concrete moral guides, particularly through Christ's teaching. Reflection on Christ's teaching through the centuries has shown us certain things about this.

Love is the great rule of morality. Sin, we saw, is at least a partial rejection of God's love, a refusal to love our fellow man as we should. All the rules are simply ways to love, and a proof of our love.

Some sins are worse than others, because they deliberately reject love and cut us off from God's grace-presence and our fellow man. In a serious matter we might fully and deliberately choose to reject God and our fellow man, to follow our own selfish way. Obviously we should avoid all sin, but particularly serious sins of this sort. Everything we do in serious sin is vitiated, empty, ultimately useless. Only when we are truly sorry and are forgiven can we enjoy God's love and grace-presence once more. Later we shall consider this further.

These normally are serious sins against love: deliberately refusing to acknowledge God or to pray; seriously injuring another or his reputation; refusing to help another in serious need; serious offenses of sexual immorality, scandal, stealing, drunkenness, refusing to use our talents, prejudice or discrimination against others.

Each sin of ours, and especially serious sin, makes it harder for us to know God's truth and follow it. Obviously the grossly immoral person—one seeking primarily his own pleasure, power, wealth—will never be able to accept God's teachings. Most people, of course, are not such deliberate sinners. But even their occasional sins make it harder for them to accept God's teachings and follow them.

Each sin of ours adds to the burden of sin in the world, and blocks the spread of God's love to our fellow man. Each sin causes us to draw away from others; we fail to do our part to spread love and happiness.

GOD'S PLAN OF GREATER LOVE

Though man went on sinning seriously against God, God did not destroy man nor abandon him. We might have expected God to reject our race, considering the accumulated sin of mankind—the continual wars, crimes, cruelty, and terrible injustices that we have inflicted upon one another. But God is infinite love and compassion.

Let us suppose that we had new neighbors who rejected our offer of friendship, and then continually insulted us, while their children destroyed our property and abused us at almost every opportunity. How long would we tolerate them?

God used man's sins to show even greater love. He promised that he would save us from our sins. His promise to save us is described as the curse which he put on the serpent; there will be a constant battle with evil, and it can hurt us, but eventually it will be overcome by the offspring of the woman: "I will put enmity between you and the woman, and between your seed and her seed; he shall bruise your head, and you shall bruise his heel" (Genesis 3, 15).

Then God gradually unfolded his plan: Despite man's sin, and in fact because of it, God sent his own Son into the world to give us his grace-presence and love beyond measure. Christ, the offspring of the woman, would crush the power of evil and bring us overwhelming grace. This is why each year during the Easter vigil service the Church says of Adam's sin: "O happy fault, that merited such a redeemer!" Out of the great evil of sin God has brought far greater good.

IN THE LITURGY

The texts of the Mass are filled with allusions to our sinfulness and our need of grace: "I confess to almighty God," "Lord, have mercy, Christ, have mercy," "Forgive us our trespasses," "Lamb of God, you take away the sins of the world, have mercy on us," etc.

DAILY LIVING: GOD'S CONSTANT HELPS

Because we are weak and prone to sin we need God's constant help. By his grace-presence God continually gives us many promptings to know what to do and strength to do it. These constant helps are called his actual graces.

Actual graces are the continuous ways in which God's grace-presence prompts us to do good or avoid evil. They come for particular "acts." They are the innumerable little ways in which God within us makes his presence known. If we are sensitive to them, we will recognize them many times a day: a prompting comes to do some good act, to pray, to help someone, to avoid a sinful situation, or to realize more clearly a truth about God or ourselves, to see another with greater appreciation, etc.

Our every good thought or action is initiated and supported by God's actual graces. We cannot do a thing to reach heaven without his help. "For it is God who of his good pleasure works in you both the will and the performance" (Philippians 2, 13).

God continually gives these promptings, makes these overtures, even to those not yet related to him by sanctifying grace. He constantly and lovingly "prods" even the worst sinners. He invites them in all sorts of ways to make their free commitment of love to him, to let him possess them and love them by his grace-presence.

God gives us these helps particularly if we ask for them, and even more so if we are determined to follow them when he gives them. We need much prompting from God's actual graces, especially as we study religion, to know and follow his truth sincerely and courageously.

SOME SUGGESTIONS FOR ...

DISCUSSION

Can you understand how sin is a refusal to accept God's love— and how it affects all of us?

Can you see how mankind would need a savior?

What do you find most effective in dealing with our proneness to sin?

FURTHER READING

* *Guilt: Man and Society,* Smith (Doubleday, 1971)—A fine anthology by varied authors on the basic questions of evil, guilt and sin.
* *Sin, Biblical Perspectives,* Maly (Pflaum, 1973)—In this book, our sinfulness is clearly shown as the bible sees it: before all else, a breaching of the intimate relationship between God and ourselves.
* *Discernment, A Study in Ecstasy and Evil,* Kelsey (Paulist Press, 1978)— A popular clergyman-psychologist gives very helpful insights into the origin and nature of evil, and how we can best cope with evil, hateful "forces" that we often realize are within us as well as without.

FURTHER VIEWING/LISTENING

This Side of Eden (Paulist Productions)—25 minutes—An award-winning, humorous yet profound examination of guilt, forgiveness and reconciliation in the lives of Adam and Eve.

PERSONAL REFLECTION

Sin from the start began "snowballing," cut our whole race off from God, and brought the horrors of death, wars, crime, cruelty, and untold suffering into our world. This is the terrible, cumulative effect of sin. My personal sins can also cut me off from God, and can affect many others, causing unhappiness and pain of which I may not even be aware.

My sins also make it more difficult, and sometimes impossible, to know and believe in Christ's teachings. Christ said, "If anyone shall do the will of my Father, he shall know my teaching, whether it be from God." I should honestly and sincerely think over my sins, especially my serious sins—perhaps during my evening prayer. I will determine to do all in my power to avoid them, especially the one that does the most harm to others.

4
God's Plan Unfolds
in the Old Testament

Has God ever shown his concern with human affairs? Can we see God's plan at work anywhere in history? What is the unique importance of the Jewish people?

THE GREAT PEOPLE OF THE COVENANT

The story of mankind after the first sin is a dreary one of continuing infidelity to God. Sin seems to dominate everywhere. But God is silently at work, and when men are ready, he steps into human history. He selects a tiny group of people and with them begins his new plan for the salvation of the world.

The Old Testament tells the story of God's relationship with his people before the coming of Jesus Christ. It is also called the Hebrew scriptures because it tells of God's special revelation of himself to the Hebrews, later called the Jewish people. It is concerned with only this one people, the Jews. Other nations are mentioned only incidentally. It does not even give a complete history of the Jewish people, but only of the events that directly concern God's plan.

We should note especially that the main themes of the Old Testament look forward to completion in the New Testament. God's people of the Old Testament are the forerunners and basis of his people of the New Testament, Christ's Church. Vatican Council II said this clearly and gratefully:

> The Church of Christ acknowledges that . . . the beginnings of her faith and her election are found already among the patriarchs, Moses and the prophets . . . that all who believe in Christ are included in Abraham's call, and that the salvation of the Church is mysteriously fore-

shadowed by the chosen people's exodus. . . . The Church, therefore, cannot forget that she received the revelation of the Old Testament through the people with whom God in his inexpressible mercy concluded the ancient covenant. Nor can she forget that she draws sustenance from the root of that well-cultivated olive tree onto which have been grafted the wild shoots, the Gentiles (*Declaration on the Relationship of the Church to Non-Christian Religions,* no. 4).

We should try to "enter into" the events of this story, since it was written as much for us as for the people of two or three thousand years ago. It is the Christian conviction that this story is meant for everyone, that it is the high point of man's relationship with God. It tells of the great events that have profoundly influenced our human situation and particularly our Western civilization. If we read of these events sympathetically and openly, trying to understand their meaning, they can tell us much about the meaning of our life and our relationship with God and other people. Countless millions have become deeper, better human beings through this story—and so can we.

God stepped into human history by making himself known to Abraham, the first of the patriarchs, about 1900 B.C. Abraham was a donkey caravaneer, the leader of his tribe, living at Ur (in modern Iran). God changed his name from Abram, and made him great promises: **Read Genesis 12, 1–3.**

God then made a covenant—an agreement or testament—with Abraham. A covenant is the ancient way by which two parties solemnly bound themselves together. It was a contract, a promise, or pledge, and those making it called down punishment on themselves if they should break it.

A covenant was made by some visible sign or ceremony signifying the internal union of the parties concerned. When Abraham asked for a sign of the covenant, God told him to cut in half several animals and lay the pieces opposite each other. Then, "as the sun was setting, Abram fell into a deep sleep; and terror came upon him, a great darkness. The Lord said to Abram, 'Know for certain . . .' (and) when the sun had set and it was dark, a smoking fire pot and a flaming torch passed between the pieces. On that day the Lord made a covenant with Abram. . . ." (Genesis 15, 8ff.)

The ceremony or ritual was sometimes, as in Abraham's case, for both parties to pass between the divided parts of an animal; sometimes there was a shedding of blood, considered the sacred principle of life by the ancients; sometimes it was an exchange of gifts, or eating and drinking together the "covenant meal."

Today we often make agreements in this way: a treaty signed by representatives of two nations; a business contract concluded at a meal and then signed by the parties; a bet made with a handshake; particularly one based on love, such as an exchange of wedding vows symbolized by an exchange of rings.

The covenant with Abraham is described in Genesis: Read Genesis 17, 1–12. By this covenant God promised Abraham great posterity, a fruitful land, and extraordinary blessings on his descendants and through them on all mankind. Abraham and his descendants for their part were to serve God and have faith in his promises. Circumcision was to be the sign of the covenant.

This is the first great and extraordinary sign of God's love: he binds himself by a covenant with man—and, further, he is faithful to it even when man is not. Now a new relationship of intimacy, a truly personal union, begins between God and man. We see how great is our worth and dignity to God—a unique concept when compared to other beliefs in which the soul often loses its identity, and where the individual means little.

Abraham was outstanding for his faith in God, so much so that he was ready to obey God's command to sacrifice his only son, Isaac. His obedience began to reverse the trend begun by Adam's disobedience:

> "Take your son, your only son Isaac, whom you love, and go to the land of Moriah, and offer him there as a burnt offering upon one of the mountains of which I shall tell you. . . ." Abraham built an altar there, and laid the wood in order, and bound his son Isaac, and laid him on the altar, upon the wood. Then Abraham put forth his hand, and took the knife to slay his son. But the angel of the Lord called to him from heaven, and said, "Abraham, Abraham." And he said, "Here am I." He said, "Do not lay your hand on the lad or do anything to him; for now I know that you fear God, seeing you have not withheld your son, your only son, from me" (Genesis 22, 2, 9–12).

God's covenant with Abraham was renewed with his son, Isaac, and with his grandson, Jacob or Israel, from whose twelve sons came the twelve tribes of the Jewish nation. The family had now settled in the land to which God had directed them, present-day Israel. Like Abraham, Jacob's name was changed to fit his new role in God's plan:

> And God said to him, "Your name is Jacob; no longer shall your name be called Jacob, but Israel shall be your name." So his name was called Israel. And God said to him, "I am God Almighty: be fruitful and multiply; a nation and a company of nations shall come from you, and kings shall spring from you. The land which I gave to Abraham and Isaac I will give to you, and I will give the land to your descendants after you" (Genesis 35, 10–12).

The scriptures tell how Joseph, Israel's son, went to Egypt and became a leader of that country. Some Hebrews followed, and increased in numbers and wealth. But then the Egyptians began to enslave them. God, however, was watching over his people and raised up their greatest leader, Moses, to lead them out of bondage.

Moses was the great Israelite leader chosen by God to deliver his people out of Egypt. We saw earlier his great experience of God, how the Lord came to him in a burning bush and revealed that he was the living God of the patriarchs:

> "Do not come near; put off your shoes from your feet, for the place on which you are standing is holy ground." And he said, "I am the God of your father, the God of Abraham, the God of Isaac, and the God of Jacob." And Moses hid his face, for he was afraid to look at God (Exodus 3, 5–6).

Then God gave Moses his mission:

> "Say this to the people of Israel, 'The Lord, the God of your fathers, the God of Abraham, the God of Isaac, the God of Jacob, has sent me to you.... I have observed you and what has been done to you in Egypt; and I promise that I will bring you up out of the affliction of Egypt, to the land of the Canaanites ... a land flowing with milk and honey' " (Exodus 3, 15–17).

Moses went to Pharaoh and demanded that he let the Israelites leave Egypt, but was refused. This Pharaoh is thought to be the famous and egotistical Rameses II, whose images cover Egypt and whose mummy can be seen today in the Egyptian National Museum in Cairo. In the records of his reign we find nothing about the Israelites, but we know that Semite slaves worked on his great store cities, and the Israelites at this time were a small, unorganized group, probably scarcely noticed in the continual migrations across Egypt's borders.

After a series of plagues—natural yearly occurrences that could be interpreted as divine interventions—Pharaoh still would not let them go. Finally, God told Moses that on a particular night each Israelite family was to slaughter a lamb, put some of its blood on the doorposts of their houses, and eat it with unleavened bread and bitter herbs: **Read Exodus 12, 1–14.**

This was the Passover or Pasch, begun by the paschal meal. It began the events leading up to the old covenant. Later Christ will eat this meal to begin his new covenant. The story continues, telling in figurative, hyperbolic language of what was probably the death of Pharaoh's firstborn son: **Read Exodus 12, 29–32.**

Saved by the blood of the lamb, the Israelites fled from Egypt and with God's help passed through the waters of the Red Sea—most probably a passage through the marshy "Sea of Reeds," aided by favorable winds which later brought high waters in which Pharaoh's pursuing soldiers were drowned. By this natural event, God again aided his people—and gave a prophetic sign of what his new people would do in Christian baptism, passing through water to salvation and freedom.

This is the great event of the Exodus, the deliverance of the Israelites from Egypt. It happened about 1270 B.C. It is the central event of Jewish history, the striking proof of God's intervention on behalf of his people, and the foundation of their hope that he would one day do so again. Strikingly unlike their pagan neighbors, the Jews retold this greatest event of their history year after year, century after century—and still recount it—as proof of God's intervention in their behalf.

THE MAKING OF THE OLD COVENANT

Free of their enemies, the Israelites now journeyed some three hundred miles through the harsh, debilitating Sinai desert. Finally they came to the Sinai mountains near the tip of the peninsula, a desolate, silent, awesome place even today.

At Mount Sinai, God made his great covenant with the Israelites: Read Exodus 19, 1–6.

This was the old covenant, or Old Testament. Moses is the mediator of this old covenant, a figure of Christ who will mediate the new and perfect covenant. Moses alone can enter God's awesome presence: **Read Exodus 19, 16–25.**

By this covenant the promises made to Abraham and his descendants are extended to all the Israelites who are now made God's own people. Here the straggling, motley and probably terrified band of ex-slaves are formed into a great people. Circumcision continues to be a sign of their unique destiny.

In return for making the Israelites his own people, God asked them to keep their part of the covenant, summarized in the ten commandments. This simple moral code was known throughout the Middle East at that period, particularly in the famous Code of Hammurabi—except that Israel's concept of God, as we shall see, was totally unique: **Read Exodus 20, 1–17.**

The ten commandments were supplemented by a whole set of other laws organizing and administering the life of the people in an orderly way. Thus much of the first five books of the Old Testament (the Pentateuch) is concerned with property and criminal laws, rules of worship and sacrifice, regulations about health and marriage, etc.

Then Moses "sealed" or accepted the covenant on behalf of the people by a sacrifice culminating in the sprinkling of an animal's blood: Read Exodus 24, 3–8. We saw that important covenants were often made by some such sign or ceremony. Later Christ will inaugurate the new, perfect covenant by shedding his blood for us in sacrifice.

This is the "church" of the Old Testament, God's people, the Israelites gathered together. This is what "church" originally meant—God's people called together by him, under the authority of their leaders, his representatives, to receive his teaching and show their acceptance of it by sacrifice.

Israel's whole future was to be judged by whether or not she kept this covenant, but almost immediately the people broke it, idolatrously worshipping a golden calf. God pardoned and spared his people through Moses' intercession, after he had fasted for forty days in reparation—here again we see Moses as the savior of his people, a forerunner of Christ. These violations of the covenant were to happen repeatedly. After the first enthusiastic acceptance of the covenant the people grew restless, dissatisfied. So God kept them in the desert for a whole generation, toughening and disciplining them until they forgot the fleshpots of Egypt. Discipline is always necessary for one to be faithful to God and resist the lure of merely material things.

The Israelites wandered for forty years through the desert, but God gave them many signs of his presence and protection: a cloud during the day, and the fire of lightning by night, a discovery of water when they most needed it, and the food of the desert manna tree to sustain them.

By these events, God reveals but also conceals himself, since they can always admit of a natural explanation. As with the signs of the Exodus—the plagues, passing over the Sea of Reeds, the thunder and lightning and earthquake of Sinai—it takes faith to realize God is acting. God is always a hidden God. "No man can see my face and live," he told Moses. And so it is with all his actions through history, and with us today.

But the story of the forming of Israel, and particularly Israel's concept of God, is strikingly unique in history. Everything in Israel's culture came from surrounding cultures, but her religion, the heart of her national life, was opposed in every way to that of her neighbors. The surrounding gods were very human, fighting, lustful, often cruel, capricious and unpredictable, needing to be placated by magic or human sacrifice, whose cults often glorified war, pillage, the degradation of women, incest, etc.

Israel's God is wholly different from man, always takes the initiative, fills him with awe, can neither be controlled by magic nor manipulated by sacrifice; he demands man's total submission. He is the Lord of all history, but yet is loving, good, always faithful to his people. Israel's unique concept of Yahweh, their God, can be summed up in two poignant passages: **Read Exodus 15, 11–16; and Deuteronomy 7, 6–12.**

If man were to form his idea of God from his desert experience, the God so conceived would be created in the image and likeness of the desert. He would be an unforgiving enemy, harsh and cruel. He would

... be not unlike the Mesopotamian Nergal who seems to exhibit the character of the murderous burning sun, or of the Syrian Hadad, a stormy warrior who flings his thunderbolts with awesome abandon. The God of Israel was not a reflection of the desert; yet the desert was the scene where man in the Old Testament encountered God. No one who is at all familiar with the Old Testament can think that the God whom Israel encountered in the desert derived his character from the desert; if he had, no Israelite poet could ever have said that his covenant of love is above all his works. Such a God could have claimed only that terrified submission which man must pay to superior irrational force ("Into the Desert" by John L. McKenzie, in *The Way*, London, Vol. 1, No. 1).

Moses died within sight of the Promised Land, and Joshua was selected by God to lead the people across the Jordan and into Canaan. They "passed over" the Jordan into the Promised Land. This was the land to which Abraham had been led by God centuries before; today, it is, roughly, the State of Israel. Eventually, with God's consistent help, they conquered the land and divided it among the twelve tribes. Judges were placed as rulers over the tribes.

Some people, reading of the bloody conquest of the Promised Land (the books of Joshua and Judges, apparently divinely authorized in Deuteronomy 20), wonder at the cruel deity portrayed there—he is certainly infinitely remote from the God of Jesus. Israel thought of its God at this relatively primitive period as a purely nationalistic deity, a God of Battles whose power was chiefly shown in the prosecution of Holy War. God would gradually manage to expand their moral consciousness over the succeeding centuries, and they would get a much different picture of him. But we might well ask today, after two World Wars and Vietnam, if we are much better.

The Exodus was over. God had kept his promise. He had given the Israelites a home of their own. But they were still unfaithful to him. **The Israelites broke the covenant again and again, but God was always faithful.** His people worshipped pagan gods and adopted immoral pagan customs. The Old Testament then portrays God as allowing disasters to come upon them—war, famine, plague, conquest, exile—in order to bring them back to repentance. He continually forgave them and allowed them to renew the covenant.

A touching description of God's love for his unfaithful people is

Hosea's tragic story of his marriage with the prostitute, Gomer. After the birth of their three children, Gomer takes up with other men, leaves Hosea, and again becomes a prostitute. Because he still loves her, Hosea seeks her out and takes her back. Thus God loves his unfaithful people and takes them back—including us today:

> She decked herself with her rings and jewelry, and went after her lovers, and forgot me, says the Lord. Therefore, behold, I will allure her, and bring her into the wilderness, and speak tenderly to her. . . . And in that day, says the Lord, you will call me "My husband," and no longer will you call me "My Baal" (false god) (Cf. Hosea, chapters 1–3).

IN THE LITURGY

At Mass the first scripture reading is normally a passage from the Old Testament, recounting some part of this great story for our benefit today.

During the first official eucharistic prayer, the priest asks God to accept our offerings "as once you accepted the gifts of your servant Abel, the sacrifice of Abraham, our father in faith, and the bread and wine offered by your priest Melchisedech."

In the Litany for the Dying, the Church asks Abel, Abraham, and the patriarchs and prophets to pray for us, and then petitions: "Deliver, O Lord, the soul of your servant, as you delivered Abraham from Ur of the Chaldees . . . as you delivered Isaac from becoming a sacrifice at the hand of his father, Abraham . . . as you delivered Moses from the power of Pharaoh, King of Egypt. . . ."

And in the burial service the Church prays: "May the angels lead you to the bosom of Abraham (heaven)."

During the Easter Vigil Service, the high point of the Church's year, the great Easter hymn is chanted, pointing out the connection between Christ and Moses, and Christ and the paschal lamb:

> Jesus Christ, our Lord, paid to the eternal Father the whole debt of Adam, blotting out the bond that still held us forfeit, with his dear blood. The paschal feast is this! Here the lamb is slain, with whose blood the doors of his faithful people are made holy. This night long ago thou didst rescue the sons of Israel, our fathers, out of Egypt.

DAILY LIVING: MEETING GOD

In human history men have met God in a decision of conscience and have been led by him to an "exodus" in search of freedom and dignity. Often, as with the Israelites, the journey was painful and confusing. The early Christians who gave up everything were an example, as were the countless peoples who sought a human identity, the waves of immigrants who peopled America, those today who risk death escaping Iron Curtain repression, and those who struggle for civil liberties.

Currently many who struggle for human rights echo this great human tradition. Aware of their weaknesses but driven by conscience, they ask: "Let my people go ... to be able to vote freely ... to advance themselves and live decently in their own land!"

God communicates with us today through the events of our life as he did to the great men of the Old Testament. But he is always the hidden God who will never overwhelm us. We must be alert to the signs he gives us, to his overtures of love. In the things that happen to us we should try to perceive what lesson he is trying to teach, what bit of love he is trying to communicate to us. Everyone and everything that is part of our life can have a meaning for us.

If we do not recognize God acting in our life, perhaps it is because we are not yet ready to take the risk of opening ourselves to his love. One who is unwilling to risk, to give of himself in love, will never perceive the love that is being offered him. To the one who is willing to love, on the other hand, life is full of wonderful meanings.

Abraham had to be willing to give up what was most dear to him, and Moses had to risk his life and the lives of many others. God may not ask this of us, but he does ask that we try to live up to our conscience, be true to ourselves, and avoid any serious sin that might alienate us from him and our fellow man.

SOME SUGGESTIONS FOR ...

DISCUSSION

Can you see the value of covenants, particularly one between God and man?

Is there an "exodus" of current or past history that has particularly impressed you?

Do you find meaningful the notion of God communicating with us through the events of life?

FURTHER READING

* *Covenant in the Old Testament,* Guinan (Franciscan Herald Press, 1975)—An easily readable, fine treatment of the various covenants in the Old Testament, and their significance and meaning for us today.
* *Theology of the Old Testament,* McKenzie (Doubleday, 1976)—An excellent study of the Old Testament as the history of Yahweh's (God's) special people, and their dynamic, living relationship with him.
* *Your Word Is Fire,* Green and Holtz, eds. (Paulist Press, 1977)—Out of the great Jewish religious revival of Hasidism, a new, moving spirit came to the Jews in the villages of Poland and the Ukraine two hundred years ago. In this small book of very wonderful little prayers, today's reader may feel something of the exhilarating, "ecstatic" Presence that moved these people.

FURTHER VIEWING/LISTENING

Moses and the Covenant (Roa Films)—A six-part filmstrip set that tells the story of Moses and the Israelites from the birth of Moses to the entrance into the Promised Land.

PERSONAL REFLECTION

A "passing over" from slavery and suffering, through the desert, to freedom and happiness was necessary for the Israelites. Later Christ will accomplish his great work by passing over from suffering and death to life. So anyone who would find God today must undergo suffering in order to enter eternal joy.

In the desert Israel was alone before God: there were no distractions, no place to run and hide. Their decision was whether to live or die. If they wanted to survive, there was only one way: total submission to God's will. Realizing that God alone could save them, Israel enthusiastically accepted his covenant.

Sometimes God must bring us "into the desert," make us realize our total inadequacy, so that we will give ourselves to him. I should ask for the faith to recognize him in my sufferings and inadequacies.

5
Priests, Kings and Prophets Prepare the Way

SACRIFICES, PRIESTS AND KINGS

After Mount Sinai, God dwelt among his people with an extraordinary familiarity. He was present especially above the Ark of the Covenant, a small gold-covered chest containing the commandments, which was placed in the tabernacle, a portable temple-tent (Exodus, chapters 25–27). From here God communicated with Moses and his other representatives among the people. In this, we have a prelude to our practice of reserving the eucharist, Christ's special presence among us, in the tabernacles of our churches.

As God's people came to know him they worshipped him, to show their feelings toward him, to give themselves to him, and be united with him. They wanted to show their recognition that he was their God, and to express their obligations to him. As with any growing love, they also wished to be transformed, united with him.

They worshipped God particularly by sacrifice—by publicly offering gifts to him. Just as men have always expressed their feelings toward one another by giving gifts, so they offered gifts to the deity.

The great events of life are celebrated by giving gifts, expressing many things, particularly a desire to be united with one we love. We give birthday presents and wedding gifts, we exchange gifts at Christmas, etc. Gifts express love, praise, thanks, repentance, and they often implicitly ask for something. A gift stands for the giver— accepting the gift means acceptance of the one who gave it, as when a girl accepts a young man's ring. Above all, then, a gift expresses our desire to be united in love with the one to whom we give it.

Sacrifice meant offering a gift, by a priest, changing it in some way, and eating of it. People would take some gift that represented themselves, and offer it to God by means of their representative, a priest. He would change or transform the gift to signify that they were giving it to God, that it no longer belonged to them—often he would kill a living gift, or victim—and then he would burn it to further show God's acceptance and possession of it. Sometimes there would be a meal or banquet, a communion, to further signify union with God by eating of what was now divine.

Abel had offered sacrifice to God, as had Noah, and Abraham had been ready to sacrifice his only son. After one of Abraham's victories, the mysterious figure of Melchisedech offered bread and wine to God in thanksgiving, a foreshadowing of what Christ and the Christian priesthood would do.

> And Melchisedech, king of Salem, brought out bread and wine; he was priest of God most high and he blessed him and said, "Blessed be Abram by God most high, maker of heaven and earth. . . ." (Genesis 14, 18–20).

A sacrifice had sealed the old covenant, and the Israelites were guided by God to lay down definite norms for sacrifices. These were offered by the priests at an altar set aside for this in the tabernacle (Leviticus, chapters 1–7). As when any group offers a gift, one person, the priest, made the offering.

The priests were men specially chosen to offer sacrifice, and to bring God's blessings to the people. They were essentially mediators, "go-betweens." God chose Aaron, Moses' brother, as his first priest and his descendants were to carry on the work of the priesthood. They were made priests at a special ceremony during which they were anointed with oil and clothed in special garb:

> "Then bring near to you Aaron your brother, and his sons with him, from among the people of Israel, to serve me as priests. . . . And you shall make holy garments for Aaron your brother, for glory and for beauty . . . and you shall take the anointing oil, and pour it on his head and anoint him" (Exodus 28, 1–2; 29, 7).

Later Christ will offer his life as the perfect sacrifice to begin the new covenant and the elements of sacrifice will then be brought to perfection. All the sacrifices before Christ prepared the way for his perfect sacrifice which would attain the perfect union of man with God.

In the most solemn and significant Hebrew ritual, the Sacrifice of Atonement, the high priest once a year sacrificed a bull and goat outside the sanctuary, then took their blood into the Holy of Holies, and sprinkled it over the covering of the Ark where Yahweh dwelt. Since their life was considered to be in their blood, these victims representing the people were united with God as far as it was possible to do so. Later the New Testament writers will show how Christ shed his blood, as he sacrificed his life to bring all mankind "once for all" into God's presence in heaven.

The Israelites also wanted a king and God inspired Samuel to anoint Saul. When he was killed, David was anointed king (c. 1000 B.C.). The job was evidently too much for Saul and he went slowly mad. The shepherd boy, David, was brought in to soothe Saul with his music, became a popular hero after he killed the giant Goliath, and then had to flee the paranoid ruler. Upon Saul's tragic death, David was chosen king by popular acclaim and made Jerusalem the capital city, bringing there the Ark of the Covenant. The biblical books 1 and 2 Samuel tell of this period.

David sinned but repented, and God promised that someday a king would come from his descendants whose kingdom would last forever. When the prophet Nathan excoriated David for his adultery with Bathsheba and his murder of her husband, he became a great figure of true repentance; then through Nathan God made him his great promise: **Read 2 Samuel 7, 12–16.**

Solomon, David's son, succeeded him and built the magnificent temple in Jerusalem in which he placed the Ark of the Covenant. There sacrifices to God took place daily. Solomon had a reign of great splendor, the high point of Israelite power and influence. But like many of his people he sinned by greed and idolatry, and eventually rebellion arose, in the midst of which Solomon died. The two biblical books of Kings tell of this and the following periods.

Because of their sinfulness, Israel was now split into the northern kingdom, Israel, and the southern kingdom, Judah, whose people came to be called "Jews." The latter, the two tribes of Judah and Benjamin, would contain the tiny "remnant" which would eventually fulfill God's promises. It is more than coincidental that as God's people of the Old Testament were split because of their sinfulness, so it was to be with his people of the New Testament: when Christendom became widely corrupted, its unity was also destroyed.

However, God did not abandon his people, but sent them in their degeneration another group of outstanding men, the prophets.

THE PROPHETS

The prophets were men especially called by God to speak in his name, his spokesmen to his people for several hundred years. They were one of the most amazing groups in history. Herdsmen, priests, noblemen, migrant workers, they shared one thing: a burning desire to return their people to faithfulness to the covenant and to deepen their understanding of it. They were the conscience of Israel. Through them Israel's religion was gradually purified and developed.

By their lives of total dedication and their outstanding deeds, the prophets gained acceptance in Israel—though, like forthright people, they were usually unpopular, and not infrequently were murdered by the people.

The great Elijah, for instance, whose cave can be seen today on Mount Carmel above the modern city of Haifa, had to contend with the weak and degenerate king Ahab and his infamous queen, Jezebel, and with the attraction of Baal-worship and its human sacrifice and other gross immoralities. The first book of Kings tells how Elijah pitted his sacrifice-offering against that of the prophets of Baal: God sent down lightning, "the fire of the Lord," to set fire dramatically to his offering, and the prophets of Baal were disgraced and slain. Jezebel then promised she would kill Elijah. He fled into the Sinai desert, weak and weary, wanting to die where God had first revealed himself to Israel. There God came to him and reassured him: **Read 1 Kings 19, 1-18.**

Then there is Amos, probably a migratory worker, a forceful man who castigated the wealthy for their oppression of the poor: ". . . they sell the righteous for silver, and the needy for a pair of shoes—they that trample the head of the poor into the dust of the earth, and turn aside the way of the afflicted. . . ." (Amos 2, 6–7).

Amos particularly condemned their smug pride over their status which would eventually destroy them: **Read Amos 3, 1–2; 4, 1–5.**

In predicting the coming disaster, he spoke of the "remnant" which would be preserved faithful to the Lord:

> Thus says the Lord, "As the shepherd rescues from the mouth of the lion two legs, or a piece of an ear, so shall the people of Israel who dwell in Samaria be rescued, with the corner of a couch and part of a bed" (Amos 3, 12).

Isaiah was the longest-lived of the prophets, and even as he foretold the destruction to come, he touchingly reminded the people of God's love:

> But Sion said, The Lord has forsaken me, my Lord has forgotten me. Can a woman forget her sucking child, that she should have no compassion on the son of her womb? Even these may forget, yet I will not forget you (Isaiah 49, 14–15).

The prophets' predictions of destruction were largely ignored by the sinful people. Then the blow fell: first the northern kingdom was destroyed by the Assyrians who swept over the country and deported many of the people. Then the kingdom of Judah fell in 587 B.C. and the people were deported to Babylon. But the prophets consoled them, and many of the most beautiful psalms (religious hymns) are from this period. From this time on many of the Jews would be scattered "among the nations," in the diaspora, eventually providing bases for the spread of Christ's teachings.

At this critical time God promised a new, more perfect covenant. Jeremiah gives this great promise (Cf. also Ezekiel 36, 24ff.): **Read Jeremiah 31, 31–34.**

The prophets' teaching now gradually converged toward the Messiah who was to come. These prophecies were given at different times and are scattered throughout the Old Testament. Many are obscure and seemingly contradictory, and evidently the prophets themselves did not understand exactly how they would be fulfilled; only when we study the life of Christ do we see how he fulfilled them.

Many of the prophecies concerned a new age, "the day of the

Lord." Joel, for instance, saw it first of all as a time of judgment upon Israel:

> Let all the inhabitants of the land tremble for the day of the Lord is coming, it is near, a day of darkness and gloom, a day of clouds and thick darkness! (Joel 2, 1–2).

But it will also be a time of great blessings, when God's spirit is "poured out on all flesh." Peter's Pentecost sermon, the first announcement of the Christian message, will quote this: **Read Joel 2, 28–29.**

The "Messiah" or "Christ" means the one anointed with holy oil, as were the priests, kings, and prophets. The word "Messiah" meant particularly the king who would fulfill Israel's destiny. While the prophecies are often obscure, one looking at them with the help of faith can discern many characteristics of the Messiah who would begin this new age: **Read Isaiah 35, 3–6.**

The Messiah would be a great king of David's lineage whose rule would never end. This, we saw, was predicted by Nathan. We should note that the ideal king in those days was Yahweh's instrument, the one through whom he saved his people, who protected them from external enemies and from oppression by the powerful. A few centuries later the prophet Isaiah also told of the kingly Messiah who would be a descendant of David; his best-known prophecies concern Emmanuel, "God-with-us" (chapters 7–11). We shall see that Christ is this kingly descendant of David: **Read Isaiah 9, 2–7.**

A mysterious "Son of Man" also appears in connection with the messianic hopes of God's people. Christ will often use this title to refer to himself:

> I saw in the night visions, and behold, with the clouds of heaven there came one like the son of man, and he came to the Ancient of Days and was presented before him. And to him was given dominion and glory and kingdom, that all peoples, nations, and languages should serve him. . . . (Daniel 7, 13–14; cf. Psalm 110).

The "suffering servant" is perhaps the best-known figure of the Messiah, given by the prophet known as Second Isaiah. He stressed two ideas difficult for the Jews to grasp, but of deep importance to

God's plan: all nations would be called to know and love God, and redemption would come about through the suffering of the innocent Servant of Yahweh—a figure of Christ: **Read Isaiah 53, 3–7.**

After the exile, a remnant of Jews returned to Jerusalem and began to rebuild. They were chastened and strongly attached to the Law—the five books of Moses (or Torah) elaborated and explained by tradition—and convinced more than ever of their destiny as the chosen people. A total theocracy, with Yahweh as their sole ruler, they considered the high priest his representative and their leader.

In the 4th century B.C. they were conquered by the Greeks, persecuted, and became somewhat hellenized. The Hebrew scriptures were translated into the Greek Septuagint about 250 B.C. Then the Assyrians swept over Palestine, and finally in the century before Christ the Romans conquered the land and installed a puppet king, Herod.

The Old Testament ends with God's people longing for the messianic age to come, but there is confusion about it. Many looked for a new time of great material prosperity. Others expected a great king, like David or Solomon, who would lead them to freedom and glory and establish once more the united kingdom of Israel.

Conscious of God's great deeds on their behalf over the centuries, they looked to his promises for the future. They were a small, almost obscure country on the fringe of a great empire. But they were a monotheistic stronghold in a world of polytheism, superstition, and rationalism; and their moral life was far above that of the rest of the Hellenistic world of the time.

We should note at this time the influential groups in Palestine who were to play a role in Christ's life: Besides the powerful priestly class, there were the **Scribes** or lawyers, the official interpreters of the Law, the most honored and influential group in the land. The **Pharisees,** originally concerned to keep the people free of foreign domination, had become narrowly nationalistic; they had added many minute traditions to the Law and exaggerated its literal fulfillment, rather than keeping its spirit.

The **Sadducees** were a proud aristocracy, more liberal in their interpretation of the Law and more open to the Gentiles, but as narrowly opposed as the Pharisees to any messianic changes. Both groups were more than content with the "status quo," and would be Christ's strongest opponents. The **Essenes,** the community of Qumran and the famous Dead Sea Scrolls, withdrew into the desert and lived a strict, celibate, community life to prepare for the coming of the Lord.

Lastly, there was the "remnant," the small number of people loyal to the Lord who were to be the start of the new Israel and the new covenant, the new people of God. Of no particular class or status, they tried to practice a purer, more perfect religion, in their hearts as well as externally. Mary, the mother of Christ, is their outstanding example. They are the "poor" of Israel, the "little ones" whose longing for the Savior is epitomized in this longing cry:

> But I am poor and needy; hasten to help me, O God! Thou art my help and my deliverer; O Lord, do not tarry! (Psalm 70, 5).

We can now sum up the main ideas of the Old Testament: God chooses the Israelites . . . makes a covenant with them, forming them into his people . . . speaking through human representatives who have his authority . . . and who guide the people in living the covenant and worshipping God by sacrifice . . . looking forward to the Messiah . . . who will establish a new and perfect covenant.

IN THE LITURGY

The Psalms are the inspired religious hymns or poems of the Old Testament. The Church uses many of them in her liturgy, and priests recite many of them each day as the Church's official prayer. They make excellent and inspiring reading for anyone.

At Mass, immediately before reading the Gospel, the priest asks God to cleanse his heart and lips as he did Isaiah's, so that he may be prepared to announce his Word. In one of the official eucharistic prayers, at the heart of the Mass, we ask God to accept our sacrifice ". . . as you accepted the offerings of your servant Abel, the just, the sacrifice of Abraham, our father, and that of your high priest, Melchisedech."

During the Advent season—which begins with the fourth Sunday before Christmas—we relive again each year the preparation for the coming of the Messiah. Passages from the prophet Isaiah are particularly set before us during this time.

DAILY LIVING: OUR FAITH EXPRESSED BY
REVERENCE AND WORSHIP

Faith is the dominant role of God's people of the Old Testament from Abraham on. They are given very little to rely on, not even the assurance of a life after death, but are simply asked to have faith that God will bless them. And he did: far beyond their desire for lands and crops and offspring, he brought them to eternal happiness with himself.

When their faith would seem to be at its breaking point, God would intervene with some sign of his presence and love. Some miraculous event would take place, or a prophet would appear to encourage them. So, if we look closely, we can discern his action when we most need it in our lives.

Reverence for God was great among his people, so much so that they would not even pronounce his name. They had a great sense of awe in his presence. Abraham was seized with terror and felt himself dust and ashes before God; Moses and Elijah hid their faces in dread at his approach; Isaiah almost despaired; Daniel fell to the ground before God, his face pressed to the earth. Perhaps if we had a greater sense of reverence for God, we would be more aware of his presence in our lives.

God's people expressed their faith and gratitude for his help by worshipping him. They did this especially at the great moments in their history, by coming together as his people to worship him by sacrifice. So also today it is natural to show our gratitude for his action in our lives, and to do this not only as individuals but by worshipping together as his people.

The Mass, we saw, is the way Catholics come together each Sunday to worship God. It, too, is a sacrifice, the prolongation of the perfect sacrifice of Christ. When we take part we try to give ourselves to God, in his special presence, to be united with him.

Finally, God's special regard for the Jewish people, so shabbily treated throughout history—and in recent years with unbelievable cruelty—should lead us all to examine our consciences. Vatican Council II forcefully went on record against anti-Semitism:

> . . . the Church, mindful of the patrimony she shares with the Jews and moved not by political reasons but by the Gospel's spiritual love, deplores hatred, persecutions, displays of anti-Semitism directed against

Jews at any time and by anyone.... We cannot truly call on God, the Father of all, if we refuse to treat in a brotherly way any man (*Declaration on the Relationship of the Church to Non-Christian Religions*, no. 4).

Perhaps Pope John Paul II best summed it up when he visited the Nazi extermination camp of Auschwitz-Birkenau and openly wept as he knelt on the ground containing the remains of several million Jews, along with many Russians and Poles. He called it the "Calvary of the modern world," and said: "Auschwitz is a place everyone should visit and ask, 'What are the limits of hatred, what are the limits of destruction of man by man?' " He concluded: "The very people who received from God the commandment, 'Thou shalt not kill,' itself experienced in overwhelming measure what is meant by killing."

A mutually profitable dialogue has been progressing between Jewish and Roman Catholic scholars, a hopeful sign of a new era emerging in world history. This dialogue also increasingly goes on in many places and at every level. It has led not only to a better understanding of the others' traditions, but to a clarification and deepening of one's own roots. This work is, of course, God's, but some noticeable progress is emerging. Some Jews, for instance, can consider Jesus as the last of the Jewish prophets. And not long ago the Catholics in the dialogue reached an unofficial but landmark consensus that there should no longer be Christian attempts to proselytize among Jews, i.e., attempts to convert them from Judaism to Christianity. (Obviously some may long since have lost contact with Judaism's own special heritage and mission, are cut off from their Jewish spiritual roots, and will come on their own to the Church seeking a meaning to life, a spiritual home.)

Given what was said above about the centuries of denigration that Jews have endured, culminating in the holocaust-horror, this emerging Catholic position of desisting from proselytizing among Jews makes much sense. It also points up a problem Catholics and other Christians have with "fundamentalist" or very conservative Christian groups, whose simplistic and distorted interpretation of St. Paul's statement about Judaism's conversion (cf. Romans 11, 23) seems typical of the inability of these groups to discern God's genuine approval of anything other than their own narrow and self-righteously judgmental Christianity.

A practical, perhaps painful, note for those contemplating a Jewish-Catholic marriage: Despite the growing understanding spoken of above, there are, in many cases, deep problems that should be thoroughly and honestly gone into beforehand. These involve not only the couple's own feelings, but also family religious traditions, and especially the future religious upbringing of the couple's children. There should be much frank discussion, learning one another's traditions in some depth, consultation with clergy, and patient, sensitive, mature communication.

SOME SUGGESTIONS FOR ...

DISCUSSION

Can you understand the role of prophets—and see how such men are needed throughout history, including today?

What action of God in the Old Testament is particularly striking to you?

Can you discern our sinful tendency to "scapegoat," to blame others, such as the Jewish people, for things we ourselves are guilty of, especially our tendency toward envy?

FURTHER READING

* *Understanding the Old Testament,* Anderson (Prentice-Hall, 1975, 3rd ed.)—A very good, comprehensive text for persons or groups interested in learning more about the entire Old Testament.
* *Israel's Prophets: Envoys of the King,* Wifall (Franciscan Herald Press, 1974)—An easily readable introduction to the meaning of prophecy, as seen in the great prophets of the Old Testament.
* *The Relevance of the Prophets,* Scott (Macmillan, 1968, 3rd ed.)—A classic work on the prophets and their message, good for anyone, on an introductory level. **The Message of the Prophets,* von Rad (Harper & Row, 1965)—A fairly scholarly book, but it is rich in theological depth. Very good for someone wanting to go deeper.
* *Faith Without Prejudice,* Fisher (Paulist Press, 1978)—Aimed at teachers and parents who are attempting to instill a "faith without prejudice" in their classrooms and homes, this is a popular presentation of the current relationship between Christianity and Judaism. Practical suggestions on family prayer, etc., make this book especially good.
* *Night,* Wiesel (Avon, 1972)—The classic work of a remarkable man who has dedicated his life to probing and spreading the message of the holocaust. A "must" for anyone concerned with our capacity for evil toward our fellow humans.

6
Christ Comes Among Us

How do we know about Jesus Christ? What was so unique about his life? Who did he claim to be? Why was he not accepted more widely? What relevance has his teaching for me today?

THE COMING OF JESUS CHRIST

We saw that the Jewish world of the first century was looking for the coming of the Messianic Age—a king, a kingdom that would fulfill the prophecies and bring God's blessings once again to his people. The New Testament tells of the coming of the Messiah and his fulfillment of these hopes.

An incident that took place during the first days of the Christian Church is recorded in the Acts of the Apostles: **Read Acts 3, 1–10.** This story of a man cured instantly "in the name of Jesus Christ of Nazareth" is typical of Christianity from the beginning. Jesus Christ of Nazareth was the inspiration and the power of Christianity from its inception. He is probably the best-known person in the history of the world. Who was he, and what do we really know about him?

The New Testament is the principal source for the life and teachings of Jesus Christ although he is mentioned briefly in a number of ancient writings. The New Testament, the second part of the bible, consists of 27 books: the four gospels, outlines of part of Christ's life and teachings; the Acts of the Apostles, some incidents in the life of the early Christian Church; the epistles, letters written by Christ's apostles to early Christian communities; and Revelation or the Apocalypse, a highly symbolic writing about the early Church and the final events of history.

The New Testament gives a substantially accurate outline of Christ's life and teachings, but not a scientific, detailed biography.

There is as much evidence for the authenticity of the main events and sayings contained in the New Testament story of Jesus as there is, for example, of Julius Caesar, or any other ancient historical figure. But the authors give only a framework, the substance of what Christ said and did. They were not writing biographies of Christ as people write biographies today.

The New Testament is the record of the early Church's growth in faith and understanding of who and what Jesus Christ is. The authors tell the story of Christ's saving deeds as seen through the eyes of believers writing for believers. Their concern is to show not only an event but its inner religious meaning. They are not greatly concerned about when or where a thing happened, the details of what happened, the exact words Christ used, etc. They show a gradual growth in understanding of who Christ was and of his revelation. To bring out the inner religious meaning of the events of Christ's life, they sometimes arrange details according to Old Testament concepts, and often express themselves in the imaginative language of their Semitic background.

To guide us in our interpretation of the New Testament, then, we use tradition, his Church's understanding of Christ's teachings. Since the New Testament came from the early Christian community, it is best interpreted in the light of the community's beliefs. This is found particularly in the other writings of Christ's early followers that have come down to us.

Since the New Testament is a record of faith, the reader must have faith—or at least be open to the possibility of faith— if he is to derive full benefit from it. The skeptic, the one whose mind is closed against the possibility of a divine intervention in Christ, will get little profit from it.

The four gospels, particularly, tell of Christ's life and teachings. They are attributed to Matthew, Mark, Luke, and John. They are really four different accounts of the single "gospel," that is, the "good news" that God has come and saved mankind, climaxing his mighty deeds of the Old Testament. This good news was first announced by the preaching of the apostles and then gradually took on written form in the Christian Church.

The gospel authors take excerpts from Christ's life and teachings, and arrange and interpret them for the particular needs of their audience. Matthew writes particularly to show that Christ is the promised Messiah; Mark's is the oldest and shortest gospel and is the basis for much of Matthew and Luke; Luke's is the most complete gospel, and shows particularly a very human and universal Christ; John's is the most symbolic of the gospels and was written to show that Jesus is the eternal Son of God who revealed himself through many "signs."

There is practically nothing known about the early life of Jesus, until he begins to preach publicly. The gospel writers are concerned primarily with his public teachings, his message through them to the world. But since the whole of the gospels was written to tell us something, we will consider briefly the story of Jesus' early years.

The life of Jesus begins with the story of the angel coming to Mary which brings out the divine origin of Jesus. Read Luke 1, 26–38. Luke tells us in this account that God somehow communicated to Mary that she was to be the mother of the Savior, and she consented. She then miraculously conceived Jesus Christ. We celebrate this event as the feast of the Annunciation, March 25.

> These initial chapters of Luke and Matthew are the Jewish style of writing, in which the sacred Christian mysteries are illustrated by prophetic Old Testament situations. Here the angel's greeting alludes to the prophecy of Zephaniah (3, 14–20) in which God expresses his love for the virgin "Daughter of Sion." Thus Mary symbolizes all that God loves in Israel. Mary is the new Ark of the Covenant, the place where God dwells, for she too is "overshadowed by the power of the Most High" (Cf. Exodus 40, 35).

Mary, the mother of Jesus Christ, remained a virgin all her life. Joseph was the husband of Mary and the foster-father of Jesus. This is traditional Christian teaching. Luke emphasizes the virginal conception of Jesus by the question to the angel: "How can this be, since I have no husband?" (1, 34), and the angel's response. Matthew tells how Joseph's doubts upon seeing Mary pregnant were settled by a revelation that the conception was miraculous (Matthew 1, 18–25).

A modern Protestant theologian writes perceptively of this:

> Her unique relation with the Spirit sets her in such close proximity to God that she must remain alone in order to point out to our eyes this unique choice of her Lord. . . . Her virginity appears at one and the same time as a sign of consecration and a sign of solitary powerlessness

which gives glory to the fullness and power of God . . . a sign of poverty, of humility, and of waiting upon God . . . a sign of emptiness and total trust in God who makes rich such poor creatures as we are (Max Thurian, *Mary, Mother of All Christians:* Herder & Herder, 1964, p. 31).

Regarding the "brothers" of Jesus mentioned in the gospels, the word "brother" was commonly used among the Jews for any blood relation (another woman, incidentally, is mentioned as the mother of two of these). Matthew says of Joseph, "And he did not know her (Mary) till she brought forth her firstborn son" (Matthew 1, 25), but the word "till" as used here need not mean any change in Mary's virginity after Christ's birth (Cf. Isaiah 46; Matthew 12, 20). Nor does calling Jesus the "firstborn" son imply Mary had other children; this title was always given to the firstborn male, even if an only child (Cf. Exodus 13, 2).

Early Christian writings widely attest to Mary's perpetual virginity: St. Basil sums up the early Christian teaching, "The friends of Christ do not tolerate hearing that the Mother of God ever ceased to be a virgin" (*Hom. in S. Christi Generationem,* n. 5). The Reformers also held strongly to this belief, echoing the Christian view through the centuries.

However, Mary's virginity should be seen as more than mere physical inviolability. For many today whether Mary is or is not physically a virgin is of small consequence; they see her virginity as symbolizing something far greater, her profound attitude of total openness to God alone, her total consecration of herself to him before anyone and anything else—and in this each of us, virginal or not, has the power to imitate her.

As we shall see (chapter 23), Mary is a figure of the Church, and her virginity is a prophetic sign of the Church's ideal purity and total dedication to Christ. She is the ideal Christian, totally given only to God.

St. Luke continues the story by telling us that Mary went to visit her cousin, Elizabeth, the mother of John the Baptist: "And when Elizabeth heard the greeting of Mary, the babe leaped in her womb. And Elizabeth was filled with the Holy Spirit, and she exclaimed with a loud cry, 'Blessed are you among women and blessed is the fruit of your womb! And why is this granted me, that the mother of my Lord should come to me?' " (Luke 1, 41–43).

This greeting of Elizabeth concludes the first part of the prayer, the "Hail Mary." Mary is the last and noblest of the long line of Israel's "poor," the humble ones who will be the start of the new Israel. Mary's answer to Elizabeth, as Luke presents it, is a mosaic of

Old Testament texts expressing joy at what God has done through her. The Church uses these verses in its blessing of a mother and her newborn child:

> "My soul magnifies the Lord, and my spirit rejoices in God my Savior; for he has regarded the low state of his handmaid. . . ." (Cf. Luke 1, 46-55).

Luke continues with the oft-told story of the birth of Jesus: Read Luke 2, 1-7.

Christmas Day, December 25, is the day on which we celebrate the birth of Jesus. It is a holyday on which all Catholics attend Mass to rejoice at this great event. The date was chosen by the early Christians to counteract a pagan feast on the same day. Jesus was actually born about 7 B.C.—our present calendar, which dates years from the birth of Christ, took the wrong year as a starting point.

Jesus' birth in poor circumstances is a lesson to us in humility and detachment from riches. The first to greet him were God's faithful poor, Mary, Joseph and the shepherds from the neighboring hills. Luke tells how an angel announced Christ's birth to the shepherds and invited them to be his first worshippers; he concludes with the song that has been immortalized in Christian worship:

> And suddenly there was with the angel a multitude of the heavenly host praising God and saying "Glory to God in the highest, and on earth peace among men with whom he is pleased" (Luke 2, 13–14).

The gospels tell of other early events of Christ's life. These stories are meant to show that Jesus is the expected Messiah-king, and that he is more than human.

His presentation in the temple forty days after his birth (Cf. Luke 2, 22–39) is celebrated each year on February 2nd, and is also called the feast of the Purification of Mary. Since Christ was hailed in this incident as the "light of revelation to the Gentiles," on this day in all Catholic churches the candles used in divine services are blessed—hence the popular name "Candlemas Day."

The coming of the Magi is told to portray the coming of the first Gentiles to worship Christ—celebrated as the Epiphany, January 6th—and the flight of the Holy Family into Egypt to escape Herod's persecution (Matthew, chapter 2).

Matthew, to show that Christ is the new Moses, the new leader of God's people, parallels the coming of each in the first two chapters: Rulers and their courts tremble at the announcement of their births; Herod consults his scribes as Pharaoh did his astrologers; both tyrants decree the murder of children, from which both heroes escape; and both saviors, persecuted and away from their people, receive a heavenly message to return.

Christ's early years are summed up by Luke: He tells us how the child Jesus had been lost by his parents in Jerusalem when he was twelve. They found him in the temple in deep discussion with the teachers of the Law who "... were amazed at his understanding and his answers." When Mary reprimanded him, his response shows an awareness of his mission: "Did you not know that I must be in my Father's house?" Then he grew up, obediently, in simple, humble surroundings:

And he went down with them and came to Nazareth, and was obedient to them: and his mother kept all these things in her heart. And Jesus advanced in wisdom and in stature, and in favor with God and man (Luke 2, 51–52).

Years pass, and then comes John the Baptist, the last of the prophets, preaching repentance and conversion to prepare the way for Christ. John developed as a strict ascetic in the desert, and one day appeared, a striking figure, proclaiming, "Repent, for the kingdom of heaven is at hand" (Matthew 3, 2).

John the Baptist asked people to be changed interiorly, to repent of their sins and be converted, to turn fully toward God. His "baptism" was a sign of this, a primitive forerunner of the Christian sacrament of baptism. When the people wanted to acclaim him the Messiah, he told them he was only preparing the way: "After me comes he who is mightier than I, the thong of whose sandals I am not worthy to stoop down and untie" (Mark 1, 7).

Jesus comes to John and asks to be baptized, and then prepares for his public life by a forty-day fast in the desert. Jesus asked for baptism to connect John's mission with what he would soon begin himself. His desert ordeal, climaxed by severe temptations from the devil, parallels the forty years the Israelites wandered in the desert, and is the model of our practice of penance during the forty days of Lent (Cf. Mark 1, 9–14; Matthew, 3, 13–4, 11).

Christ starts his mission in the harsh desert, as Israel had, to show that he is the beginning of God's new people. He is to be the "new Israel," the one who takes on himself all the aspirations and inadequacies of God's people, and begins a new, transformed people. In the desert he also faces God in stark loneliness, emptiness, fear, and the temptation to discouragement and rebellion—and thus purified he begins his mission or public life.

Christ's public life is the two or three years that he spent preaching, teaching, and working miracles, leading up to his suffering and death. He became known as a great preacher, a reader of hearts, and a wonder-worker:

> And he went about all Galilee, teaching in their synagogues and preaching the gospel of the kingdom and healing every disease and every infirmity among the people. So his fame spread throughout all Syria, and they brought him all the sick, those afflicted with various diseases and pains, demoniacs, epileptics, and paralytics, and he healed them. And great crowds followed him from Galilee and the Decapolis and Jerusalem and Judea and from beyond the Jordan (Matthew 4, 23–25).

THE KINGDOM OF GOD IS HERE!

The central theme of Christ's preaching is the good news of the kingdom of God: ". . . Jesus came into Galilee, preaching the gospel of the kingdom of God, and saying, 'The time is fulfilled, and the kingdom of God is at hand. Repent and believe in the gospel' " (Mark 1, 14–15).

Jesus' announcement of the kingdom was what the Jewish people had been anticipating for hundreds of years. We saw how they were awaiting this new, wonderful messianic age of great blessings. Christ now revealed that it was coming about. This was the best possible news they could hear—and thus it is called the gospel, the good news.

But when Christ revealed that his kingdom was an interior, spiritual one, only a comparative few accepted him. These were the small remnant, the poor ones whose hearts were truly open to God's teaching and rule. We saw how most people expected a great political king, or one who would bring many material blessings, or who would perfectly observe the Law—but Christ asked an interior change in oneself to belong to his kingdom.

The kingdom of God is his loving rule, his reign over us, and our submission to him. When we believe in him and do his will, we belong to his kingdom. God's reign or kingdom is his guiding presence, his grace-presence, within us; to submit to his loving guidance is to belong to the kingdom.

To be a part of God's kingdom, Christ said, we must undergo an interior conversion. We must have a change of heart, repenting of our sins, determined to begin a new life: "Repent and believe in the gospel"—here Christ was fulfilling what John the Baptist had announced. Then in the beautiful and famous "Sermon on the Mount" Christ tells us how to live this conversion in order to be a part of his kingdom (Cf. Matthew, chapters 5–7). He begins with the eight beatitudes, the way to true happiness (the word "blessed" means "happy"): **Read Matthew 3, 3–12.**

In this kingdom the poor, the humble, the oppressed, the "little people" are the happy ones—a complete reversal of the world's usual standards whereby the rich and powerful are the favored ones. Everyone who has experienced injustice and looked to God for a better life knows what Jesus was talking about.

A new commandment, love, is the one important rule in this kingdom. The Jews, we saw, lived by the Law, particularly the commandments. Now Jesus summed up the whole law of his kingdom: "A new commandment I give to you, that you love one another; even as I have loved you, that you also love one another" (John 13, 34).

We will live in this new kingdom forever. Those who follow Christ and become part of his kingdom will be raised up from death: ". . . whoever sees the Son and believes in him, shall have everlasting life, and I will raise him up on the last day" (John 6, 40). This was indeed tremendous news to the Jews who, we saw, had only begun shortly before the time of Christ to think of the notion of a personal life after death, and were not at all clear about it. It has also been tremendous news to those who have grasped it down through the centuries.

Now on earth, those who follow Christ pray and work to extend God's kingdom of love more and more to all men. One day in heaven the kingdom will be completed—God's love will rule over us all—and we will see creation in all its glory and understand the "why" of suffering and injustice. During our present life we pray as Christ taught us: ". . . thy kingdom come, thy will be done on earth as it is in heaven."

Christ chose apostles to help spread his kingdom. They were the beginning of his Church: "And he appointed twelve that they might be with him and that he might send them forth to preach" (Mark 3, 14). Inspired by Christ, they would try to make themselves and all men submissive to God's love. He gave them "the keys of the kingdom," the power to guide men to his truth and love.

THE PROMISED MESSIAH—AND HIS REJECTION

"I am the way and the truth and the life. No one comes to the Father but by me" (John 14, 6).

Jesus thus proclaimed that he was the one sent by God as the perfect king, priest, and prophet. This summed up his earthly mission. As the "way" Jesus is our king, the perfect king predicted in the Old Testament, now come to begin an eternal spiritual kingdom. As the "truth" Jesus is the perfect prophet or teacher looked for in the Old Testament, come to give us the fullness of God's truth. As the "life" Jesus is, as we shall see, the perfect priest who sacrificed himself for us.

There is the very human story of Jesus' encounter with the Samaritan woman who had five husbands and was then living with another man. Jesus revealed her past to her, and she typically tried to distract him by launching a defense of her Samaritan worship. Then she referred to the coming Messiah whom the Samaritans thought of as a great prophet to come. Jesus told her simply, "I who speak with you am he" (John 4, 5–42).

Christ proclaimed that he was sent by God—the Messiah, but in a new, fuller, spiritual sense. We saw that the Jewish people expected the Messiah to be a great worldly leader, the inaugurator of a new age of political power and material blessings. Christ, however, did not accept the title of Messiah in this sense; while he never denied it, he seemed always uncomfortable with it. His ministry was to establish a spiritual kingdom among men, not just a material one. He was bringing messianic blessings that were eternal, beyond his people's fondest dreams. But only those who are willing to hear the truth can know of this: **Read John 18, 33–37.**

Jesus continually spoke of himself as the "Son of Man," who would one day come on the clouds of heaven (Daniel 7, 13–14). (In Ezekiel this term simply means "man.") As he was on trial for his life "... the high priest began to ask him, and said to him, 'Art thou the Christ, the Son of the Blessed One?' And Jesus said to him, 'I am. And you shall see the Son of Man sitting at the right hand of the Power and coming with the clouds of heaven'" (Mark 14, 61–62).

He shocked his followers by speaking of himself as a humiliated and suffering Son of Man, the "suffering servant" who had been predicted (Isaiah 52, 13—53, 12).

And he began to teach them that the Son of Man must suffer many things and be rejected by the elders and chief priests and scribes, and be killed, and after three days rise again. And he said this plainly. And Peter, taking him aside, began to rebuke him (Mark 8, 31–32).

Many who had heard him were skeptical, but he offered proof of his divine mission by working miracles, fulfilling the messianic prophecies, and making prophecies of his own. In particular, he predicted that he would return alive after his death; so astounding was this that only a chosen few later grasped it: **Read John 2, 18–22.**

In his teaching Jesus purged the old Law of its formalism and legalism, and completed it by his more perfect law of love. "Do not think that I have come to destroy the Law or the Prophets," he said. "I have not come to destroy but to fulfill" (Matthew 5, 17). He "spoke with authority" about the Law, and declared that what God wants is love, mercy, justice, honesty. He rebuked the Pharisees for their hypocrisy, their elaborate system of observances, mistaking the means for the end. Chapter 23 of Matthew is one of the most scathing condemnations in all literature. Finally, Jesus told them, because of their blindness "the kingdom of God will be taken away" from them, and given "to a people yielding its fruits" (Matthew 21, 43).

Most of the people did not accept Jesus, but a small number did. They were to be the beginning of his Church. The crowds who had been drawn to him by his miracles largely deserted him when he refused the role of the long-awaited political Messiah. Because he loved all men without exception, most men rejected him; Matthew quotes him as wryly commenting:

> For John came neither eating nor drinking, and they say, "He has a demon"; the Son of Man came eating and drinking, and they say, "Behold, a glutton and a drunkard, a friend of tax collectors and sinners!" (Matthew 11, 18–19).

Stung by his fearless preaching, the hypocritical leaders of the people decided that he would have to die. As his influence over the people grew, they saw him as a threat to their autocratic authority. Despite his holiness and miracles they rationalized that he was an incorrigible troublemaker and for the good of the people he would have to be eliminated. Like many who try to suppress freedom movements today, they became very much concerned with the public safety and order. They then approached Judas, Christ's traitorous apostle, and made a deal to seize his master for what a cheap suit of clothes would cost today.

After a triumphal entry into Jerusalem on Sunday, Jesus began the last week of his life, called by Christians "Holy Week." On Holy Thursday he ate his last supper with his apostles. That night, with Judas' help, he was seized by his enemies.

A farcical trial was held, Christ's enemies convicted him of blasphemy, and he was condemned to death. Like many bigots of our own day, they wanted everything to be legal. Pilate, the Roman governor who alone had the power of life and death, seems to have been convinced that Jesus was innocent. But when the Jewish authorities threatened to report him to the emperor for tolerating a rival to Caesar, he gave Christ to them.

Mocked and beaten and scourged, Jesus carried his cross to Calvary, and there he was crucified. After three hours on the cross, he died. It was the first "Good Friday." To his followers, this looked like the end of all their hopes.

But on Easter Sunday morning Jesus came back alive again as he had predicted he would. For forty days he appeared to his followers, and then finally disappeared from the earth on Ascension Thursday.

His followers returned to Jerusalem, somewhat encouraged, to await the coming of the Holy Spirit, as he had told them.

IN THE LITURGY

The "liturgical year" is the way in which we relive each year the great events of Christ's life by a series of feasts. It is centered around the two great Christian feasts of Christmas and Easter.

The Mass, our great act of worship, is centered on Christ. We learn his words and teachings especially in the scripture readings. We should remind ourselves that Christ is speaking to us as they are read.

The rosary is a devotion meaningful to some Catholics, centered around the life of Christ. It is a series of prayers, mostly "Hail Marys," repeated on fifty beads, combined with meditations on the important events in the life of Jesus, and Mary's connection with him. For many people who use the rosary, the repetition of the "Hail Marys" serves as an aid to meditation, a sort of "mantra" that holds one's attention on God, while one's specific attention is usually not concentrated on the particular words of the prayer.

DAILY LIVING: THE LIFE OF HIS KINGDOM IS LOVE

Jesus taught us above all to love God and our neighbor: Love is the cornerstone of his teaching. It was so important in his eyes that he exhorted us to love even our enemies—a teaching that was nothing short of revolutionary: **Read Matthew 5, 43–48.**

He lived all his teachings, but particularly that of love. He proved his love by dying for us, and as he was dying he prayed for his enemies: "Father, forgive them, for they do not know what they are doing" (Luke 23, 34).

Each one of us, in some small way, can imitate Christ's love. Christ showed his love in many ways during his life. In our life there is usually some one aspect of love, some virtue, that we particularly need. We might consider what one characteristic—or more—we need especially.

Jesus loved God humbly, perfectly submissive to his will. This desire to do the Father's will was so outstanding that he could say, ". . . I always do the things that are pleasing to him" (John 8, 29). Even in terrible anguish, contemplating his coming sufferings and death, he prayed: "Father, if it is possible, let this cup pass away from me; yet, not as I will but as you will" (Matthew 26, 39).

Jesus taught us that we learn how to love by prayer. He taught us to pray by his constant example. He frequently spent the whole night in prayer; he began all his important actions with prayer; he prayed especially in suffering and crisis (Cf. Luke 6, 12; John, chapter 17; Matthew 26, 36–44; Luke 23, 34 and 46). He particularly taught us **humble prayer** in the parable of the Pharisee and the publican (Cf. Luke 18, 9–14).

Jesus had courage in doing the Father's will, and in speaking the truth, no matter what people thought or what it cost him (Cf. Matthew 15, 12–14).

Jesus showed a special love for the sick, the poor, sinners, and those despised by others—the social outcasts, those who hadn't "made it" in society (Cf. Luke 7, 1–7; John 9, 1–38; Luke 7, 36–50).

He taught us to love our neighbor, regardless of his race, sex or social status, particularly in the parable of the good Samaritan (Cf. Luke 10, 30–37).

He taught us pointedly to forgive those who injure us, or else God will not forgive our misdeeds, in the parable of the unmerciful servant (Cf. Matthew, 8, 21–35).

Jesus' whole life exemplified a detachment from wealth and human possessions. We saw his humble birth and background. During his public life he showed a special love for the poor, and had no home and few possessions of his own. One day he remarked, "The foxes have dens, and the birds of the air have nests; but the Son of Man has nowhere to lay his head" (Matthew 8, 20). The ultimate foolishness of greed is shown in the parable of the rich man and Lazarus (Cf. Luke 16, 19–31).

Jesus continually taught us that God will always forgive us, no matter what we have done, as long as we are truly sorry. The wonderful parable of the prodigal son illustrates God's love and mercy (Cf. Luke 15, 11–32).

SOME SUGGESTIONS FOR . . .

DISCUSSION

What, to you, is the most meaningful thing about Christ's life and preaching?

What particular characteristic of Jesus Christ do you think you need most?

Can you see modern parallels to the action of Christ's enemies, particularly in their trying to legally dispose of him?

FURTHER READING

Note: We said that the basic source for the life of Christ is the New Testament, the second part of the bible. Here, in the four gospels, are the records of Jesus' life, his words and actions as remembered and written down by his first followers. There are various translations of the bible into English, and these are listed (with a few words of commentary about each) at the end of chapter 11, "The Great Book in Which We Meet God," along with other suggested books for studying the bible. An excellent introduction to the New Testament, easily understandable, is Pheme Perkins' *Reading the New Testament* (Paulist Press, 1978). We suggest this as the best single introduction to Jesus' life and teachings. On a deeper level, *New Testament Theology* by Joachim Jeremias is a fine biblical investigation into the life and mission of Jesus. Listed below are some others:

* *Jesus, A Gospel Portrait,* Senise (Pflaum, 1975)—A fine overview of the gospels, the world in which Jesus lived, and his central message of God's kingdom.
* *Jesus According to a Woman,* Wahlberg (Paulist Press, 1975)—A fresh, insightful portrait of Jesus from a woman's viewpoint. Excellent for both men and women.
* *The Parables of Jesus,* Jeremias (Scribner's, 1972)—A popular, easy-to-read explanation of the parables—Jesus' basic way of teaching—and their background. This is truly a classic.

FURTHER VIEWING/LISTENING

The Gospel According to Matthew (Brandon Films)—A feature-length, widely acclaimed, powerful and moving portrayal of Christ's life.

Ecce Homo (Paulist Productions)—Half-hour color life of Christ, excellently put together from art masterpieces.

The Stories of Jesus in Pastoral Ministry, Shea (NCR Cassettes)—Four cassettes by a very gifted storyteller who is also a priest/theologian/poet. He shows how storytelling can effectively get across to people Christ's ministry—and ours.

PERSONAL REFLECTION

Christ asked for a change of heart, a conversion, a rejection of one's sins and a turning more fully toward him. I should get the inspiration and strength to do this if I meditate on his life each day, perhaps by reading at least a page of the New Testament, and then trying to apply to it my own life.

We suggest reading Luke's gospel since it is the most complete. A good book on the life of Christ can give a background to enrich this reading.

The great way Catholics believe they come into special contact with Christ is at Mass. By the power of God Christ becomes present among us, particularly under the appearance of bread and wine, and prolongs or re-presents his death and resurrection. He does this so we can all take part and offer ourselves to the Father with him. At holy communion especially we are united in a most intimate way with Christ under the appearance of bread, and with one another. This, then, is our great expression of worship and love.

In order to see and experience the Mass for yourself, we suggest that you attend Mass if you are not already doing so, each Sunday if possible. Later we shall discuss the Mass in detail.

7

Christ Reveals to Us the Father, the Spirit, and Himself

What did Jesus tell us God is like? How can we have a meaningful contact with God? Can we be sure that Jesus Christ is divine and that his teaching is God's own?

It is natural to want to reveal ourselves to someone we truly love. We want that person to know as much as possible about us—to come to know our family, our friends, our daily life, our hopes and fears—and to accept us as we really are.

Jesus Christ gradually revealed to us his origin and background, his innermost life and those with whom he shared it. He did this because he loves us and wants us to know about it.

"I am from him (God), and he has sent me" (John 7, 29). Jesus said this, and meant it in its fullest, deepest sense. To understand Jesus Christ, we must try to penetrate the mystery of God's inner life. This he has opened to us. But this is not all.

Jesus Christ told us how we can ourselves share in God's own inner life, in the life of heaven itself, while here on earth. This, he said, is God's plan: that we should even now begin to share most intimately in his very life. To understand ourselves, then, our yearnings and fantastic capabilities, we study God's own life as Jesus revealed it.

OUR FATHER

In the Old Testament, God had revealed himself as one God, the Father of his people. Amid pagan polytheism many Jews had died for this truth. They came to think of God as a Father, from whom all things come, whose love was poured out on them, even when they turned from him: "Israel, says the Lord, is my first-born son. . . . Israel in his boyhood, what love I bore him! It was I, none other, that guided those first steps of theirs, and took them in my arms, and healed, all unobserved, their injuries" (Hosea 11, 1–4).

Then gradually God came to be seen as the Father, in a special way, of the future king-Messiah: "I shall be to him a father, and he shall be to me a son" (2 Samuel 7, 14).

When Jesus came he spoke many times of God as a loving Father, his Father and ours. When he was twelve years old he was missing for three days; Mary and Joseph found him in the Temple and asked why he had left them. "Did you not know that I must be in my Father's house?" he replied. Like many a young man today, he had become aware of what his vocation in life was to be. He went to Nazareth, then, and was subject to Mary and Joseph, but his heart was more and more with his heavenly Father.

When he began preaching, Jesus continually spoke of God as our Father. He told us how to pray: "Our Father, who art in heaven, hallowed be thy name. . . ." To any who might see God as a righteous or distant figure, Jesus made clear that he is a loving Father who cares for all our needs: **Read Luke 12, 24–31.**

Jesus was completely caught up in doing his Father's will. One day when his apostles realized that he needed food and begged him to eat, he said, "I have food to eat of which you do not know." They wondered at this and he explained, "My food is to do the will of him who sent me, to accomplish his work" (John 4, 31–34). When his enemies badgered him, he told them, ". . . I preach only what the Father has taught me. I do always the things that are pleasing to him."

This total, selfless dedication to goodness has made Jesus history's most attractive figure.

THE HUMAN SON, ONE OF US

In Leningrad, Soviet Russia, the Museum of the History of Religion (the "Museum of Atheism") has large displays devoted to the abuses of organized religion and its supposed incompatability with the modern, scientific world. But in the world building there is nothing about Christ, no deriding of him, no attack on him.

In the larger art museums of the city there are many paintings of Christ by various masters—usually of the compassionate, very human Christ healing the sick or preaching to the poor—before which thousands of men, women and children quietly pass. Even in this professedly atheistic state, Christ is a unique and respected figure.

Even for many today who say one can have no real contact with God—who proclaim that "God is dead"—the figure of Christ, the "man for others," is at the center of their life and thought. They are attracted by him, and even as they debate who he was, they live to imitate him.

In the first three gospels particularly, we see how very human Jesus Christ was. For the first thirty years of his life he led the uneventful life of a small town carpenter. He gradually became more aware of his mission in life and when he began to preach he suffered antagonism, insults, and the misunderstanding of his own friends and neighbors. On one occasion they even tried to kill him (Luke 4, 16–28). He was often hungry, thirsty, tired, with no home to call his own (Luke 4, 2; John 4, 6; Matthew 8, 20).

He was sometimes sad, and cried over the death of his friend Lazarus (John 11, 33–35). He could enjoy himself, too, and liked to see others enjoy themselves. His first recorded miracle was changing water into wine at a young couple's wedding reception (John 2, 1ff.); he often accepted dinner invitations from his friends (Luke 7, 36ff.); and he liked to be with little children, despite his followers' attempts to chase them away (Matthew 19, 13ff.).

He was acutely conscious of the difficulties, frustrations, uncertainties and fears that any of us experience. Throughout his life he "increased in wisdom. . . ." (Luke 2, 52). As his preaching continued he was constantly frustrated by the growing opposition of his enemies, the powerful leaders of the people. He realized that his preaching of conversion to the kingdom had failed, and that now he would have to suffer and die to bring salvation to his people. He saw that he was to be the suffering servant of God predicted by Isaiah (chapters 50–53) who was to die to bring others to God.

He was strongly tempted from the outset, drawn to sin as if he could fall—though he never did (Matthew 4, 1–11). His lifelong struggle to do his Father's will reached its climax in his agony before his death: "Father, if thou art willing, remove this cup from me; yet not my will but thine be done" (Luke 22, 42). And as he was dying, he cried out in anguish and darkness of soul, "My God, my God, why have you forsaken me?" (Matthew 27, 46).

But to his closest followers, Jesus was a paradox, a mystery. He was close to them, spent many hours instructing them to the point where they argued with him and almost took him for granted. But there was always something of a mystery about him. His personality was powerful, he spoke with a unique authority, but yet he was open, asked questions to learn what people thought of him (Matthew 16, 13), and was shaken by the death of a close friend (John 11, 33–36).

He worked wonders unlike anyone before: " 'Girl, I say to thee, arise.' And the (dead) girl rose up immediately" (Mark 5, 41–42). But yet he confessed that there were some things he did not know: ". . . of that day or hour (the Judgment) no one knows, neither the angels in heaven, nor the Son, but the Father only" (Mark 13, 32). He said, "All things that the Father has are mine" (John 16, 15), but on another occasion he said, "The Father is greater than I" (John 14, 28).

Gradually he was unfolding his innermost self . . .

THE DIVINE SON

Jesus' great revelation is that the God who is our Father has an only Son, also God, and that he is this divine Son of God. Others are sons and daughters of the loving Father—but Jesus is *the* Son. Gradually this unfolds in the gospels. He calls the Father by the intimate term, "Abba" (Mark 14, 36). He says that he is so close to his Father that he alone knows and reveals him:

> "All things have been delivered to me by my Father; and no one knows the Son except the Father; nor does anyone know the Father except the Son, and anyone to whom the Son chooses to reveal him" (Matthew 11, 27).

The infancy stories of Matthew and Luke show the Church's belief that Jesus' origin was with God. At the start of his public preaching, after he was baptized, " . . . heaven was opened, and the Holy Spirit descended upon him in bodily form as a dove, and a voice came from heaven, 'Thou art my beloved Son, in thee I am well pleased' " (Luke 3, 21–22). And in his last prayer, before his death, Jesus summed up his work as the Son of the Father: **Read John 17, 1–5.**

Jesus showed that he was more than human, by his evident holiness, his knowledge and superhuman insights, and his miracles. People began saying, "Never has man spoken as this man" (John 7, 46), and "Who, then, is this, that even the wind and the sea obey him?" (Mark 4, 40). Then one day he made the bold claim:

"Abraham your father rejoiced that he was to see my day. He saw it and was glad." The Jews therefore said to him, "Thou art not yet fifty years old, and hast thou seen Abraham?" Jesus said to them, "Amen, amen, I say to you, before Abraham came to be, I am." They therefore took up stones to cast at him; but Jesus hid himself, and went out from the temple (John 8, 56–59).

John here tells us that Jesus is claiming the sacred name of God, "I am." His hearers understood his claim, since they wanted to stone him to death as punishment for blasphemy. He claimed to forgive sins, and his hearers concluded, "Who is this man who speaks blasphemies? Who can forgive sins but God only?" (Luke 5, 21). On another occasion he said openly, "My Father and I are one." His hearers again took up stones to cast at him, saying, "Thou, being a man, makest thyself God" (John 10, 33).

The gospels tell us that Jesus was a wonder-worker, who performed many miracles. They mention some forty miracles of all kinds, including three occasions on which he brought dead persons back to life. We do not know the details of his miracles, or how many he really performed—the gospels, we saw, are records of faith and are not greatly concerned about historical details. But even the 1st-century Jewish historian, Josephus, and the anti-Christian pagan writers conceded that Christ was a wonder-worker. In John's gospel especially, Christ's miracles are called his "works," performed to prove his divine power:

" . . . do you say of him whom the Father has made holy and sent into the world, 'Thou blasphemest,' because I said, 'I am the Son of God'? If I do not perform the works of my Father, do not believe me. But if I do perform them, and if you are not willing to believe me, believe the works, that you may know and believe that the Father is in me and I in the Father" (John 10, 36–38).

Only gradually, however, did it become clear who Jesus really was. The Jews for centuries had abhorred idolatry, the giving of divine honor to anyone or anything created. God had gradually become remote to them—even his name was too holy to be pronounced. So, though the people were awaiting a Messiah, they were totally unprepared for him to be divine. Then, too, Christ's mission on earth was to establish the kingdom of his Father among men, not to claim anything for himself. He shows his divinity more by his actions than by direct claims.

It is evident from the New Testament that there was a development in his followers' grasp of Jesus' divinity, that his apostles had no real understanding of this during his ministry. After the resurrection and the coming of the Holy Spirit they gradually came to understand—gradually, because they were not so much concerned with the abstract question of precisely who or what Jesus was, as with the great things God had done for us through him. They were caught up in preaching the tremendous good news of our salvation by Jesus to eternal life, and with trying to convert all mankind to share in this. But by the time of John's gospel and the epistle to the Hebrews, for instance, the realization of his divinity is expressed clearly (Cf. John 1, 1; 20, 28; Hebrews 1, 8–9).

We should not be surprised that Jesus' full identity took a while to penetrate the understanding of his followers. We who so glibly call Jesus divine should try to realize how difficult it must have been for his first followers to come to understand this—that the man with whom they had so intimately associated had within himself the fullness of the infinite God. Their every instinct as monotheists was to reject as utterly blasphemous any implication that a man could in any way be divine. Only with the light of the Holy Spirit through the years after Pentecost did they begin to realize that this was so.

Then, too, there is a sense in which Jesus developed in the knowledge of himself and his mission. He "increased in wisdom, and in stature and in favor with God and man" (Luke 2, 52). What he always was and what he basically knew in the depths of his consciousness, that he was divine, he only gradually came to grasp in the context of his life situation. This is an extraordinarily difficult thing for us who are only human to understand—and ultimately it is a mystery—how a human intellect could come to grasp the fact that one is a divine person.

Perhaps as we know that we are spiritual beings, that we have a soul, but cannot directly conceive of or reflect on this aspect of ourselves, and as we only gradually come to realize through the experience of living what it means to be a human person—so Jesus only gradually became reflexively conscious of his divine personality, gradually came to know himself more and more deeply.

How much Christ's divinity "broke through" or was communicated to his human consciousness is currently the subject of much discussion.

Many scholars today look at the scriptural evidence and think that while Jesus was always aware of a uniquely intimate relationship with his Father (God), he fully realized his divinity at his resurrection, when he was filled with the Spirit and glorified.

In any event, one thing is becoming clearer today: Jesus is a more "human" figure, much more one of us, than many Christians, accustomed to thinking of him primarily as divine, had previously supposed.

The resurrection of Jesus, his return to life after his death, is the great testimony to his divinity. He is the only person in human history to have such striking testimony of his return to life. Not only the early Christians, but billions of people through history have staked their belief on this.

The gospels go into detail to show that Jesus really died and came back alive again:

> And as Jesus was going up to Jerusalem, he took the twelve disciples aside by themselves, and said to them, "Behold, we are going up to Jerusalem, and the Son of Man will be betrayed to the chief priests and the scribes; and they will condemn him to death, and will deliver him to the Gentiles to be mocked and scourged and crucified; and on the third day he will rise again" (Matthew 20, 17–19).

After a merciless scourging, Jesus had to carry his heavy cross through the city to the place of execution; the soldiers, fearing that he would die on the way, got someone to help him carry the cross (Matthew 27, 32).

After hanging on the cross for three hours, Jesus died. Soldiers examined Christ, saw that he was already dead and pierced his heart with a spear. His body was placed in a new tomb, and a heavy stone was rolled across the opening to seal the tomb; Christ's enemies, remembering his prediction that he would rise on the third day, placed a guard of soldiers around the tomb (John 19, 31–37; Matthew 27, 62–66).

On Easter Sunday morning, several women followers of Christ arrived at the tomb and were amazed to find it empty; an angel told them that Christ had risen. Then, Peter and John, hearing the news, ran to the tomb, and they too found it empty. Mary Magdalen, seeing the empty tomb, concluded his body had been stolen; when Christ appeared to her, she thought he was the gardener (Luke 24, 1–3; John 20, 1–18).

On Easter Sunday evening, Christ appeared to the apostles in a closed room. That same evening, Christ appeared to two of his followers on a road outside Jerusalem (Luke 24, 13–35). St. Paul says that at another time Christ appeared to more than 500 people (1 Corinthians 15, 6). Apparitions of Christ are mentioned eleven times in all.

Christ's resurrection transformed his followers once they realized its meaning. Demoralized by Christ's death, they were not all disposed to believe that he had risen from the grave. They tell us that when Christ did appear, they thought he was a ghost, and he had to eat something to convince them that he was truly alive (Luke 24, 36–43)—that the apostle Thomas would not believe until he could examine the wounds in Christ's body—then he exclaimed, "My Lord and my God!" (John 20, 24–29).

After Christ's several appearances, he ascended into heaven, and his followers awaited the coming of the Holy Spirit as he had instructed them. They had begun to believe, but were still confused. Then the Spirit came and the staggering fact now began to penetrate—it would take some years yet, but gradually they came to realize: God had come among them in Jesus Christ. The wonderful person with whom they had talked and eaten and toiled, who had led them and inspired them and who now was gone from them—this man had had within himself the full power of the divinity.

They went forth to proclaim his resurrection and his message throughout the world. They called Christ "Lord" in the same way that the Old Testament had spoken of God; he is God's power and wisdom (1 Corinthians 1, 24), the perfect reflection of his glory (Hebrews 1, 3). They worked miracles in his name, and they willingly went to their death for him.

Belief in Christ's resurrection was, and is, the impetus behind the spread of Christianity. The early Christians never spoke of Christ as a dead hero, but as one living in their midst. As the early Christian Church developed, this was its key teaching, and it has been so through the centuries. The belief of billions of Christians through history is summed up by St. Paul:

... and if Christ has not risen, vain is your faith, for you are still in your sins. Hence they also who have fallen asleep in Christ have perished. If with this life only in view we have had hope in Christ, we are of all men the most to be pitied. But as it is, Christ has risen from the dead, the first-fruits of those who have fallen asleep (1 Corinthians 15, 17–20).

It is important to remember what we assert, as Christians, when we say that Christ is risen. We are saying that his complete manhood is glorified, that it is perfect, unrestricted, unlimited, endowed with the fullness of divine power. We cannot imagine a risen humanity, and we should be careful of picturing the glorified Christ as being "here" or "there." When he wished his followers to realize that he was truly alive, he "appeared" to them, was "seen" by them, i.e., they realized that he was alive and glorified. We, too, by faith, "meet" the glorified Christ when we realize that he is alive and acting among us.

In the history of the ancient Christian Church at Antioch there is recorded the story of St. Marina, a 3rd-century girl of pagan parents who became a Christian and was eventually beheaded for her beliefs. At her trial, the pagan governor exclaimed, "How stupid to worship a man as if he were a god—above all a man who came to such a disgraceful end as crucifixion!" Marina answered, "Why do you always bring up his crucifixion and never speak of his resurrection? His death shows that he was a man, yes—but his resurrection shows him to be God!"

John's gospel particularly gives the reflection of the late 1st-century Christian Church about Christ when it calls him the Word of God who became a man. This gospel shows a maturing reflection about Christ's divinity-in-humanity. It continually points to his "works," his miracles, as signs that he is divine. It begins: "In the beginning was the Word, and the Word was with God, and the Word was God . . . and the Word was made flesh, and lived among us" (John 1, 1–14). The prophets had proclaimed God's Word, his message, as best they could—now the living Word, the perfect expression of God the Father, has come among us.

To believe in Christ's divinity one must have an open mind and a willingness to live his teachings—and the power of faith. Skeptics, those whose minds are closed to his teachings or to moral improvement like Herod, Pontius Pilate, and the Pharisees, probably would have seen nothing had they been with the apostles when Christ appeared after his resurrection. Others' minds may be open but they lack the power of faith. (We shall consider this more fully in chapter 14 when we discuss faith.) St. Peter says,

God raised him on the third day and caused him to be plainly seen, not by all the people, but by witnesses designated beforehand by God, that is, by us. . . . (Acts 10, 40–41).

One should consider Christ's whole teaching before accepting or rejecting his divinity. Christ gradually reveals himself, usually, through his message. As with Christ's first followers, it takes time to grasp the reality of who he is. If one is open to the truth and tries to live by what one discovers to be true, faith in Christ often comes as one ponders his teachings. The rest of this book concerns these teachings.

Jesus Christ is the perfect man, the "new Adam," the new head of the human race, the perfect lover of God and of us. He never sinned, nor did he ever turn aside from his Father's will. He is the only one in history who responded perfectly to God's outpouring love, and who never faltered in his constant, all-embracing love for his fellow man. St. Paul stumblingly grasps the reality of Jesus when he says that he is " . . . the image of the invisible God, the firstborn of every creature. For in him were created all things in the heavens and on the earth, things visible and things invisible. . . ." (Colossians 1, 15).

Divine and perfect man though he is, Jesus Christ yet experienced all our human weaknesses and emotions, our joys and sorrows, our hopes and pain. St. Paul says that he "emptied himself" of his divinity, that he is " . . . one tempted as we are, like us in all things except sin." He struggled, as we must, to know the Father's will and to do it. As we saw previously, he underwent all our difficulties, frustrations, uncertainties and fears—and because of his perfect sensitivity he experienced these things even more acutely than we ever could.

Jesus Christ, then, is both God and man. This is the mystery of the incarnation, the fullness of God in human flesh. " . . . the Word was made flesh and dwelt among us" (John 1, 14). Other cultures in their mythologies have had savior gods who came among men, but no one dreamed that the infinite, unique, "totally Other" God would become one of us.

By his incarnation, the Son of God has united himself in some fashion with every man. He worked with human hands, he thought with a human mind, acted by human choice and loved with a human heart. Born of the Virgin Mary, he has truly been made one of us, like us in all things except sin (*The Pastoral Constitution on the Church in the Modern World*, no. 22).

God the Son became a man through Mary, his human mother, whom we call the Mother of God. We call her this because her son, Jesus, is God. Mary is a human being, infinitely below the Almighty. She was chosen to give Christ his human body, but obviously not his divinity nor his human soul. But Mary is truly a mother—she is to Jesus all that any mother is to her son. Jesus is God the Son; the "I" or "ego" of Jesus is divine. Therefore, anything that Jesus has, he has as God. We can say that God had relatives, that God had a mother. The title "Mother of God" came to be used in early Christianity as a test of one's orthodox belief in Christ.

The "Hail Mary" is one of the most ancient prayers of the Church. The first part is Luke's portrayal of the angel's words to Mary at the moment of the incarnation, and also Elizabeth's greeting to her. The second is an ancient, popular petition.

> Hail, Mary, full of grace, the Lord is with thee; blessed art thou among women, and blessed is the fruit of thy womb, Jesus. Holy Mary, Mother of God, pray for us sinners, now and at the hour of our death. Amen.

Another ancient Christian belief is that Mary was conceived free from sin. This is Mary's immaculate conception, celebrated on December 8, a holyday in the United States on which Catholics take part in Mass to rejoice in this privilege Christ has given Mary, the model Christian.

St. Augustine expressed the early Christian belief about Mary when he said that all men are sinners ". . . except the Holy Virgin Mary, whom I desire, for the sake of the honor of the Lord, to leave entirely out of the question when the talk is of sin" (*De nat. et grat.* 36, 42).

Mary's freedom from sin is something we should expect since she was chosen for the unique dignity of being God's human mother. Since Christ came to conquer evil, it is fitting that he should take his human body from a woman who was untainted with sin. Luke describes Mary's awe-filled realization: "He who is mighty has done great things for me, and holy is his name. . . ." (Luke 1, 49).

This doctrine has often been a stumbling-block to ecumenical relations with non-Catholic Christians, since there is no biblical evidence for it, and some of the early Church Fathers spoke of Mary's moral faults. Catholics consider it an example of a development of doctrine, not appearing clearly in Catholic life and teaching until the Middle Ages.

A better way to view this is not so much as a personal privilege of Mary, but in its actual purpose: a part of the preparation for the coming of the Son of God into the world. It is actually, therefore, a statement about Christ. It was a privilege given to Mary for the sake of further sustaining the uniqueness of Jesus Christ. This, like everything else in her life, and indeed her very being, existed only for Jesus Christ.

By these privileges which God gave to Mary, we see that he always prepares people for their roles in his plan. As Mary was given great graces for her great role, so God gives us all the graces necessary to carry out his plan in our life.

The meaning of all this is that God loves us so much that he became one of us, to share his happiness with us. In our world, when a man loves a woman he wants to be with her, to share experiences, to make her happy. God loves us and comes among us, to share our experiences, to give us happiness beyond anything we can imagine. Perhaps this is why he became one of us, to convince us of this love and happiness. Otherwise we would never have believed our destiny.

THE HOLY SPIRIT

Christ spoke about the Holy Spirit who would be sent by the Father and himself to complete his work. Sometimes called the Holy Ghost, Christ calls him the Paraclete or Advocate, that is, a Helper or Comforter. The Spirit is to help the apostles to at last understand Christ and his teachings:

> But the Advocate, the Holy Spirit, whom the Father will send in my name, he will teach you all things, and bring to your mind whatever I have said to you.... But when the Advocate has come whom I will send you from the Father, the Spirit of Truth who proceeds from the Father, he will bear witness concerning me (John 14, 26; 15, 26).

In the Old Testament the Spirit of God was thought of as a manifestation of the Father, his life-giving "breath" which takes possession of a man, renewing him from within, making him responsive to God's Word. Thus the prophet Isaiah proclaims his mission: "The Lord has anointed me, on me his spirit has fallen" (61, 1). And Ezekiel beautifully proclaims the Lord's promise to his people: "I will give you a new heart, and breathe a new spirit into you; I will take away from your breasts those hearts that are hard as stone, and give you human hearts instead. I will make my spirit penetrate you, so that you will follow in the path of my law, and remember and carry out my decrees" (11, 19–20).

The Spirit worked within Jesus, a personal reality, guiding and inspiring him. At his baptism, " . . . the Holy Spirit descended upon him in bodily form as a dove. . . ." (Luke 3, 22). "Then Jesus was led by the Spirit about the desert" (Luke 4, 1), before beginning his mission. As he starts his mission, the Spirit gives him power: **Read Luke 4, 14–19.**

Near the end of his life Jesus told his followers that the Spirit would make his teachings clear to them: ". . . it is expedient for you that I depart. For if I do not go, the Advocate will not come to you; but if I go, I will send him to you" (John 16, 7). After the Spirit came on Pentecost, Christ's disciples began to understand his teachings, among them the fact that the Father, Son and Holy Spirit are one God.

The Holy Spirit is the successor of Jesus, who continues his work among us and within us. He continually moved the early Christian Church, and today he is the source of God's life in the Church and in each Christian. He is the power that enables us to believe in Christ and live his teachings: "No man can say Jesus is Lord except in the Holy Spirit," says Paul (1 Corinthians 12, 3). He is also our invincible power in the battle with sin and ignorance—though often we never suspect his presence, or suspecting it, we are afraid to open ourselves to him.

Reflecting on Christ's revelation, the Church has slowly penetrated into the mystery of the Father, Son, and Holy Spirit. As Christianity developed, scholars and people alike tried to understand Christ better, and his relationship to the Father and the Spirit. Guided by the Spirit, some facets of this mystery began to emerge, and were proclaimed by the Church in several councils.

There is but one God, but in God there are three divine, completely equal Persons. This is the mystery of the Blessed Trinity. Each of the Three Persons is really distinct from the other Two. Each is wholly God, equal to the other Two. One did not come before the others. Yet there is only one God.

> *Traditional Catholic theology puts it this way:* the three divine Persons, distinct as Persons, possess the same one nature of God. This is based on the difference between the idea of "person" and that of "nature," taken originally from Greek philosophy and expanded by Christian thinkers: *person* tells *who* we are; *nature* tells *what* we are. Each of us, for example, is aware that he is a distinct person, different from everyone else. But each of us is also aware that he is human, has a human nature, and in this we are similar to everyone else. Each of us, then, is one person with one nature. It is quite possible—and this is the case with God—to have One who is Three Persons with one nature.

The Second Person of the Blessed Trinity, God the Son, took on a human nature, became a real man, and lived and died among us as Jesus Christ. St. Paul tells us, "Christ Jesus, who though he was by nature God, did not consider being equal to God a thing to be clung to, but emptied himself, taking the nature of a slave and being like unto men" (Philippians 2, 5–7). This is the mystery of the incarnation.

> Jesus Christ, then, has two natures—a divine nature and a human nature. Jesus has his divine nature as God from eternity, together with the Father and the Holy Spirit. He took on a distinct human nature 2,000 years ago.
>
> But Jesus is only one Person, God, the Son, who "uses" these two natures. With the power of his divine nature he acts as God; with the power of his human nature he acts as man. But whenever Jesus did anything it was the one Person of God the Son who did it.

It is good to remember that the Blessed Trinity is a mystery. We can know something about the Trinity, but in the final analysis very, very little. Life is full of mysteries—the ultimate composition of an atom, what life itself is, etc.—and so we should not be surprised that the inner life of God is the deepest of all mysteries. Whether or not one can accept our belief in the Trinity depends on God's gift of faith.

> *Through history men continue to achieve new insights into God's existence and nature.* He is ever leading us to a truer, more profound

knowledge of himself and our relationship to him. What is proof of God for one man is not for another; what is widely accepted in one period of history may not be later. We believe the Church's insights are true. But they are only a few stumbling words about One who is immense, immeasurable, impenetrable love.

The work of any man's lifetime should be an endless quest for the infinite—to try to know, to understand a bit more, to make some sort of contact with God. The tragedy is that men who give their lifetime to penetrating nature or organizing society never stop to study or reflect on the infinite God. If persevered in, no quest can be as rewarding. To this some of the greatest men of our civilization have testified.

The names of the Three Persons tell us something about them and their personal relationship to us. What one Person does for us the other Persons also do; yet each has a distinct role in God's plan. By grace we are joined to each in a distinct way:

The First Person is called the Father because he produces a Second Person, the Son. He is spoken of as our creator; the word "God" usually refers to him. He is the source from whom everything comes to us, and to whom our worship is ultimately directed. We address him personally when we pray the "Our Father"—the Lord's Prayer—and all the great prayers of Christian worship.

The Second Person is called the Son because he has his origin from the Father, and receives the same divine nature from the Father. Similarly, a boy is called "son" because he has the same human nature as his father, received from his father. We saw that this Second Person is also called the "Word," the perfect expression of the Father.

Jesus Christ is the Son become man, our brother, through whom every grace comes to us, and through whom we worship the Father. By being joined to Jesus Christ, we share in the very life of the Trinity—we somehow become sons in the Son. Our whole life is to be a gradual reproducing of his life of sonship in ourselves. There is truly no limit to what we can do when united with him.

Though we pray *to* Christ, this prayer should lead us to pray *through* Christ and *with* Christ to the Father. We then share in Christ's perfect prayer to the Father. Our stumbling prayer becomes the prayer of Christ. This is the way the Church usually prays.

The Third Person is called the Holy Spirit because he is produced by the love of the Father and Son for one another. So great is their love that it produces another Person, Love himself, the Holy Spirit; our word "spirit" is taken from a word meaning breath or sigh, a universal sign of life and love.

The Holy Spirit is the gift, the love, of the Father and Son to us. He is the one through whom we enter the life of the Trinity. He comes from Christ into us; within us, he unites us to Christ and the Father.

The Spirit is the one who is the source within us of our Christian prayer and worship. Our ability to pray is from him. When we pray he prays within us. He gives form, meaning, power to our prayers. Thus we pray "in the Spirit."

The Spirit comes to the aid of our weakness; when we do not know what prayer to offer, to pray as we ought, the Spirit himself intercedes for us, with groans beyond all utterance. And God, who can read our hearts, knows well what the Spirit's intent is (Romans 8, 26).

One of the great lessons we derive from Christ's teaching about the Blessed Trinity is that God is not unlike us. Rather, God is Three Persons, a "family" who love one another with a joy and happiness that we can hardly begin to imagine.

To summarize our relationship to the Three Persons:

Everything comes to us from the Father, through the Son-made-man, Jesus Christ, and we receive it by means of the Holy Spirit within us.

We, in turn, return our love to the Father, through and with his Son, Jesus Christ, and we do this by the power of the Holy Spirit within us.

... be filled with the Spirit, speaking to one another in psalms and hymns and spiritual songs, singing and making melody in your hearts to the Lord, giving thanks always for all things in the name of our Lord Jesus Christ to God the Father (Ephesians 5, 18–20).

IN THE LITURGY

Almost every prayer and ceremony of the Church is done in the name of the Blessed Trinity. The Sign of the Cross and the Doxology are ancient prayers in their honor. We celebrate Trinity Sunday on the first Sunday after Pentecost each year.

At Mass, the Sign of the Cross is used several times from the beginning to the last blessing. The "Lord, have mercy on us ..." asks their mercy; the "Glory to God in the highest," which follows, praises them. The Creed summarizes our belief in the Trinity.

Most other Mass prayers are addressed in the Church's ordinary way: to God the Father through the Son, in union with the Holy

Spirit—for example, the conclusion of the collects. The climax of the offering of our gift in every Mass is when we silently pray: "Through him (Christ), with him, and in him all honor and glory is given to you, God, Almighty Father, in the unity of the Holy Spirit."

At Mass, we also affirm our belief in the incarnation. In the Creed, for instance, we profess that God the Son, the Word of God, "was made flesh . . . and became man." In the eucharistic prayer, at the heart of the Mass, we recount the fact that God the Son has become man in Jesus Christ.

DAILY LIVING: OUR DIGNITY AS BEARERS OF THE TRINITY AND BROTHERS AND SISTERS OF CHRIST

In revealing the Blessed Trinity to us, Christ showed us something of God's inner life, and his amazing desire to be known to his creatures.

But this is not all. Christ said, "If anyone loves me, he will keep my word, and my Father will love him, and we will come to him and make our abode with him. . . ." (John 14, 25). And speaking of the Holy Spirit, he said, ". . . you shall know him, because he will dwell with you and be in you" (John 14, 17).

The Blessed Trinity dwells intimately within us. This is God's grace-presence. As long as we have grace, what we really have with us is this presence of God, united to us in the most intimate way possible. This is the "indwelling" of the Blessed Trinity.

This indwelling presence means that even now we are beginning the life of heaven. Anywhere, anytime—as long as we are not isolated by serious sin—we can communicate with the Trinity within us, and be confident of their help.

By this indwelling presence we can come to know and experience the divine Persons. The Father, we realize, is *our* Father who loves us and shares his life with us. The Son is our brother, Jesus Christ, who is like us and communicates the Father's love to us and leads us to the Father. The Holy Spirit is most intimately within us, uniting us to Jesus, joining us to the Father—and to one another—through and with Jesus.

This indwelling presence means that we must respect our body and

the bodies of others. St. Paul's words to his Corinthian converts who had been abusing their bodies might also be reminders to any of us:

> Or do you not know that your members are the temple of the Holy Spirit, who is in you, whom you have from God, and that you are not your own? For you have been bought at a great price. Glorify God and bear him in your body (1 Corinthians 6, 19–20).

We respect our own self as a person by realizing that we each are unique in all of creation, and by developing our unique identity and sense of self-esteem. Each of us is known and loved by God within us in a most personal, understanding way. Thus, regardless of how others treat us, and regardless of our own weaknesses and needs, we are totally known and intimately loved by the only One who really matters, who holds the universe itself in existence. This should give each of us a deep sense of our dignity as a person of lasting worth, with unique powers and God-derived talents. So our concept of ourself as a person of limitless value, beauty, and lovableness should never depend on others' approval (or even that of a special other).

Concretely, we respect ourself as a person by developing our talents, our unique giftedness. This means courage and imagination, the ability to rise above peer pressures, to avoid overindulgence in alcohol, drugs, smoking, and the abuse of sex. Young people especially can be carried away by our overly-permissive society, by an attitude of "everybody's doing it" (sometimes tacitly tolerated even by their parents, adults-in-years who are really children in emotional maturity).

We respect the dignity of others by treating them with true love and consideration. We should desire for all men everything that we seek for ourselves. We fail in this if we take advantage of anyone or abuse anyone, for example, by unjustly overworking him, showing prejudice against him, by unjust anger, bearing a grudge, etc.

Another reason for respecting ourselves and others is because God the Son became one of us, thereby teaching us that a human being is something wonderful indeed in God's eyes. He is the "firstborn among many brethren" (Romans 8, 29). In what better way could God bring home to us our tremendous dignity?

Because of the incarnation our earth is now especially sacred and

worthy of our best efforts to develop it, to make it a better place for us all. While we are interested in space and the possibility of rational beings on other planets, yet we know that we have had God the Son among us, on our planet. He thought enough of us to become one of us—this should be a constant spur to our efforts.

> God's Word . . . entered the world's history as a perfect man, taking that history up into himself and summarizing it. He . . . taught us that the new command of love was the basic law of human perfection, and hence of the world's transformation . . . that the effort to establish a universal brotherhood is not a hopeless one (*Pastoral Constitution on the Church in the Modern World,* no. 38).

A perceptive modern writer puts it this way:

> In the Christian experience . . . God does not dip his finger into history; he totally immerses himself in it. When he visits the world he does not come slumming. He comes to stay (Dewart, *The Future of Belief,* Herder & Herder, 1966, p. 194).

SOME SUGGESTIONS FOR . . .

DISCUSSION

If you are a Christian, how do you think of the Persons of the Trinity?

What does the Christian belief that God became a man mean to you?

Is the presence of God real to you, at least sometimes?

FURTHER READING

** *Jesus, God and Man,* Brown (Macmillan, 1976)—In typically clear style, this outstanding New Testament scholar lays before us who and what the New Testament writers considered Jesus to be, as well as the question: "How much did Jesus know?" Also, in ** *Biblical Reflections on Crises Facing the Church* (Paulist Press, 1975), Fr. Brown sets forth in beautifully simple form various 20th-century views on the "Christology" of the New Testament.

** *The Christ,* Schoonenberg (Seabury)—This book is a "breakthrough" modern look at the problem of God-in-man, Jesus Christ, by an outstanding Dutch theologian. **What Are They Saying About Jesus?* O'Collins (Paulist Press, 1977)—A brief, clearly-written, and superb book on current theological insights and speculation about Jesus Christ and their implications for our Christian faith. This is a "must," masterfully done.

* *To Whom Shall We Go? Christ and the Mystery of Man*, Hays (Franciscan Herald Press, 1975)—This is a fine booklet on Christ and his message for the average person. It can also be used profitably as reading for discussions on the meaning of Jesus Christ in our daily lives.

FURTHER VIEWING/LISTENING

Jesus B.C. (Paulist Productions)—27 minutes—A delightful and inspiring parable on why God became man.

The Christ (Teleketics, Franciscan Productions)—Four concise filmstrips/cassettes that clearly present who Jesus Christ is, his message, and what difference his life, death and resurrection make for us today.

The Clown of Freedom (Paulist Productions)—27 minutes—A striking contemporary parable of Jesus' death and resurrection, set in a Latin American dictatorship.

PERSONAL REFLECTION

The Blessed Trinity lives within us as long as we do not deliberately cut ourselves off from this grace-presence. The more I try to be aware of this presence during the day, the greater is my power of love, the easier it is to do good, and the greater will be my happiness and that of everyone with whom I come in contact.

The Blessed Trinity also lives within the bodies of others; an awareness of this will lead me to respect them.

I should set aside time, even just a few minutes each day, to communicate with the Trinity within, asking help to know what to do and to have the courage to do it.

8

Christ Saves Us by His
Death and Resurrection

What is the ultimate reason why God came among us? What is the high point of human history? Why did Christ suffer and die? Is there any meaning to the suffering, humiliation, frustration in our lives? Why are joy and hope natural to a good Christian?

IN CHRIST WE DIED AND ROSE AGAIN

We have seen how God himself came among us in Jesus Christ. He told us of God's own innermost life, the Blessed Trinity, and how the divine Persons dwell intimately within us. He shared our human joys and afflictions, and gave us a whole new way of life. He showed us by his own example how to live totally for God.

Jesus Christ, however, not only taught us how to attain heaven. More fundamentally, he made it possible for us. From Adam on, man had been cutting himself off from God by sin. Pride and selfishness had become imbedded in human nature. Men were divided within themselves, from one another, and from God.

God's plan was to share his own life with us forever—and God's love is unwavering. He would save man from the predicament into which his sins had put him. We call God's actions toward man a "history of salvation." Its high point is the coming of the Savior.

God prepared our race for many years, from the first humans through the whole Old Testament period. He tried to attract men by being generous with them, giving his love in the measure that men could respond to it. Even when his chosen people violated their covenant with him again and again, he continued to reach out with his love and forgiveness. He worked slowly, by our standards, because he will never force men to come to him. Our love must always be given freely.

Men had become so sinful that it seemed that God's plan had failed, that the living God was dead—or at least missing. Widespread slavery, degradation of women, religious prostitution, human sacrifice, cruelty to the weak, average citizens taking their recreation watching other humans being torn apart—this was the world of 2,000 years ago. But it was the "fullness of time" for which God had been preparing. Men had experienced the depths of sin. A faithful remnant acutely realized their need of a savior and longed for his coming. The Father then responded in an undreamed of way.

God sent his own Son, Jesus Christ, to overcome the power of sin and fill us with his grace-presence. In his plan we are to grow in this gift of himself, this new life, until we are with him face to face forever in heaven. Jesus summed up his mission: "I came that they may have life, and have it abundantly" (John 10, 10). Those who knew that mankind needed a savior, never dreamed it would be God's own Son.

Jesus could save us because he opened himself totally to the Father. He alone perfectly responded to the Father's will. "I seek not my own will, but the will of him who sent me" (John 5, 30). He was the perfect man, truly human, but untouched by the pride and selfishness around him. He is the "new Adam," the fresh starting-point, the new and perfect head of our race. His obedience made up for the disobedience of Adam and all of us. He showed us how to respond to love. He "emptied" himself, and the Father could then fill him with life and love for all mankind. **Read Philippians 2, 5–11.**

We must remember that each of us is in need of Christ as our Savior, because each of us is a sinner. We are all born into the situation and environment of sin that we call original sin. We all need to be freed, raised up from our own prideful disobedience. We fall again and again into sin. We need to be opened to God's love. We need someone to pick us up, to carry us beyond our sins to God.

What we could never do because of our sins, God did for us by becoming a man in Jesus Christ. As a loving parent stoops to a helplessly crippled child and carries it along, so God accomplished for us what we could not do for ourselves.

Jesus Christ saved us by his death and resurrection. While every action of Christ's life helped to save us, his great central act of love was his death and resurrection. St. Paul says succinctly, "Jesus our Lord . . . was put to death for our trespasses and raised for our justification" (Romans 4, 25).

Christ's death and resurrection were able to help us because he united us to himself, so that we could share in what he did. In a mysterious and wonderful way we died and rose again with him. We know how love causes one to suffer with his beloved: parents suffer anguish at seeing their children in pain, a wife's sufferings cause her husband mental torments. Some people love enough to give up life itself for the one they love.

> In Vietnam some time ago a young American officer risked sniper fire by crawling out to save a poor, dying peasant, and was killed by a bullet through the head. Some years ago a California mother offered, quite sincerely, to die in place of her criminal son who had been sentenced to the gas chamber for murder.

So Christ identified us with himself, and died for our sins. Totally innocent himself, he yet gave himself totally for us. He is completely, unreservedly the "man for others." He said, "Greater love has no man than this, that a man lay down his life for his friends."

But Christ did even more. We were his enemies, because of our sins, and yet he laid down his life for us and made us his friends. St. Paul exclaims,

> Why, one will hardly die for a righteous man—though perhaps for a good man one will dare even to die. But God shows his love for us in that while we were yet sinners Christ died for us (Romans 5, 7–9).

By dying for us Christ made up for our sins. When he was killed, he killed sin's power over us; when he was buried, the power of sin was buried with him. **Read Romans 6, 4–11.**

> Theology expresses in several ways what Christ did: He "redeemed" us, bought us back from our subjection to sin; "satisfied" for our sins, made "reparation" for them, i.e., repaired the damage they had done; he brought about our "justification"; he "merited" grace for us; he "atoned" for our sins, made us "at one" again with God.

By rising to new life Christ obtained for us the new life of God's grace-presence. Christ is now the head of a revitalized human race, the "firstborn of many brethren." He offers us this new life, a sharing in God's own life, God himself within us. If we accept it, it is the beginning of an unimaginable intimacy with him that will never end.

> *After his death Jesus "descended into hell"*—he went, not to the hell of the damned, but through the "underworld," the state of being cut off from God, abandoned, powerless—the consequence of his decision to die the death of a sin-laden man. Then "he preached to the spirits in prison" (1 Peter 3, 19)—those who had lived since Adam and were awaiting salvation. He freed them and brought them with him when he ascended into heaven.

Christ's death and resurrection is the great turning-point in human history. An old world ended, and a whole new way of life, a new vision of reality began. Now we can have a life of unimaginable love and intimacy with God himself.

THROUGH CHRIST'S PERFECT WORSHIP WE CAN NOW REACH GOD

Through Christ's death and resurrection we can be sure of reaching God. Men have always sought to contact God, to know if he is there, if he is interested. We wonder how we can reach him. As with men from primitive times, we want to be united with him, transformed, "taken up" into a new life with him. So it is that men have always worshipped God, attempting to reach him particularly by offering him gifts in sacrifice. But men were only too aware of the inadequacy of their offerings.

Christ's death and resurrection was the one, perfect sacrifice by which man reached God. We saw how God's people had worshipped him by sacrifices of animals and crops, offered by their priests. These sacrifices prepared the way for Christ's perfect sacrifice in which he offered his life as our gift to the Father.

> For if the sprinkling of defiled persons with the blood of goats and bulls and with the ashes of a heifer sanctified for the purification of the flesh, how much more shall the blood of Christ, who through the eternal Spirit offered himself without blemish to God, purify your conscience from dead works to serve the living God (Hebrews 9, 13–14).

Christ is our mediator, our perfect yet understanding priest. His obedience and love made his death the perfect sacrifice. He was the perfect "go-between." The Old Testament priests had offered sacrifices to God in the name of his people, and brought blessings from God. Christ offered his life to his Father and brought us the gift of eternal happiness. The priests of the old law were imperfect men. Christ is the perfect man, yet one like us who understands our weaknesses. He is the greatest priest of all, our one perfect mediator. **Read Hebrews 5, 1–10.**

As Melchisedech had offered bread and wine in thanksgiving for one of Abraham's victories, so Christ offered bread and wine—and transformed it, as we shall see—as a prelude to his sacrifice.

Christ's ascension into heaven completed his resurrection. His mission on earth was now totally fulfilled. He has returned to the Father and is glorified at his "right hand" in heaven.

Christ's glorification dramatically showed that the Father accepted his sacrifice and that we could now be united with God forever. To have meaning, a gift must be accepted by the one to whom it is given. In the Old Testament the death and burning of the sacrificial victim was meant to show God's acceptance of the gift, its transformation into something divine. Christ's resurrection and ascension strikingly showed that his gift of himself on our behalf was accepted by his Father.

THE NEW AND UNENDING COVENANT OF LOVE

Christ fulfilled beyond all expectation the passover of the Old Testament: he passed from death to life and from this world to the Father, bringing us all with him. God had passed over Egypt, saving his people from death and slavery, and the Israelites had passed over the waters of the Red Sea and the Jordan, to become united with God in the Sinai covenant and the Promised Land. Whenever the Jews ate the annual paschal meal, they looked forward to a new passover, a new exodus to a new freedom and happiness.

Christ fulfilled this longing by making it possible for us to pass with him to eternal happiness. He is the "Lamb of God" (John 1, 29) sacrificed to save us all. "Christ, our paschal lamb, has been sacrificed," says St. Paul (1 Corinthians 5, 7). **Read John 8, 32–36.**

By dying and rising Jesus Christ brought us from slavery under sin to the perfect freedom of God's redeemed people. This is the new exodus and Christ is the new Moses leading us all to freedom and eternal happiness. If we join ourselves with him, our sins can no longer enslave us or prevent us from attaining true happiness.

Christ timed his passover to coincide with the annual commemoration of the first passover. He began his passage from death to life by eating the Jewish paschal meal, his last supper. As Moses had done, Christ gave his followers a ritual by which his passover would be commemorated for future generations. He said over the bread, "This is my body which is being given for you. Do this in remembrance of me"—and as he passed the last cup of wine, "This cup is the new covenant in my blood, which shall be shed for you" (Cf. Matthew 26, 17–29).

Christ's ritual meal, however, would enable his followers through the centuries to rise above time and actually share in his very death and resurrection. This is the Mass, the great sacrifice and family meal of his Church.

By dying and rising for us Jesus Christ began the new, perfect, eternal covenant. The ancient covenants of God with his people culminated in the old testament of Mount Sinai. Moses had sealed this covenant by sprinkling the people with the blood of sacrificed animals; so now Christ shed his own blood in sacrifice to begin the new and unending covenant, the new testament. At the last supper before he died, he said, "This cup is the new covenant in my blood, which shall be shed for you" (Luke 22, 20; Cf. Hebrews, chapters 8–10).

In the Old Testament the blood of sacrificed animals was brought by the high priest into the Holy of Holies, the part of the tabernacle where God dwelt among his people. Now Christ offered his blood and entered God's dwelling place in heaven, bringing us with him, fulfilling man's yearning for union with God which could only be hinted at before. "Christ ... by a great and more perfect tabernacle, not made with hands, that is, not of this creation, neither by the blood of goats nor of calves, but by his own blood, entered once for all into the Holies" (Hebrews 9, 11–12).

By this new covenant God promises us a life after death of unending, unimaginable happiness, sharing his own life, living as he does. By the old testament God gave his people land and temporal prosperity if they lived up to their agreement; they did not even suspect an unending life after death, much less know how to attain it. Now God is offering us himself forever. This is the most perfect gift of love possible, the closest personal relationship that we could have with him.

Our part of this covenant of love is simply to accept Jesus Christ and live by his teaching of love. So close, so personal is this relationship of love which God offers us, that his own Son, Jesus Christ, is the living, walking, flesh-and-blood sign of it. Jesus Christ, in fact, is the new covenant. He unites in himself God and us. By believing in him we enter into this covenant. He, personally, is the great proof, the great sign that such a love relationship is for real. By accepting him we begin eternal life, God's grace-presence within us, here and now.

When we accept Christ and this new covenant we pledge ourselves to love. He showed us that this was a covenant of love in the best way he could, by dying for love of his Father and us, to unite us in love. If we make this new covenant we must determine to love. As marriage is the covenant which seals the deep love relationship of a man and woman, so our covenant with God supposes that we have fallen in love, that we want to commit ourselves to a life of love with God and our fellow man.

WHAT THIS COST AND WHY

We should pause and meditate on the gospel story of Christ's sufferings and death, in order to appreciate God's great love in saving us. As we do this, we should remember that our sins contributed to his sufferings.

As Jesus went about preaching and teaching, his death seemed more and more imminent, constantly present before his eyes. He said he ". . . must suffer many things and be rejected by this generation" (Luke 17, 25). His disciples were shocked and scandalized by these predictions; when they went up to Jerusalem for the last time ". . . they were in dismay, and those who followed were afraid" (Mark 10, 32).

After the last supper with his apostles, Jesus went to pray in the garden of Gethsemani where he came to realize vividly the sins he was taking upon himself and the death that awaited him. This caused a mental agony so terrible that "... his sweat became as drops of blood running down upon the ground" (Luke 22, 44).

He shrank from the ordeal ahead, but clung to his Father's will: "Father, if it is possible, let this cup pass away from me; yet not as I will, but as you will" (Matthew 26, 39). Meanwhile, his apostles slept.

Judas, one of his chosen twelve apostles, betrayed him with an embrace of friendship, and he was seized by his enemies (Matthew 26, 47–49).

His followers deserted him. As he had predicted, Peter, their leader, crumbled before a maidservant's mockery and denied him with an oath: "I do not know him!" (Luke 22, 57).

He was taken before the Jewish high priests where he unequivocally declared his divine mission. For this he was slapped, humiliated, found guilty and sentenced to death (Matthew 26, 63–67).

During the night and next morning he was mocked, beaten, spat upon, and made the butt of a condemned fool's game. He was then taken before Pontius Pilate, the Roman governor. Pilate found him innocent of any offense, but the mob, undoubtedly including many he had helped, were aroused by his enemies and demanded his death: "Crucify him! Crucify him!" (Luke 23, 21).

Then Pilate, to appease them "... took Jesus and had him scourged"—a flaying with spikes, leaden balls, and razor-like metal—from which men not infrequently died.

And they stripped him and put on him a scarlet cloak; and plaiting a crown of thorns, they put it upon his head, and a reed into his right hand; and bending the knee before him they mocked him ... and they spat on him, and took the reed and kept striking him on the head (Matthew 27, 28–30).

At last Pilate "... handed him over to them to be crucified." Crucifixion was the death reserved for the lowest criminals. "And so they took Jesus and led him away" (John 19, 16). As he carried his cross to the hill of Calvary outside Jerusalem, he had to be helped lest he die along the way. Arriving at Calvary, "... they crucified him there, and the robbers, one on his right hand and the other on his left. And Jesus said, 'Father, forgive them, for they do not know what they are doing' " (Luke 23, 33–34).

He hung dying for three hours—a death since analyzed as a kind of asphyxiation. After forgiving his enemies, he promised heaven to a repentant thief and murderer. He saw his mother standing humiliated and desolate beneath the cross, and he commended her to his one still-faithful disciple. Later his Church would take her as its own.

Then he felt depths of desolation, cut off from his Father, estranged, abandoned, and he cried, "My God, my God, why hast thou forsaken me?" (Matthew 27, 46).

This is the way Jesus showed his love for the Father and for us. The cost never mattered. He always put God first, living and dying in total, trusting obedience to his Father's will.

In doing this he gave himself totally for others—for us. God "made Christ to be sin" for us—thus Paul tries to describe Christ's fearful experience of taking on our sins as if they were his own, of being totally abandoned by his Father for us.

God willed that Jesus should redeem us in this way so that his love would be unmistakably plain to us. When we see his own Son humiliated and killed, we can begin to realize what it is for a God to love. In no other way could he have made so clear his unfailing love. In no other way would we have been convinced that we are lovable in the eyes of the infinite God.

> In this is love, not that we loved God, but that he loved us and sent his Son to be the expiation for our sins . . . that those who believe in him may not perish, but may have life everlasting (John 3, 16; 1 John 4, 10).

This is how God establishes his kingdom, his rule of love over our hearts. Jesus came as a humble, loving prophet rather than as a powerful king. Where people might have expected a great display, Jesus made clear that he wanted to convert our hearts through love. This is always God's way: instead of compelling submission or awed adoration, he wants our freely-given love.

Christ's death on the Cross shows strikingly the "powerlessness of God" in this world, that is, that he does not save us by means that seem effective to us, but rather overcomes evil by his apparent defeat at its hands. This is the paradox of the Cross and this is freshly evident in today's world. It is becoming more and more apparent that God cannot be expected to intervene in our affairs with displays of power—that his followers are decreasing in worldly and institutional importance—but by this apparent absence from the world he is prodding us to use our human resources to work with him to bring it to perfection. Though God is truly present, close, acting in our lives—and some are especially aware of this—yet he is there to show us how to help ourselves. Too often in the past we have depended on his intervention instead of becoming truly involved ourselves in the mundane struggles of the "terrible everyday." And too often we have tended to judge our success as Christians by worldly standards.

Thus the false image of a God who continually intervenes at our behest, who can be coaxed and cajoled, is dead. This is perhaps expressed best by the influential German Lutheran theologian who was hanged by the Nazis in 1945, Dietrich Bonhoeffer:

> God is teaching us that we must live as men who can get along very well without him. The God who is with us is the God who forsakes us (Cf. Mark 15, 34). The God who makes us live in this world without using him as a working hypothesis is the God before whom we are ever standing. Before God and with him we live without God. God allows himself to be edged out of the world and onto the cross. God is weak and powerless in the world, and that is exactly the way, the only way, in which he can be with us and help us. Matthew 8, 17 makes it crystal clear that it is not by his omnipotence that Christ helps us, but by his weakness and suffering.

> *Christ died for the sins of all of us, not merely because his fellow Jews wanted him killed.* Though many of his countrymen rejected him, some accepted him, the men who began his Church. After the destruction of Jerusalem (which was taken as a sign of God's rejection of the Jews), a tragic hatred developed between Christians and Jews. The beginnings of this are evident even in the New Testament: Pilate is gradually exculpated and the Jews are held increasingly guilty. The Fathers of the Church, the leaders of the developing Christian world, often expressed bitter sentiments against the "Christ-killers," and the Jews reacted by vilifying Christ. From the ghettos of the Middle Ages to the savagery of the Nazi "final solution" (all too frequently tolerated by Christians) we see how man can even use religion in a strange and distorted way. Spurred by the memory of the Nazi horrors, a new era may be opening today in Jewish-Christian relations. Vatican Council II says emphatically:

> ... what happened in his passion cannot be charged against all the Jews without distinction, those then alive, nor against the Jews of to-

day.... The Jews should not be presented as rejected or accursed by God.... The Church ... decries hatred, persecutions, displays of anti-Semitism, directed against Jews at any time and by anyone (*Declaration on the Relationship of the Church to Non-Christian Religions,* no. 5).

Catholics are asked to perform some act of penance each Friday as a gesture of grateful love. Until recently American Catholics abstained from eating meat each Friday, but now may do this or some other act of penance of their own choosing (except for Ash Wednesday and the Fridays of Lent which are still days of abstinence from meat). On Friday, the day Christ sacrificed his life for us, we make this small sacrifice to discipline ourselves and to overcome our sinful tendencies, that we might be more fully joined to him.

The American Catholic bishops have made some practical suggestions for Friday penance: "It would bring great glory to God and good to souls if Fridays found our people doing volunteer work in hospitals, visiting the sick, serving the needs of the aged and the lonely, instructing the young in the Faith, participating as Christians in community affairs, and meeting our obligations to our families, our friends, our neighbors and our community, including our parishes, with a special zeal born of the desire to add the merit of penance to the other virtues exercised in good works born of living faith."

CHRIST IS IN GLORY AMONG US

Christ's resurrection is the key truth of our Christian faith. The first proclamation of the "good news," the pattern of the message that was to convert billions and change the world's history, stressed Christianity's basic and unique fact: Jesus Christ, who had been murdered, came alive from the grave by God's power and entered a perfect, glorified state. **Read Acts 2, 22–36.**

Christ's resurrection is the divine "seal of approval" on himself and his message, and tells us that, joined to him, we too shall live on forever as he said. He delivered us from the fear of death, and brought joy and hope to our lives: "I am the resurrection and the life; he who believes in me, even if he die, shall live; and whoever lives and believes in me, shall never die" (John 11, 25–26).

The New Testament says that Christ appeared on earth for forty days after his resurrection to complete the training of his apostles, and so that they could be absolutely sure that he was truly living among them. Forty is a Jewish "perfect number," one that recurs again and again in the scriptures.

After his resurrection Jesus could exercise his lordship in a way he had not done before. By overcoming death, the ultimate frustration of all human efforts, he began the full exercise of his superhuman, divine power among us. His mission will be fulfilled only at the end of the world, when all evil powers have been overcome.

Jesus shares his victory with us, for now we too have the power to rise and be glorified forever. Christ has a glorified body, impervious to space, time, pain, etc., perfect in every way. He promises that we, too, shall have a body when we rise. "If the Spirit of him who raised Jesus from the dead dwells in you, then he who raised Jesus Christ from the dead will also bring to life your mortal bodies, because of his Spirit who dwells in you" (Romans 8, 11).

We must join ourselves to Christ and take part in his death and glorification to attain eternal life with God. Everyone who is saved is somehow joined to him, whether he realizes it or not. Christ is the one mediator for all. But some are called to join themselves to him more consciously, more fully.

We first join ourselves to Christ's death and glorification by faith and baptism. Baptism, we shall see, is the sacrament by whose ceremony we first take part in these great events. Sin dies within us and we rise from its water with the new life of God's grace-presence.

The Mass is the great way Christ himself prolongs for us his death and resurrection, so we can take part in it and thereby conquer our sins and receive his grace-presence. In each Mass Christ becomes present among us, and through a human priest presents for us his death and resurrection by means of signs or ceremonies. Taking part in the Mass is, we believe, the greatest way of sharing in Christ's love.

We call Jesus Christ the King of the universe, of angels and of men, because all things belong to him as God, and because as man he redeemed us. The Church celebrates the Feast of Christ the King on the last Sunday of October. To the extent that he was humbled for us, now he is exalted: **Read Philippians 2, 8–11.**

What if there are rational "people" on other planets, in other star systems—are they saved, able to attain heaven? There are many possibilities: they might be in an original innocence; they might be as yet unredeemed; they might also have been redeemed by Christ—God could have taken on other created natures besides our own. The possibilities are limitless. God can bring his creatures to happiness with himself in an infinite number of ways. What we do know is that he himself has come and brought us to himself forever.

Alice Meynell pictures what may be the scene when all creation is gathered in eternity:

> O, be prepared, my soul!
> To read the inconceivable, to scan
> The million forms of God those stars unroll
> When, in our turn, we show to them a Man.
> ("Christ in the Universe")

We are to be God's instruments for restoring harmony to material creation, to bring it to perfection by our work and love. The material universe is also God's good creation, but it became tainted by the sin of Adam and all of us. Now it "cries out to redeemed man" to become perfect, to share fully in Christ's redemption. Every advance in perfecting the universe in which we live carries out God's plan for this.

Jesus Christ is among us here and now, more fully than when he was visibly among men 2,000 years ago. "I am with you always, to the close of the age" (Matthew 28, 20). Though invisible, he is closely united to us. He is not in some place beyond outer space. He is as much around us, beneath us, within us, as above our heads. He is personally giving us all the graces by which we attain heaven and by which we bring others and the universe itself to perfection. He is especially united to us in his Church.

At the end of the world he will appear visibly once more to judge the whole human race. Then his work among us will be done. He will deliver all men in this kingdom of love to his Father forever.

Christ's work among us was to be completed by the Holy Spirit whom he would send. At his resurrection Christ was filled with the Spirit. He could now release the full influence of this Spirit of love upon men. The Spirit would enable us to understand Christ's teachings and give us the courage to follow them: **Read The Acts of the Apostles 1, 4–8.**

IN THE LITURGY

In each Mass Christ is present, prolonging his sacrifice, his own death and resurrection, so we can make it our own. Each time we take part, we can offer perfect worship to God. We renew our covenant of love. We take a gigantic step, the greatest possible on this earth, toward our transformation into the divine, our union with God.

The prayers of the Mass emphasize that it is a re-presentation or prolonging for us of Christ's death and glorification.

At the consecration of each Mass we are particularly reminded of Christ's death, as the priest says separately over the bread and wine, "This is my body . . . this is the chalice of my blood." And immediately after the consecration, we are "calling to mind the blessed passion of the same Christ, your Son, our Lord, and also his resurrection from the grave and glorious ascension into heaven. . . ." Immediately before communion we call on Christ, the "Lamb of God," to have mercy on us.

The communion of each Mass particularly brings to mind Christ's resurrection: a meal gives life, and at communion we are united to the living Christ to share in his life of grace.

The Church offers all the great prayers of her liturgy to the Father through Christ, our mediator. The formula ". . . through Christ our Lord" occurs again and again.

We relive annually the event of our salvation by the ceremonies of Holy Week, the most sacred time of the year:

On Palm Sunday palm branches are blessed and distributed to the people and there is a procession as on the first Palm Sunday. During the Mass following, the gospel story of Christ's passion is read.

On Holy Thursday evening we celebrate the anniversary of the last supper by a Mass which expresses our gratitude for the great gift of the eucharist and our sorrow at the sufferings of Christ which began on that night.

The service on Good Friday commemorates the death of Christ by means of readings, prayers, and the singing of the passion, along with veneration of the cross and holy communion. After the service of Good Friday, the tabernacle is empty and the altar bare. From now until Holy Saturday we relive the time when the dead body of Christ was in the tomb.

On Good Friday also in many churches there are special services to commemorate the Three Hours during which Christ hung on the cross.

Easter Sunday, on which we commemorate Christ's resurrection, is the greatest feast of the Christian Church. Our Easter service begins with the Easter Vigil on Holy Saturday night: a new fire is lighted and blessed, to represent Christ the "light of the world." From the fire we light the paschal candle, also representing Christ, and then the candles of the congregation. A hymn of triumph is chanted, and then the several instructions telling the story of God's care for his people over the centuries. Baptismal water is blessed and Christ's resurrection is symbolized by drawing the paschal candle from the "tomb" of the water.

At this time, there may be the baptism of new converts, the heart of this service. In the ancient Christian Church, the Easter Vigil was the great occasion for baptizing converts—they were united to Christ's resurrection and received his new life of grace during this celebration of his resurrection. Then all present renew their baptismal vows, once more committing themselves to Christ. The first Mass of Easter is celebrated, preferably about midnight. Christ reenacts in person his death and resurrection for us.

Each Sunday is a "little Easter." The reason Christians worship and Catholics take part in Mass on Sunday is to celebrate this great day of Christ's victory over sin and death. Sunday is the center of the Christian week.

From Easter to Ascension Thursday, the Masses have a joyous theme. The paschal candle, representing Christ, is lighted at the main Masses.

Ascension Thursday, forty days after Easter, is a holyday in the United States on which Catholics attend Mass to celebrate Christ's triumphant ascent into heaven.

In popular devotion, the Stations of the Cross are a series of fourteen pictures or crosses on the walls of Catholic churches. They commemorate the journey of Christ to Calvary, his death and his burial.

Their purpose is to help us realize God's love and mercy in saving us, and incite sorrow for our sins which have caused Christ such suffering. Many churches now have a 15th Station commemorating the resurrection. There are booklets available with suggested meditations for the Stations.

Devotion to the Sacred Heart of Jesus is for some, particularly older Catholics, a way of showing their love for Jesus Christ. The heart of Jesus, pierced for us, has become the symbol of his love for us and his mercy toward sinners.

Some people take part in Mass and Holy Communion on the first Friday of every month, to show their love of Christ and to atone for his rejection by men.

The five sorrowful mysteries of the Rosary commemorate Christ's sufferings, and the first two glorious mysteries, his resurrection and ascension.

Every Catholic church not only has many crosses throughout, but also has a crucifix, or image of Christ on the cross, as a constant reminder of his death for us. It is a common Catholic custom to have a crucifix in one's home, on one's person, one's rosary, etc.

The "Sign of the Cross" is a way of outwardly professing one's belief, not only in the Blessed Trinity, but also in the suffering and death of Christ for us on the cross.

DAILY LIVING: OUR ATTITUDE
TOWARD SIN AND SUFFERING

Christ chose his suffering and death freely to show us the seriousness of sin. He did not have to suffer and die, but he—God himself—went through this humiliation and anguish to free us from our sins, to make it possible for us to attain heaven. He thereby tried to convince us to do all in our power to avoid sin, since serious sin is the one thing that disrupts the universe and that might cut us off forever from God.

A genuine awareness of what Christ suffered should also make us keenly anxious to help others avoid sin—and perhaps eternal alienation from God.

We can have some insights into the often agonizing mystery of why God allows us to suffer. We cannot understand fully the "why" of pain, but we can see something of its inevitability: If we were perfectly happy, possessing everything we want in this world, we might become smug, complacent, proud, and cease reaching out longingly for God and the life beyond, which is our true destiny. We might also cease working toward our "new earth" of universal love and peace (Cf. 2 Peter 3, 13).

Also, God alone sees the whole picture. He asks us to trust him, much as a father might tell his child who must undergo a painful operation: "This is going to hurt, and you won't understand why—but trust me when I tell you that it will help you."

To say that God is not good because the innocent suffer, or to cease believing in him because of this, is shortsighted and childish. It is to want a God who will conform to our notion of what is ultimately good for us. Our good is not necessarily whatever we happen to desire, approve, or even greatly need, and we cannot expect the universe to be shaped according to our needs and desires. The Christian revelation is sure above all of one thing: that God draws the suffering ones to himself forever and engulfs them eternally in his love.

The cause of evil and suffering is not God, but rather our own clinging to the passing things that we must grow beyond if we are to attain our destiny, the total perfection in love that God wants us to have for eternity. So much of our human misery is brought about by our clinging to passing things, to status, to other persons, to material things, to spiritual feelings, etc. Our will, instead of aligning itself willingly with God's, struggles, holds itself aloof, clutches at these passing goods. Only slowly and painfully do we submit to Love, and let God take us over.

Then, too, for one who believes in an eternity of happiness, the sufferings of this life are only a brief instant by comparison—like a painful injection that takes but a moment, in return for which we have unending health.

Why innocent people so often suffer will be fully answered only at judgment after death. Meanwhile, Christ's example shows us strikingly how suffering can bring about great good.

Christ showed us that suffering has great power to spread love in the world, to bring ourselves and others to heaven. God could have saved the world from its sin in any way that he chose. The suffering and death of his only Son was the way he used. He thereby taught us that if we accept our sufferings, frustrations, humiliations, they too can have great power for good—how much we will realize only in eternity.

The follower of Christ, then, must suffer with Christ. Jesus said, ". . . he who does not carry his cross and follow me, cannot be my disciple" (Luke 14, 27). And Peter says, "Unto this, indeed, you have been called, because Christ has suffered for you, leaving you an example, that you may follow in his steps" (1 Peter 2, 21). There is simply no other road for a Christian.

When suffering comes, we should unite with Christ's sufferings, asking him to help us bear it and profit from it. Besides spreading love in the world, suffering can teach us humility, patience, tolerance, and our utter dependence on God. Many of us learn in no other way. St. Paul put it: "I die daily . . . with Christ I am nailed to the cross" (1 Corinthians 15, 31; Galatians 2, 20).

The Christian must continually die with Christ to rise with him— disciplining himself, controlling his sinful instincts, that the new life of grace might grow in him. "And they who belong to Christ have crucified their flesh with its passions and desires" (Galatians 5, 24). This is mortification—we die in order to live. **Read Matthew 16, 24– 26.**

As Christ's sufferings led to his triumphant glorification, so our sufferings will someday end in the eternal joy of heaven. A transition from death to life—a passing through suffering to attain joy—is the way God's plan is carried out in history. The Israelites underwent the slavery of Egypt and then passed on to freedom. Christ's suffering and death had to precede his resurrection and glory: did not Christ have to suffer these things before entering the eternal happiness of heaven? Our daily life often consists of innumerable "dyings" and "risings" by which we become like Christ. Vatican Council II sums up our human situation:

> On earth, as yet pilgrims in a strange land, tracing in trial and oppression the paths he trod, we are made one with his sufferings, as the body is one with the head—suffering with him, that we may be glorified with him (Romans 8, 17) (*Constitution on the Church*).

Joy and hope are natural, then, to true followers of Christ. We know that whatever we suffer now will someday end in the joy of heaven with our glorified Savior.

SOME SUGGESTIONS FOR . . .

DISCUSSION

What does Christ's death and resurrection mean to you personally?

Does our human pain, the suffering of the innocent, frustration, etc., make more sense in view of the Cross?

Can you agree that a Christian must be basically an optimist?

FURTHER READING

* *The Challenge of Jesus,* Shea (Doubleday Image Book, 1977)—An excellent little book—practical, inspiring, easy to read—on the effect Jesus can and should have in our daily life.
* *Christ is Alive,* Quoist (Doubleday Image Book, 1972)—A simple but profound little book on the relevance of Jesus Christ to the mysteries and aspirations of our lives.
* *Jesus,* Jacobs (Paulist Press, 1978)—A simple, short book about the greatest event in the history of the cosmos. In our analyzing of Christ's life and of particular things he did or said, we can miss the simple, overwhelming message summed up here.

FURTHER VIEWING/LISTENING

Resurrection (Paulist Productions)—27 minutes—Jesus is pictured in limbo, tempted to see his life as a failure—until he realizes that his Father is confirming his mission.

God in the Dock (Paulist Productions)—27 minutes—A striking film on the age-old problem of evil. God is on trial for his life because he has let innocent people suffer.

PERSONAL REFLECTION

Each time I look at a cross or crucifix, I realize that God loved me enough to die for me. That God should become a man, should suffer and die—that he should put himself in a position where the selfishness and cruelty of men could touch him—that he should ever both-er with man at all is a mystery—and the only possible answer is his love. "By this we know his love, that he laid down his life for us. . . ." (1 John 3, 16).

To be united with God by love, to have his grace-presence growing within me, is the most important thing in life. At this moment I am either united with him, or separated from him by unforgiven sin. It would be the ultimate tragedy to go through life cut off from God's great love by an attitude of unrepentance.

An act of kindness or self-discipline on Friday can show my love for Christ on the day he died, and help free me from the self-enslavement of my sins. This Sunday I might worship God with Christ at Mass, thanking him for his death and resurrection on our behalf, and seeking to be more a part of it.

9

Christ Sends the Holy Spirit
to Form His Church

What provision did Jesus Christ make for his teaching, his work among us, to be carried on through the centuries? What special characteristics did Christ's Church have from the beginning? What is the real, inner meaning and purpose of Christ's Church?

THE SPIRIT FORMS GOD'S NEW PEOPLE

Read Acts 2, 1–4. Christ sent the Spirit, as he had promised, to complete his work. Christ had told his followers to await the coming of the Holy Spirit who would give them power to carry his teachings "... even to the very ends of the earth" (Acts 1, 8). He also had promised "... when the Spirit of truth comes, he will guide you into all the truth" (John 16, 13). Now on Pentecost the time of the Holy Spirit began.

With the coming of the Spirit Christ's followers went forth as God's new people. As God had chosen the twelve tribes of Israel in the Old Testament, so Christ chose the twelve apostles. As God had come down upon Mount Sinai to make Israel his people amid a storm, lightning, and earthquake, so now on Pentecost the Spirit comes amid fire and a roaring wind, to send Christ's followers forth as God's new people.

As God had begun his people of the Old Testament by making a covenant with them at Sinai, so Christ had begun the new People of God, his Church, by the covenant made in his death and resurrection. He had shed his blood on Calvary to establish the new covenant, as the old had once been sealed by the blood of animals on Sinai. The Church of the New Testament, then, "came forth from the side of the dying

Christ." But only with the coming of the Spirit were Christ's followers aware of what he had done and of who they were.

Christ's followers are the new People of God, the Church of the New Testament. God had chosen the Israelites and made them his church: he gathered them together, gave them his teaching, made a covenant with them, and lived in their midst. When God became man and dwelt among us in Jesus Christ, he also chose for himself a people, a Church.

> *Thus Vatican Council II, the greatest Church gathering of this century (discussed in chapter 10), calls the Church of the New Testament the "People of God" who, "like a pilgrim in a foreign land,* presses forward amid the persecutions of the world, and with the consolations of God. . . ." (*Constitution on the Church,* nos. 8 and 9). This description of the Church as God's "pilgrim people" is particularly apt for so many today who think of themselves as on a journey, trusting in God to bring them to their destined eternal home.

The twelve apostles were its first and leading members, the remnant which would grow mightily. As God had dwelt among the Israelites, so Christ now lives among us in his Church. Christ said, "I have come not to abolish . . . but to fulfill" (Matthew 5, 17). God's plan is consistent. The early Christians were reminded:

> . . . you are a chosen race, a royal priesthood, a holy nation, God's own people, that you may declare the wonderful deeds of him who called you out of darkness into his marvelous light. Once you were no people, but now you are God's people; once you had not received mercy, but now you have received mercy (1 Peter 2, 9–10).

The Spirit, symbolized by the unbridled, mighty wind, means power and freedom for Christ's followers. As ancient Israel had been freed from Egyptian slavery and made God's free people, so the Spirit now guarantees the freedom of Christ's followers. In the baptismal ceremony the priest breathes over those who are becoming Christians to symbolize the coming of the Spirit with power and freedom. No longer need we be slaves to sin, held back from happiness by sin. The Spirit brings us the power to be truly free, to attain unending happiness.

THE COMMUNITY OF THE SPIRIT

The Spirit enabled the apostles finally to understand Christ's teachings and courageously to go and spread them. Before the Spirit came they had been huddled together, weak, fearful, and confused. Now they began to realize that Christ, who had chosen them, was truly divine. They grasped the meaning of his teachings, and became eloquent and courageous witnesses.

They were led by Peter whose Pentecost sermon proclaimed Christ as the divine Messiah (Cf. Acts 2, 12–36). He assured his hearers that the apostles were not drunk, but filled with the fervor of the Spirit as the prophet Joel had foretold, "I will pour out my Spirit upon all flesh. . . ." He told them that they had killed their Messiah, and then boldly concluded:

> This Jesus God raised up, and of that we are all witnesses. Being therefore exalted at the right hand of God, and having received from the Father the promise of the Holy Spirit, he has poured out this which you see and hear. . . . Let all the house of Israel therefore know assuredly that God has made both Lord and Christ this Jesus whom you crucified (Acts 2, 32–36).

The Spirit constantly guided Christ's first followers. The Acts of the Apostles, a sort of brief history of the first Christians, shows the Spirit acting again and again, and Paul's epistles mention the Spirit several hundred times, He is present at their meetings, guiding their decisions: "It has seemed good to the Holy Spirit and to us. . . ." (Acts 15, 28). He guides the activities of the apostles: "And while Peter was pondering the vision, the Spirit said to him. . . ." (Acts 10, 19). On some occasions his presence deeply stirs them:

> And when they had prayed, the place where they had gathered together was shaken, and they were all filled with the Holy Spirit, and spoke the word of God with boldness. . . . And with great power the apostles gave their testimony to the resurrection of the Lord Jesus, and great grace was upon them all (Acts 4, 31–33).

This community formed by the Spirit had several very noticeable characteristics. These are given in the Acts of the Apostles, in its picture of the Jerusalem community of Christians.

—the community was above all united in love. Christ made clear that this was to be the outstanding characteristic of his followers:

> A new commandment I give to you, that you love one another. By this all men will know that you are my disciples, if you have love for one another (John 13, 34–35).

They practiced love to the extent of sharing all things in common (Acts 2, 44–45; 4, 32–35). As the Church grew this was replaced by a more practical but equally generous spirit of helpfulness to one another—such a spirit that a pagan contemporary said of them, "See how they love one another."

—under the authority of the Twelve, with Peter as their leader (Acts 1, 13; 6, 1ff). We shall see this more fully in the next chapter.

—preaching constantly the good news that God had come and saved us in Christ (Acts 2, 14ff; 3, 12ff).

—admitting new members to their community by baptism, which had to be preceded by an interior conversion, a true change of heart:

> Now when they heard this (Peter's Pentecost sermon) they were cut to the heart, and said to Peter and the rest of the apostles, "Brethren, what shall we do?" And Peter said to them, "Repent, and be baptized, every one of you, in the name of Jesus Christ for the forgiveness of your sins; and you shall receive the gift of the Holy Spirit" (Acts 2, 37–38).

—celebrating together the eucharistic "breaking of the bread," the primitive Mass, as Christ had told them to. It was by this particularly that they felt united with Christ and one another (Acts 2, 42; 20, 11).

The Spirit fills and guides Christ's Church today so that it has these same characteristics. He is in the Church as a whole, and in each member, giving understanding, power, love, and freedom. He will be with Christ's Church "forever . . . the Spirit of truth" (John 14, 16–17).

A UNIFIED, UNIVERSAL COMMUNITY

Christ's followers were to be particularly united, as God's people had always been. One of the great concerns of the Old Testament was that God's people should always be united. When Israel was split, it was regarded as an intolerable situation which would someday be healed by God. Christ refers constantly to the unity his Church should have. "There shall be one flock and one shepherd" (John 10, 16). It is the one vineyard, one tree, one building, the bride, the one vine. Christ stressed this unity particularly the night before he died, when he prayed several times that his followers would be one, so that men would believe his teachings: **Read John 17, 20–23.**

We would expect Christ's Church to be united, in order to avoid confusion and needless disputes, to better spread his teachings and love throughout the world, to give a confused world some certainty about eternal happiness.

The unity of the first Christians was an evident, visible thing. They were united in love, under the authority of the apostles, sharing the same basic doctrines and the same worship that made them one. St. Paul rebuked some who began dividing into factions: "Has Christ been divided up?" (1 Corinthians 1, 13; 12, 25). Speaking of their common worship, he said:

> The bread which we break, is it not a participation in the body of Christ? Because there is one loaf, we who are many are one body, for we all partake of the same loaf (1 Corinthians 10, 16–17).

On another occasion St. Paul gave his converts the ideal for Christians: **Read Ephesians 4, 1–6.**

Perfect unity is the ideal, never quite achieved but always to be striven for. Christ's apostles argued among themselves. The first Christians at Jerusalem tended to form two factions, the "Hellenists" and the "Hebrews." Soon, as the Church's mission became clearer, a better unity was achieved; but disputes still arose, so that St. Paul wrote from trying experience (words that could be repeated in any period since):

> I appeal to you, brethren, by the name of our Lord Jesus Christ, that all of you agree and that there be no dissensions among you, but that you be united in the same mind and the same judgment (1 Corinthians 1, 10).

Catholics consider their Church to be particularly united. Everywhere among every social group, it has the same basic teachings, the same basic moral code, the same authority to which all submit, and the same ritual of Mass and sacraments. It has always had a basic, visible unity of structure throughout its history. This unity was especially evident in Vatican Council II: 2,700 bishops representing over half a billion Catholics, meeting together, often disagreeing, but all concerned for unity in essential doctrines and morality.

Catholics also must work to heal the disunity of Christians for which they are partly to blame. The unity for which Christ prayed, the Christian ideal, is closer today than for centuries. But it is still a long way from reality. The weakness and sinfulness of Christians has caused our divisions. Striving to love more will bring us together.

Christ expanded the old law by making his Church catholic or universal. He would give all men the opportunity to become members of his new people, whatever their race or social position: "Go into all the world and preach the gospel to the whole creation" (Mark 16, 15). "Go therefore and make disciples of all nations. . . ." (Matthew 28, 19).

Peter on Pentecost announced that anyone, Jew or Gentile, could now be saved through Christ. Inspired by the Spirit, he quotes the prophet Joel:

> And it shall come to pass on the last days, says the Lord, that I will pour forth my Spirit upon all flesh. . . . And it shall come to pass that whoever calls upon the name of the Lord shall be saved (Acts 2, 17. 21; Joel 2, 28).

But it took some years for this idea of catholicity to penetrate the thinking of the early Christians. Imbued as they had been with the notion that God's people was restricted to the Jews, they made no attempt to convert the Gentiles. Then Peter was given a special vision which prompted him to baptize the first Gentile convert, Cornelius. He explained his action by saying, " 'God has shown me that I shall not call any man common or unclean. . . .' While Peter was still speaking these words, the Holy Spirit came upon all who were listening to his message. And the faithful of the circumcision . . . were amazed because on the Gentiles also the grace of the Holy Spirit had been poured forth. . . ." (Cf. Acts, chapters 10 and 11).

St. Paul, the great "apostle of the Gentiles," was personally chosen by Christ to spread his teaching to all mankind. He had been

Saul, a fanatical Pharisee, hater of Christians, and was one day on his way to Damascus to take as prisoners the Christians there. The story of his conversion is one of the most striking of all literature. **Read Acts 9, 3–22.**

He then took his Roman name, Paul, and directed his restless zeal to preaching Christ throughout the Roman empire, to Gentiles as well as Jews. Harried, misunderstood, driven by the Spirit, he travelled unceasingly spreading the gospel until his death in Rome as a martyr. Most of his epistles (letters written to young Christian communities) have come down to us; they comprise about half of the New Testament. Paul's own description of what he endured makes it easy to understand why he is the model of all Christian missionaries: **Read 2 Corinthians 11, 23 to 12, 9.**

This missionary aspect of Christ's Church—that it is to be preached to all mankind, as a way of love for everyone—came to be one of its distinguishing characteristics. This was in contrast to other sects of the ancient world. The label "catholic" was as well known as, and synonymous with, the title "Christian." Paul could say, finally, "I thank my God through Jesus Christ for all of you, because your faith is proclaimed in all the world" (Romans 1, 8). Very soon the Church came to include all types of people, from every level of society, to the astonishment of the pagan world.

Throughout history Christians have tried to spread Christ's teachings to all mankind, at the cost of much suffering and a great sacrifice of human lives. Sometimes nationalism, forced conversions, or a lack of appreciation of native religious insights has weakened their witness. But in the great majority of cases they have been impelled by love and preached love above all else. Along with Christianity they spread civilization, peace and progress.

The enormous achievements of missionaries in Africa, for example, came to the world's attention with Pope John Paul II's overwhelming welcome by millions when he visited there in 1980. One American newsmagazine commented: "Africans are still surprised and touched by the willingness of missionaries to struggle in the hinterlands, helping to dig wells, teaching reading and writing, commanding life-giving sacks of grain during periods of famine, risking their lives trying to cure the sick" (*Time*, May 12, 1980).

Catholics find their Church to be particularly catholic. It is for them a universal home, a place for anyone. It has often been remarked that every type of person, whatever his intelligence, background, race, or social position, can find satisfaction in Catholicism. Sometimes its very catholicity, its multiplicity of ways to God, confuses those looking at it from without. But of its many practices, a few are essential, many more are optional. There is a basic unity and certitude and yet "something for everybody."

> ... each individual part contributes through its special gifts to the good of the other parts and of the whole Church. Through the common sharing of gifts and through the common effort to attain fullness in unity, the whole and each of the parts receive increase (*Constitution on the Church,* no. 13).

True catholicity, however, is an ideal, as yet unrealized, toward which we strive. The Church continually seeks to be more "whole," to learn from all, so that it can more truly be "all things to all men" (1 Corinthians 9, 22). "The Church must somehow find expression in all languages, all historical situations, in all the personalities who will ever come into human history" *(Constitution on the Church in the Modern World).*

UNION WITH CHRIST AMONG US

People in love want to be with each other. United with one another they give each other love, strength, encouragement. Sometimes they can be united only by thought, at a distance, and then they long to be physically united.

Christ remains invisibly but really among us, in order to be united with us in the closest possible intimacy. Though he saved us 2,000 years ago, his love impels him to remain with us now, personally drawing us to the Father and eternal happiness.

It is by being united with Christ that we learn his teachings and receive his grace. Glorified, invisible among us, he is the source of all the helps by which we attain heaven.

> St. Paul calls Christ's risen body a "spiritual body" which is "life-giving" (1 Corinthians 15, 44–45). By Christ's "body" St. Paul means the person of Christ himself, body, soul and divinity. He gives us from himself the new life of grace. This new life with Christ is invisible but

real: ". . . your life is hidden with Christ in God" (Colossians 3, 3). Our life is truly a life in Christ—we are "incorporated" into him. We can say with St. Paul, "I live, now not I, but Christ lives in me" (Galatians 2, 20).

This is what the Church really is: Christ among us, working through his Spirit, uniting us to himself and to one another in order to bring us to his Father. Christ is more involved now in human affairs, in our lives, than he was during his visible life on earth. Now glorified and all-powerful, he works among us through the Spirit. The Church is simply Christ reaching us through his Spirit with his teachings and grace-presence—and the way we return with him to the Father.

The Church, then, is Christ and all those who are united with him in the Spirit. It is Christ extended through space and time, joining us to himself, the "fullness of him" (Ephesians 1, 23). "By communicating his Spirit, Christ made his brothers, called together from all nations, mystically the components of his own body" (Vatican Council II).

Christ gave many descriptions of the way we are united to him in his Church. The New Testament gives some ninety different images of the Church—all attempting to describe the mysterious and wonderful reality of Christ among us and one with us. Here are some of them:

The Church is *the bride*, and Christ is its loving bridegroom (Matthew 9, 15; Ephesians 5, 26ff). For many this is a particularly striking image.

It is a "*little flock*" of which he is the shepherd; "I am the good shepherd, and I know my own and my own know me, as the Father knows me and I know the Father; and I lay down my life for the sheep" (John 10, 14–15).

It is the field, the *vineyard* cultivated by God. Christ says, "I am the vine, you are the branches . . . apart from me you can do nothing" (John 15, 1ff).

It is *God's building*. Christ is the rejected stone that became the cornerstone (Matthew 21, 42). It is built on the foundation of the apostles (1 Corinthians 3, 11) and of Peter (Matthew 16, 18). We are to be "living stones" built into it (1 Peter 2, 5).

It is *our mother* meant to give us understanding, tender love and guidance (Galatians 4, 26).

It is *an exile* journeying on earth as in a foreign land (2 Corinthians 5, 6; Colossians 3, 1–4).

It is the place where the kingdom of God is particularly found, "the germ and beginning of that kingdom on earth ... (which) strains toward the completed kingdom" (Vatican Council II).

It is *God's family* (Ephesians 2, 19). Our Father gives us his own life, and brings us into the loving life of the Trinity. The members of this family love one another and are dependent on one another. Each is important, each has something to contribute to the others; the weak members are given more honor, as a handicapped child might be the center of his family.

It is made up of sinners as well as good people, a "field" with weeds and wheat growing together (Matthew 13).

To express the union of Christ with his Church, St. Paul often called it Christ's body, of which Christ is the head. "Christ is the head of his body, the Church" (Colossians 1, 18). The head was considered by the ancients the dominant part, controlling and giving life to the rest of the body. Christ the head leads us and gives us his life of grace. The Holy Spirit can be called its soul. The soul gives unity to a body, and so the Holy Spirit is the invisible unifier of the Church; he joins the members to one another and to Christ the head; he inspires every good action in the members of the body.

All the members, as parts of the body, are united with one another as well as with Christ the head. Each member is important and what one does affects the others: Read 1 Corinthians 12, 12–27. As our physical body has millions of tiny cells, all working together and contributing to the life of the whole body, so the Church has millions of members helping one another spiritually. If one part of our physical body is sick or in pain, other parts often feel poorly; so if a member of the Church is "sick" in sin, he hurts not only himself but others as well. As the healthy parts of our body come to the assistance of a sick part, so the members of the Church by their prayers and good works can aid those who are in sin.

As each part of our physical body has a particular function, so each member of the Church has a particular role in bringing grace and holiness to the rest. "For just as in one body we have many members, yet all the members have not the same function, so we, the many, are one body in Christ" (Romans 12, 4–5). Some humble, "hidden" member may be helping the others far more effectively than those in positions of prominence.

Our physical body grows and adds new cells; so the Church strives to grow in love and add new members. "(We) grow up in all things in him who is the head, Christ. For from him the whole body . . . derives its increases to the building up of itself in love" (Ephesians 4, 16).

Through the members of his Church particularly Christ teaches us how to attain heaven and gives us his grace. He teaches us by using certain members to whom he has given the power to teach. He enables us to work with him in spreading his grace-presence to ourselves and others. "And the eye cannot say to the hand, 'I do not need your help'; nor again the head to the feet, 'I have no need of you . . .'" (1 Corinthians 12, 21). God's plan, therefore, is that we "gain" Christ's grace for one another, helping others attain heaven, and others helping us. Paul deeply realized this:

> I rejoice now in the sufferings I bear for your sake; and what is lacking of the sufferings of Christ I fill up in my flesh for his body, which is the Church. . . . (Colossians 1, 24).

We work with Christ by praying for others, offering our work and sufferings for them, and as we shall see, by taking part in his sacraments. There are people whom Christ's love will not help as it might have, people who will suffer needlessly unless we help them.

Because we are all joined together, the power of our love knows no bounds. We saw how each child is born into a situation of sin—an environment of selfishness, pride, dishonesty, hatred, etc., which we call original sin, and which has been snowballing since the first sin. Each child, in turn, will influence others as he grows by the evil which he does, adding to the accumulating sin of the world. But good also snowballs. Whenever we do an act of kindness, or act justly, patiently, honestly when tempted to do otherwise, this adds to the accumulating good and love in the world—and since our redemption by Christ this has a new power to affect men eternally. Often we can see this in practice: we do a kindness to someone, that person is moved by our consideration to be kind to another, etc.

We are never alone or without help in Christ's body. Even if it seems that we haven't a friend in the world, Christ is always helping us and countless other members—including people we will not know until the next life—are working with him to help us. At this very moment someone on the other side of the world may be praying or suffering, and Christ may be using their love to help us attain heaven.

IN THE LITURGY

At Mass during the eucharistic prayer we pray for the Church, for its guidance, peace, and unity throughout the world.

In the Prayer of the Faithful and particularly during the eucharistic prayer, we pray for all the types of people within the Church: the clergy and laity, the living and dead, and "us sinners" that we might be united with the saints.

Before communion we pray that Christ will give his Church peace and unity. At the handshake or embrace of peace we show our desire to be united with one another. Communion, which is the body of Christ, as we shall see, both symbolizes and brings about the unity of Christ's Church.

DAILY LIVING: LOVING OUR FELLOW MEMBERS OF CHRIST AND ALL MEN

So close is the union of Christ with the members of his Church that what we do to them, we do to him. This was brought home to Saul on the road to Damascus as he was on his way to persecute the early Christians—Christ said, "Saul, Saul, why do you persecute me?" (Acts 22, 7). Christ himself tells us pointedly how he will judge us one day: **Read Matthew 25, 34–40.**

Since we are joined with one another in Christ's body, what we do to another we also do to ourselves. When we hurt another, we hurt ourselves, making it harder for both of us to achieve happiness. "For no man ever hates his own flesh, but nourishes and cherishes it, as Christ does the Church. . . ." (Ephesians 5, 29).

Love, therefore, is the test of being a Christian. It is the Spirit that must infuse anyone who claims to be a Christian—and it is the Spirit who is Love within us. We must love others just as we would Christ, and as we love ourselves.

Christians should witness to love by loving their fellow members of the Church in a special way. Because Christians should be conscious of their union in Christ, people today should be able to say of us as of the first Christians, "See how they love one another!" We should work and pray especially for full Christian unity, that all Christians will one day show the united, universal love for which Christ prayed.

But we should treat all men as we would Christ himself, with love. Christ died for all men, not just Christians. Others may be called partial or "hidden" members of Christ's Church. We know they often show a great deal of love in their lives. They can be brought to fully appreciate Christ's love by your love.

The true Christian, then, treats everyone with kindness, regardless of race, class, nationality, politics or religion. In his daily actions, at work, at home or school, he tries to avoid anger, and particularly deliberate hatred or seeking of revenge, just as he would avoid injuring Christ himself. In his speech, he is careful of any calumny or detraction. He associates with all, particularly those who need a friend. "Who is weak, and I am not weak?" says St. Paul.

The true Christian is mindful of today's particular test of love. Any refusal to work with, live with, or associate with someone because of his race is a rejection of Christ himself.

> In Chicago, a neighborhood group of Christians from several denominations joined with their priests and ministers in going from door to door to block a group of unscrupulous real estate speculators who were panicking people into selling their homes, which would then be sold to Negroes at an exorbitantly high profit. The canvassing was a difficult task, but now, by the common effort of these Christians, the neighborhood is peacefully integrating.

The true Christian is honest in his dealing with others. In dealing with them, he recalls, he is dealing with Christ himself. Cheating, lying, or any form of dishonesty is unworthy of a member of Christ. "Therefore, putting away falsehood, let everyone speak the truth with his neighbor, for we are members one of another" (Ephesians 4, 25).

Finally, the true Christian respects his body and the bodies of others, by temperance and sexual self-control. Our bodies are united to

Christ. When we abuse them, we abuse Christ himself: **Read 1 Corinthians 6, 15–18.**

SOME SUGGESTIONS FOR . . .

DISCUSSION

Can you understand the necessity of a worldwide unity among Christ's followers?

Can you see how the Church, in its true, inner reality, is Christ among us?

What for you right now would be a concrete test of Christian love?

PERSONAL REFLECTION

Christ lives in my fellow human beings, even the most lowly and despicable. He thinks enough of them to die for them, and to live now in a most intimate union with them. Trying to see Christ in all men, especially those who seem most unlike him, is reaching out for a great reality.

I might perform an act of kindness, if possible, toward someone different from myself: someone retarded; one of another race who needs help in obtaining decent housing or a good job; one of another religious belief that I have difficulty understanding, or of another political persuasion with whom I have clashed.

10

Those Who Serve as Our Guides

What is the origin of the pope and bishops of the Church? How can a human be infallible? What place does authority have in religion?

CHRIST CHOOSES THE APOSTLES AND PETER

God's way has been to come to us through other human beings. While each man must find him in his own heart, yet God gives us his love and help most often through others. He uses other men to draw us to himself. We realize his presence to the extent that we are loved by others and give love to others.

In the Old Testament God always taught his people and led them through men specially chosen by him—the patriarchs, kings, priests, and prophets. This is the pattern of God's plan. Christ also chose men to spread his teachings and his grace.

Christ chose the twelve apostles as leaders, among God's new People, to give his teachings and grace to mankind. They are the leaders of the faithful remnant who began spreading God's kingdom among men. An apostle is a witness of the resurrection sent by Christ to testify to this. More than twelve were apostles, but the Twelve were the nucleus mentioned in all the gospels; as Israel's twelve sons had founded the twelve tribes, so the twelve apostles would lead the new Israel, Christ's Church.

Most of the twelve apostles were simple Galilean fishermen. One, Matthew, was a tax-collector. Another, Judas, betrayed Christ; after he hanged himself, Matthias was chosen in his place. The greatest apostle, Paul, not one of the Twelve, was a persecutor of Christ's Church whom Christ converted on the road to Damascus. Christ's choice of Simon Peter, the leader of the apostles, his brother Andrew, and Matthew, is related by Luke: **Read Luke 5, 1–11 and 27–28.**

While on this earth Jesus Christ travelled only through the small country of Palestine, and spoke to comparatively few people. He was concerned with bringing God's kingdom among men, rather than setting up an organization. The Twelve and the others he chose would work out the best way of carrying his teachings to others, guided by the Spirit. Luke tells how he set the Twelve apart after a night of prayer: **Read Luke 6, 12–16.**

The apostles were to carry on Christ's own work as prophet, priest, and king. They were to teach all mankind, as prophets of the new law of love:

> "He who receives you, receives me; and he who receives me, receives him who sent me. He who receives a prophet because he is a prophet, shall receive a prophet's reward; and he who receives a just man because he is a just man, shall receive a just man's reward" (Matthew 10, 40–41). And Jesus drew near and spoke to them saying, "All power in heaven and on earth has been given to me. Go, therefore, and make disciples of all nations, baptizing them in the name of the Father, and of the Son, and of the Holy Spirit, teaching them to observe all that I have commanded you; and behold, I am with you all days, even unto the consummation of the world" (Matthew 28, 18–20).

They were to teach with Christ's own authority, to share in his kingly power: "He who hears you, hears me; and he who rejects you, rejects me; and he who rejects me, rejects him who sent me" (Luke 10, 6). ". . . whatever you bind on earth shall be bound in heaven, and whatever you loose on earth shall be loosed in heaven" (Matthew 18, 18).

They would continue Christ's priestly work of offering worship to the Father, and giving his grace to man. They were to be his instruments, as when he told them to forgive sins: "As the Father has sent me, even so I send you. . . . Receive the Holy Spirit. If you forgive the sins of any, they are forgiven. . . ." (John 20, 21–23). He would use them to make himself present in a special way and to offer a sacrifice commemorating his death: "This is my body . . . this cup is the new covenant in my blood. Do this, as often as you drink it, in remembrance of me." Of this St. Paul comments, "For as often as you eat this bread and drink the cup, you proclaim the Lord's death until he comes" (1 Corinthians 11, 23–26).

When the Spirit came upon the Christian community at Pentecost, they went forth under the leadership of the apostles, to spread Christ's teachings. Before Pentecost they were confused and frightened; afterward, though still imperfect men who could quarrel among themselves, they taught clearly and fearlessly. The community ". . . devoted themselves to the apostles' teaching. . . ." (Acts 2, 42). After Samaria had been evangelized, "the apostles who were at Jerusalem sent there Peter and John. . . ." (Acts 8, 14). Also Paul, though chosen personally by Christ to be an apostle, yet wanted to be united and recognized by the apostolic group of Jerusalem (Galatians 1).

The apostles taught with a clear authority. When a dispute arose, the apostles met in Jerusalem and issued a decree which began ". . . the Holy Spirit and we have decided. . . ." (Acts 15, 28); they knew they could speak with the authority of the Spirit. John wrote of himself and the other apostles: "We are of God. He who knows God listens to us. He who is not of God does not listen to us. By this we know the Spirit of truth and the spirit of error" (1 John 4, 6; 2 John 1, 10).

The apostle Paul forcefully reminded his converts of his authority when he wrote about a faction that opposed him: **Read Galatians 1, 6–9.**

Finally, whenever people join together to accomplish anything there is usually one person in charge. A nation has a president; a city, its mayor; a business firm, its president or chairman of the board: in a family, the father has the final authority. In the Old Testament God was represented among his people by some leader, a patriarch, king, or high priest. So too Christ chose one man as the leader of his followers. This would assure unity, that all might work together to spread his teachings.

Christ chose Simon Peter as the leader of the twelve apostles. A reading of the gospels shows clearly that Peter was the leader of the group—he is mentioned six times as often as any other, is listed first and is the one who speaks for the others. Three of the gospels tell us how Christ singled out Peter and gave him a special authority over the others. These testimonies come from different parts of the Church and this despite the fact that all knew he had denied Christ. John and Luke describe Christ's first meeting with him at which he changed his name from Simon, son of John to Peter which means "rock" in the language spoken by Christ (John 1, 42; Luke 6, 14).

Matthew described Christ's choice of Peter as leader in this incident: **Read Matthew 16, 13–19.**

> A rock is strong, permanent, the base which holds a structure together; to the Jews of Christ's time *the* rock was Mount Sion which according to legend shut off the underworld and therefore provided protection against the devil's powers. The keys given Peter symbolize authority, power (Cf. Isaiah 22, 22; Revelation 1, 18). To bind and loose means a law-making power.

Luke describes Christ at the last supper telling Peter to strengthen the other apostles, and this despite the fact that Peter will deny him: "... when you have turned again, strengthen your brethren" (Luke 21, 32). John portrays Christ after his resurrection making Peter the shepherd or leader over his flock, his followers: **Read John 21, 15–17.**

> Christ had often referred to himself as a good shepherd and his followers as his flock (Cf. John 10, 11ff; Luke 15, 1–7; Luke 12, 32; Matthew 10, 16; Acts 20, 28). Later, others came to be called shepherds or pastors (1 Peter 5, 1–3). To "feed" expresses teaching, ruling; the triple repetition means a solemn, binding affirmation, like a modern oath.

Peter went eventually to Rome where his position as leader of the early Christian Church was passed on to his successors, the bishops of Rome. Peter's leadership is evident in the early Church, yet not as one endowed with supreme jurisdiction; all the apostles had been commissioned by Christ and evidently felt little need to refer to Peter. They spread the faith independently of each other. Peter went to Rome, because it was the center of the civilized world, and was martyred there. As time went on and the Church grew throughout the world, the unifying authority of Peter's successors grew with it and they became recognized as the leaders of the Christian Church, eventually called popes.

Peter's leadership is shown by his presiding over the election of Matthias; he also works the first miracle, is the first to preach the gospel, the first to receive a pagan convert, and he constantly speaks for the others. On starting his ministry, Paul visited Jerusalem to speak to Peter (Galatians 1, 18); when Paul "opposed him to his face" because of his vacillating conduct, this description of the incident (Galatians 2, 11) shows Peter's special position—though he certainly did not exercise the authority the popes would a few centuries later.

THE COLLEGE OF BISHOPS

We have seen how Christ began an organized community, under leaders he had chosen, to carry on his teaching and loving service to mankind. It is a fact of history that any great leader—religious, political, social reformer, etc.—chooses followers to carry on his insights, his work and his teachings. He thus forms an "organization," small at first, which grows and develops after he has died. We saw how the Christian Church began with the small community of Christ's first followers after the Holy Spirit came upon them at Pentecost—and how they began to organize and spread Christ's teachings, bit by bit, throughout the known world.

Most people, at one time or another, see organizations and institutions as a somewhat regrettable necessity of human life. Most of us undoubtedly wish there were fewer organizations and institutions with which we had to deal. Organizations have a way of developing bureaucracies, rules and "red tape," and it seems that more and more people are needed to run them. Yet we also know that as human beings we need organizations and institutions.

No idea or insight—good or bad—can be passed on and be effective among us humans without some sort of organization. "Large" insights, ones that affect many people at a basic level, that originate with some great leader, tend to grow and develop, be somewhat changed, and spawn disagreements among their adherents. For example, insights of Freud in psychology, of Einstein in physics, of our "founding fathers" about democratic government, developed, grew, gave birth to further insights, and have had inevitably conflicting notions of what is true and best in the particular field. Jesus' insights into the whole meaning of life itself, despite his clear provision for unity and peace among his followers, have resulted in all sorts of interpretations of what he meant, how best to apply his teachings today, etc. This is our fallible human way, even with the greatest of ideas.

So, in the matter of religion, of people's relationship with God, and of living out their life according to its most basic meaning, people naturally tend to come together, to organize. Though religion is always very personal, people join together to share, to develop and spread their insights—particularly if they have been inspired by a truly great vision of their founder.

And if the founder is divine and has taught uniquely insightful, profoundly inspiring and revolutionary ideas about love, service, and what is of ultimate importance in life—as Jesus Christ did—his followers form a community, organize, share, study, and even give their lives in the hope of serving and renewing all mankind, of one day making all people brothers and sisters in love.

And just as with a team, an idea of human service, or government, any movement that is going to be lastingly effective needs people to take the lead in organizing it and guiding the group to most effectively carry out its renewing mission to mankind so as to provide a unity among those inspired by the idea. There is, then, a natural need for guidance, organization, and authority in religion, as in all of life.

From the early years of the Church there has been a hierarchy, that is, different degrees of authority: bishops, priests, deacons. Bishops have the full power of the apostles, priests some of the powers, and deacons lesser powers. As in the Church of the Old Testament, and as in any organization, so there are various offices in Christ's Church.

The organization of the early Church, however, was formed only gradually. Many offices are mentioned in the epistles and in Acts, but the terms do not always have the precise significance that they have today: elders, presbyters, bishops, priests, shepherds, superintendents, presidents, deacons, etc. Some if not most local Christian communities were governed by a "college" of "presbyter-bishops" of whom one was the president or overseer, and all had been appointed by the apostles or their delegates.

In the very early Church, there seem to have been two types of organization, one hierarchical and the other not. Luke pictures Paul as appointing presbyter-bishops in the communities where he worked (Acts 14, 23; 20, 17), and Paul in Philippians 1, 1 mentions bishops in the church he had founded there. On the other hand, the church at Corinth had no evident hierarchical leader, but people with different charisms. What soon prevailed, however, was the hierarchical form. (At the end of the first century, for instance, a letter of Clement of Rome to Corinth shows bishops leading the church there.)

In John's writings, the early "Johannine" Christian communities did not have an authoritative or hierarchical structure, but they considered the Paraclete, the Holy Spirit, as their sole authoritative Teacher; later this group split, and those who held to the pre-existing divinity of Jesus came to accept the need of authoritative presbyter-bishops to preserve the true teaching regarding Jesus' full divinity and full humanity.

What emerges by the turn of the second century is a "monarchical" episcopate: the bishop presides as the head of the local church and the priests form a college around him, assisting him. Thus Ignatius, the influential bishop of Antioch, writes c. 110 A.D.: "You must all follow the lead of the bishops as Jesus Christ followed that of the Father; follow the presbyterium (college of priests) as you would the apostles; and reverence those in the diaconate as you would a commandment from God. . . . Let no one do anything touching the Church apart from the bishop. . . . Where the bishop appears, there let the people be, just as where Jesus Christ is, there is the Catholic Church" (*Letter to the Smyrnaeans,* 8; cf. also *Constitution on the Church,* no. 20).

A bishop is the leader of the local Church or diocese, its spiritual father and center of unity. Each diocese is the Church in miniature: each is a family under the bishop's fatherly guidance; as in any family, the talents of the members of the diocese are to be used for the good of all; each must contribute what he can.

A common early method of selecting bishops was election by the local congregation. Soon local choices had to be approved by the more important "metropolitan" bishops or archbishops, in the West by the bishop of Rome—this to safeguard the episcopacy from unfit men. Since the early Middle Ages bishops have been selected by the pope usually upon recommendation of the other bishops of the area. Civil rulers have often had—and a few still have—a voice in selecting bishops, sometimes with unfortunate results. Today there is discussion of again giving the local people of God, perhaps through select clergy and laity, a voice in choosing their bishop.

The "College of Bishops" is the successor of the group of apostles. Although the bishops are appointed by the pope, they are not his agents, nor do they get their authority from him. It is as a member of the group of bishops, the successor of the group of apostles commissioned by Christ, that the bishop has authority.

Each bishop also has a responsibility toward the whole Church. The apostles and their delegates worked jointly for the conversion of the whole world, and the early bishops showed great charity even to distant Churches. This responsibility of the bishops, obscured for a time, has been stressed again by Vatican Council II:

> Each of them . . . is to be solicitous for the whole Church . . . to instruct the faithful in love for the whole mystical body of Christ, especially for its poor and sorrowing members and for those who are suffering persecution . . . and to supply to the missions both workers and also spiritual and material aid, and . . . to gladly extend their fraternal aid to other churches, especially to neighboring and more needy dioceses. . . . (*Constitution on the Church*, no. 23).

The bishop, by the laying on of hands, shares some of his powers and duties with priests and in some cases with deacons. Just as Moses was helped by many elders when he led the Israelites through the desert, as a priesthood always existed in Israel, as Christ chose other disciples besides the twelve leaders, so too the bishop is helped particularly by his priests and sometimes by deacons. They assist in worshipping God and bringing his grace-presence and teaching to men.

THE PAPACY

The bishop of Rome, the pope, is Peter's successor among the bishops and the visible leader of Christ's Church on earth. Later we shall see how the pope is chosen.

The title "pope" means "father of fathers" and was once used for the heads of all important dioceses; it came to be used solely of the Roman bishop in the 11th century. The popes have rejected other titles such as "universal bishop," which might seem to derogate from the position of their brother bishops. "Pontiff," which has been sometimes used, comes from Imperial Rome and means "bridge-builder" or priest connecting God and man.

The pre-eminent authority of the Roman Church was recognized from the early centuries by most of the Christian world. Ancient Christian documents tell us that the Roman Church was the only one that claimed a primacy over the others, as the center of unity and settler of disputes. It was the only one recognized as universal leader, at least to some extent, by the Christian world in general. It consistently upheld what came to be recognized as orthodox Christian teaching.

As the Christian Church developed, the great dioceses became leaders of their areas and centers of unity. In the East these were particularly Alexandria, Antioch, and Constantinople. Their bishops were called metropolitans, archbishops, or patriarchs. The other bishops became to some extent limited; for example, the metropolitan had to consent to their election. Rome, the only apostolic patriarchate in the West, thus developed as the unifying center and leader of Italy and the West.

Its actions showed that Rome more and more considered itself pre-eminent throughout the whole Christian Church. Near the end of the 1st century, for instance, Clement, Peter's third successor, settled a dispute at Corinth in Greece. Irenaeus of Lyons near the end of the 2nd century expressed the growing conviction that it was necessary to be united to the Roman Church to have the true teaching of the apostles: ". . . the superior pre-eminence of that Church is such that every Church—I mean the faithful of any country whatsoever—necessarily agrees with her, that is, every Church in any country in which the apostolic tradition has been preserved without interruption" (*Adv. Haer.*, III, 3.2). Rome came to be considered more and more the center of Christian unity and its teaching the test of orthodoxy; many accused of heresy, for instance, felt obliged to explain their teachings to the bishop of Rome.

However, during the first four centuries recourse to Rome by the Eastern Churches particularly was rare. It became more frequent from the 5th century on when the strong leadership of the papacy as we know it began to take form; thus the bishops assembled for the Council of Chalcedon in 451 stated their acceptance of the view of the current pope, Leo: "Peter has spoken through Leo."

It was natural that Rome should develop as the leader of the Christian world. The Roman empire's traditions of stability, law and order, practical justice and discipline, its penchant for institutionalism and its conservative regard for tradition—all these worked to make the Church of Rome the stabilizing influence and center of unity of a developing Christendom. Particularly after the barbarian invasions, it became evident that the Roman Church was the only one that could effectively reform and reorganize the often scandal-ridden, weakened local churches. Catholics see in this developing authority of the Roman Church an evolution planned by God to give a center of unity and certainty to his Church as it grew.

Jesus Christ himself working through his Spirit is the real leader of the Church; the pope is his vicar or visible representative. Christ is the true rock, the one shepherd, and all human authority only represents him and is his instrument. The hierarchy of human leaders is necessary, but it is only temporary until Christ comes again in glory.

The college of bishops under the leadership of the pope has the authority of governing Christ's Church. The pope has supreme power, but when he uses it he acts on behalf of the whole college of bishops; the episcopal college has full power, but the "keys" to the use of the power are in the hands of the head of the college, Peter's successor, so that it can never be used against his will.

This authority can be used in several ways. The bishops can exercise their supreme power in union with their head, the pope, as in an ecumenical council. Or the bishops can teach or act in union with the pope while remaining dispersed throughout the world. Or again, the pope himself can teach or legislate for the whole Church, speaking for all bishops, but not dependent upon the consent of the Church or of the bishops, though he does consult the Church and particularly the bishops before he speaks.

Vatican Council II thus sums up the governing authority of the Church:

"Just as in the gospel ... St. Peter and the other apostles constitute one apostolic college, so in a similar way the Roman Pontiff, the successor of St. Peter, and the bishops, the successors of the apostles, are joined together (carrying on) the very ancient practice whereby bishops ... in all parts of the world are in communion with one another and with the Bishop of Rome in a bond of unity, charity and peace. In virtue of his office ... as vicar of Christ and pastor of the whole Church, the Roman Pontiff has full, supreme and universal power over the Church. And he is always free to exercise this power. The order of bishops, which succeeds to the College of Apostles ... is also the subject of supreme and full power over the universal Church, together with its head, the Roman Pontiff, and never without this head. This power can only be exercised with the consent of the Roman Pontiff. ... This college, insofar as it is composed of many, expresses the variety and universality of the people of God, but insofar as it is assembled under one head it expresses the unity of the flock of Christ" (*Constitution on the Church,* no. 22).

An ecumenical council, a gathering of the bishops of the world in union with the pope, best shows this "collegiality" or co-responsibility of the bishops and pope for teaching and guiding the Church. Such a council is to be called by the pope, presided over by him or his delegates, and its decrees approved by him.

Councils have undergone an historical development. Some early councils were convoked by the emperors and presided over by them or their representatives, though the papal delegates had positions of honor, and the popes' previous attitudes guided the orthodox course of most councils; conciliar decrees were often promulgated by the councils on their own authority, receiving papal approbation later. For a council to be truly ecumenical, then, it must have been representative of the bishops of the whole Church, and its decrees at least eventually accepted by the pope.

Today many wish to have future councils or their equivalent open to lay participation, pointing out that a council should truly represent the Church. The Church itself is the "council" called together by God, comprising the whole people of God. As many levels as possible should be present at these gatherings, pope, hierarchy, priests, religious, and people of all sorts: married, unmarried, scientists, laborers, etc. Early and medieval councils had lay participation and when the present Church law is changed, they may once again.

Vatican Council II was held from 1962 to 1965, with approximately 2,500 bishops in attendance. It was the major event in the Church's history in this century. It was the twenty-first ecumenical council of the Church (by the reckoning of most authorities). Only the bishops voted, but much influence for its decrees came from the Church's leading theologians, non-Catholic observer-delegates, and lay people and religious who were also invited to give their views.

A "synod" of bishops meets regularly with the pope (at present every three years) to help him guide the Church. Most of these bishops are elected by national bishops' groups around the world, and their smaller number enables them to function as a "senate" within the Church. Commissions of bishops from all over the world are also carrying out the decrees of Vatican Council II; many meet regularly with clerical and lay experts in various fields.

To help the pope in the day-by-day governance of the Church there is a "curia," various "congregations" or groups of cardinals, bishops, priests, and a small number of lay people. As scholars and administrators, they study and advise the pope in matters of doctrine, seminary formation, marriage, liturgy, ecumenical relations with other churches, etc. Some act as the pope's (and the Vatican State's) representatives with the various governments of the world. They can issue decrees in matters pertaining to their field, subject to the pope's approval.

There are also scholars, or theologians, in the Church who research, reflect on, and work at expressing various aspects of the Church's teachings and the experience of Christians in living out those teachings. They try to discern the ways in which the Spirit is acting in the Church, its future possibilities, and the ways it can profit from other fields of knowledge (and vice versa). Theologians often represent different approaches to better understanding and developing the core truths that Christ gave to his Church. They work with the pope and the bishops, contributing the expertise of their scholarship and reflection.

THE GIFTS OF ALL TO SERVE ALL

Christ showed his followers how to use their authority by being the servants of others. He gave himself totally in serving others, even to dying for them. He told his apostles: "You know that the rulers of the Gentiles lord it over them, and their great men exercise authority over them. It shall not be so among you; but whoever would be great among you must be your servant, and whoever would be first among you must be your slave; even as the Son of Man came not to be served but to serve. . . ." (Matthew 20, 25–28).

Just before he died, he dramatically showed Peter and the other apostles that their authority should be humble service (this ceremony is re-enacted in the Holy Thursday liturgy each year by the pope and by many bishops): **Read John 13, 2–16.**

Christ's followers realized they were to serve not only God but others. They served God by serving others. Paul constantly calls himself a "slave" who does not want to "lord it over" others. "Be servants of one another," he says (Galatians 5, 13). Peter exhorts the elders to "tend the flock . . . not as domineering over those in your charge but being examples of the flock" (1 Peter 5, 2). The usual New Testament word for authority, used again and again, is "diakonia," i.e., service, ministry.

Some, the hierarchy, are to be leaders in service. They lead in order to unify, structure, and organize the service of all, so that it can be truly communal and effective; they are chosen to be mediators, priests, instruments in a special way. Their service is to be given in a more intense manner—sometimes as a model to their flock by dying for them, as their master did and many have done through history.

The pope is called "the servant of the servants of God." He is the

"shepherd" who leads, but he leads only in order to take care of the Church, to serve it, and perhaps to die for it. The Caesars killed thirty of the first popes, almost one after another. Many others have suffered much, as they bore the burdens of Christendom's leading figure.

> Unfortunately popes and bishops have not always remembered their duty of service. Particularly in medieval times, they were more often worldly lords than spiritual leaders serving their people. Much of this was historically inevitable as European civilization developed, but great evils came to the Church because Christ's representatives ruled in an autocratic manner.
>
> Recent popes and bishops have been much more conscious of this duty of service. Vatican Council II says of the bishops' mission: "That duty, which the Lord committed to the shepherds of his people, is a true service, which in sacred literature is significantly called 'diakonia' or ministry" (*Constitution on the Church*, no. 24).

The Church is a living community of people with different gifts or "charisms" for the service of all: Read 1 Corinthians 12, 4–11.

> Vatican Council II has stressed these gifts of the Spirit once again: "The Spirit . . . equips and directs the Church with various hierarchical and charismatic gifts. . . . Among these gifts the grace of the apostles is pre-eminent . . . (but) he distributes special graces among the faithful of every rank. . . . These charisms, whether they be the more outstanding or the more simple and widely diffused, are to be received with thanksgiving and consolation, for they are perfectly suited to and useful for the needs of the Church" (*Constitution on the Church*, nos. 4, 7, 12).

Each member of the Church, clergy and laity, has something to contribute. We saw how each member of Christ's body has a vital function, how the Spirit dwells in each member. Some of the extraordinary gifts St. Paul mentions above existed primarily in apostolic times, to help the Church get underway. But many exist today in modern form, together with other gifts particularly suited to our present needs.

Each must try to use his gifts. Some are called to be leaders, administrators or organizers, while others have gifts for taking care of the "little ones," the poor, sick, neurotic. Some excel in teaching, others in works of charity, art, or Christian witness. One is gifted in speaking out boldly, another tempers our works by prudent observations, and still another does day-to-day tasks extraordinarily well.

The greatest gifts are those of loving, not those of authority. Christ makes clear that we will one day be judged on our works of charity, not on our status (Matthew 25, 31ff). St. Paul says, "Love never ends; as for prophecy, it will pass away; as for tongues, they will cease; as for knowledge, it will pass away" (1 Corinthians 13, 8). The most notable member of the Church is a woman, Christ's mother Mary, who never exercised any hierarchical function. Ultimately, only holiness matters.

The leaders of the Church must try to be aware of, judge, and use the gifts of all. Much of what is best in the Church has been initiated by the Spirit among the laity and priests, reaching the attention of the bishops only later. The bishop's role is to engage in a continual dialogue with his people, trying to be open to the Spirit who often speaks through their gifts. "Judgment as to their genuineness and proper use belongs to those who are appointed leaders in the Church, to whose special competence it belongs, not indeed to extinguish the Spirit, but to test all things and hold fast to that which is good" *(Constitution on the Church,* no. 12; *1 Thessalonians 5, 12; 19, 21).*

The Church, then, exists to serve God and the world. Its organization, which will one day pass away, exists only that it might better serve by witnessing to truth and love. It must imitate its founder in service particularly to the "little ones," the poor, sick, ignorant, and in trying to further the good in all men.

THE GIFT OF INFALLIBILITY

We would expect that Christ would give his followers some guidance when they set out to spread his teachings. Even the most brilliant men can disagree or be mistaken, and Christ's followers were to communicate God's own special revelation of truth. To be sure men would get his message, and to avoid confusion, Christ gave his Church infallibility.

Infallibility means Christ's guidance of the Church through the Holy Spirit so that it cannot make a mistake in teaching his message. We saw how Matthew shows Christ telling the apostles as a group, and Peter as an individual: "Whatever you bind on earth shall be bound in heaven, and whatever you loose on earth shall be loosed in heaven" (16, 19; 18, 18). Sending them out to teach, he says, "He who hears you, hears me. . . ." (Luke 10, 16). Before leaving his followers Christ told them that he would be with them "always, to the close of the age" (Matthew 28, 19). He promised them also that the Father would give "another Counselor, to be with you forever, the Spirit of truth. . . ." (John 14, 16–17). The apostles knew that they had the authority to speak for God himself, as we saw; Paul thus speaks of "the Church of the living God, the pillar and bulwark of the truth" (1 Timothy 3, 15).

Infallibility is expressed by the belief of the people of the Church who are in union with the pope and bishops. When the people as a whole believe a doctrine, it must be true. "The entire body of the faithful, anointed as they are by the Holy One . . . cannot err in matters of belief" *(Constitution on the Church,* no. 12).

The people sometimes express the faith better than their leaders. Cardinal Newman has shown, for instance, that during the 4th century it was the belief of the people that was largely responsible for keeping the true Christian doctrine about the nature of Christ's divinity, while the bishops were either silent or divided (Cf. Newman, *On Consulting the Faithful in Matters of Doctrine* (New York: Sheed & Ward, 1961).

Christ's infallible guidance also passed on from Peter and the apostles to the popes and bishops. It was inevitable that disagreements and confusion would creep in among Christians, particularly as we get further from the time of Christ. Therefore the successors of the apostles and Peter would have an even greater need of an infallible guidance.

Infallibility is expressed by the bishops as a group, as a college. As the successors of the apostles they use this charism when teaching or protecting Christ's revelation concerning belief or morality. Sometimes they teach "solemnly," in an extraordinary way, gathered in an ecumenical council together with the pope. Usually they exercise "ordinary infallibility," that is, they separately teach the same doctrine throughout the world.

Infallibility is expressed by the pope when teaching "ex cathedra," that is, under these conditions: when he teaches as the visible head of the Church, to all Catholics, on a matter of religion or morality, intending to use his full authority and give an unchangeable decision. Infallibility refers only to the pope's power or charism of correctly teaching Christ's revelation to mankind. In *personal* belief or morality, in science, politics, etc., the pope can be wrong. He can sin, and make mistakes—and many have—in governing the Church.

> By this power the pope does not give new revelation, but rather serves and protects the revelation Christ has given us. It is not something of which the pope is proud; it is no guarantee of the soundness of his personal faith, good judgment or prudence. It is rather a testimony to his, and our, human weakness that needs this guidance.
>
> In using this power the pope is the "mouthpiece" of the Church. He speaks on behalf of all the bishops and the believing people. He does not act arbitrarily, pulling teachings out of the air. He rather expresses more clearly a teaching already within the life of the Church; assisted by the Holy Spirit, he can clarify or bring out further implications in what the Church has been believing.

Infallible teachings about God's revelation (dogmas) are the Church's basic, unchanging beliefs. Catholics see a proof of God's guidance in the Church's use of infallibility over the centuries, for the popes and councils have never contradicted the solemn infallible teaching of other popes and councils. Considering the evident weaknesses of some popes and bishops of history, their corrupt lives, the pressures upon them and the fact that some personally held erroneous beliefs, such consistency in infallible teaching is seen to be truly extraordinary.

There is a development of doctrine in the Church, however, a deepening understanding and clearer expression of the doctrines revealed to the apostles. Though the Church's basic teachings are unalterable and can never be negated, their formulation can change, grow, develop to express the truth more fully. As one entering a darkened room gradually makes out the shapes of the furniture, etc., or as a film being developed gradually becomes clearer, so the Church's teachings develop. The Church might be compared to a flowerbox in which many seeds—God's revelation to man—have been planted; some are now blossoming, others are partly grown, and others have only just begun to appear—so the Church's teachings are in various stages of development.

A dogma is proclaimed solemnly only when there seems need to do so, usually when it is attacked, and only after long study and careful consideration. The dogma of papal infallibility was itself not solemnly proclaimed until the year 1870—it took that long for it to be clearly formulated and its solemn proclamation considered necessary—although it can be seen in the Church from the early centuries as a part of the developing concept of papal authority.

Actually, the Church's infallible teachings, while giving us a basic measure of certainty in our service of God, say very little. By its infallibility the Church does not claim to possess the whole truth of God and his relationship to man, but only what we humans are able to see of his revelation at this particular point in history. Any teachings (or all of them together), while true, do not claim to express the whole truth.

St. Paul put it: "Now we see in a mirror, dimly, but then face to face. Now I know in part; then I shall understand fully, even as I have been fully understood" (1 Corinthians 13, 12).

Infallible teachings might best be compared to launching pads used to send satellites millions of miles into space. They begin the satellite or probe on its journey of millions of miles, and it is very important that the launching pads be carefully constructed and that they direct the satellite properly so it may achieve its goal; a relatively small miscalculation here can result in an error of thousands of miles or more in space. But the launching only begins the satellite on its journey. So, too, infallible teachings are truths that can point us, guide us on our journey of love through life to a limitless eternity of love. Thus it is important that they be carefully arrived at and that their meaning be taken seriously. But they are only the merest beginnings of the infinite Truth that is God, only the start of God's giving of himself to us forever as Unlimited Love.

For those concerned over the concept of infallibility as expressed by papal pronouncements, seeing in this a barrier to Christian unity, it might help to remember that only one such infallible pronouncement has been made since the declaration of papal infallibility in 1870, namely, the assumption of Mary, declared in 1950 (after the then Pope Pius XII had consulted all the world's bishops about their belief and that of the people of their dioceses, down through the centuries). And as we shall see in chapter 23, the assumption of Mary, when properly understood, may not be that much of a problem for other Christians after all.

Infallible teachings are being seen more and more today (by Protestants and Orthodox Christians, as well as Catholics) as being more than statements of literal truths (thus the renowned psychoanalyst, Carl Jung, rejoiced at the proclamation of Mary's assumption, seeing its more profound, universal meaning).

Teachings must also be seen in their historical setting, i.e., in the light of the time and circumstances in which they were formulated. Phrasing that was relatively clear in a particular historical time and cultural setting may not express the teaching as clearly to people in today's world, especially to those in a largely different cultural situation. For example, some scholars today are trying to express the dogma of the true humanness of Jesus Christ in a clearer, more relevant way, while also emphasizing Jesus' true Godness or divinity.

The whole tenor of Vatican Council II, of recent popes, and of almost all theological thinking is to avoid making any further infallible pronouncements, but rather to go deeper into the truths we already know, to probe their fuller meanings, and to express them in concepts understandable to our modern world.

Several decades ago, the renowned English writer and dramatist, George Bernard Shaw—certainly one of organized religion's most biting critics—observed ironically in the preface of his famous play, *Saint Joan:* "Compared with our infallible democracies, our infallible judges, and our infallible parliaments, the pope is on his knees in the dust confessing his ignorance before the throne of God. . . ."

Catholics also follow the guidance of the pope and their bishops in religious matters when they are not teaching infallibly. These are the more common laws of the Church. Some have greater authority than others. They can and do change, according to the circumstances and needs of the times. They are given in decrees, encyclical letters, etc. At times, even ecumenical councils deal with non-infallible or disciplinary concerns.

It is obvious that we must have these, too, just as a city must have health regulations, parking laws, etc., which good citizens obey. To have unity instead of confusion we have this authority to which all give their free allegiance.

Among the Church's teachings some are more important and meaningful than others. The Church's basic teachings about the nature of God, Christ, our salvation by Christ, the bible, baptism and the eucharist are a far greater part of an educated Catholic's life than, for instance, truths about Mary and the saints, the nature of purgatory, or papal infallibility. ". . . in Catholic doctrine there exists an order or 'hierarchy' of truths, since they vary in their relation to the foundation of the Christian faith" (*Decree on Ecumenism,* no. 11).

IN THE LITURGY

Pentecost Sunday, fifty days after Easter, is the feast on which we commemorate the coming of the Holy Spirit on the apostles. It is often called the birthday of the Church.

At Mass in the beginning of one of the eucharistic prayers we offer our gifts "in the first place ... for your holy Catholic Church throughout the whole world ... together with your servant our pope, with our bishop, and with all who faithfully teach the Catholic apostolic faith." Since these men are God's special instruments, they need special help.

Then we recall the fellowship we have with "your holy apostles and martyrs, Peter and Paul, Andrew ... Linus, Cletus, Clement (the first successors of Peter) ..."—reminding us that this is the same Mass in the same Church as that of the apostles and Peter.

A **"novena"** is nine days of public or private prayer in preparation for some feast. This practice comes from the nine days the apostles prepared after Christ's ascension for the coming of the Holy Spirit at Pentecost.

DAILY LIVING: OUR ATTITUDE TOWARD AUTHORITY

To the Catholic believer an infallible authority is natural and what one would expect from God. If God has come among us to teach us a way to himself, we would expect him to provide us with a certain amount of surety in knowing his teachings. In human affairs, we always try to come as close as we can to an infallible truth—if one has a disease, he wants a doctor who knows as much as possible about curing it—and it is obviously much more important to have at least a minimum of truth about God and eternal happiness.

An infallible authority, far from limiting our freedom, can give us greater freedom. Christ says of his teaching, "You will know the truth, and the truth will make you free" (John 8, 32). Knowing the truth about anything frees us from ignorance, doubt, insecurity—if we know our watch is correct, we are freed from uncertainty about the time. The more truths science discovers about man and the universe, the greater freedom we can have from disease and calamities. A Catholic, following the infallible authority of his Church, can have a basic freedom from ignorance and error in the most important of all things.

On the other hand the more truth we possess, the greater is our responsibility. Now that nations control the power of the atom, we can also destroy ourselves; we must use this knowledge for the good of all. So, too, God expects those who have his infallible guidance to love more, to use their insights and bring others to his truth and love.

Obedience to authority is natural, too, in less important, non-infallible matters. All day long we obey authorities, sometimes reluctantly, but seeing the necessity for it—conforming to parking laws, paying taxes, obeying those we love or those over us at work, school, etc. We realize that we are free to disobey but then we must face the consequences. We realize, too, that we must live with the weakness and inequalities of any human authority.

There may be extraordinary situations in which a Catholic, after sincere attempts and discussion with theological teachers, cannot make his own some authoritative, non-infallible teaching (e.g., the present papal teaching on birth control): he cannot reconcile it with his grasp of the total gospel preached by the Church. He should then tell his convictions to his spiritual leaders and responsibly work toward a revision of the Church's position. This can be a difficult process in which one has no certitude about how to proceed.

In all of this one's conscience must be his ultimate guide. However, because ignorance or selfish motives may cause one to form an erroneous conscience, there is always a need to try to conform one's conscience to the teaching of the Church.

One's attitude toward religious authority is conditioned by his lifelong relationships to other authorities. One who has experienced little loving authority in his personal life will rarely be able to relate to a Church that speaks with authority. Another might have a personal need for constant authoritarian "props" and so will be overly dependent on a structured religious system. Between these extremes people vary in their need for or independence of religious authority.

A Catholic gives his free obedience to the Church's authority. He tries to be open, ready to learn, to make the teaching his own. He knows that his bishops are gifted by the Spirit to pass on Christ's saving truth. He tries to obey as intelligently as he can.

But this obedience is not just a blind keeping of rules, obeying minimal laws which make a person's decisions for him. Rather it is an openness to guidance in making decisions oneself, a readiness to apply to oneself the general principles of authority, an openness to the Spirit as he acts in our life.

SOME SUGGESTIONS FOR . . .

DISCUSSION

Does it seem logical that the Church should have a center of authority and unity?

What to you are the advantages—and/or liabilities—of an infallible guide?

Can you see the reasonableness of a development of doctrine in the Church?

FURTHER READING

** *Priest and Bishop, Biblical Reflections*, Brown (Paulist Press, 1970)—A brief, excellent study by an outstanding biblical scholar about the biblical background of the priesthood and the hierarchy of the Church.

* *A Pope for All Christians?* McCord, ed. (Paulist Press, 1976)—An excellent study by scholars of various Christian faiths into the possibilities of a future spiritual leader for all Christians.

* *Papal Ministry in the Church*, Küng, ed. (Herder 1971) is another imaginative book on the possibilities for a future, universally acceptable papacy.

* *I Will Be Called John,* Elliott (Pittsburgh Press, 1973)—An inspiring, well-written biography of Pope John XXIII, who "opened the windows" of the Church, convened the Second Vatican Council amid much opposition and changed the Catholic Church for all time. "Good Pope John"

was the much-loved old man who presided at the birth of a new Church.

* *Illustrissimi, Letters from Pope John Paul I (Albino Luciani)* (Little, Brown, 1978)—He was pope only thirty-three days, but "the pope of goodness and of the smile" captured the hearts of almost everyone by his simplicity, humanity, and warmth. This delightful book is a collection of his warm, erudite, and witty open letters to everyone from Jesus to Mark Twain to Pinnochio.
* *The Documents of Vatican II,* Abbott, ed. (Angelus Book, 1966)—The documents of Vatican Council II, with an explanatory introduction to each and comments by non-Catholic authorities.

FURTHER VIEWING/LISTENING

Circus (Roa Films)—22 minutes, color—A powerful parable about you, Christ, and his Church. Thought-provoking.

PERSONAL REFLECTION

To attain salvation we all need the help of others. I should try to realize that some guiding authority is natural and necessary, and in giving it my free allegiance I follow, not just the men involved, but ultimately God. I will humbly seek whatever guidance I feel necessary to reach God and his truth.

The Apostles' Creed is the ancient Christian profession of faith, having come to us from the time of the apostles. It is a good prayer to say frequently as a profession of Christian faith.

I believe in God, the Father almighty, Creator of heaven and earth, and in Jesus Christ, his only Son, our Lord, who was conceived by the Holy Spirit, born of the Virgin Mary, suffered under Pontius Pilate, was crucified, died, and was buried. He descended into hell; the third day he arose again from the dead. He ascended into heaven, and sits at the right hand of God, the Father almighty; from thence he shall come to judge the living and the dead. I believe in the Holy Spirit, the holy, catholic Church, the communion of saints, the forgiveness of sins, the resurrection of the dead, and life everlasting. Amen.

11
The Great Book in Which We Meet God

Why is the bible a special book? How can one better understand the bible? How can one be helped by reading the bible?

THE BIBLE, GOD'S WORD AND MAN'S TOO

We have seen how God revealed himself and his plan to mankind through the men and events of the Old Testament, and then finally revealed himself fully in Jesus Christ. God's revelation to man culminated in the teachings of Jesus Christ as set down in the New Testament. We saw that over the centuries the Church has been developing new insights into his teachings, and he is himself continually among us, revealing himself to his followers in a number of ways. But the basic source of what we know about God and Jesus Christ, the Church's great contact by which all other claims to contact with God are tested, is the revelation given us in the bible.

The teachings of Christianity and of the Catholic Church have their basis in the bible. This was dramatically demonstrated at Vatican Council II when, each day, the book of gospels was solemnly placed before the assembled bishops at the start of their deliberations. Near the close of its last session the Council thus summed up the Church's dependence on the bible:

> . . . All the preaching of the Church must be nourished and regulated by Sacred Scripture. For in the Sacred Books, the Father who is in heaven meets his children with great love and speaks with them; and the force and the power in the Word of God is so great that it stands as the support and the energy of the Church, the strength of faith for her sons, the food of the soul, and the pure and everlasting source of spiritual life (*Constitution on Divine Revelation*, no. 21).

The bible is called the "Word" of God because through it God communicates himself, expresses himself, to us. As we communicate ourselves to others through our words, so by the bible God communicates himself to us.

The Second Person of the Trinity is the almighty Word, the perfect expression of the Father. The bible is God's created Word. He expresses himself through it by guiding the human authors. The Word-made-flesh, Jesus Christ, and the Word-that-is-the-bible are mysteriously and intimately connected: Today's theology speaks of the "sacramentality" of the bible, because through it man is offered a special opportunity to encounter God in Jesus Christ. This is brought about by the bible's direct contact with the human intellect, imagination, and emotions. In some ways it can excel the encounter with God that comes through the sacraments because it is more tangible and offers more substance to man.

The bible is inspired by God, that is, he guided the human authors so that they wrote what he wanted. Even though the human authors sometimes may not have been aware of his guidance, nevertheless they set down in their writings what he wanted them to. Thus we read it as the world's most sacred and special book.

The bible is also the work of men who expressed their own thoughts as they wrote in their own way. The human authors were not merely passive instruments of God, but wrote freely, using the language and style of their time and culture to communicate their message in the way that seemed most appropriate to them. The writers were like us, sinful, subject to error. Sometimes they did not grasp the fullness of God's revelation.

The prophet Jeremiah shows an awareness of his human limitations by opening his book thus: "The words of Jeremiah . . . to whom the word of the Lord came" (Jeremiah 1, 1–2). Luke in his prologue (1, 1–4) wrote: "Inasmuch as many have undertaken to compile a narrative of the things . . . it seemed good to me also . . . to write an orderly account. . . ." Thus the scripture is the words of men seeking to express the word of God which had come to them.

The bible gives the inspired record of God's revelation from the time when the revelation was originally given. God guided his Church to put together the bible because he wanted us to have his teachings in the actual form in which they were first given—when the great, "breakthrough" events of our salvation were still fresh in men's minds—so that down through the centuries we might draw inspiration from them.

A person might set down in a diary an account of some great event in his life soon after it took place, and then years later upon rereading it, be deeply stirred. Reading the words of the bible makes God's great actions seem very close to us—and helps us realize that he is just as truly acting in our lives today.

The bible is a special type of literature and its books must be understood as God and the human authors intended. It contains many different kinds of writing, or literary forms, each of which presents the truth but in its own way—e.g., poetry, parables, hyperbole, metaphors, satire, etc. "Since God speaks in Sacred Scripture through men in human fashion, the interpreter of Sacred Scripture, in order to see clearly what God wanted to communicate to us, should carefully investigate what meaning the sacred writers really intended, and what God wanted to manifest by means of their words" (*Constitution on Divine Revelation,* no. 12).

We saw previously the purpose of the bible and its style of writing. Cf. "The Source of Our Story" in chapter 2. To understand particularly the literary style of the New Testament, cf. "The Coming of Jesus Christ," chapter 6.

The reliability of the historical setting of the books of the bible, once challenged by critics, has been confirmed again and again by modern archeological findings. Just as Christian scholars have come to see the importance of understanding the literary forms of the biblical books, so the discoveries of modern archeology have confirmed the bible's antiquity and the authenticity of the historical setting in which its events took place.

In 1947, the "greatest manuscript discovery of modern times" occurred in the finding of the first of a collection of ancient scrolls in a cave near the Dead Sea. Since then, ten additional caves within a radius of a few miles of Qumran have yielded more material. To date there have been found the remains of some 600 manuscripts, consisting of about a dozen complete scrolls and thousands of fragments dating from the third century B.C. to the early Christian decades. About a fourth of the material comprises copies of the Hebrew Scriptures including a well-preserved scroll of Isaiah and manuscripts representing every Old Testament book except Esther. Of the deuterocanonical books, fragments of Tobit, Sirach, and the Letter of Jeremiah were found. These ancient writings were used by the Essenes, a separatist Jewish sect living in a monastic community at Qumran. The other writings of this priceless discovery consisted of commentaries on various books of the Old Testament, the theology of the sect, and the organization of the community and their disciplines.

These momentous discoveries gave us a Hebrew text of much of the Old Testament over a thousand years older than anything that previously existed. They showed that the final redaction of the Hebrew text was considerably older than what some textual critics had held heretofore. New Testament scholarship has been strikingly illuminated by the material containing the theology and disciplines of the Essenes. It has been held by some that Jesus was strongly influenced by the sectarians of Qumran. Responsible scholarship today does admit to some similarity in his teachings, but the resemblances are outweighed by the differences; the objectives, ideals, and motivation of Christianity greatly differed from that of the Essenes, though quite possibly John the Baptist had some early connection with them, and probably many of them were numbered among the first Christians.

There are also the more recently discovered and already famous Ebla tablets, found in northern Syria. The milieu of the culture which produced these writings has many similarities to the world of the bible. Important cities of the Old Testament are mentioned, and there appear to be parallels in family and clan names, reflecting a period just prior to the patriarchal period.

More recently come to our attention are the discoveries made at Nag Hammadi in Egypt, in 1945, of many early Christian writings, mostly by Gnostic Christians—among them the Gospel of Thomas, of Philip, of Mary (Magdalene), and other writings, giving sayings and incidents of Jesus' life from a gnostic point of view. These give us much information on the development of early Christianity, and especially of this cult-like group which died out after the second century. The gnostics are so-called from their claim to a secret self-knowledge ("gnosis") which enabled them to become divine as, they believed, Jesus had done. Some writings express a beautiful, mystic, inner spirit, but the gnostics also rejected the body as evil—since it was material—and sexual intercourse as a turning of one's spirit into a slave of one's body (which may account, in part, for their dying out so quickly).

Many other discoveries of manuscripts and papyri in the Middle East have been, and are, shedding further light on biblical times. Biblical archeology, a relatively new scientific discipline, is continually expanding our knowledge of the background and meaning of the biblical texts.

None of the original manuscripts of the Old or New Testament books remain today, but our copies are more ancient and numerous than any other books of that period. Our earliest copy of Horace, for instance, is dated 900 years after his death; of Plato, almost 1,300 years. But we have a complete copy of the gospels dated 250 years after its writing, an almost-complete copy dated 100 years earlier, plus fragments from the 2nd century. Compared to the few dozen ancient copies we possess of the best-preserved classics, we have a few thousand of the scriptures. Also, in other early Christian writers we find thousands of biblical quotations and citations, from the New Testament particularly, all testifying to its authenticity.

Because the biblical authors did not write a scientific detailed history in our modern sense, some critics have said that we cannot arrive at a true picture of the historical Christ. They say that what we have in the New Testament particularly are only testimonies of the writers' faith, fragmentary and mythological accounts. However, a conclusive majority of Christian scholars, while agreeing that the faith of the Christian community shaped the writing of the New Testament and that it does use some mythology, nevertheless hold firmly that at the basis of the gospel accounts is a real person, Jesus Christ, who said and did certain definite things.

One writer puts it: "Faith in Christ is not a spontaneous creation, a satellite which never had a launching pad." The evangelists wrote within the early Christian community, amid either eye-witnesses or those who had intimately known eye-witnesses. There is no explaining the faith and influence of these Christians unless the Christ portrayed in the gospels is real. Otherwise no one would believe in such a totally unique character, preaching such a doctrine: perfect and yet very human, claiming to be the unique revelation of God among men, assuming absolute authority over the sacred Law of Judaism, demanding that men change their lives for him even to loving one's enemies and dying for him, finally going to his death and appearing alive again as proof of his teaching.

Unless this portrayal is real, there is no logical reason why Christians should ever have believed in him or convinced so many others of his teachings. There is no other explanation of his great impact and following.

THE BIBLE'S ORIGIN AND DEVELOPMENT

The scriptures used by the apostles and the primitive Christian Church was a Greek translation of the Old Testament called the Septuagint. This translation had been originally made of the then-existing writings of the Old Testament in the 3rd century B.C. at Alexandria in Egypt for the Jews of the diaspora (those living in foreign lands away from Palestine and the temple). Certain other sacred writings were added to this original translation in the next century and a half (some Psalms, Daniel, Esther, Tobias, Judith, Wisdom, Sirach, Baruch, and 1 and 2 Maccabees). When the Christian Church expanded beyond Palestine and began to evangelize the Hellenistic world, this Greek bible was used with great enthusiasm. It became the bible of the Church during its first generation.

The New Testament canon, the Christian writings considered the inspired Word of God, was slow in developing. At first the early Christians were not concerned with providing written records for posterity because they believed that Christ's second coming would occur in their immediate lifetime. With this in mind, missionary efforts were primarily directed toward preaching the oral gospel. Not until the death of most of the first generation Christians—the apostles and others who were actual witnesses of Christ's public ministry, passion, and resurrection—did a concern arise to preserve the gospel for future generations.

With the last half of the 1st century Christian literature began to develop. Some of these writings would eventually make up the New Testament. St. Paul's first letter to the Thessalonians is the earliest of all New Testament writings to reach us in its original form. It was written from Corinth about 50 A.D. Paul followed this with additional letters to various and scattered groups that he had converted to Christianity. His letters were written for the practical purpose of encouraging, instructing, and admonishing these far-flung churches.

The earliest gospel that we have in its original form is Mark. Written sometime after 64 A.D., it is historically the most important of the gospels, for it is the earliest surviving record of Jesus' life and virtually the only record; it is the basis of most of Matthew and Luke and it underlies John.

Irenaeus, an historian of the late 2nd century, says that "after the deaths of Peter and Paul, Mark, the disciple and interpreter of Peter, also handed down in writing the things which Peter had proclaimed" (Harper Bible Dictionary).

From this point on there was a great increase in Christian writings. The other extant gospels were written within a decade or two. Many other writings were highly regarded by local churches, e.g., the Epistle of Clement, the Didache, Gospel of St. Thomas, Shepherd of Hermas, etc. But it was almost unanimously held that the writings which had some apostolic origin were to be placed in a special category. Between 150 and 200 A.D. our present New Testament books came to be basically accepted by the Christian world, though some books were not widely used.

There is a development in Christian theology among the books of the New Testament. From its earliest book, Paul's first epistle to the Thessalonians, to the second epistle of Peter, the last to be written, there is an evident development in the Church's understanding of Christ and his teachings. Under the influence of the Holy Spirit, Christ's first followers were coming to understand and set down in words what God had done in Christ.

The canon or list of books of the Old and New Testaments was established by the end of the 4th century for all practical purposes. Certain early Church "fathers," scholarly and holy churchmen who were often bishops, particularly influenced the selection of the books that would comprise the New Testament. More and more these 27 books were used by the Church, and the other writings fell into comparative disuse.

Clement of Alexandria (150–215 A.D.), Eusebius (d.c. 340 A.D.), and Jerome (d.c. 420 A.D.) were some of these Church fathers. Athanasius in 367 A.D. issued a list of 27 books which is the same as our present New Testament; this was accepted as canonical by the synods of Hippo (393) and Carthage (397, 419). About this time Pope Damasus I commissioned Jerome to translate the Septuagint and the canonical Christian writings from Greek to Latin, the spoken language of the Roman empire. This translation is known as the Vulgate and was used as the Church's official version until recently.

The Catholic Church, within whose influence the bible was formed, has always reverenced it, and today especially the Church urges her people to read it daily. The bible has always been the basis of the Church's teachings and of her liturgy. Its use was not as widespread in past centuries as today, mostly because people generally could not read and understand it. Yet before the Reformation there were translations of the bible into almost every modern language, and many in Latin which was understood by most educated people.

The Church, however, particularly in post-Reformation times, banned certain translations of the bible because they were considered to have distorted some passages or were being used to teach erroneous doctrines. Because of this defensive mentality, the post-Reformation Church placed too little emphasis on the bible, and sometimes discouraged private bible reading altogether.

Today there is a great biblical revival in the Church, and the bible has become the great force for Christian unity. Christian scholars of all faiths are working together on the ancient biblical manuscripts, sharing their discoveries with one another. They are in almost unanimous agreement on the bible's translation, and the more biblical studies progress the closer they draw together on its meaning.

Regarding vernacular translations of the bible in modern languages:
Before the Reformation there were a number of versions of the bible available to the people in French, Spanish, Italian, and German; these were translations from the Latin Vulgate.

Beginning with Tyndale's translation in 1526, there appeared in rapid succession eight English versions of the bible, culminating in the King James version in 1611. One of these was the Douay-Rheims bible translated from the Latin by Roman Catholic scholars—the New Testament in 1582 and the Old Testament in 1609. This version became the official bible for English speaking Roman Catholics, and the source for the later Knox and Confraternity translations.

The English bible owes more to William Tyndale than to any other man, not only because he was the first to translate the bible from the original Hebrew and Greek, but because the basic structure of his translation has endured through all subsequent changes. The King James version used much of his translation. One third of the New Testament is worded exactly as Tyndale's and the balance follows his general underlying structure.

The King James version came to be called the authorized version of the English people. For two and a half centuries it remained unchallenged. In 1870 a revised version was made in which something like 36,000 corrections were entered; other revisions have been published since.

In America the most widely used edition today is the Revised Standard Version; the New Testament was published in 1946, the Old Testament in 1952, and the Apocrypha in 1957. This is the authorized version of the National Council of Churches. The **Oxford Annotated Edition** with Apocrypha has excellent footnotes, maps, and supplementary information. Both of these bibles are available in Roman Catholic editions.

The New American Bible completed in 1970 is the first translation of the entire bible from the original language into English under Roman Catholic auspices. It replaces the Confraternity edition, and it has been authorized for the readings used in the Mass. Because of this, it will probably become the most widely used bible by American Roman Catholics. It is in modern English and some editions have excellent footnotes.

The Jerusalem Bible, translated by English Roman Catholic scholars in 1966, is another modern English text with a wealth of explanatory notes and other supplementary information. It is unexcelled in its marginal cross references to other parts of the bible which contribute to an understanding of the text.

In 1970 the **New English Bible,** authorized by the Church of Scotland and other British churches, was completed. It is exceptionally effective in its use of modern English. Yet, it retains a continuity with the older versions that have been hallowed with centuries of use. Another very fine translation in modern English is the **J. B. Phillips New Testament.**

Good News for Modern Man, the New Testament in Today's English, published by the American Bible Society in 1966, has surpassed all records as a best selling paperback. It has outsold the best seller of every year since its publication, and its total sales exceed any book ever sold. A companion volume of the Old Testament is being prepared because of the overwhelming success of the New Testament.

In recent years bible scholarship has been bringing together men of all faiths in cooperative ventures. An example of this is the scholarly **Anchor Bible** being published with an extensive commentary, one book at a time. It is being translated by the most renowned scripture experts of Judaism, Protestantism, Catholicism, and Orthodoxy.

In the Old Testament, Catholic bibles have seven more books than most non-Catholic versions. There is no substantial difference in the New Testament. Though some early Christian writers had reservations about seven Old Testament books, scholars today agree that they were generally accepted and used throughout the Christian Church from the beginning. The books, called the Apocrypha or deutero-canonical books, are Tobias, Judith, Wisdom, Sirach (Ecclesiasticus), 1 and 2 Maccabees, and parts of Daniel and Esther.

The difference of opinion about the books is an ancient one:

The Jews at the time of Christ had no fixed list of books. The theory that the Greek Septuagint, translated and used by the Jews of the diaspora, had a fixed canon which was eventually adopted by the early Christian Church is questioned today. The great codices of the Septuagint—Vaticanus, Sinaiticus, and Alexandrinus—which should bear witness to this supposedly fixed collection, are in disagreement. The same situation existed among the Palestinian Jews, and is attested to by the fact that the Essenes of the Dead Sea included some of the deuterocanonical books in their collection of scripture. It is generally believed that the Rabbinical schools of Palestine, because of the growing controversy with early Christianity and the development of Christian writings being used as scripture, did establish a canon in the late second century—although there are echoes in rabbinic literature well into the 3rd century of individuals questioning the status of some of the writings.

The Jewish historian, Josephus, alludes to a rabbinical tradition that Ezra closed the canon of the bible; this tradition which is in fact unfounded is probably an attack on the Septuagint. Another rabbinical tradition attributes the delineation of the canon to a synod at Jamnia in Palestine about 100 A.D., but there is little reliable information on the activities of this synod.

At the time of the Reformation, Martin Luther made a translation of the bible using the Palestinian canon as the basis for his Old Testament—thus eliminating Judith, Tobias, Wisdom, Sirach, Baruch, 1 and 2 Maccabees, and parts of Daniel and Esther. These books were placed in an appendix to the Old Testament. He also rejected Jude, Hebrews, James, and Revelation from the New Testament. The other Reformation churches, however, did not dispute the New Testament canon, and Lutherans returned to the traditional New Testament listings in the 17th century. By the end of the 19th century most bibles published by non-Catholic sources did not include the disputed seven books of the Old Testament.

The Catholic bishops at the counter-reformation Council of Trent declared in 1546 that the 73 books which had been used to that time by the Christian Church were canonical and the inspired Word of God.

"The quarrels over the authority of the Apocrypha are now largely matters of the past. A generation that has witnessed the discovery of the Dead Sea Scrolls will probably agree with the statement by Prof. Frank C. Porter, in Hastings' *Dictionary of the Bible* (1901), that 'modern historical interest . . . is putting the Apocrypha in their true place as significant documents of a most important era in religious history' " (Preface of Thos. Nelson & Sons R.S.V. Apocrypha).

Most of the best recent versions of non-Catholic bibles are available in editions with the Apocryphal books. To quote E. Jacob: "These books do not appear to be a roadblock but rather a bridge between the two testaments. Certain doctrines such as the resurrection of the dead, angelology, the concept of retribution, have assumed in the apocryphal (deuterocanonical) literature the aspect under which they materialize in the New Testament. To not include them is to run the risk of removing a precious link in the web that constitutes the unity of revelation." This prominent European Protestant bible scholar goes on to say that it is highly desirable that these books be inserted at the end of the Old Testament, as they were during Reformation times.

Catholics and Protestants are now working together to produce common bibles, especially in the minor languages of the mission fields, and these bibles will contain the apocryphal (deuterocanonical) books.

THE CHURCH'S TRADITION INTERPRETS THE BIBLE

Christ did not leave his followers a religion in the sense of a "package" of clear, well-defined truths. His teaching was to be completed by the Holy Spirit and undergo development in the course of centuries. While he gave us the fullness of God's revelation, yet much was implicit, not able to be grasped by the ones to whom it was given—and today much is not able to be grasped by us. To help each age understand Christ's teachings, his Church must adapt their expression to the mentality of that time. The teachings remain basically the same, but we progressively see into them more fully, more relevantly. The Holy Spirit guides each generation to add its own understanding to them.

Nor did the apostles sit down and write a handbook of the Christian faith. Their religion was still "finding itself," growing in an understanding of its true mission—sometimes through painful controversy, as in the battle over the "Judaizers" who would have kept Christianity an aspect of the Jewish Faith. These were the problems of the humans who tried to carry on after Christ. They were inspired by the Spirit, but still remained very human.

The primitive Church developed through the oral teachings of the apostles and others who were the witnesses to the great events of Christ's life. The Christian writings which later made up the New Testament were comparatively slow in developing, so that in the first decades of Christianity the faith was based solely upon oral apostolic traditions. In fact the people based their faith almost entirely on the preaching Church until near the end of the 2nd century. The basic elements of the faith were being revealed during the full period of the apostolic age. Only slowly did the Church arrive at a definite creed in the sense of a clearly defined set of truths.

> An example of the development of revelation can be seen in the formula for baptism. In the earliest oral proclamation as recorded in the sermons of the book of Acts, the apostles stated that one must be "baptized in the name of Jesus Christ" (Acts 2, 38; 8, 16). As a deeper understanding of the faith was revealed to them, they baptized "in the name of the Father, and of the Son, and of the Holy Spirit" (Matthew 28, 19).
>
> Christian traditions were expressed in both oral and written form. St. Paul wrote to the Church in Thessalonica, "So then, brethren, stand firm and hold to the traditions which you were taught by us, either by word of mouth or by letter" (2 Thessalonians 2, 15). Christianity did not simply become a religion of a book. The Church often asserted apostolic sanction for traditions and usages that could not be traced to apostolic writings.

The bible came from the living Church—the Old Testament from the living community of God's people, Israel, and the New Testament from the apostolic community that Christ founded, his Church, the new Israel. The books accepted as part of the New Testament, particularly, had to be orthodox, to match the belief of the Church. For every accepted book, the Church rejected a similar one. God's truths are revealed to us in the bible, but to understand them in their fullness, they must be seen along with the traditions of the Church from which they first came.

Tradition is the way Christ's Church understands and lives his teachings. It is not merely the quaint customs of the Church, things like our practice of shaking hands upon meeting a friend. It is the way Christ's teachings were and are lived by his Church.

Tradition comes from many things: The Church's creeds, the records of the Church's worship and liturgical practices, the writings of scholars and Church leaders, the decrees of popes and councils, the prayers of the Church's people, etc.

> The Church pays particular attention to the tradition that comes from the ancient Church, from those who were closest to Christ. This

is called "apostolic tradition." It is found in the early records of the
Church's worship, the writings of the early Church "Fathers," ancient
Christian inscriptions, paintings, etc.—anything that tells us what
Christians believed and did from the time of the apostles.

**Tradition is also continuing and developing today. It is the way
the Church here and now understands and lives Christ's teaching.** It
is going on now, in the writings of scholars, the decrees of Church
authorities, the practices of the liturgy, the Christian practices and
devotions of the people, etc. Since Christ and his Spirit guide the
Church, they are continually forming this tradition.

**Tradition, then, is the way in which the teachings of the bible are
understood and put into living application in the Church.** The teachings of the Church, contained in the bible, are interpreted for us by
the Church's tradition. To understand Christ's teachings we look
both to the bible for the "Word" and to tradition for the "Spirit" in
the interpretation of sacred scripture. It is something like looking at
a house from the outside and from the inside—in either case you are
looking at the whole house, but both points of view are necessary to
grasp it fully.

**While the bible contains God's original revelation, yet the bible
cannot be understood alone.** The Church's living tradition is necessary to understand it. Sometimes all that it gives us is a hint of a particular teaching, and while some of its teachings are explicit, others
are only implicit. To try to interpret the bible without the aid of
Christian tradition would be like trying to interpret the American
Constitution while ignoring the other writings of the Founding Fathers, the constitutional interpretations of the courts, commentaries
of legal scholars, etc.

> None of the biblical authors had any idea of writing a book which
> would of itself give us all of God's revelation. John wrote the last and
> longest gospel and says at the end of it: "There are, however, many oth-
> er things that Jesus did; but if every one of these should be written, not
> even the world itself, I think, could hold the books that would have to
> be written" (John 21, 25). St. Paul says, ". . . hold the teachings that
> you have learned, whether by word or by letter of ours" (2 Thessalo-
> nians 2, 15). We saw that Christianity was in existence almost two hun-
> dred years before the biblical writings were known throughout the
> Christian world, and even after this the books were accepted and
> passed on under the aegis of the Church's authority.

So we cannot arbitrarily use biblical texts to "prove" a teaching apart from the Church's tradition. Through the centuries men have tried to "prove" almost everything by quoting biblical texts without regard for the living tradition of the Church. We recognize that each individual cannot be given his own copy of the American Constitution to interpret and live as he sees fit; so we cannot understand and live the teachings of the bible without the traditions of the Church.

"There exists a close connection and communication between sacred tradition and sacred scripture. For both of them, flowing from the same divine wellspring, in a certain way merge into a unity and tend toward the same end. Sacred tradition and sacred scripture form one sacred deposit of the Word of God committed to the Church" (*Constitution on Divine Revelation,* no. 9).

God's revelation, then, is something that is happening to God's people today, as well as what the Church has possessed from the beginning. In the events of their daily lives, Christians should be making personal contact with Christ revealing himself to them. They should experience this especially when they gather together for the liturgy, as we shall see, or when they pray, or when they encounter God in some deed of kindness, justice, fortitude, etc. For the committed believer, everything that happens is divine.

AN OUTLINE OF THE BIBLE

The Old Testament tells the story of God's revelation of himself and of his plan leading up to the coming of Christ. It contains forty-six books, written by various authors over a period of many centuries. (The older, alternate titles of the books are shown in parentheses. The books are arranged in the order of their appearance.)

The Pentateuch, the first five books—Genesis, Exodus, Leviticus, Numbers and Deuteronomy—also called the Law (Torah)—

This begins with a primitive history of mankind presented in a mythological setting. It continues with God's choice of his people, given in an historical setting. Its high point is the making of the old covenant. It also contains religious legislation covering the way of life of God's chosen people.

The Historical Narratives

Joshua (Josue), Judges, Ruth, 1 Samuel (1 Kings), 2 Samuel (2 Kings), 1 Kings (3 Kings), 2 Kings (4 Kings), 1 Chronicles (1

Paralipomenon), 2 Chronicles (2 Paralipomenon), Ezra (1 Esdras), Nehemiah (2 Esdras), Tobit (Tobias), Judith, and Esther—

These books give a general history of Israel. They tell us of the conquest of the promised land, Canaan, the development of the kingdom of Israel as an ancient world power under the reign of Kings David and Solomon, and the divided kingdoms of Israel and Judah, the destruction of these kingdoms, followed by the captivity in Babylon, and finally the return and attempt to rebuild Jerusalem and the temple to their former glory.

Wisdom Literature and Poetry

Job, Psalms, Proverbs, Ecclesiastes (Qoheleth), Song of Solomon (Canticle of Canticles), Wisdom, Sirach (Ecclesiasticus)—

Historically these books have been classified as the seven "sapiential books," or collections of wisdom sayings, though they contain poetry, prayer, liturgy, and love songs as well.

The Written Prophets

Isaiah (Isaias), Jeremiah (Jeremias), Lamentations, Baruch, Ezekiel (Ezechiel), Daniel, Hosea (Osee), Joel, Amos, Obadiah (Abdias), Jonah (Jonas), Micah (Micheas), Nahum, Habakkuk (Habacuc), Zephaniah (Sophonias), Haggai (Aggeus), Zechariah (Zacharias)—

These men of God are unique not only among the men of ancient times but in the entire literary history of the world. Their office was not filled by human choice but by God. Occasionally and rarely predictors of the future, their main concern was the current situation among God's people. They were a comparative handful of extraordinary preachers who dramatically exhorted, inspired, and tried to reform God's people at times of great crisis.

An historical bridge to the New Testament: 1 and 2 Maccabees (Machabees)—Saga of the period in Israel's life from 166 to 37 B.C.

The New Testament gives the early Christian Church's view of Christ's life and teachings. It contains 27 books, written between 50 A.D. and the early years of the 2nd century A.D.

The four gospels, as we saw, give a rough outline of Christ's life and teachings. The first three, called the synoptic gospels, closely resemble one another; in their composition there was some copying, either from one another or from identical sources, though each author has his own distinctive arrangement and purpose.

Matthew was written particularly to show that Christ is the promised Messiah, the new Moses. It therefore stresses how Christ fulfilled the messianic prophecies, and it arranges things according to five booklets as does the Pentateuch. It was probably written in Syria or Palestine in the 80's A.D. Both Matthew and Luke show that they got much material from Mark, and some material from another source which is now lost (designated as "Q," from the German word quelle = source). Matthew is the first gospel in the sense that it was the one most widely read in Christian assemblies and so did more than any other gospel to form the Christian image of Jesus.

Mark, the oldest and shortest gospel, is very descriptive, and is mainly concerned to show that God has come and saved us in Jesus; everything leads up to the climax: Christ's suffering, death, and resurrection. It was probably written in Rome and shows an awareness of its Gentile Christian readers.

Luke, described as a physician and disciple of Paul, shows Christ as the friend of the poor, the sinner, the sufferer. His is the most complete of the gospels, and has something about almost everybody. This gospel was probably written at about the same time as Matthew, perhaps at Rome, but unlike Matthew it has in mind Gentile Christian readers.

John, written from the viewpoint of one who loved Christ very much, is the loftiest of the gospels. It is quite different from the other three. Its purpose is to show that Jesus is the eternal Son of God, and shows a developing Christian theology about Christ—hence it probably comes from the last decade of the 1st century. It stresses Christ's "signs" and particularly the sacraments of baptism and the eucharist.

The Acts of the Apostles, also written by Luke, takes up where the third gospel stops. It tells of some outstanding incidents in the beginning of the Christian Church. The second part is concerned chiefly with Paul. This book is fascinating and easy to read from beginning to end.

The fourteen epistles attributed to St. Paul are letters written to early Christian communities or to individuals. They are letters of instruction, guidance, and admonition, written to strengthen the faith of the early converts and to put down errors. They were either dictated by Paul himself, or were written by his followers from the teachings he gave them. In their pages is a summary of Christian theology as presented by the great apostle of the Gentiles. The reader should notice how Paul's inspired insights develop in these, how he grows in his perception of Jesus as the eternal, divine Son of God and how he expands upon the relatively simple sayings and stories of Jesus given especially in the first three gospels. Like the author of John, much of his knowledge comes from his own mystical experiences of his Lord.

> The letters written by Paul himself include Romans, 1 and 2 Corinthians, Galatians, 1 Thessalonians, Philippians, and Philemon. Paul's authorship of Hebrews is universally rejected among critical scholars, along with the "pastoral" epistles (1 and 2 Timothy, and Titus). Some question the Pauline authorship of Colossians, Ephesians, and 2 Thessalonians; however, there is no doubt that these last letters were written in the spirit of Paul's theology.

The seven "catholic" epistles are letters addressed to the Church in general, one of James, two of Peter, three of John, and one of Jude. Attributed to these apostles and reflecting their thought, these letters were written mostly by their followers.

Revelation or the Apocalypse concerns the "hidden things," and gives a series of figurative visions in symbolic and mysterious language. It concerns the time between the ascension of Christ and his return at the end of the world, and was especially meant to console the early Christians struggling against imperial Roman paganism.

IN THE LITURGY

The bible forms the basis of our worship. Most of the prayers of the Mass, the sacraments, the daily prayer of priests and religious, etc., are composed of prayers from scripture.

The best way to receive God's Word is when the scriptures are read to us at Mass. The first part of the Mass is called the Liturgy of the Word, because it gives us God's Word, especially in the scripture readings and the sermon which should be based on these. It is then that God addresses his Word to his people. At Mount Sinai, the chosen people assembled to hear God's Word read to them; they then agreed to his Word and a covenant was established by sacrifice. God's people assembled today at Mass likewise listen first to his Word, and then show their acceptance by taking part in the renewal of Christ's perfect new covenant sacrifice.

Sacred scripture, then, is at the heart of the Mass. Just as we receive Christ in the sacrament, so also we receive Christ in the "Word." There are now normally three scripture readings in the Sunday Mass. The first is from the Old Testament, and is chosen for its relationship to the gospel, thus stressing the unity of the Old and the New Testaments. The second reading consists of semi-continuous passages from the letters of Paul and James. The gospel, the final reading, follows the theme of the liturgical season. The lectionary of the Mass provides a more varied reading of the bible by arranging the texts in a three-year cycle.

> We are fully confident that priests and faithful alike will prepare their hearts together more earnestly for the Lord's Supper, meditating more thoughtfully on sacred scripture, nourishing themselves daily with the words of the Lord. The fulfillment of the wishes of the Second Vatican Council will be inevitably the consequence of this experience of God's word: sacred scripture will become a perpetual source of spiritual life, and an important instrument for transmitting Christian teachings, and the center of theological teachings (Introduction to the Lectionary, Chapter I, Part IX).

DAILY LIVING: THE BIBLE IN OUR LIFE

When we meditatively read the bible and try to apply its words to our lives, God communicates with us. He helps us to know what to do and have the courage to do it. The bible's words are addressed to us as much as to the men among whom it was written. The deeds related in the bible are meant to show us that God is continually present among his people, that he acts to help us here and now as he once helped them.

> *The bible's power in one man's life is illustrated by this real-life story:* Raised as a midwest minister's son, a young man was accustomed to daily bible reading in the home, but upon attaining adulthood and financial success he abandoned any practice of the Christian faith. Then a crisis caused the breakup of his marriage and he gradually turned again to reading his deceased father's bible. Eventually he was converted to Catholicism, and now, several years later, he leads an outstanding group of lay apostles and is in constant demand for his penetrating talks on the bible.

SOME SUGGESTIONS FOR ...

FURTHER READING—

BIBLE STUDY AIDS

Many people become discouraged in their attempts at bible reading because they are using an older version in which the style and language are obsolete and difficult to follow. Thus it is important to look over the newer versions of the bible. A number of these are listed earlier in this chapter. In addition, there are other study aids available:

A **bible dictionary** is a collection of articles offering facts and data about persons, places, ideas, words, and themes from the bible. It provides pertinent information from other sources dealing with history, geography, archeology, and language studies that can further illuminate one's bible study. Recommended texts in this category are McKenzie's *Dictionary of the Bible* and Harper's *Bible Dictionary.*

A **bible atlas** contains maps of important historical periods in bible history, with a commentary on the events occurring in those eras. Among the many good atlases available are *The Oxford Bible Atlas* and Grollenberg's *Atlas of the Bible.*

A **concordance** lists alphabetically all the words that are found in the bible. This helps one find particular bible verses, and also helps locate material topically. Some good concordances are Cruden's, Young's, and Strong's.

A **commentary** provides an explanation of the bible passages book by book and verse by verse. It illuminates difficult and obscure passages, and gives an interpretation of the meaning. One of the best available today in one volume is the *Jerome Biblical Commentary.* The *Interpreter's One-Volume Commentary of the Bible* is also excellent.

Also valuable are *A Commentary on the Gospel of Matthew* and *A Commentary on the Gospel of John,* both by Kirk and Obach (Paulist Press 1979, 1980), and *A Commentary on the Gospel of Mark,* Keegan (Paulist Press, 1981).

Among the excellent **general introductions** to the bible are *The Bible Makes Sense,* Bruggemann (St. Mary's College Press, 1977), and

God's Word and God's People, Deiss (Liturgical Press, 1976) which is especially good for connecting the bible with our worship at Mass.

For **bible study groups** there are some fine books available, including *Sharing of Scripture,* Roberts (Paulist Press, 1978) and *A Guide to Reading the Bible,* a four-pamphlet set issued by ACTA Publications. A series of booklets issued by the Liturgical Press on the books of the Old and New Testaments is simple and well done.

DISCUSSION

Can you understand how Christ's teachings spread and how the bible enjoyed a natural and gradual development?

Does it seem natural to you that God's revelation should be continuing today in our lives?

What parts or books of the bible are the most meaningful to you?

PERSONAL REFLECTION

We should all read a bit of the bible each day, asking the Holy Spirit to open our mind as we do so. Below are suggested readings, with a prayerful response to each. As I read one of the suggested sections, I should ask myself "What is God saying to me here?"

When temptations are great read Matthew 4, 1–11; James 1. Pray Psalm 139 (140).

If you have fallen into serious sin read Luke 7, 36–50; 1 John 1 or 2. Pray Psalm 50 (51). Then express your sorrow as perfectly as you can to God whom you love.

When you need strength to overcome your weakness read Romans 8; Ephesians 6, 10–24. Pray Psalm 31 (32).

If you need reassurance read 1 John 3. Pray Psalm 26 (27) or 90 (91).

When you are lonely read John 14. Pray Psalm 22 (23).

If you are facing a crisis read Colossians 1 or 1 Peter 1. Pray Psalm 15 (16) or 120 (121).

When ill or in pain read 2 Corinthians 1 or 4 or 12, 1–10 or James 5. Pray Psalm 40 (41).

If you fear death read John 11 or 20 or 2 Corinthians 5, or Revelation (Apocalypse) 14, 12–13. Pray Psalm 85 (86).

When you are bereaved read Wisdom 3, 1–9 or 1 Corinthians 15 or 1 Thessalonians 4, 13–18, or Revelation 21 or 22. Pray Psalm 102 (103) or 115 (116).

When following the crowd seems easier than following God read 2 Corinthians 6. Pray Psalm 36 (37).

12
The Great Signs in Which We Meet God

Can we reach God by our worship? How can we be sure of his presence in our lives? Of what value are religious ceremonies?

THE SACRED LITURGY, CHRIST'S SIGNS OF LOVE

We have just studied the bible which tells us of God's great works among his people in times past. Now we will take up the sacred liturgy, in which God is present and acting among us today. We can meditate on the bible, but far better, we can actually relive its great events ourselves by taking part in the ceremonies of the liturgy.

To understand the sacred liturgy, we must have some appreciation of the meaning of love. Love is not only the basic concept of Christianity, but indeed of all human existence. We cannot be happy, even in this life, unless we are loved and can give love. Love means giving ourselves to the one we love, in order to be united with our beloved, to bring our beloved happiness.

Christianity is simply a love affair between God and us. God first gave himself to us, and we respond by giving ourselves to him. Through this intimate, mutual giving, we attain union with God and happiness forever.

God draws us to himself by giving us his teaching and his grace. He teaches us how to come to him and he gives us his own presence, grace, to raise us to himself.

We give ourselves to God by worshipping him. We saw that this is man's basic, most natural attitude before God—to honor him, to try to make contact, to ask his help.

It is by being united with Christ that we worship God and receive

his grace and teaching. We saw that Christ is our Savior and Mediator, risen and living among us in his Church, acting through his Spirit. God gives himself to us to the extent that we are united with Christ, and we can give ourselves to God only in and through Christ. Many do not know Christ, but are united to him as "anonymous Christians."

The believer, united to Christ, can meet God as an individual, worshipping him by himself and receiving his grace and truth. He might do this in the prayer of his own heart, in the silence of his room or in the stillness of a forest. Or he can meet God in his fellow man—by an act of kindness or courage or honesty—worshipping God by this and being more filled with his presence.

Christians, however, can unite themselves with the worship of the whole Church—meeting God in the sacred liturgy. No longer do they approach God merely as individuals. Now they are united in a special way to Jesus Christ and to all the members of his Church. Their poor pleadings become those of Jesus Christ himself and of everyone in the Church expressing his or her love.

The sacred liturgy is the "signs"—the symbolic ceremonies—by which Christ and his Church worship God and are filled with his grace-presence. In the liturgy, we express our love together, as a community of God's people, in ceremonies that symbolize our feelings toward God and one another. Signs of this sort, expressing our feelings of love, our needs and hopes, are as natural as the many ceremonies that play a part in anyone's life. Often they express our deepest feelings—the vastly "more," the inexpressible—better than our words can.

By a "sign" we mean something visible, some action, which conveys our inner feelings, our love. A kiss is a visible sign of love which is something spiritual, invisible. A handshake is a sign of friendship. Because we are human, it is natural and necessary for us to express our love and be assured of God's love by means of visible signs. A child spontaneously shows his regard for his father by many little actions, a husband expresses his affection for his wife. So our love affair with God expresses itself in the signs and ceremonies of the liturgy.

Christ is present in a special way in the sacred liturgy, acting on our behalf, joining us to himself. His worship becomes ours. We receive grace as part of him. We no longer appear alone and inadequate before God the Father, for now Christ is pleading for us. We are behind him, in a sense, in his shadow. He is our High Priest, ". . . able at all times to save those who come to God through him, since he lives always to make intercession for them" (Hebrews 7, 25). To take part in the liturgy, Christians receive a "character," a special power joining them to Christ so they can share in his work as priest and mediator.

When we take part in liturgy, our worship has a great, new power to help others as well as ourselves. The worship of the whole Church is now with us and becomes ours. We pray in the name of the whole Church, with its power behind us, like an ambassador speaking for his country. " . . . every liturgical celebration, because it is an action of Christ the priest and of his body, the Church, is a sacred action surpassing all others; no other action of the Church can equal its efficacy. . . ." (*Constitution on the Sacred Liturgy,* no. 8).

The liturgy is the worship of the whole Church and comes from the Church. It is the Church's official, "public" worship. To have liturgy, with all its power, requires more than assembling a group of Christians to pray together; although Christ would surely be in their midst, yet his presence in the liturgy is more. The Church determines what is liturgy, for the liturgy belongs to all of us, to the whole Church. It has a sacredness, a power transcending any individual or group. This is why it must be guided by the spirit and rules of the Church.

The liturgy is the greatest thing we have in the Church. "The liturgy is the summit toward which the activity of the Church is directed; at the same time it is the fount from which all her power flows. . . . (It) is the outstanding means whereby the faithful may express in their lives and manifest to others the mystery of Christ and the real nature of the true Church. . . ." (*Constitution on the Sacred Liturgy,* Introduction and no. 10).

Rituals, symbolic ceremonies and signs are part of our daily lives. We use symbolic ceremonies, rites, or rituals to celebrate, to express and to bring home to ourselves the meaning of the significant events of life: for example, celebrations at our work for promotions and retirement, rites of initiation, graduation from school, a couple's marriage commitment, a nation's annual ceremonies commemorating the great men and events of its history, etc.

In the liturgy we "ritualize" or "symbolize" the great events of Jesus' life, bring them into the present, and powerfully link them

with what we go through in our daily lives. The many "dyings" and "risings" of our daily lives, the experiences of hurt, pain, and confusion, as well as those of joy, hope, and love—those that are small, and those that change our lives—all these we join with the same events in Jesus' life, and above all with his dying and rising for us. The power of his death and resurrection gives meaning to our "deaths" and "resurrections" and gives us strength to persevere and grow in faith, hope, and love. The liturgy vividly reminds us of what God-made-man went through for us, and contains his powerful grace-presence, his own strength, confidence, and love, so that we can cope and can grow spiritually when we go through these things every day.

Vatican Council further summed up how the liturgy shows what Christ is and what his Church is: ". . . she is both human and divine, visible and yet invisibly equipped, eager to act and yet intent on contemplation, present in this world and yet not at home in it. . . . In her the human is directed and subordinated to the divine, the visible to the invisible, action to contemplation, and this present world to that city yet to come which we seek" (*Constitution on the Liturgy,* no. 2).

When we take part in the liturgy we are plunged into the past and are also living in the future. Mysteriously the liturgy brings together past, present, and future. Time, relative even to us, cannot restrict God. By the ceremonies of the liturgy time is "stretched out" for us. Christ conveys to us here and now the actions by which he saved us 2,000 years ago—and by these same signs we are actually beginning now our life in eternity, the future "heavenly liturgy," the worship and love that will absorb us forever. Of all the moments of our life, then, we are the most in contact with God, the most "in eternity," when we are taking part in the liturgy.

Through the liturgy Christ prolongs through the centuries his death and resurrection, his great acts of love for us, so we can share in them. Through the ceremonies and feasts of the liturgy we live "in Christ," actually taking part in these great events of his life. We continually die with him to sin and rise with him to the new life of grace, offering perfect worship with him and growing more and more in love.

The liturgy is, then, the great way in which Christ speaks to us now and tells us of his love, not only by the words of scripture but by actions or signs of his love. As a couple in love dwell on each other's words and gestures, even those that appear to others the most ordinary, so to the Christian in love with God the words and ceremonies of the liturgy convey God's own personal and tender love. As God in the Old Testament reassured and strengthened his people assembled together, at Mount Sinai, for example, and as Christ spoke so lovingly and intimately to his followers at the last supper, so today he speaks to us, tells us of his love by his Word given us in the liturgy. And more than this, God through his Son is communicating his love to us in each ceremony of the liturgy—each is meant to be a sign of himself and his love reaching out for us—and each has a meaning for the Christian truly in love with him.

> . . . in order that the liturgy may be able to produce its full effects, it is necessary that the faithful come to it with proper dispositions, that their minds should be attuned to their voices, and that they should cooperate with divine grace, lest they receive it in vain (*Constitution on the Liturgy*, no. 11).

The rites and ceremonies of the liturgy must express our inner love. Without a sincere attempt to love, the ceremonies are valueless, empty signs. Christ stresses that we must adore God "in spirit and truth." He continually condemned the Pharisees, the "whited sepulchres," "hypocrites," whose lives were a mere external observance of rituals that lacked inner meaning and sincerity.

The Mass and the seven sacraments are the great ceremonies of the liturgy. We prepare for them by the "little things" of the liturgy, the sacramentals.

THE SACRAMENTALS—REACHING OUT FOR CHRIST

> Little children were brought to him then that he might lay his hands on them and pray; but the disciples rebuked them. But Jesus said to them, "Let the little children be, and do not hinder them from coming to me, for of such is the kingdom of heaven." And when he had laid his hands on them, he departed from that place (Matthew 19, 13–15).

Just as Christ himself did during his life on earth, so today his Church calls down his blessing on us at different times in our lives. The story of creation concludes, "God saw that all he had made was very good." The Church asks God to bless not only us but many of the ordinary things of life, so that they might lead us to him.

A sacramental is the Church's prayer asking Christ's blessing on someone or something, or it is an object that is thereby "blessed." The Church's prayer asking Christ's blessing is usually given by a priest; however, parents can bless their children, people ask God's blessing on their food, or bless themselves with the sign of the cross. Some blessings are given to dedicate a thing to a sacred use.

Some of the more common sacramentals are: the sign of the cross, blessed candles, blessed pictures, statues, medals, scapulars, holy water, the rosary, the stations of the cross, benediction of the blessed sacrament, the Divine Office.

Statues, pictures, etc., are not prayed to as having power of themselves; rather they remind us of God's presence. God commanded the Jews long ago: "Make two cherubim of beaten gold . . . which you shall then place on top of the ark" (Exodus 25, 18–20). Christian art from the early centuries has used images of Christ and the saints to stimulate devotion.

Some sacramentals are given on certain days during the year: Candles are blessed and distributed on Candlemas Day, February 2nd; throats are blessed on St. Blaise Day, February 3rd; on Ash Wednesday, blessed ashes are placed on our foreheads; palms are distributed on Palm Sunday; fields are blessed on August 5th. Other blessings are given at any time, e.g., the blessing of a mother before or after childbirth.

A sacramental is a reminder, but it is also something more: it is a special way of putting ourself in Christ's presence, asking his help and blessing. The woman who reached out for Christ acted as we might in using a sacramental: **Read Luke 8, 40–48.**

When we use a sacramental with faith and devotion, we reach out for Christ—and somehow, the entire Church joins with us. We can be sure that he will help us in some way. When a mother receives the Church's blessing on herself and her newborn child, she comes into Christ's presence, asking his blessing on herself and her baby. Having our automobile blessed, with a determination to drive carefully, is asking Christ to drive with us and protect us.

We should use the sacramentals reverently, but also avoiding superstition. What we derive from them depends on God's will, the Church's prayer, and our own faith and devotion. We must be careful not to look on them as magical, producing effects automatically. If we use them with a living faith, they are wonderful ways to make us aware of God's presence in our everyday lives, in everyone and everything around us.

The sacramentals are particularly meant to prepare us for the sacraments, which are the all-important signs by which we come into a most intimate grace-giving contact with Christ. The sacramentals are the less important signs by which we reach out for Christ. They prepare us for our meeting with Christ in the sacraments by stirring our faith and devotion, and they prolong the effect of the sacraments in our lives.

The difference between these was instinctively understood by a woman, not a Christian, who recently visited a Catholic priest. Her husband, unfaithful for years, had gone off with another woman, leaving her to care for their four children. Introduced to the rosary by a Catholic friend, it had been a great comfort to her for several turbulent years. But recently she had been attending Mass and now yearned to take part in holy communion, realizing that this would be the best possible help for her and her family. One had led to the other.

CHRIST'S SEVEN SACRAMENTS—
OUR GREAT, INTIMATE CONTACTS WITH HIM

After relating Christ's healing of the woman with a hemorrhage, Luke continues with the incident of the dying twelve-year-old daughter of Jairus: **Read Luke 8, 49–56.**

While visibly present on earth, Christ often used physical actions, his own ceremonies, as instruments of his divine power. In this incident he gives life by calling out to the girl, taking her hand, raising her up.

Christ also communicates the divine life of grace through ceremonies or signs. Just as his human body was the instrument of his divinity 2,000 years ago, so today he uses the human members of his body, the Church, to give us the life of grace through these ceremonies. These are the all-important signs of the liturgy, the seven sacraments.

A sacrament is a sacred sign of worship by which we come into intimate personal contact with Christ and receive his grace—a ceremony in which we meet Christ most intimately and receive his grace—and by which we join with Christ particularly in his great action of dying and rising.

> By these meetings with Christ we are joined most intimately with the whole Trinity. It is the Spirit within us that unites us with Christ in the sacraments, and they join us ultimately with the Father. Our love relationship with each Person is deepened by each sacrament.

Christ gave us the sacraments two thousand years ago. He instituted them, that is, he provided that his grace would be given especially by some suitable signs. These he left mostly to his Church to determine.

Christ gives us the sacraments here and now. Through them we come into intimate, personal contact with him giving us grace—each is a "sacramental meeting" or "encounter" with him, like the meeting on the road to Emmaus: **Read Luke 24, 15–32.**

When we take part in a sacrament, Christ's presence is also concealed, but he is there, affecting us intimately by his love. We on earth cannot yet bear to look upon Christ glorified in heaven—but in each sacrament he is with us, using this ceremony to reach out to us, taking hold of us as one in love embraces his beloved, as a mother embraces her child. We know that sometimes a single contact with one we love, even a glance or smile, can greatly affect and even change our life—so Christ in his sacrament can totally renew us.

Christ uses human beings within his Church, usually bishops and priests, to give us his sacraments. But the man who gives the sacrament is only Christ's instrument; Christ himself communicates his grace to us through the words and actions. The goodness or badness of the human instrument makes no difference as far as our receiving grace is concerned. We are always assured of contact with Christ, of deepening God's grace-presence within us.

> *Christ is the "sacrament" of God, and his Church is the "sacrament" of Christ.* We saw that a liturgical sign is something visible that conveys a spiritual reality. In Christ we meet visibly, palpably, the invisible God. And through Christ's visible Church we make contact today with Christ among us. The Church's sacraments are Christ's actions among us.

The seven sacraments are "signs" in this way: when the visible ceremony takes place, Christ brings about an invisible spiritual

change within us. Every sign or ceremony conveys an idea, but it does not actually produce an internal change—a handshake conveys the idea of friendship, but it does not make two men friends. The sign of a sacrament, however, not only tells us about the spiritual change taking place within us—Christ uses it actually to produce that change. A sacrament gives the grace it signifies. In baptism, for instance, as the priest pours the water and says the words, Christ is bringing about an invisible change in us—we are receiving grace and being freed from sin.

Christ gives us these visible signs so that when we go through them, we can be sure we have been in contact with him and have received his grace. The ceremony assures us that he is there. Just as it is not enough for a child merely to know of its mother's love, but needs her actual embrace, just as a husband and wife need to show their love by signs of affection, so we need these sacramental signs of Christ's presence and love.

> Vatican Council II sums up what the sacraments do for us: "The purpose of the sacraments is to sanctify men, to build up the body of Christ, and . . . to give worship to God. Because they are signs they also instruct. They not only presuppose faith, but . . . they also nourish, strengthen, and express it" (*Constitution on the Sacred Liturgy*, no. 59).

A sacrament, if entered into with faith and love, always affects us interiorly, always gives us grace. It is Christ's powerful gesture of love, causing us to respond, as a firm handshake compels a firm grip in return. Christ always gives us grace unless we deliberately block him. One might block Christ's grace by receiving certain sacraments in serious sin, e.g., confirmation, holy orders, marriage; if the sin is later forgiven, Christ then can give us the grace.

The sacraments intensify our faith and our love for God and our fellow man, as well as making our sufferings bearable and meaningful. They unite us to the humiliated and glorified Christ. They do not eliminate suffering from our lives, but they help us bear it. They deepen our Christian joy, assuring us of our ultimate resurrection with Christ.

Each sacrament, then, makes us more like Christ, assimilates us to him so that his thoughts and words and actions become ours—or rather, ours become his. The more we share in his sacramental life, the more we are transformed, drawn to him. Through the sacraments we gradually acquire his love, his sensitivity for others, his zeal and passion for justice, his compassion for the sick and "little ones," his single-mindedness in doing his Father's will.

The sign or ceremony of each sacrament teaches us about its special effect upon us. While all the sacraments increase God's presence within us Christ does something special for us in each. The ceremonies are often difficult to understand today, but originally were taken from the people's ordinary life and given a religious meaning.

> *The basic rites, while particularly meaningful to the people of the bible, are fundamental human symbols found in almost every culture;* e.g., washing with water, placing hands on another's head, eating a symbolic meal together, anointing with oil. Obviously many symbols that came from a simpler pastoral society, or from among people accustomed to court ceremonial, are not as meaningful to an urban, democratic, mechanistic culture like ours.
>
> Many now think that much of this symbolism, which is based on the old cultural forms of the Mediterranean area, should be replaced by signs more obvious to today's people. It will take much patient and prayerful effort to develop signs that keep our link with the past and yet are meaningful in the present. The Church must supervise this development, and the Council has given a basic norm for this: "The rites should be distinguished by a noble simplicity; they should be short, clear, and unencumbered by useless repetitions; they should be within the people's powers of comprehension, and normally should not require explanation" (*Constitution on the Sacred Liturgy,* no. 34).

Through his Church, Christ tells us how his sacraments should be given. Christ's Church is the guardian and giver of his sacraments. He has let his Church choose the sign which best expresses the grace he has attached to a particular sacrament (except the eucharist and probably baptism whose signs seem to have come from Christ himself); thus the essential sign of some sacraments has changed in the Church's usage over the centuries.

The power to give a sacrament is communicated to men especially chosen by Christ's Church in the sacrament of holy orders. A man must be empowered by this sacrament—a special laying on of hands—in order to communicate Christ's grace sacramentally to others (except for baptism and matrimony).

In each sacrament Christ unites us in a particular way with the other members of the Church so that we can help and be helped by them. He uses the sacraments to build up his Church. Baptism joins us to Christ's body, his Church. Confirmation makes us adult Christians, specially empowering us to help spread Christ's body. The eucharist unites us most intimately not only with Christ, but with the other members of his Church. Reconciliation (penance) gives us the forgiveness of the mystical body and is a reconciliation with Christ and all whom we have offended by our sins. The anointing of the sick either restores us to the Church on earth or it prepares us to enter the Church in heaven. Holy orders and marriage provide for the continuation of Christ's Church on earth.

A sacrament is a sign of our worshipping love. Our part is vital in this meeting with Christ. When we take part in a sacrament, we express our faith, love, and worship. The greater our faith and love, the more sincere our worship, the more of his grace-presence Christ can fill us with.

Therefore, we should prepare well to meet Christ in each sacrament. We must come to it with the proper intention, with sorrow for our sins, with faith and love. A sacrament is not a mechanical "thing," something magic, that gives us grace automatically without any contribution on our part. It is a meeting in which we must respond to Christ reaching out for us. As we would prepare ourselves for any special meeting with one we love, so the better we prepare the more we will receive from our meetings with Christ in the sacraments.

To help us prepare and to bring out its full meaning, each sacrament has some lesser signs, or sacramentals, along with its essential sign. The ceremony by which each sacrament is given, including the prayers and sacramentals connected with it, is called the "rite" of the sacrament.

Christ's help for us in the sacraments is intensified or weakened by our everyday actions, and vice versa. The more we consciously try to get strength from the sacraments, the more they help us to use countless other daily opportunities to grow in grace—much as a soldier in combat might derive strength from the memory of his last meeting with his loved ones. A sacrament is a powerful beginning—comparable to the first stage of a missile—whose purpose is to impel us to a more Christian life moment by moment.

The sacraments are the great ways in which Christ encounters us and gives us his grace, but he also uses many other ways. Like a stone thrown into a pond, making ripples that spread out in continuous circles, so grace flows from Christ's Church to mankind: the inner, distinct circles are the sacraments, beyond these are the less clearly defined sacramentals, and still further from the center are the other good actions of men.

One might experience God more intensely and receive grace more fully outside the sacraments, but normally they are the great moments at which Christ meets us and helps us on our way to heaven. A boy and girl in love, separated for several months, finally come together again—their meeting is a special moment of sharing in love, to which our encounter with God in the sacraments is comparable.

Christ gives us the sacraments, then, to help us at the important moments of life. Men have always surrounded the great moments of life with sacred symbols and ceremonies. Christ uses these occasions to give us his saving grace: birth, growth to maturity, our daily need for nourishment, moral failure, marriage, serious illness and death, a need of human help to reach God—these are the pivotal points of our lives on earth and at these Christ stands with his sacraments.

> These are the seven sacraments, and briefly, what Christ does through each:
>
> *Baptism* joins us to Christ and his Church, gives us grace, and takes away all sin.
>
> *Confirmation* makes us adult apostles for Christ.
>
> *The Holy Eucharist* is Christ himself coming to us under the appearance of bread and wine.
>
> *Reconciliation or Penance* Christ uses to forgive us our sins after baptism.
>
> *The Anointing of the Sick* Christ uses to strengthen us in serious illness.
>
> *Holy Orders* is the way Christ ordains priests for his Church.
>
> *Marriage* is the way Christ unites a Christian man and woman in a lifelong union.

Among the sacraments, baptism and the eucharist are the most important. Baptism begins in us the Christian life, and the eucharist is our main source of strength along the way.

WORD AND SACRAMENT

To sum up: The great means by which God gives himself to us are the bible and the liturgy—"Word and Sacrament." Each is a special meeting with Christ and the Trinity. God uses them above all else to give us his grace and teaching. Together they form the Christian's way to God.

There has always been an intimate connection between the Word of God and the worship of God. The books of the bible, both Old and New Testaments, came from the community's liturgy in the sense that the scriptural narratives, hymns, and prayers were either meant to be used at worship or they came from the actual worship services of God's people. Even the New Testament epistles or letters were intended to be read when the Christian community assembled for the liturgy (Cf. 1 Thessalonians 5, 27).

The bible gives us God's teaching, and at the same time prepares us to receive his grace in the sacraments. Christ speaks to us through the scriptures, arousing faith in us, leading us to respond by the sacraments. The better prepared we are by the scriptures, the better is our worship and the more of God's grace-presence the sacraments bring us.

It is in the liturgy, on the other hand, that we best hear, understand, and respond to God's Word given in the bible. The ceremonies of the liturgy not only teach us in a living way the sacred events of the bible, they also enable us actually to take part in them here and now. Our reading of the bible is meant to lead to the sacraments in which our most powerful and most lasting bond with Christ and our fellow Christians is established.

DAILY LIVING: SIGNS OF GOD'S PRESENCE

If we believe in God, in Christ, we should have some sign of this in our home. Many people find that they need some reminder of God's presence, particularly since our lives today are becoming more and more secularized.

One might in one's home have a cross or crucifix, a bible placed

where we will read it, or perhaps a picture or statue that appeals to us and will inspire us.

We should also take advantage of what the Church has to visibly remind us of God's presence. Anyone, including one who is not Catholic, can receive the sacramentals of the Church. If used with sincere faith they can help anyone to be aware of God's presence.

> ... for the well-disposed members of the faithful, the liturgy of the sacraments and sacramentals sanctifies almost every event in their lives.... There is hardly any proper use of material things which cannot thus be directed toward the sanctification of men and the praise of God (*Constitution on the Sacred Liturgy,* no. 61).

SOME SUGGESTIONS FOR ...

DISCUSSION

Can you understand the naturalness of using signs to express our feelings, in the liturgy as well as in our daily life?

Do the sacramentals of the Church seem meaningful?

What sign of God's presence seems particularly meaningful to you?

FURTHER READING

* *Christ, The Sacrament of the Encounter with God,* Schillebeeckx (Sheed and Ward, 1963)—Still a theological classic for those who want a thorough understanding of the notion of sacrament: it shows how Christ is the sacrament of God and the Church is the sacrament of Christ, as well as the reality and depth of the Church's seven sacraments.
* *Signs of Love: The Sacraments of Christ,* Foley (St. Anthony Press, 1976)—A popular, easy-to-read presentation of the Church's sacraments, emphasizing that each is a tangible sign that we are personally meeting with Christ. *A New Look at the Sacraments* by Bausch (Fides, 1977) has some fine insights about the sacraments as both divine-life-giving and truly humanizing. It is a good historical, theological and personal exploration.
* *The Meaning of the Sacraments,* Hellwig (Pflaum, 1972)—A brief, clear explanation of what the sacraments are all about. This book includes many valuable insights from the bible, history and theology.

FURTHER VIEWING/LISTENING

The Changing Sacraments (Teleketics, Franciscan Communications)—A seven-part filmstrip series explaining the history and development of the sacraments, with skillful use of whimsical cartoons and humorous art. Each is brief and very good. Also quite good is the Teleketics series, *Of Sacraments and Symbols.*

PERSONAL REFLECTION

Each time I look at an inspiring cross or crucifix, or work of religious art, I should be reminded of God's presence in my daily life.

If I am alert to them, there are many other signs of God's presence around me: the beauty of a landscape, a sunset, the laughter of a child, the peaceful countenances of an old couple, the eager joy of young lovers, the infinite patience of a face worn with suffering, the quiet dignity of many of the poor.

13

Christ Unites Us to Himself and One Another by Baptism

Why is baptism so important? What is the meaning of the ceremony of baptism? What is meant by saying that a person is converted? What of most of the human race who are not baptized as Christians?

WHAT CHRIST DOES FOR US IN BAPTISM

We saw how God uses the signs of the sacred liturgy, particularly the sacraments, to come into our lives today. By entering into these signs we meet Christ most intimately and go with him to the Father. These are the great meetings by which we are filled with his grace-presence.

The first of these great signs is baptism. Here Christ unites us with himself in a new, deeper way, to live more truly and fully with him. Somehow, mysteriously but really, we now go with Christ through the great actions of his life, particularly his death and resurrection. We begin journeying with him to the Father. We will suffer and die with him, and one day we shall rise with him to our real, full life after death.

Baptism is the sacrament in which Christ joins us to himself as a member of his Church. Baptism is often called a "christening," expressing how we are made one with Christ, a completely new person. St. Paul tells how baptism unites us to Christ, so that we are "in" him as in a garment:

> For all you have been baptized into Christ, have put on Christ. There is neither Jew nor Greek; there is neither slave nor freeman; there is neither male nor female. For you are all one in Christ Jesus (Galatians 3, 27–28).

Scripture tells us how baptism is to be given. Matthew attributes to Christ himself this ancient formula:

> Jesus . . . said, "All power in heaven and on earth has been given to me. Go, therefore, and make disciples of all nations, baptizing them in the name of the Father, and of the Son, and of the Holy Spirit. . . ." (Matthew 28, 17–19).

The sign or ceremony of baptism is to pour water on the person's forehead while saying the words, "I baptize you in the name of the Father, and of the Son, and of the Holy Spirit." To "baptize" means to wash with, to immerse in water. The water is ordinarily poured on the person's forehead, but baptism can also be given by immersing a person in water while saying the words—the ordinary way it was done in the early centuries—or by sprinkling water on the forehead while saying the words.

By baptism, Christ initiates us into his Church, joins us to his body, the Christian community. He thereby gives us the ability to take part fully in the other sacraments. "For in one Spirit," says St. Paul, "we were all baptized into one body, whether Jews or Gentiles, whether slaves or free" (1 Corinthians 12, 13).

In baptism the new Christian is pledged to the Christian community and the community in turn pledges itself to him. It is the entrance into the Christian family with a pledging of love and service on both sides. The new Christian now will seek God particularly within this Church community, and the community promises its love, prayers, and help to him. Just as belonging to a natural family is far better than being an orphan, so being a part of the Christian family can give love and support one would not have on one's own. The growing custom of baptizing at the Sunday eucharist brings out beautifully this mutual pledge of love and service.

Baptism gives the new life of grace to one who does not have it: Read John 3, 1–6.

The new birth of which Christ speaks is baptism; the new life it gives us is sanctifying grace, God's living and loving presence within us.

By baptism Christ forgives us all our sins. If we are truly converted, we make a fresh start, we begin living a new life with and in Christ. ". . . if anyone is in Christ, he is a new creation" (2 Corinthians 5, 17). All our sins are totally made up for; it is as if we had never sinned. When Peter on Pentecost preached the gospel to its first hearers, they were ". . . cut to the heart" and asked, "Brethren, what shall we do?" He replied:

> Repent, and be baptized, every one of you, in the name of Jesus Christ for the forgiveness of your sins; and you shall receive the gift of the Holy Spirit (Acts 2, 37–38).

Christ frees us from sin and gives us grace in baptism by joining us to himself in his own death and resurrection. We saw that his death and resurrection was the great action by which he freed us from the power of sin to keep us from heaven, and by which he obtained for our whole race the new life of God's grace-presence. By baptism we first unite ourselves to Christ's death and resurrection. St. Paul explains: **Read Romans 6, 3–11.**

Sin's power "dies" within us and is "buried" as we go under the water, and we rise to a new life of grace as we come up out of the water. We are thus united with Christ's death which overcame sin, and to his resurrection which brought us the new life of grace. The ordinary ancient way of baptizing fully expressed this: the person was immersed or "buried" in water and then drawn out of it.

The ceremony of baptism fulfills in a perfect way the deliverance to life and freedom that was begun in the Old Testament. God's people were saved by the waters of the Red Sea from Pharaoh's army, and given a new life of freedom. Christ leads us through the waters of baptism to free us from sin and death and give us the new and eternal life of grace. Baptism is our Christian passover, our own personal exodus.

> The use of water to overcome death and slavery and give new life is often foreshadowed. Water has always been a symbol both of death and of life; the ancient Hebrews feared the waters of the sea, and yet as a desert people they knew that water also meant life.

By baptism one is drawn into the new covenant. Under the old covenant God was present among his people in the Ark of the Covenant which they brought with them through the desert and later enshrined in the temple at Jerusalem. Now, under the new covenant, God lives within each of his people, most intimately, and they in him. He is himself the new promised land; instead of a geographical territory, he gives us himself—and for all eternity.

Baptism, then, is the sign of our true, interior life, God's grace-presence within us. Now we are publicly (and consciously, if old enough) pledged to live with an awareness of this presence within us: the Persons of God are within us, transforming us, giving a new meaning and power to everything we do. Mysteriously, wonderfully, we are joined in a particular and intimate way to each of the Three Persons. Within us, surrounding us, filling us, guiding and loving us, the Trinity draws us into their own life. This is the "indwelling" of the Blessed Trinity—it is heaven already begun within us.

> "Grace" is simply our relationship to the divine Persons, the "state," the life situation in which the Persons come to us, live with us and love us. By this we have a special relationship to each of the Persons. Now that we have penetrated further into God's plan, and have seen something of the actions of the divine Persons in human history, we might reread the part of chapter 7 dealing with our personal relationship to each Person. This should now have a deeper meaning.

Like any personal love relationship that fulfills, elevates and transforms one, so grace makes us more and more like God. A deep friendship, the love of a man and woman—these raise and fulfill one's personality wonderfully. We become fuller persons ourselves, even as we take on more and more of the characteristics of our friend or loved one. So here we are raised to the very level of God, transformed more and more into him. ". . . it is no longer I who live, but Christ who lives in me" (Galatians 2, 20).

This is the "kingdom of God" which Christ preached: God's grace-presence within us. To have God's grace-presence within us is to belong to the kingdom, to submit to his loving guidance from within. When we believe in him and try to do his will, we belong to this kingdom. We might recall what Christ said about this kingdom: the poor, the humble, the oppressed are the happy ones, and the one law in the kingdom is that of love. The kingdom is not yet completed—we must suffer and work for its fulfillment, that God's grace-presence will fill all men—and so we pray ". . . thy kingdom come, thy will be done on earth as it is in heaven."

To help us live the Christian life, Christ gives us special powers: the virtues. The virtues are powers or attitudes within us: faith, hope, charity; they are explained in detail in the next chapter. Christ also promises us all the day-by-day helps, the "actual graces" necessary to live as his followers. One's Christianity may never develop, through no fault of his own; Christ guides him through life nevertheless, giving him more than sufficient help to attain heaven.

At baptism the Christian receives the power to share in Christ's own work as priest, prophet, and king. This is the "priesthood of the laity," the power to offer Mass fully with Christ and take part in the other sacraments, to act as a mediator in prayer and other ways. It is a prophetic and kingly power in that we must now openly witness to the faith, hope, and love within us—to the kingdom of God, God's grace-presence within us.

WHO CAN BE BAPTIZED?

For those who know about and believe in Christ's teaching, baptism with water is the necessary first step Christ has given us to eternal happiness. The words of Christ to Nicodemus express this clearly: ". . . unless a man be born again of water and the Spirit, he cannot enter the kingdom of God" (John 3, 5). This has been the Church's belief from the beginning, as is evident again and again in the Acts of the Apostles, the epistles, and other early Christian writings.

Therefore we baptize infants so that they can begin growing in the life of grace within the Christian community. Infant baptism—a whole family, for instance, being baptized together—was practiced in the Christian Church almost from the beginning.

Infants being baptized should not be looked upon as if they were somehow interiorly evil, needing to be washed "clean" or "purified" by the waters of the sacrament. Rather, they are good and beautiful in God's eyes, and certainly free of moral fault. But they share the inherent human weakness that we call original sin and experience what it is to be unloved, beginning in the womb, and will be unloving in return. Baptism sets up a new relationship by giving infants a new orientation, pointing them in the direction of God through Christ and the Church; now the vision of God and a new, perfect world is before them. Baptism is thus a new birth, to eternal life, and a new creation, for by it one shares in the vision of a new universe. Now it is up to the parents of those baptized—and the whole local Christian community—to help develop their part in this new universe.

The 1980 statement from the Sacred Congregation for the Doctrine of the Faith—Instruction on Infant Baptism—reiterates the importance of infant baptism, even in the event that parents are not prepared to profess their own faith. The statement notes that baptism is not merely a sign of faith but a cause of faith, and thus is not to be denied to an infant. Furthermore, infants are baptized into the faith of the whole Church, and it is the Church—not solely the child's parents—that is responsible for proffering an education in the faith.

Regarding what happens to unbaptized infants, we have no clear teaching of Christ or doctrine of the Church. Some older theologians thought that they went to "limbo," which they regarded as a state of perfect, unending, "natural" happiness, but much less than the happiness of heaven. However, most by far today think that such an infant would attain heaven. They say simply that God accepts each of us (unless we have totally rejected him by living in a state of serious sin); our conscious response to his love is secondary, and certainly not necessary for these innocent little ones. The renewed process of Christian initiation, mentioned above, and the possible deferral of baptism now being experimented with, should do away with this notion once and for all.

A priest usually gives baptism. However, in case of danger of death anyone can baptize, even one who is not a Christian. Such people, of course, must baptize correctly and have the intention of giving Christian baptism.

At baptism we have sponsors or godparents—a Catholic man and woman chosen to help their godchild live his or her Catholic faith fully. An adult convert usually has one sponsor of the same sex. A sponsor should be a practicing Catholic, at least fourteen years of age, and someone other than one's parents or marriage partner. Today, for sufficient reason, there need be only one Catholic sponsor; the other may be a knowledgeable committed non-Catholic Christian, called a "Christian witness" to the baptism.

It is a privilege to be a baptismal sponsor, and that privilege involves a sacred duty. It is a ministry in the Church for which preparation is normally necessary. Sponsors should be active, mature Catholics who realize that they must keep in touch with their godchild, and help the young person grow in the faith. Sponsors often honestly realize that they themselves need more mature study in order to be "updated" in

their own knowledge and practice of their faith. The priest arranging
the baptism may help them to do this. They can take advantage of
classes, updating them—and the child's parents as well—in a mature,
renewed faith. Sponsors for adult converts should take part in each step
of the process of initiation into the Church. It can be a wonderful experience of growing together into a mature faith.

Parents should choose as a sponsor not just a relative who will have
little continual contact with the growing child, but someone who will
be able to be in regular, continual contact as the child grows into Christian maturity.

**Since we become a new person interiorly at baptism, some take a
new name, that of a saint.** This saint becomes our patron, a lifelong
model to imitate as he or she imitated Christ. St. Paul says, ". . . be
imitators of me, as I am of Christ" (1 Corinthians 4, 16). An adult
convert today usually retains his or her own name, whether or not it
is that of a saint. Some may take this additional patron's name; some
may not.

We should learn something about our patron saint in order to better
imitate him or her. Our patron, in turn, is vitally interested in us and
helps us attain heaven, as will be explained later.

**Infants are usually baptized in the parish of their parents; adult
converts are generally baptized where they take instructions.** Converts are baptized when the one instructing them judges them ready,
ideally when the process of Christian initiation has sufficiently prepared them. An infant is normally baptized within several weeks
after birth. But the infant's parents (and sponsors) should be knowledgeable about and freely committed to the child's Catholic Christian upbringing; thus the infant's baptism should wait until they are
sufficiently ready for this mature, free commitment—and this usually involves instruction, reflection and discussion on their part.

A priest may have to refuse to baptize someone if he judges that the
person (usually an infant) will probably not live an active Catholic life.
There may be no indication that an infant of non-practicing Catholic
parents has much chance of learning about Catholicism, as a viable
adult faith, from his mother's and/or father's example. Baptism is the
beginning of a new way of life, not just a formality of family tradition,
nor insurance against "limbo," nor a sort of magic inoculation of godli-

ness that somehow takes effect despite a child's lack of religious up-bringing.

There are, however, many couples who, though they do little or nothing formally "Catholic" (no longer take part in Mass for instance), still regard themselves as Catholic and wish their child to be baptized. Some see it as illusory, even hypocritical, to baptize their baby, since the growing child has little chance of being taught about or of living a Catholic Christian life. Yet the practice of the Church has never been to declare such parents cut off from membership in the Church. Though they do not currently practice Catholicism, i.e., are not actively participating in a church community, yet the Church's teachings—and God's grace-presence—may be operating in their lives of overall moral goodness, private prayerfulness, and a real, if passive, belief in God and Jesus Christ. Also, a good test of what parents really believe, and of their basic aspirations in any matter, is often what they want for their children, not what they presently (often regretfully) have not been able to find meaningful for themselves.

A couple should have a frank, imaginative talk with a priest, and afterward they may want to update themselves on the Church's teachings, including the part they will play in their child's religious upbringing (and particularly the more active role of the Catholic partner in an interfaith marriage). Then baptism might be given the child.

The couple in this situation usually rethinks deeply (and hopefully discusses together) their own life-values and the place of God and religion in their own lives. Frequently they find after a course of study updating them on their faith, that they can recommit themselves to a now more mature and growth-producing practice of their religion in a parish church-community.

Some dioceses and parishes offer such parents an option of either taking the "updating" course of study mentioned above (usually a kind of "mini-series"), or of taking an "inquiry" course, a fuller series of discussions on Catholic Christianity.

If one who was baptized a Christian wanted to become a Catholic, he or she would not be baptized again, unless there was doubt about the validity of the previous baptism, i.e., whether it had been done correctly. If there is a real doubt, the priest would baptize conditionally with these words, "If you are not baptized, I baptize you in the name of the Father, etc." One previously baptized as a Christian should obtain a certificate of this baptism so that the information can be entered on the records of the Catholic Church.

The already baptized Christian who wishes to become a Catholic would make a Profession of Faith, a statement of his or her belief in the teachings of the Catholic Church. But before becoming a Catholic Christian, one must be converted.

Together with baptism, confirmation is the other sacrament of initiation into the life of Christ and the community of the Church. In the early Church, confirmation was usually celebrated along with baptism. Today Catholics who are baptized as infants receive confirmation later, usually in their teenage years. Still, it is part of the full initiation of the "new" Christian into the people of God. When an adult is baptized, confirmation is usually celebrated at the time of the baptism—a way which more closely resembles the practice of the early Christians. It is always important to link the two sacraments together (even when there are some years that separate them) because it is through the *two* sacraments together that we become fully members of the Church "by water and the Holy Spirit." We will consider confirmation and the role it has in the Christian life in more detail in chapter 17. Now we will see its place in the Rite of Christian Initiation of Adults where, thanks to the renewal of recent years, it is more tangibly and visibly associated with baptism as a sacrament of initiation.

CONVERSION

The Acts of the Apostles tells how the deacon Philip one day met an official of the Queen of Ethiopia and told him the good news about Christ, as they were driving along the road from Jerusalem. They came to a stream, and the official said, "See, here is water; what is there to prevent my being baptized?" Philip said, "If you believe with all your heart, you may." And the official answered: "I believe that Jesus Christ is the Son of God." Then they stopped the chariot and went down into the water where Philip baptized him (Cf. Acts, 8, 26–39).

Of course, the whole incident is condensed (when it was written, around the end of the 1st century, the much more lengthy process of Christian initiation had been developing for some time). But the incident tells us very succinctly what conversion is all about: One has to believe "with all his heart." So anyone wanting to be baptized and/ or converted to Catholic Christianity must not only accept intellectually the teachings of the Church, believing them to be true, but must also be determined to live up to those teachings as best he or she can. Peter's Pentecost sermon expresses it similarly: "You must reform (convert, turn around your life, have a change of mind and heart) and be baptized. . . ." (Acts 2, 38). St. Paul, too, reminds his converts ". . . how we entered among you, and how you turned to God from idols, to serve the living and true God" (1 Thessalonians 1, 9).

A conversion, therefore, is a total "turning" toward Christ and a new way of life. We accept the Church's teachings as true, and, repenting of our sins, are determined to live a good Christian life. It is a total interior change of mind and heart. With all our heart we turn away from our sins, toward Christ and his Church. We make a total commitment of ourselves to Christ. We may have sincerely tried to serve God before, but now we are determined to do so to the full extent of our new and fuller knowledge of the truth.

Conversion means a firm determination, but not a certainty, that one will never sin again. Perhaps converts are realistically fearful, even quite certain, that they will fall again into their old sins, but they commit themselves nevertheless, trusting in God to help them and pick them up should they fall.

The power to be converted is given by God, and is often called the "gift of faith." It presupposes our own sincere efforts, as we shall see. But it is God who first attracts us, motivates us, "calls" us by a loving invitation that is perhaps gradual but nonetheless persistent to turn completely to himself.

To express their conversion adult converts to Catholicism make a Profession or Act of Faith. They solemnly read this profession before a priest and, ideally, the assembled Christian community, affirming their acceptance of the Church's basic teachings and their commitment to live by them. If one cannot make one's profession before the community, there is present at least one witness or "sponsor" (usually an adult of the same sex who can help the new Catholic adjust to his or her faith and live it out most fully). If the new convert is to be baptized, this profession is done immediately before baptism, as part of the rite of Christian Initiation.

Vatican Council II, however, has provided a new way for one who is converting—baptized or not—to become a Catholic Christian. It is the Rite of Christian Initiation of Adults.

THE CHRISTIAN INITIATION OF ADULTS

The Christian Initiation of Adults—the last of the significant reforms in Church life initiated by Vatican Council II—is an updated version of the way the first Christians became followers of Jesus Christ. This process of initiation grew up in the period shortly after Jesus Christ left his followers without his visible presence, and yet was very much with them, in still-vivid memories and especially by his guiding, invisible presence. The recently renewed rite is a series of steps allowing aspiring Catholic Christians to gradually and maturely develop in an understanding and practice of the faith to which they will be committed for life.

In those early days, Christian initiation might also be a commitment to death for one's beliefs (the Emperor Nero began persecuting Christians in the 60's A.D.). The rite of initiation, therefore, was—and is again today—far more than a formality of outwardly joining a church. Today, though the odds are against one's actually dying for Christian principles, it is happening in some places in our world. But, more importantly, the renewed rite of initiation is meant to bring to the Church mature Christians who have fully and freely studied, reflected on, prayed over and experienced living as adult, committed Christians in our sophisticated, largely materialistic society. To become and to live as a committed Christian today is, in many ways, as demanding as it was 2,000 years ago.

The Rite of Christian Initiation of Adults (or RCIA), the process by which adult converts are received into full communion with the Catholic Church, takes place in four parts or stages, each expressing a further development or deepening of one's faith-commitment. Coming to a mature, adult-level grasp of the Catholic Christian faith takes time, as we said, to bring home to converts what they are undertaking for the rest of their lives. During this time, God is marvelously working within these persons, deepening their faith, hope and love—and more and more uniting them with Jesus Christ and all the people who make up his Body, the Church. The local church-community supports the person at each step along the way, by their prayers, giving what active help they can, and by deepening their own loving belief in the process.

This process has been found to be very rewarding by many who have been baptized as Catholics, but are Catholics in name only. They have never made a truly mature, adult commitment to the Church. This process can bring about a deep and joyous conversion—one that perhaps had been taken for granted since their baptism as infants, but which had never been made wholeheartedly, with adult-level knowledge, conviction, and commitment. There may be spiritual stirrings, yearnings, hopes deep within them—and a vague desire for a place to once again go to find support, inspiration, and an intelligent, mature alternative to the cynicism, materialism, greed, and "me-ism" that are so much a part of our society. The whole process of adult Christian initiation is designed to help one to grow spiritually, to better love others and oneself, and to find and love God as he really is. It can be the start of a new, more loving, and more wonderfully fulfilling way of life.

The first stage of initiation is that of Inquiry. This usually consists of a series of classes and/or discussions for those who are interested, but are making no commitment to the Church (though some may have already decided to join). Here one learns the basic teachings of Catholic Christianity. (These are given in this book, mostly in the material in regular print. We suggest also reading and reflecting on the related scriptural references, entitled, e.g., **Read Luke, Chapter 1.** There may also be something of special individual interest or concern in the *FURTHER READING* or *FURTHER VIEWING* sections.) One also tries to grow in prayer, in doing acts of everyday, caring love, and in openness to where God is guiding him or her. One should have some experience of the caring hospitality of the local church-community; some meetings, for instance, might take place in the homes of those who are daily trying to live out their own Catholic Christian journey to God.

Co-instruction, discussion, and especially honest questioning should take place here, not only with priests and deacons, but with lay people and perhaps religious involved as well. People may want to share their personal "stories" of how God has acted in their lives—but the inquirer should also and always feel free to just sit and listen.

The decision to go on and to enter the next stage, or Catechumenate (and when), is a mutual one—of the priest (and/or whoever is conducting the inquiry sessions), and especially of the one who is inquiring. Some people may want to go through the inquiry sessions again, or perhaps take time for further reflection, prayer, reading, other classes, and also further discussions with the priest one has come to know, and with others. One should never feel pressured to go on to a further stage, for this is a most intimate matter between oneself and God (who may or may not be leading one to formally enter the Church). Every priest keenly understands this and has learned to respect every person's unique relationship with God; family members and friends, too, should and probably will have a like respect. Some of the most loving and selfless people in history have been "inquirers" all their lives.

The second state is the Catechumenate, which consists of further instruction and living as a committed Catholic Christian. Designed for those who have decided to join the Catholic Church, it is begun with the ancient and beautiful Liturgy of Enrollment. Ideally this takes place before the bishop in the diocese's cathedral. The catechumens express their belief, and are "examined" (i.e., can express in their own way the teachings and practices of Catholic Christianity to which they are now committing themselves); they sincerely renounce the evil that could block their journey to God, and they are lovingly welcomed into the worldwide Church community. They are now "Catholics," but in the learning stage (and so are called catechumens, or believing learners, and are enrolled as such in the Catechumenate Register).

In some places the catechumens follow the ancient custom of leaving Mass after the Liturgy of the Word; this is meant to emphasize that they need more preparation before they can take part fully in the eucharist and share in the eucharistic meal, or holy communion. The catechumens may be married as members of the Church and receive a Christian burial.

Catechumens choose a sponsor, a Catholic who knows them well and will accompany and help them during their catechumenate and the remaining two stages of initiation—and hopefully assist them to grow in faith and love for the rest of their life. During this period catechumens deepen their knowledge and practice of Catholicism—usually following a course of learning and practical living based on "salvation history," the way in which God himself revealed to us the way to salvation and unending life.

This book uses this approach for the most part. During this stage the more detailed aspects of Catholicism are reflected on—mostly, the indented parts of the book in smaller print, and ideally with some of the *FURTHER READING* and *FURTHER VIEWING* that may be recommended by the priest conducting the catechumenate, and also according to the individual catechumen's particular interests and needs. Most important of all are the *DAILY LIVING* and *PERSONAL REFLECTION* sections that conclude each chapter; an intellectual understanding of Catholic Christianity is sterile and meaningless unless it is accompanied by daily attempts to live, pray, and meditatively reflect on Christ's way of love.

The third stage is that of "Election," or of "Choice." This is meant to take place during the Lenten season, and it begins with the Rite of Election on the First Sunday of Lent. It is a recognition by the local church community that those who have completed the Catechumenate have been truly chosen by God to be full members of his Church. Lent then becomes a time of spiritual deepening—of prayer, penance, and quiet recollection—for both those just acknowledged as chosen, and for the whole community. It is like a time of "retreat" for all—of honest self-examination, repentance, inner purification, strengthening, and growth. As much of the local Christian community as possible gathers (usually at the Sunday eucharist) for the ancient rites of the "Scrutinies," a deepening discernment of what is weak and what is strong in us, and the "Presentations" of the Creed and the Lord's Prayer, expressing for all the core of what we as Christians believe and how Christ taught us to pray. Holy Saturday should be for these newly chosen a day of rest, fasting, and prayerful recollection or meditation.

(In this book, during the Election period, special attention might be given to chapters 16 "The Inner Life of a Christian," and 17, "Our Christian Presence in the World," but particularly the former. Then chapters 18 and 19, "Sin and Its Effects" and "Our Continuing Conversion," might be pondered; then one can conclude with an honest examination of one's conscience, using chapter 25, "Living Daily the Christian Life," as a springboard for one's examination. Finally, chapters 14 and 15, on the Mass and the eucharist, can be pondered, to especially bring home the significance of this greatest of Christian sacraments, and our uniquely privileged way to worship God together with one another and with Jesus Christ himself.)

Then, at the Easter Vigil, the elected new converts take part in the ancient Sacraments of Initiation. Their long period of preparation is completed, and now before the whole congregation they make their Profession of Faith and are baptized. Then they are anointed, receiving confirmation and completing their baptism. Finally they celebrate and take part fully for the first time in the meal of the holy eucharist—the culmination of their initiation, and Christ's greatest act of love, in which they can now share as often as they wish.

It should be noted, parenthetically, that the sacrament of confirmation—though it completes baptism and is properly part of an adult's initiation—is usually given chronologically to those coming into young adulthood, as the sacrament of Christian maturity and Christian witnessing. Thus this book discusses confirmation in chapter 17, "Our Christian Presence in the World."

The fourth and final stage of Christian Initiation is meant to take place through the whole post-Easter season. It is a period during which the new converts deepen or grow in their Christian baptismal commitment—by sharing in the eucharist with interior meditation on the meaning of what they have undertaken for life, by doing grateful acts of kindness or charity toward others, and by trying to develop a particular way of ministering within the community. The local Christian community, in turn, should help them find the particular ministry in which they can best use their particular gifts. In many places, the new Catholic Christians want to learn more, to take part in further classes and discussions, and thus to continue to grow in knowledge and love.

IN THE LITURGY

The full rite of baptism—and of Christian Initiation—brings out its full meaning for the new Christian. Ideally, the baptism of adults—on their reception into the Catholic Church, if they are already baptized Christians—is done as part of the full rite of Christian initiation. The Easter Vigil service is the ideal time for this today, as it was in the Church of almost 2,000 years ago. As has been explained, the Rite of Christian Initiation is meant to take place in stages, with its climax before the whole local church community at the Easter Vigil service.

It is important to remember, incidentally, that an already baptized Christian who enters the Catholic Church is a member of the Body of Christ, and therefore does not have to go through the whole process of Christian initiation. But this is very much an individual matter. Some may be Christians in name only, and will want to go through all the steps of initiation, since they are really coming as adults to a mature Christian commitment for the first time. Others may have a good knowledge of Christianity and may have been practicing it for many years; they will obviously want and need less instruction, less time for getting used to their new commitment, than those spoken of above. Perhaps one who has been baptized as a Catholic Christian, but who has never been raised as such, will want to go through the whole process. It is a wonderful experience of gradual growth into a mature faith, and many have found the whole process very rewarding. Obviously, each person's situation should be discussed with the priest who is conducting the classes, and worked out to their mutual satisfaction.

The Easter Vigil service, the climax of the Church's liturgy, is the time for the whole congregation to join in a renewal of their own baptismal vows, as the new Christians make theirs. They together renounce Satan, i.e., evil in their lives, and then together renew their Catholic Christian commitment, so that the new Catholic Christians can fully realize that they have a whole community to support them and care for them, as they grow together in faith, hope, and love.

The use of holy water, particularly when making the sign of the cross upon entering or leaving church, is a reminder of the water of our baptism; as it cleansed us originally from sin, so now we are reminded to live free of sin. Holy water is ordinary water blessed by a priest with the official prayer of the Church that whoever uses it reverently will remain cleansed of sin. The "Asperges" ("Sprinkling") of the congregation before some Masses also indicates this.

THE MAJORITY WHO ARE NOT BAPTIZED

There are other ways of being united to God besides baptism. Most of the human race has never heard of or cannot believe in Christ or baptism. And as the world population increases, Christians become proportionately less. The Christian life begun by baptism is becoming more and more the privilege and the responsibility of a few. Most of humanity is united with God in other ways.

An adult who believes in God and basically desires to do his will, and who has sorrow for his sins out of love of God, has God's grace-presence by this sincere desire. His sins would be forgiven. This is called "baptism of desire." So, too, a potential convert would receive grace if he desired to receive baptism and had sorrow for his sins out of love of God; if such a person died before baptism he would attain heaven. Also an unbaptized person who gives his life for his belief in God or some Christian teaching—though he may not recognize it as Christian—is said to be "baptized" in his own blood and thereby receives grace and salvation.

People come to God in this way through other, non-Christian religions. They would not normally have available the fullness of helps which Christ gives to his Church. Since he is "the way, the truth, and the life," the privilege and responsibility of being fully and consciously united with him belongs to Christians. But God is present among these others, as Vatican Council II points out:

> The Catholic Church rejects nothing that is true and holy in these religions. She regards with sincere reverence those ways of conduct and of life, those precepts and teachings which, though differing in many aspects from the ones she holds and sets forth, nonetheless often reflect a ray of that Truth which enlightens all men (*Constitution on the Church in the Modern World,* no. 2).

So, too, one who cannot believe in a personal God, through no fault of his own, but is committed to following his conscience, receives God's grace-presence. The basic orientation of his life would be to some worthy ideal outside himself, perhaps the good of society or the welfare of those he loves. In seeking this he is unknowingly seeking God—and God comes to him.

Some who sincerely seek truth oppose Christ and his Church, sometimes to the point of actively persecuting it. Often they have a false image of Christ or his Church. Perhaps they have encountered believers whose behavior is blatantly unchristian, and who, as Vatican Council II says, "conceal rather than reveal the authentic face of God and religion." Perhaps they see the glaring deficiencies in the Church's institutional framework, while not realizing how the framework can foster what is best in man. God lives within many of these unbelievers, though they may oppose him or those who try to work for him.

But these other ways of being united in God's grace-presence do not normally produce the full, deep union that can begin by Christian baptism. Baptized Christians who try to live out their baptismal commitment can know more of the basic truths about God, man, the universe, and life's purpose. They have the power to love and serve others more effectively, share in a special way in Christ's priesthood, and be more conscious of God's Presence in our world—in worshipful prayer, in our fellow human beings. With the Christian community's continuing help, committed baptized Christians can see opportunities for growing in love and union with God and others, where they might otherwise miss them.

One who knows about and believes in Christ's sacrament of baptism must receive it, with all its privileges and responsibilities. Otherwise he would be untrue to his conscience, and he should realize that he will have to answer for this, not only to himself but to God. It would be tragic to refuse Christ when he invites one in a special way, as he did his first disciples: "Come, follow me!" (Mark 1, 17; Matthew 9, 9).

Yet Christian baptism is only the beginning. Its power can be frustrated by an unchristian upbringing or environment, or by a deliberate rejection of its consequences. Unfortunately some baptized Christians live as if they were inoculated by their Christianization against true Christianity—they have long since convinced themselves that they are living as Christians, but by their smugly sinful lives they are hardened against its message. On the other hand, some who are not baptized may by their sincere and open lives grow much more fully in God's presence and spread far more love in the world.

Some words should be said here about "born-again" Christians. These comprise a broad spectrum of people. They have in common a usually sudden, often unexpected experience of being "saved" or "accepted" by Jesus, to whom, in turn, they commit themselves wholeheartedly as their personal Savior (or in some similarly expressed way). Those who have had this conversion experience seem to fall into two general types (with many shades in between):

The first group has evidently had a genuine experience of conversion, and as a result their lives are changed; faith, hope, and Christian love come through and begin to shape their lives, perhaps for the first time, perhaps as a profound reconversion to the faith in which they were baptized, but which has been dormant, unlived, for years. Most of these take place in the context of a conservatively-oriented Christian church, which usually stresses a simple experiencing of Jesus and God that more intellectually-oriented, socially liberal Christian groups find hard to understand. Conservative Christians generally place more emphasis on one's living out of traditional Christian values (expressed best for them usually in the Ten Commandments) than with changing society's structures to promote justice, peace, and equality. They are more concerned about the erosion of family life, sexual immorality, and the hedonism of much of our society.

They also generally place special emphasis on "bearing witness," on publicly professing and zealously spreading their belief in Christian "basics." They have a deep regard for and love of the bible as God's Word. Yet they don't take every word literally. While they accept much of modern biblical scholarship, they also tend to look to the bible mostly for guidance—a book to be lived by daily, rather than one to be overly-analyzed. Sometimes conservatively-oriented Catholics find much in common with these, for instance in some charismatic Christian groups.

The other type of "born-again" Christian is the one that Catholics in general find hard to accept. Without judging the genuineness of these people's conversion experience (obviously something only God can and should do), it is especially their basic attitude toward the bible and social issues that Catholics (as well as "main-line" Protestants) object to. These are often contrary to the Church's teaching, especially as expressed by Vatican Council II, recent popes, the American bishops, and lay groups within the Catholic Church.

These people are more "fundamentalist" than conservative; they tend to take literally the words of scripture, regarding its every word as inerrant, and allow for no symbolism, mythology, etc. They thus reject modern scripture scholarship, whether Protestant or Catholic, and tend to emphasize the Old Testament traditional strictness of the law and Commandments, more than Christ's forgiving and all-embracing love. They display a narrow, unshakably absolute certitude about the truth of their beliefs, and the sinfulness and even damnation of those who violate the Commandments and refuse to "repent." They are usually little concerned with racial and sexual justice and equality, and with the poor and deprived of other nations. They seem overly-concerned with combatting "godlessness" "tolerance," and "humanism," and are too little interested in social evils.

DAILY LIVING: RENEWING
OUR BAPTISMAL CONVERSION

We have seen that baptism does not give us faith permanently, nor "magically" enable one to live a truly Christian life. We must continue to grow and to cooperate with what God is continuing within us. Believers must continually be open to the Spirit as they practice their faith, expecting difficulties, doubts, and failures in their attempts to live and love as a Christian should—and also in the attempts of churchmen to communicate Christ to them.

They realize that, especially in today's rapidly changing world, they must be continual learners, trying to assimilate the Church's new insights into ancient truths, and to be involved with whatever loving causes they can—and particularly to develop a life of prayer and appreciation of the eucharistic Christ. Thus, in growing and developing a truly adult faith, there gradually comes a more intimate relationship with Christ and a realization of God's continual, loving Presence . . . even in the midst of adversity and wrenching pain.

Thus a Christian's life is one of continual conversion—or periodic "reconversions." Christians may fail in their baptismal commitment and may fall into a state of serious sin—perhaps again and again. When they are sorry, they renew their baptismal commitment (and express it by a well-prepared-for and sincere confession, being once again reconciled to Christ and his Church). They humbly ask God's help and begin again. If they are truly wise, they know that God's love is endless as it draws them on and on. The great St. Paul, as close to Christ as he was, thus expressed his own continuing weaknesses, and their deep lesson for him: **Read 2 Corinthians 12, 7–10.**

SOME SUGGESTIONS FOR . . .

DISCUSSION

Can you understand the significance of the sacrament of baptism?

Can you see the need of a true conversion before an adult's baptism or Profession of Faith?

What advantages and responsibilities does one who is baptized normally have in contrast to one who is not?

FURTHER READING

* *A Parish Guide to Adult Initiation,* Boyack (Paulist Press, 1980)—An excellent guide, full of practical suggestions from a concrete parish program that has "worked," for making evangelization and the Rite of Christian Initiation of Adults a way of renewing a whole parish.
* *The Shape of Baptism: The Rite of Christian Initiation,* Kavanagh (Pueblo Publishing Co., 1978)—An insightful, broadly based book that builds on the author's long experience as an excellent theological and pastoral guide for the crucial beginning-period of the Christian life.
* *Christian Initiation Resources* (Sadlier, 1980ff.)—A quarterly publication giving a packet of pertinent materials for implementing the RCIA and restoring the catechumenate to a central position in parish life.
* *The Way to Christianity,* Chilson (Winston Press, 1980)—An imaginative, fresh approach to the teachings of Jesus, especially good for those who are somewhat educated and are turned off by the laws and structures of institutionalized religion. This is pre-evangelizing, pre-inquiry done meditatively, as a beginning "search for spiritual growth."
* *Renew* (Paulist Press, 1980)—A three-year program for the spiritual growth of people within a vibrant faith-community. It has been working effectively within the archdiocese of Newark, both as a diocese-wide program and by individual parishes without diocesan involvement. It skillfully blends reflection, sharing, scripture and prayer.

FURTHER VIEWING/LISTENING

Baptism—Journey of Faith (Teleketics, Franciscan Communications)—Five films/videotapes presenting five dramatic stories, tying each to a different aspect of baptismal initiation. Quite useful to parents preparing for their child's baptism, for adult inquirers, discussion groups, etc.

The Radical Rite: The Vision of Christian Initiation of Adults, Guzie (NCR Cassettes)—Three cassettes with guide and album by a leading expert on the sacraments. Also good, from NCR Cassettes, is *Sacraments of Christian Initiation: A Pastoral Perspective,* Gusmer, consisting also of three cassettes and related materials, and *Initiating Adult Catholics: A Pastoral Approach to the New Rite,* Mick, which has four cassettes and related materials, and is done by one who has pioneered in using the rite, including relating it to various parts of this book.

PERSONAL REFLECTION

God's special Presence or closeness, received in baptism, or by the sincere desire to do what God wants, is the only important thing in life. It is God himself, intimately within me, the beginning of heaven while here on earth. I should resolve to do all in my power to avoid sin, particularly habitual serious sinning which robs me of God's love and cuts me off from others.

14
Our Worship Together: The Mass

What is the meaning of the Mass? Why go to Mass at all? Why is the Mass the greatest thing in this life? Why is it arranged the way it is? How can we derive real value and help from the Mass?

WHY WE GATHER TOGETHER TO WORSHIP

We saw that worship is an expression of what God is worth to us—our deepest feelings of reverence, need, and gratitude—and our confidence that we are uniquely loved, worth very much to him. Worship is our trusting "yes"—however difficult, even painfully given at times—to the Mystery of caring Love we call God. And it is a "yes" to the whole wonderful mystery of our own life, its joys and sorrows, its peaks and pits, its loves and its times of crushing rejection.

We saw, too, that worship means joining others to express and share together our feelings of reverence and need toward God, and our feelings of caring and need for one another. As human beings, as people needing people, it is as natural to worship together as it is to eat together, to work together, to love together. "No man is an island," as a poet put it, and we surely cannot find God only in isolation; it is too easy to come up with a magnified version of our own ego. We need others' experiencing, insights, encouragement, and honest proddings—just as they need ours.

As Christians we are not ashamed to say that we need one another, that we need to gather together in church as we go on our particular journeys through life. We saw the beautiful image of Vatican Council II for Christ's Church: God's people, pressing forward "like pilgrims in a foreign land ... amid persecutions and consolations," to our destined home with God and one another in heaven. But we also gather together in worship to learn how to better love one another in this life, how to best and most caringly co-create a "new earth" in space and time.

> *To get anything out of going to worship together, we obviously need a mature, realistic patience and openness.* We must make sure we are doing our part, if we are to be aware that God is there and doing his part. Each liturgy will touch, be truly meaningful to, only so many people; worshipping together is not something magical, a quick fix of inspiration for all present. We need to remind ourselves that someone (perhaps many others) will receive help—that if this week's worship does not come home to me, perhaps next week's will. And perhaps during the week we will help bring this about by preparing: by lovingness toward others, by honest moments of private reflection.

CHRIST GATHERS US TO SHARE IN HIS GREATEST ACTION

We have seen God's love for us and his desire to be with us. He came among us in Jesus Christ. He lives among us today in his Church. He reaches out to us through the sacraments: baptism, by which he unites us to himself, and confirmation by which he sends us his Spirit.

Wonderful though it is that God should come among us, more wonderful yet is the destiny he has prepared for us. He wants to raise us to himself, to the very level of divinity, to know and love him most intimately in unending happiness.

Mankind had rejected the grace that made this possible, but Christ came and redeemed us, making it possible once more. This, our salvation by Christ, was the greatest act of his life and the central event of all history. By it mankind could attain union with God, face to face, forever.

Yet in order to profit by this great act of Christ's love, we must unite ourselves freely to it. We must make it our own. We must somehow take part in Christ's life, but especially in his death and resurrection in order to attain the perfect union of love with him that is heaven. This is because he loves us and wants us to be with him, freely and most intimately.

It is natural to share in the things that happen to those we love, and particularly in the great events of their life. We want to be with those we love, particularly in their great moments of joy or suffering. A husband wants to be by the bedside of his critically ill wife, parents want to take part in their child's graduation, friends take part in one another's weddings, etc.

Jesus Christ in his love has made it possible for us to share in what happened to him. We can read a biography of a great leader and be caught up by his or her spirit, courage, and example. In a way, we can pass over into the lives of such people and to some small extent share their great experiences. Jesus has made much more than this possible for us. We can actually relive his life, mysteriously but really. We try to imitate Jesus, but even more we can actually go through—with him—what he did. His actions, his way of experiencing things, gradually become our own. So St. Paul, perhaps his greatest follower, says: "I have been crucified with Christ. It is no longer I who live, but Christ who lives in me. . . ." (Galatians 2, 20).

Above all, Jesus Christ wants us to take part with him in his death and resurrection so that our own "dyings" and "risings" can be a part of his—and his a part of ours. He wants us especially to enter into these great events of his earthly existence so that he can come with his power and love into the "pits" and the "peaks" of our life— our daily deaths and resurrections, our plunges into pain and our small triumphs. He wants us to share his own "passage," his own experience of death and new life, his going back to the Father and unending happiness. He wants to catch us up into himself, so that what we go through will be part of what he went through and so that our sufferings and joys will have sense and meaning and be filled for us with his own loving power.

> We saw how Christ unites us for the first time in his death and resurrection at baptism. After baptism, each sacrament unites us in a special way to Jesus Christ as he saves us. But the greatest partaking possible is by the sacrament of the holy eucharist.

The holy eucharist is Jesus Christ living among us under the appearance of bread and wine. When the priest at Mass says the eucharistic prayer over the bread and wine (at the heart of which are Christ's words, "This is my body. . . . This is the chalice of my blood. . . ."), where there were before only bread and wine there is now the living Jesus Christ. This is the sacrament of the holy eucharist. By the power of Christ working through the priest as he leads the people in the eucharistic prayer, the bread and wine, though still appearing to be bread and wine, are now Christ, present and acting among us in a special, powerful way.

> We are aware that this sounds strange indeed to some and is open to misunderstanding. When we say that the bread and wine "become Christ" we are not saying that bread and wine are Christ, nor are we practicing some form of cannibalism when we take this in communion. What we mean is that the bread and wine are a sign of Christ present, here and now, in a special way—not in a mere physical way, as if condensed into a wafer. Somehow his presence has "taken over" the bread and wine, so that, for us who believe, it is no longer merely bread that is present, but Christ himself. And Christ is here present, not just to be eaten as if in a cannibalistic sense, but rather present and doing something for us: putting us in touch with and sharing with us his death and resurrection.

Jesus Christ lives among us in the holy eucharist for a purpose—to make present for us his death and resurrection so that we can take part. This is the Mass. Jesus said, "This is my body given up (to death) for you. . . . This cup is the new covenant in my blood." Christ's death and resurrection, his going to the Father, is made present in this ritual so that Christians till the end of time can take part in them, gradually going with him to the Father. The Mass is the great way we are drawn to God, and our great source of strength for the journey to him.

There are various ways in which we can take part in a great historical event, for example, a political rally. We might have heard of it, we might see a film of it on TV, or we might have actually been a part of it. The more we enter into it and the more we are involved in it, the more we will get out of it and the more it will mean to us and affect our actions toward others.

At Mass, we are not only present at Jesus Christ's actual death and resurrection, prolonged through time and space. We also really take part in them to the extent we want to. Christ's death and resurrection are here; we are present at them, but they are hidden—they are present here under the ritual signs of bread and wine. The more these signs mean to us and the more we consciously join our daily "dyings" and "risings" with the great struggle of Christ's death and resurrection, then the more we actually are part of them, the more our life and our pain become meaningful, the more hope we have, the more love we will spread in the world, and the closer we come to eternal life and oneness with God himself.

THIS IS OUR COVENANT MEAL

The night before he died Christ gave us the great way of continually sharing in his death and resurrection—by means of a meal, the last supper: Read 1 Corinthians 11, 23–29. To understand this incident we must remember that this meal was the passover meal, eaten to commemorate the salvation of God's people from slavery and death, and the old covenant of Mount Sinai. Whenever the Jews ate this meal they looked forward to a new passover to come, a new salvation, a new exodus to a new freedom. Our redemption was Christ's great new passover, from death to life, from this world to the Father—and he began it by eating this paschal meal, his last supper. He gave this paschal meal a new power and new meaning. He made it the way his followers could actually share in his passover, in his death and resurrection.

By the words, "This is my body given up for you.... This cup is the new covenant in my blood," Jesus Christ mysteriously but really made himself present where before there were only bread and wine. Thus Jesus Christ gave us the sacrament of the holy eucharist. The bread and wine, though still appearing to be bread and wine, were now transformed. Jesus Christ was present in a new and wonderful way, though the bread and wine still had their original qualities. And it was the whole living Christ present under the appearance of bread, not only his body, and the whole living Christ present under the appearance of wine.

But above all, Jesus was presenting before his apostles his death and resurrection which would take place the next day, and which would begin his new covenant. The bread was his body which would, he said, be "given up" in death for us all. The cup was his blood which would be shed to establish his new covenant. By these words he made present at the last supper, mysteriously but really, his bloody death and his resurrection. It was a living preview of what would happen the next day, Good Friday, and on Easter Sunday morning.

This meal by which Christ began his passover also began the events by which he made his new, perfect covenant. "This cup is the new covenant in my blood," he said. As he and his apostles ate the meal which commemorated the old covenant, he was looking forward to the new covenant which he would shortly begin. Then as Moses had once sealed the old covenant by sacrifice and the sprinkling of animals' blood, Christ shed his blood in sacrifice on Good Friday to begin the new covenant. As the greatest event of the Old Testament had been celebrated by a meal, so Christ made this meal the occasion of celebrating the greatest event of his life and of all history.

Then Christ gave his apostles the power to do what he had done, to make present his death and resurrection after changing the bread and wine into himself—"Do this in remembrance of me," he said. By this he gave his apostles the power to prolong his sacrifice, to extend it, to somehow continue it down through history. Each time this took place, his passover, his covenant would be renewed again. Every other action of history is bound by limitations of time and space, except this.

Every priest by his ordination receives the power of making Christ present and re-presenting his death and resurrection. This power has been passed on in the Church from the apostles by the sacrament of ordination, holy orders. By giving this power to his priests, Christ provides that his Church down through the centuries can continually take part in the great events of our salvation. Christ chose his apostles to be the first priests of the new testament, just as God had chosen Aaron and his sons as the first priests of the old testament. As the powers of a special priesthood were passed on in Israel, so the full powers of Christ's priesthood are passed on today to those he chooses through his Church.

Every Christian also shares in Christ's priesthood and in this offering of himself which is his death and resurrection prolonged. We saw how, by baptism and confirmation, each Christian receives this power of the lay priesthood. The ordained priests of the Church, the successors of the apostles, act as Christ's instruments making him present in the eucharist. Then the whole Christian congregation uses its priestly powers to offer him, and itself with him, to the Father.

... AND OUR PERFECT SACRIFICE ...

One way of understanding the Mass is to recall that the great events of life are celebrated by giving gifts or presents—as on birthdays, weddings, anniversaries. Giving gifts is as old as humanity and as widespread. Our gift can express many things: love, praise, thanks, repentance, and it can implicitly ask for something. A gift stands for the giver—accepting a gift often means acceptance of the one who gives it, as when a girl accepts a ring from a boy. A gift, then, particularly expresses our desire to be united in love with the one to whom it is given.

From ancient times, we saw, men have offered gifts in sacrifice to God (or their concept of God). They have done this to show their feelings toward him and their desire to be united with him. We saw in the Old Testament sacrifices how God helped his people express their feelings toward him, guiding them to offer their gifts to him.

Sacrifice means offering a gift through a priest, changing it in some way, and sometimes eating of it. People would take some gift that represented themselves, and offer it to God by means of their representative, a priest. He would change or transform the gift to signify that they were giving it to God, that it no longer belonged to them—often he would kill a living gift or victim—and then he might burn it to further show God's acceptance and possession of it. Sometimes there would be a meal or banquet, a communion, to further signify their union with God by eating of what was now divine.

Something was lacking even in the Old Testament sacrifices. Men never had a suitable gift for almighty God, nor did they have a worthy priest; then, too, they were unable to be as fully united with God as they wished.

If I were hungry, I should not tell you, for mine are the world and its fullness. Do I eat the flesh of strong bulls, or is the blood of goats my drink? (Psalm 49, 12–13).

When mankind was ready, Jesus Christ offered the perfect sacrifice by his death and resurrection. He was the perfect gift and the perfect priest making this offering. The best gift, after all, is that of a living person, as when a couple give themselves to one another in marriage—and Christ is the divine Son giving himself to the Father.

By his death he gave himself to his Father; his resurrection and ascension showed that the Father accepted his gift.

Christ gave us the power to offer this same perfect gift, himself, to continually share in his death and resurrection by the holy eucharist. We would expect that Christ would not leave his followers without a way of communicating with God by sacrifice. But he went beyond our greatest expectations. He gave us the holy eucharist, his living presence among us, so we could join ourselves to him and continually share in his own great sacrifice.

The Mass, then, is the renewal of Christ's sacrifice, of his passover, and new covenant, by him and us, his Church. At each Mass Christ becomes present; he prolongs and renews his sacrifice so we can be a part of it, so we can pass with him through this world to eternity, and with him continually renew our own covenant.

Christ is present among us at Mass with the same intention or desire to give himself for us, but now he shows this by the separate signs of bread and wine. Instead of showing it by a bloody death, he now expresses his giving of himself by this ceremony with bread and wine. In our own actions for example, it is our inner intention, our sincere willingness to do something, that really matters. There is a great difference between a person giving up his life voluntarily and one who is forced to die. Christ becomes present among us at Mass with the same inner intention, the same desire to be sacrificed for us that he had on Calvary 2,000 years ago. However, now, instead of carrying out his intention by a bloody death, he expresses it by the separate signs of bread and wine.

> A person can show his love by giving his life, or equally by being ready and willing to do so. Christ is present at Mass with the same willingness, the same desire to give his life for us that he had when he actually died. It is somewhat as if our war dead could come back alive on Veterans' Day, inspired by the same interior willingness to give their lives, and go through a pageant reenacting the way they died, that we might now unite our feelings with theirs. "Do this for a remembrance of me," said Christ—the Mass is a living remembrance, a living memorial which brings the past into the present.

At Mass Christ does not suffer or die again. Rather he represents, prolongs, continues, renews his great moment of sacrifice down through the centuries so that we can be a part of it. There are millions of Masses, but only one sacrifice of Christ. If we at Mass were to close our eyes it would be the same as if Christ's followers on Calvary closed theirs; the same great action is taking place before us and we are able to be an intimate part of it.

Through the Mass Christ does many things for us. Above all, he enables us to offer perfect worship and be perfectly united with God. The men of the Old Testament strove to bring this about but never could. Now at Mass we are joined with Christ as he appears before his Father and ours. The Father no longer sees the poor actions of mere men—you and me with our sins and weaknesses—but only the gift that God himself cannot resist.

If our eyes could see what is really happening at any Mass, we would see Christ at the altar and among us, leading us and drawing us all into himself. Then, with him, we would ascend to the Father's presence. We would also see the Holy Spirit within each of us, uniting us, inspiring our offering. We would see the Father giving us in return his Son, Jesus Christ, the best gift God can give mortal man, and we would see ourselves being drawn into an indescribable union with divinity.

THE MASS IS GOD'S WORD, OUR GIFT, AND HIS GIFT

When giving a gift, there is conversation, some sort of preparation to bring out its meaning and significance. We do not merely thrust our gift at its recipient. Particularly if it is a noteworthy gift, there is conversation and ceremony with it. When a national hero is presented with the Medal of Honor there are speeches, music, etc. So too we prepare to offer our gift in sacrifice to God by conversation with him, by listening to his Word, and by ceremony.

God had called his people together at Mount Sinai to hear his Word and respond to it by sacrifice (Cf. Exodus 24, 7–8). This assembly of the Israelites established the old covenant, making them his people. This "assembly of Yahweh" is the same as the New Testament word for "Church." The basic meaning of a Church, then, is this: God's people assembled by him to hear his Word and respond to it by sacrifice.

After Christ's ascension his followers assembled to receive his teaching from the apostles and offer the eucharistic sacrifice. This is the Church of the New Testament. The eucharistic meal, called the "breaking of the bread," and the teaching that went with it would gradually develop into the pattern of worship that would be the Mass.

> And they devoted themselves to the apostles' teaching and fellowship, to the breaking of bread and the prayers (Acts 2, 42). On the first day of the week, when they were gathered together to break bread, Paul talked with them, intending to depart on the morrow; and he prolonged his speech until midnight. . . . And when Paul had gone up and had broken bread and eaten, he conversed with them a long while, until daybreak, and so departed (Acts 20, 7. 11).

Many scripture scholars see in the 6th chapter of John's gospel an excerpt from an early Christian liturgical service; John himself may have conducted primitive services in this way. Verses 35–50 give the doctrine or teaching, and verses 51–58 the eucharistic part of the service. This, then is the pattern: The Word of God followed by the eucharist.

The Mass, then, is the assembly of God's new people, his Church, called together by him to hear his Word and to take part in his perfect sacrifice. When we come together for Mass we are not only going to church—we are a Church. The Mass welds us into one people as we renew our common covenant, offer our gift and share our meal which is Christ. It is by the Mass that the Church is continually renewed in what it is.

The Mass as the meal which renews Christ's sacrifice can be compared to the main meal of a family. First, the family comes home; they wash up, and talk to one another, learning the events of the day. The table is set and the food is prepared. Then the family prays together over their food, offering thanks to God for all he has given them. Finally, they eat together, taking part in the food and in one another's companionship.

So too at Mass we first come together and prepare ourselves, cleansing ourselves of sin, speaking with God, and learning from him the great events of our salvation. Then we prepare our food, the bread and wine. We then join in the great eucharistic prayer of thanksgiving to God over our food which is now Christ his Son. Finally, we take part together in our meal of holy communion, nourishing ourselves on Christ and joined with one another in the companionship of our Christian family love.

The arrangement of the Mass also expresses the fact that it is an exchange of love:

God gives to us—his Word, the scriptural teaching.

We give to God—our sacrifice-offering of thanksgiving, Christ, and ourselves with him.

God gives to us—his Word, the eucharistic Christ.

The Mass begins with some introductory prayers, usually recalling our sins and asking God's pardon that we may be worthy to worship him, and briefly praising him for what he is and has given us.

The first main part of the Mass is the Liturgy of the Word, the scripture readings. We have assembled together as God's people and have prepared ourselves by prayer. Now God addresses his Word to us. Later we will respond to his Word by our sacrifice. This, we saw, was the way God's people worshipped in the Old Testament, and the way Christ's first followers continued to worship. Christ himself had followed this pattern when he prepared his apostles by his last discourse (John, chapters 13–17), and then went forth to his death and resurrection. The first Christians originally adopted this part from the Jewish synagogue service of prayers, readings, and commentary.

Faith is aroused and we are enlightened and made eager for Christ by the scripture readings and the preaching that follows. Before our gifts of bread and wine are changed into Christ, our hearts must be changed, opened, by this instruction. Usually there are three readings: the first is from the Old Testament; the second is from one of the New Testament epistles; and the third reading is from one of the gospels. In the sermon or homily Christ addresses his message to us through the priest who represents him.

The importance of this first part of the Mass is stressed by Vatican Council II when it says that here "God speaks to his people and Christ is still proclaiming his gospel" (*Constitution on the Sacred Liturgy,* no. 33). And again, "From the table of both the Word of God and the body of Christ . . . the Church unceasingly receives and offers to the faithful the bread of life" (*Constitution on Divine Revelation,* no. 21).

We then respond to God's Word on Sundays and great feasts by professing our faith, saying together the Creed. Then, in the Prayer

of the Faithful, we respond to the exhortations of the scriptures and
the sermon by praying for all those who need help and for the things
we and the world particularly need.

**The second main part of the Mass is the Liturgy of the Eucharist
(or the Liturgy of Sacrifice).** Here we prepare our gifts, they are
transformed into Christ, and through him and with him we offer
ourselves in thanksgiving to the Father. The Father, in return, gives
us the same perfect gift, Jesus Christ, who unites us to himself and to
one another.

**We begin our sacrifice with the offertory during which we prepare
our gifts, the bread and wine, and make them ours by uniting ourselves to them.** As a mother prepares a meal for her family, as Christ
sent his apostles to prepare for the last supper, so we do here. We
also unite ourselves and all we wish to pray for with these gifts, so
that later when they have become Christ we will be united to him in
his offering to the Father.

**With the preface we begin the great eucharistic prayer (or canon),
during which Christ's presence transforms our gifts and we offer
ourselves with him, in this great prayer of thanksgiving to the Father.** This is the heart of the Mass, its most solemn part. We call this
the eucharistic prayer, that is, a prayer of remembrance and thanksgiving. We remember the great love God has shown us by his actions
for us, and we are particularly grateful for what he has done for us in
Jesus Christ. We then give him the best possible thanks by offering
him Jesus Christ, his Son, and ourselves with him.

> The term "eucharist" comes from the long prayer of thanksgiving
> said by the Jewish people at the end of a meal, gratefully recounting
> God's mighty deeds for them over the centuries. So Christ at the last
> supper ". . . took bread and when he had given thanks he broke it and
> gave it to them. . . ." (Luke 22, 19). During the eucharistic prayer we
> remember everyone and everything, joining all creation in our thankful
> worship.

**At the center of this prayer are Christ's words, said over the bread
and wine: "This is my body which will be given up for you. . . . This
is the cup of my blood, the blood of the new and everlasting covenant. . . ."** This is called the consecration. These core words bring
home to us how our gifts are being transformed into Jesus Christ
himself in this eucharist, and how he is making present his death for

us. The words said over the bread tell us that it is his body "given up" to death that is before us; in a moment the bread will be broken to further bring home to us his death. The words said over the wine tell us that it is Jesus shedding his blood for us who is before us, dying in order to begin his new covenant-commitment of unending love and life for us.

The separate signs of bread and wine bring home to us how his blood was drained from his body as he hung dying for us on the cross. He is present among us with the same willingness to die for us as on Calvary two thousand years ago, but now he shows his total, unending love by these separate signs of "consecrated" bread and wine. His powerful presence here gives us the strength to go through the "dyings" necessary in our daily life as a Christian—to more and more let go of the things that can keep us from him—in order to "rise" to a new aliveness, a new lovingness with him.

Then the priest sums up the Christian memory of what Christ did for us, his death and resurrection, now marvelously before us in "this life-giving bread, this saving cup," so that we can share in it. He calls on the Holy Spirit to truly unite us as we share in Christ's body and blood. Then we pray for those in the Church on earth who need our prayers and for those among us who have died, and we ask to be united with those who have already attained heaven.

Our eucharistic prayer culminates in the offering of ourselves and of all creation with Christ to the Father. Christ has taken our poor gifts and transformed them into himself. Now, joined with him, everything we are and have is offered in a great thanksgiving gift. This prayer concludes:

"Through him, with him, in him, in the unity of the Holy Spirit, all glory and honor is yours, almighty Father, for ever and ever." The congregation responds with their great "Amen!"—"So be it!"

Our gift has been offered in sacrifice, and now we prepare for our sacrificial meal, holy communion, God's gift to us. God now shows us strikingly that he has accepted our gift, that we are truly united with him. He comes to us himself in the form of food—something of which men in times past would not even dream. This is the greatest gift he could give us. He unites each of us to himself in the most intimate way possible, through Christ his Son. Christ comes to us in this sign of food to bring home to us that he is our spiritual strength and nourishment.

We say or sing together the prayer that Christ himself taught us, the Lord's Prayer or "Our Father." Then we pray for freedom from sin and anxiety "as we wait in joyful hope for the coming of our Savior, Jesus Christ."

With the prayer for peace we give the handshake or embrace of peace to one another. This is an outward sign of the peace and unity in which we are trying to grow as a Christian community.

Then there is the breaking of the bread, which tells us how Christ's body was "broken" for us as he died for us. Also, at the last supper his followers shared the same loaf to symbolize their oneness with and in him. The priest breaks a particle off the sacred bread and drops it in the chalice or cup to symbolize our unity through this eucharist (in the ancient Church a particle from the sacred bread used at the bishop's Mass was sometimes taken to the other churches and dropped in the chalice as a sign of the unity of the Church).

Now Jesus Christ unites himself with each of us in holy communion. First the priest takes part in communion under the form of bread and then under the form of wine—as at the last supper, the priest always takes both the bread and the wine. Then the people take part in communion with Christ, either under the appearance of bread alone, or under both forms. Sometimes the bread may be dipped in the wine and then consumed.

Holy communion is our great and joyous meal of love, unity, and thanksgiving. People have always expressed their happiness, friendship, thanksgiving, and particularly their unity by having a meal together. We saw that the joining of two parties in a covenant was often celebrated by a meal together; today a couple has a wedding meal, often, to celebrate their lifelong covenant of love. We saw that Israel celebrated its union with God through the old covenant by the passover meal which also looked forward to a new, more perfect union. Now we have a far more intimate and perfect union with God in this sacrificial meal of the new covenant. But this is not all Christ does:

> The cup of blessing which we bless, is it not a participation in the blood of Christ? The bread which we break, is it not a participation in the body of Christ? Because there is one loaf, we who are many are one

body, for we all partake of the same loaf. Consider the practice of Israel; are not those who eat the sacrifices partners in the altar? (1 Corinthians 10, 16–18).

Christ through holy communion also unites us with one another, making us "one body," one Church. Just as many grains make one bread, so we, by eating the eucharist, become one. Eating together draws people together, especially when celebrating a great event, as Christmas or Thanksgiving dinner, a wedding breakfast, or a banquet. A family meal is normally the center of its life together.

Christ chose this custom of eating together to draw his followers together, to unite us not only with himself but with one another. Holy communion, then, is the great banquet of God's family, his Church, by which the members are drawn together in love. We are so truly united with one another that St. Augustine could say, "You are the body of Christ, and when you receive the body of Christ you receive yourselves." Singing together when taking part in communion particularly emphasizes our unity.

The communion meal is the part of the Mass that particularly reminds us of Christ's resurrection. A meal symbolizes life—we must eat to live. This eucharistic meal not only symbolizes but gives us Christ resurrected, living again, communicating to us his own life of grace.

> Christ usually appeared after his resurrection during meals and ate with his followers. The authentic witnesses of the resurrection, says Peter, are those "who were chosen by God as witnesses, who ate and drank with him after he rose from the dead" (Acts 10, 41). When Christ appeared to two of his followers on the road to Emmaus, they did not realize who it was until "he took the bread and blessed, and broke it, and gave it to them. And their eyes were opened and they recognized him. . . ." (Luke 24, 30–31). After his ascension Christ's followers felt that he was living in their midst especially when they gathered for the eucharistic meal, and they looked for his second coming one day at this event.

After the communion, the Mass concludes with a few prayers of thanksgiving and the final blessing. Strengthened and united with Christ and one another, we are now sent back into our daily lives to live the life of Christ.

This, then, is the Mass—the wonderful way in which Christ continually joins us to the great actions by which he saved us, the greatest events of human history. Now we can take part in them most intimately, continually drawing strength from them for our journey to the Father. We who take part in Mass today are as truly a part of Christ's greatest deeds as if we were his followers standing on Calvary, and in some respects we can join in even more intimately. This privilege is ours as Christians—for many, it is their privilege every day.

DAILY LIVING: THE MASS AND OUR DAILY LIFE

All the actions of a Catholic's daily life should lead up to the Mass and flow from it. When we take part in the Mass, we unite ourselves with Christ and through him we reach out and are drawn to God. This act of worship is certainly the most significant and important action of the day and of the week.

At Mass we personally renew our covenant with God for that week. The more we prepare for it, and try to remember and prolong it in our daily life, the more truly Christian—Christ-filled—our life will be.

Our offering at Mass must be interior and sincere. Christ sacrifices himself at Mass by his interior desire to give himself for us. The more we unite ourselves interiorly, by our own sincere desire, to Christ's offering—the more we offer something that is really of ourselves—the more effect the Mass will have on our daily lives.

SOME SUGGESTIONS FOR . . .

DISCUSSION

Can you understand the idea of the Mass, as a sacrifice and as a meal?

Can you understand why the Mass is arranged the way it is?

How, in your opinion, could one get more out of the Mass?

PERSONAL REFLECTION

Each Mass is a renewal of my covenant with God. He pledges himself to give me eternal and unimaginable happiness, if I will only be faithful this little while here on earth. I should take every occasion I can to renew my covenant with him, to open myself in sincere acceptance of his love. The Mass is the great way in which I can do this.

15

The Eucharist in Christ's Church Today

Why is the Mass changing today? What further developments might we expect in the Mass? How are Christians drawing closer in their worship? Why do we call the Mass the greatest thing in Catholicism?

HOW THE MASS DEVELOPED

The Mass at first was a simple service that took place after a meal, as at the last supper. The meal was the "agape" and the eucharistic service was called the "breaking of the bread" or the "Lord's supper." In Jerusalem the first Christians continued to attend the temple together, but then "breaking bread in their homes, they partook of food with glad and generous hearts" (Acts 2, 46). We read of Paul's visit to Troas: "On the first day of the week, when we were gathered together to break bread, Paul talked with them. . . ." (Acts 20,7ff).

Soon, however, abuses crept in, and gradually the eucharistic service was separated from the agape-meal: Read 1 Corinthians 11, 17–22. When the eucharistic meal became a separate service and gradually took on a regular form, it was begun by the reading of the Word of God and prayers. The Christians at first had continued taking part in the Jewish service of prayer and instruction in the temple or synagogue; now this became a part of their own service in their homes. We saw how the gospels came from the narratives, prayers, and hymns used at worship, and the epistles were written to be read at the assembly's worship.

An early Christian writer has left us the first full description of a Christian Mass celebration, about the year 150 at Rome:

> ... And on that day which is called after the sun, all who are in the towns and in the country gather together for a communal celebration. And then the memoirs of the apostles or the writings of the prophets are read, as long as time permits. After the reader has finished his task, the one presiding gives an address, urgently admonishing his hearers to practice these beautiful teachings in their lives. Then all stand up together and recite prayers. After the end of the prayers ... the bread and wine mixed with water are brought, and the president offers up prayers and thanksgivings, as much as in him lies. The people chime in with an Amen. Then takes place the distribution, to all attending, of the things over which the thanksgiving has been spoken, and the deacons bring a portion to the absent. (He had previously remarked, "... this food itself is known amongst us as the eucharist. No one may partake of it unless he is convinced of the truth of our teachings and is cleansed in the bath of baptism. ...") Besides, those who are well-to-do give whatever they will. What is gathered is deposited with the one presiding, who therewith helps orphans and widows.... (Justin Martyr, *First Apology*, c. 67).

As time passed, other prayers were added, but the pattern of worship was: God's Word, the eucharistic offering of thanks, and the eucharistic meal. The key actions were central, done in comparative simplicity; everyone stood closely about and had an active part in the ceremonies, which were in the people's language. By the 3rd century, the simple meal aspect had disappeared, and the pattern became: reading of the Word, the eucharistic prayer of thanksgiving, and communion.

Gradually, after the persecutions ended, the Mass became more complicated, had many forms and elaborate rites, and became distant from the people. By the early Middle Ages, many court ceremonies had become incorporated into Christian worship in an attempt to make it more solemn: genuflections, bowing, kissing, incensing, etc. Then too the Arian heresy which denied the divinity of Christ became widespread; to stress Christ's divine presence, altars gradually were moved away from the people, the priest turned his back on the people and alone said the eucharistic prayers, communion railings went up to separate the sanctuary from the people, at which they knelt to receive the consecrated bread from the priest who alone could touch it, and prayers expressing our unworthiness became common in the Mass. Also, to weld together the various conquered tribes, the Franks had imposed on them the Latin language and liturgy which was less and less understood by the people.

By the high Middle Ages the Mass had become largely separated from the people and the business almost exclusively of the clergy, who often did little more than say "their" Mass which was felt to have an almost automatic value. The great cathedrals of Europe reflect the devotion of the people but also their growing distance from the mysteries of worship. Communion became less and less frequent and was taken more and more under only one form. The sacrifice aspect of the Mass was overstressed. Private devotional practices multiplied, especially those to the saints, and began to partake of superstition; relics were sold and stolen. The clergy in many places became smug and corrupt in their status. Then the inevitable happened—the Reformation took place. Luther's first demands included the reform of the clergy and Mass in the vernacular.

The Church reacted at the reform Council of Trent by curbing the abuses that had crept into its worship as well as other aspects of its life. However, in the Church's view the reformers had gone too far in setting aside the separate, hierarchical priesthood and the sacrificial aspect of the Mass. Its Counter-Reformation, though, swung the pendulum too far—it "froze" the ceremonies of the Mass, the use of Latin, the stylized role of the priest and the silent and non-scriptural participation (or non-participation) of the people.

With the beginning of the 20th century, however, a healthy counteraction began: Under Pope Pius X the Church began gradually moving toward restoring the Mass to its early, ideal form. But the progress was sporadic and only among a comparative few. Few had any idea of the great reform that would shortly take place.

The Constitution on the Sacred Liturgy of Vatican Council II was the culmination of the work of those who were trying to make our worship more meaningful. It has been called by many, non-Catholics as well as Catholics, the most revolutionary and far-reaching document of its kind in the Church's history. Some of its main points follow:

Full and active participation by all the people is the aim to be considered before all else. . . . The Christian people, so far as possible, should be able to understand (the texts and rites) with ease and take part in them fully, actively, and as befits a community. . . . The people as well as the priest have different functions, and the people should be encouraged to take part by means of acclamations, responses, psalmody, antiphons and songs, as well as by actions, gestures, etc.

There is to be more reading from holy scripture and it is to be more varied and suitable. . . .The ministry of preaching is to be fulfilled with exactitude and fidelity. . . .

The rites should be distinguished by a noble simplicity; they should be short, clear, and unencumbered by useless repetitions; they should be within the people's powers of comprehension, and normally should not require much explanation. . . .

The use of the mother tongue . . . frequently may be of great advantage. . . .The Church has no wish to impose a rigid uniformity . . . (and) elements from the traditions and cultures of individual peoples might appropriately be admitted into divine worship.

The liturgical reforms of the council have had a good beginning, but there is always much to be done to make meaningful the Mass-mystery to the diverse needs of all of us as we gather to worship. Much has been done to arrive at ceremonies that will retain the meaningful things of two thousand years of worship, and yet be meaningful to contemporary man. The American bishops years ago asked for the broadest possible powers to experiment with different types of Masses.

The liturgical authorities in Rome have the final decision about when and what major changes should take place so as to keep a certain uniformity throughout the worldwide, changing Church. National bishops' conferences work to integrate local customs into the Mass, aided by "input" from the laity. Today, the new norms, used with sensitive imagination, allow the Mass to be a genuinely God-filled experience, suitable to our modern needs.

The ceremonies and language of the Mass may differ from place to place, according to the Church's different "rites" or liturgies. There are several dozen different rites, most as ancient or more so than the Latin, especially among the churches deriving from the Middle East. But the essential actions of the Mass are the same throughout the worldwide Church. A Latin Rite Catholic would derive a good deal of profit from taking part in an Eastern Rite Mass.

The Mass throughout most of the Church is in the Latin Rite, but the Latin language has been replaced by the vernacular so the people can better take part. Latin was retained over the centuries as a reminder of the antiquity and universal sameness of the Mass; today, however, it is seen that universal unity does not depend on uniformity of language and ceremonies.

The vestments worn by the priest at Mass remind us of the antiquity of the Mass, and also that Christ is present working through the priest. In a sense the vestments "hide" the priest, bringing home to us that he stands at the altar as Christ's instrument. They came originally from the ordinary clothes worn in the early centuries when the Mass began. Today many want to simplify these, particularly when Mass is said in homes, so it will be more meaningful to modern worshippers.

The setting, solemnity, and music of the Mass can vary greatly. In a "sung Mass," usually celebrated on special occasions, the priest-celebrant may be assisted by a deacon or perhaps a subdeacon, incense is often used (a symbol of our prayers rising, pleasing to God), and there are other marks of special solemnity. To have a special solemnity when there is only one ordained minister, certain parts of the Mass may be sung or chanted by him, with a choir and the congregation and/or choir responding. The singing, chanting, and special prayers done by the priest and people can vary a good deal from place to place.

Mass is sometimes "concelebrated," that is, a group of priests may take part with the presiding celebrant, sharing in the prayers and readings and all exercising their power to consecrate. This brings out strikingly the unity of the priesthood, particularly in its great role of celebrating the eucharist.

Today there are often different types of Masses for different groups, with the prayers and readings adapted to the particular group—e.g., school children, teenagers, college students, office workers, those in the inner city, suburbanites, professional people, etc.—besides being adapted to the occasion on which the Mass is celebrated.

One modern development, very meaningful to many, is the folk Mass, in which popular folk music is sung in a religious context; for the young, particularly, this type of Mass can be deeply stirring—and, surprisingly, for many older Catholics as well. Also, in some places, during the Liturgy of the Word, slides, films, dancing, and brief dramatic presentations are being used to instruct the people and bring home to them the lessons of God's Word.

A close sense of participation and oneness in love is often best attained when Mass is celebrated among smaller groups. For this reason, some get much out of Mass being celebrated regularly in their homes, for instance, when a group of young people go camping on a retreat weekend. All can participate more fully, adding their insights to the priest's homily.

THE MASS AND CHRISTIAN UNITY

Since the worship of God is the greatest thing we can do on this earth, the way we worship is vitally important. When giving someone a present, we try to find out what will please that person, how we can best express our love by our gift. God in his love helps our worship by showing us how best to do it. As he once guided the Israelites in their worship (cf. Exodus, Leviticus), so now he guides our worship through his Church. Through Christ he gave us the best way we could possibly worship him, the eucharistic service, which developed in the Church as the Mass. This is why many Christians, and especially Catholics, have always been particular about worshipping with other church groups.

However, worship among separated Christians can express the unity we have and also powerfully ask God to unite us further. The Vatican Council here opened new doors: "In certain special circumstances, such as in prayer services for unity and during ecumenical gatherings, it is allowable, indeed desirable that Catholics should join in prayer with their separated brethren" (*Decree on Ecumenism,* no. 8). Nothing is as effective as praying together, to make us experience the unity we have and to make us yearn for further unity.

There are two main principles upon which the practice of such common worship depends: first, that of the unity of the Church which ought to be expressed; and second, that of the sharing in means of grace. The expression of unity very generally forbids common worship. Grace to be obtained sometimes commends it. The concrete course to be adopted . . . is left to the prudent decision of the local episcopal authority . . . the Bishops' Conference . . . or the Holy See. . . . (*Decree on Ecumenism,* no. 8).

Intercommunion between Catholics and other Christians is not yet normally allowed, since this has always been considered the fullest expression of Christian unity—and we are as yet disunited on some basic teachings. However, there could be circumstances in which the grace to be gained by such a practice would outweigh any wrong impression of a premature unity, and intercommunion might be allowed; the eucharist could be a means of unity as well as a sign of it.

The Church's recognition of eucharistic sharing as a means toward unity, and a sign of the unity we already have, is expressed especially in a Vatican Instruction which says that the eucharist may be given to non-

Catholic Christians on particular occasions, determined by the local bishop, and that the bishop may issue guidelines for his priests to follow in this—the Vatican Council's *Decree on Ecumenism,* the Ecumenical Directory of 1967, and the Vatican Instruction of 1972–73. This is not "open communion" by which any baptized Christian would be invited to communion in the Catholic Church; this is not permitted in the Church. Nor is this "intercommunion" in which mutual eucharistic sharing takes place between Catholics and other Churches which have preserved "the substance" of the eucharist.

This refers to the admission to communion of individual non-Catholic Christians who freely and spontaneously "request" it in the Catholic Church. The following summarizes the special circumstances in which a non-Catholic Christian may there take part in communion. It can be done if he or she (1) experiences a serious spiritual need for communion; (2) is physically or psychologically unable to have recourse to a minister of his or her own community; (3) has the same fundamental belief in the eucharist as that of the Roman Catholic Church; (4) is leading a genuinely Christian life; (5) is not forbidden by his or her own church from requesting communion in another church.

Obvious occasions on which a non-Catholic Christian might freely and spontaneously request communion in a Catholic church might include an interfaith marriage, an anniversary, and a first communion.

Often this central, symbolic sacredness of the eucharist and the rules surrounding it are difficult for non-Catholic Christians of good will to understand (and for some more "progressive" Catholics as well). This should be seen not as a denigration of others' status as Christians, but (as with Orthodox Christians) as a way of affirming our particular expression of rootedness in Christ's continual Presence in the midst of a somewhat rootless and swiftly changing world.

Intercommunion among Catholics and Orthodox Christians was allowed by Vatican Council II (if no church of one's own tradition was available) because both have the same Mass and priesthood by apostolic succession; in the United States, however, this is not yet acceptable to both groups. Being unable to communicate together should make Christians yearn for the day when they can do so in full unity—and make them work all the harder for ecumenical understanding.

In the Catholic view the full sacramental sign of unity and grace comes about only through the instrumentality of a priest at Mass. Yet when the eucharist is celebrated in another Church, there is present in some way the reality of the eucharistic mystery; despite the frequent lack of valid priestly orders which express the unity of the Church, there is yet some real presence of Christ in these "other eucharists." A devout non-Catholic receiving the eucharist in his church might have more of the reality of the eucharist than a lukewarm Catholic (*Decree on Ecumenism,* no. 22).

The theological dialogues between Roman Catholic and Anglican theologians, and also between Catholic and Lutheran theologians, have produced statements saying, in effect, that their churches were in substantial agreement in their teaching on the eucharist, and recommending that steps be taken toward intercommunion between their churches. The Roman Catholic-Presbyterian dialogue, and some others, are also moving in this direction.

Certainly Christians who truly desire to be united with Christ and their fellow Christians through communion, and who have sorrow for their sins and love in their heart, are really united in love with Christ and the rest of the Church when they take part in communion in their own particular church. Perhaps, then, one great thing that all Christians can do to bring about unity among themselves is to take part in communion in their own churches whenever they can.

Many today, particularly young people, feel that if they can work together as Christians, they should also, at least on occasion, worship and take part in communion together—and they simply take part in communion together when an occasion seems to warrant it. The theological issues that so divided their elders seem to them to be of no immediate importance, while the need to express their Christian unity in worship and mutual love seems to them to be a movement of the Spirit.

Christians today are drawing closer and closer in their forms of worship. Vatican Council II stressed things dear to non-Catholic Christians: Christ's presence among the people at worship, their full participation, the Word of God read and preached upon, an openness to spontaneity and change in worship, etc. Protestant Christians, on the other hand, are stressing more and more things that Catholics consider vital, particularly the inclusion of the eucharistic prayer and communion as a regular part of the liturgy, and belief in the presence in some way of Christ's unique sacrifice in the eucharistic act.

CHRIST AMONG US AT MASS

When Christ becomes present among us in the eucharist, it is not as if he were coming among his followers for the first time. Christ is already present in the hearts of his people by faith, grace, and love, when they come together to take part in the Mass.

At Mass Christ is among us in several ways. He is in the signs of the eucharist prolonging his sacrifice, and uniting us with himself in his passage to the Father; this great action, we saw, is what the Mass basically is. But Christ is also present in the priest who represents him and who leads the people in worship. He is present speaking to us and opening our hearts through the scripture readings and sermon. And he is present in the communion meal by which he comes to us as food.

Christ is present also in the Christian community as it worships. He is in the midst of his brothers and sisters, the Christian people, worshipping the Father in and through them. He is in each and all, inspiring their love of one another and of the whole human family. "Where two or three are gathered together in my name, there am I in the midst of them" (Matthew 18, 20; Cf. *Constitution on the Sacred Liturgy,* no. 7).

The presence of Christ in these various ways should make us realize why the Mass is so important. Christ loves us so much that he uses all these ways to communicate himself to us, to become united with us, to strengthen us, and to give us his love. "Christ is present from the first word to the last, from one wall of the church to the other" (Fr. Bernard Cooke).

Christ is with us at Mass in all these ways above all to unite us, the Christian community, as one body. He unites us to his sacrifice, presides through the priest, speaks to us in the scriptures, comes to us as food—all in order that we might be truly united in love, that we might become one body with him and with one another. It is at Mass above all that we are united. It is at Mass that we best show our unity. And it is at Mass that we become the presence of Christ in the world.

At Mass we are continually becoming a Church. We saw that the Church is not a static "thing," but the growing, developing way we are united to Christ and one another. It is basically a love relationship, and like any such relationship it must express itself, continually grow and develop. The Mass is the great way the Church grows. Here the Church is continually renewed, cemented, strengthened. Here it worships, grows in love, and receives God's love and teaching.

Were Mass no longer celebrated, the Church would cease to exist. A good gauge of the spiritual health of the Church is the participation of the people in the Mass. Historically, those who have attacked the Church have almost always begun by prohibiting the Mass. "It's the Mass that matters" is an old adage that sums up its place in the Church.

THE CHRISTIAN PEOPLE AT MASS

In the liturgy we pray and sing together because, though many, we are one—and we want to become one. The liturgy should bring about a great awareness of one another—that we need one another and are helped by one another, in worship as in life. We are joined together as we offer our common gift and receive God's gift to us. We join our incompleteness to that of others, and together, as a worshipping family, we most perfectly express our stumbling attempts at union with divinity.

The Mass, then, is not only the best sign of our unity—it also is the great cause of our unity, particularly when we partake together of our great family meal, the "Lord's Supper" (1 Corinthians 10, 17). During the week we are scattered in our homes, factories, schools, and offices. At Mass we come together for the great banquet that makes us one. The more closely we take part in it the more we will appreciate and love our fellow Christians. Christ is here among us in the closest possible way, joining us with himself and one another.

The Mass is our great weekly Christian social event, the family worship of God's people gathered together with Christ. The priest who leads the people never prays in his own name or for himself alone, and the congregation's prayers also are for one another: "The Lord be with you.... Let us pray.... Let us give thanks to God...." The frequent "Amen" of the whole congregation perfectly expresses their unity in love and offering.

Particularly at Mass God's new chosen people use the power of their "royal priesthood. " By their baptism, and again by confirmation, they share in the priesthood of the laity, able to offer perfect worship to God for themselves and others and to bring his graces to the world. They do not claim to be holier than others, but they know Christ is in their midst, using them in a special way, poor instruments though they may be, to spread his love to others. What was said of the Israelites in the Old Testament is now said in the fullest sense of the Christians of the New Testament: **Read 1 Peter 2, 4–10.**

The Mass is meant to bring out the true unity in catholicity of the Church. All races, classes, and social strata should be one in this worship. When we gather together for Mass we should heed St. James' reminder to the first Christians: **Read James 2, 1–4.**

Since the Mass is a family worshipping and eating together, each member has a part to play. Christ is among us, invisibly present as our real head and leader. The bishop is his visible representative who guides our worship so that it is truly a part of the liturgy of the whole Church. The ordained priest is Christ's representative and instrument, and also the leader of the people at this particular Mass; through his Word Christ becomes present in the eucharist, and then he leads us all in offering Christ and ourselves to the Father.

The people's part is to respond to God's Word, to unite themselves to the offering of Christ and to join in the banquet of holy communion. They express their part by praying and singing together, by contributing in some way to the offering, by responding to the great prayers of offering, and above all by taking part together in the eucharist.

> The Church . . . earnestly desires that Christ's faithful, when present at this mystery of faith, should not be there as strangers or silent spectators; on the contrary, through a good understanding of the rites and prayers they should take part in the sacred action, conscious of what they are doing, with devotion and full collaboration. They should be instructed by God's Word and be nourished at the table of the Lord's body; they should give thanks to God; by offering the immaculate victim, not only through the hands of the priest, but also with him, they should learn also to offer themselves; through Christ the Mediator, they should be drawn day by day into ever more perfect union with God and with each other. . . . (*Constitution on the Sacred Liturgy*, no. 48).

Some of the people have special roles, proclaiming the scripture readings (except the gospel) and briefly commenting on the scripture reading, giving other readings, assisting the priest, leading the singing, bringing up the offerings, and acting as lay ministers of the eucharist by helping to distribute communion at Mass.

It takes time to appreciate the liturgy fully, to feel at ease in community worship and to participate actively. The Mass prayers will be led by priests at varying speeds; the Mass becomes so much a part of a priest that it reflects his temperament and background. Some congregations respond with more uniformity and seeming devotion than others. Distractions occur constantly. To adjust to the great reality behind all this takes time and patience.

We should remember, too, that while the Mass is primarily a social and sharing event, there are times when we want to—and should—

pray in our own way during it, expressing our most personal feelings toward God, our deep longings, particular needs, our secret fears and joys — or just being quiet in his presence. There are periods of silence in the Mass to allow this, and it is important that they be respected.

Catholics are expected to assemble for Mass each Sunday, and also on the holydays scattered throughout the year. Only a Catholic with a poor understanding of the meaning of Mass would take this responsibility lightly. Of course, important work, sickness in the family, etc., excuse us from taking part, though perhaps one could join in the Mass prayers at home, or take part on another day. In most places the Sunday or the holyday Mass may be anticipated on the previous evening to make it more meaningful for those taking part.

The holydays in the United States are six: Christmas (Dec. 25), the Octave of Christmas (New Year's Day, Jan. 1), Ascension Thursday (fortieth day after Easter), the Assumption of Mary (Aug. 15), All Saints (Nov. 1), and the Immaculate Conception of Mary (Dec. 8).

We can offer our Mass for anyone, living or dead or for any good intention. Naturally we derive from the Mass what we bring to it. The more faith and love in our worship, the more it will unite us with God and help others. The prayers of the liturgy are not just external ceremonies but actions into which we must enter with our minds and hearts. Two people might attend Mass, one getting a great deal from it, and the other almost nothing.

Even if it is impossible for us to attend Mass daily we should unite ourselves by our sincere intention with Christ's offering in all the Masses of that day throughout the world. During the day, working, suffering, struggling to be good, we can offer ourselves with Christ for the salvation of others, uniting ourselves to his continuing sacrifice.

The priest usually offers each Mass for some particular person or intention, and people sometimes ask a priest to offer Mass for their intention. It has been customary for the person requesting this to make an offering of money (a "stipend") to the priest—not to pay for the Mass, but to help support the priest and the church. This custom comes from the early Church when the people brought to the Mass the things necessary for the sacrifice, for the support of the priests, the poor, etc. St. Paul wrote, ". . . the Lord directed that those who preach the gospel should have their living from the gospel" (1 Corinthians 9, 13–14).

Every Mass, however, is an offering to the whole Church, and the whole Church and each member benefit from each Mass. To better emphasize this, and for other practical reasons, many today want to abolish the practice of Mass stipends, and to provide for the support of priests by a larger regular salary.

The eucharist and the Mass, then, are the center of the Catholic faith. The other sacraments converge on this. Baptism and confirmation lead up to it, and are ideally given at a Mass so that the whole community can take part; penance and the anointing of the sick prepare one for it, and the anointing is ideally done at Mass, so that the whole congregation can join in praying for their ill members; holy orders is given at Mass, and a Catholic couple usually take part in a nuptial Mass when they are united in marriage. After death one's body is brought to the church for a Mass of Christian Burial.

So, then, nothing else has meaning or power except in relation to the eucharist and the Mass. This was brought out at Vatican Council II when each day's session began with a Mass in which all the assembled bishops took part.

Each day Mass is celebrated, normally, in every Catholic parish. It can be a source of daily graces to that whole neighborhood, not in some magical way, but as a special presence of Christ among us radiating his love to *all who take part,* and to all in the vicinity who (believers or not) are in need of his love and help. The Mass, too, can be the center of a priest's day, from which he regularly draws strength for his other activities. Many Catholics take part in Mass on weekdays, and some come daily to draw help from it for their daily lives.

RELIVING CHRIST'S LIFE THROUGH THE LITURGICAL YEAR

Since Christ's life and sacrifice is such a tremendous, infinite reality, we cannot grasp it all at once. It takes time to grasp and be changed by it. The Church in the liturgy presents Christ's life and sacrifice in parts, so that we can live them out event by event.

The liturgical year is the way we relive each year the great events of Christ's life. It is the way the Church each year teaches us in a living way about these events. It is the Church's yearly cycle of feasts, beginning with the First Sunday of Advent (the fourth Sunday before Christmas) and ending with the last Sunday after Pentecost.

Each Mass has an ordinary or unchanging part, and a proper or

changing part which varies according to the liturgical year. Some of the proper or changing prayers may be said or chanted together by the people: the entrance antiphon, the gradual (or tract or alleluia), the offertory antiphon, and the communion antiphon. The lay lector reads the epistle for that day, and the priest or deacon the gospel. The priest reads the collect, the prayer over the gifts, and the prayer after communion.

Through the events of the liturgical year we actually relive, with Christ, the events of his life, death and resurrection. People attend a movie or a play or watch a TV presentation that reenacts the events in the life of a great person. During the liturgical year we reenact the events of Christ's life—but unlike a movie, Christ is actually present in each Mass, and we not only watch, we actually take part in the great events of his life. He is present in a special way at each feast, communicating something special to us each time.

> The liturgical year . . . is not a cold and lifeless representation of the events of the past, or a simple and bare record of a former age. It is rather Christ himself who is ever living in his Church. Here he continues that journey of immense mercy which he lovingly began in his mortal life, going about doing good with the desire of bringing men to know his mysteries and . . . live by them (Pope Pius XII, *Mediator Dei*).

Throughout the liturgical year the Church brings before us God's Word, the bible. The most significant passages are selected and arranged to bring home to us the great events of our salvation. A three-year cycle of scripture readings brings before us all the significant parts of the bible, and the most important parts are repeated each year.

The liturgical year is built around the great cycle of events called the proper of the seasons. The two central feasts, and the two great seasons, are those of Christmas and Easter. Each of these has a season of preparation, the central feast itself with its minor feasts, and a continuation or prolongation of the spirit of the feast:

1. THE CHRISTMAS SEASON—Theme: The Coming of Jesus Christ—The Incarnation

Preparation during the Advent Season—Four Sundays before Christmas (violet vestments). Through prayer, reflection, and self-discipline we prepare ourselves for the coming of Christ.

Celebration—Christmas, December 25. We rejoice that God has come among us and that we have been born with him into the new, eternal life of grace. The lesser feasts that follow are: Holy Family Sunday; the Octave of Christmas or Feast of Mary, Mother of God, on January 1; the Epiphany on January 6 (or the Sunday between January 2 and 8), on which we celebrate the call of the Gentiles to follow Christ; and the Baptism of the Lord (the Sunday after January 6)—(white vestments during this time).

Continuation—Sundays in Ordinary Time, leading up to Lent (green vestments). Here we continue the joy of the Christmas season, the coming of Jesus Christ, and the beginning of his ministry among us with his baptism.

2. THE EASTER SEASON—Theme: Christ's Death and New Life—Our Salvation

Preparation during the Lenten Season, from Ash Wednesday on through Lent (violet vestments). Through this time of special prayer, fasting, and voluntary self-discipline, we repent of our sins which caused Christ's sufferings and bring pain to others. We try to "die" to selfishness, greed, and self-indulgence so that we can "rise" to a new commitment to our life in him at Easter. The last Sunday of Lent is Passion Sunday (Palm Sunday), and we enter Holy Week, the most sacred time of the year.

During Holy Week, the last week of Lent, we reenact in the liturgy the sufferings and death of Christ, taking part in them as much as possible, so that we can bear our sufferings and put aside our sins which are the cause of all suffering. The "Easter Triduum" of Holy Thursday, Good Friday, and Holy Saturday celebrates the great events of these days, each with special services, leading up to the climax of the Church year and of human history.

Celebration of the Triumphal Resurrection of Jesus Christ at Easter—the greatest feast of the Church, and the basis of our faith—begins with the Easter Vigil service on Holy Saturday night and climaxes with the Mass of Easter. The two lesser feasts following upon this are the Ascension of Christ (forty days after Easter) and Pentecost Sunday (fifty days later) (white vestments, except for the red of Pentecost). Through the Sundays after Easter we rejoice at Christ's new life and the triumph of our faith; we try to rise with him from a life dead in sin to one of new fervor, holiness, and love.

At Pentecost we celebrate the coming of the Holy Spirit, the "birthday of the Church," the sending-forth of the community that would spread Christ's teachings and love through the ages. Trinity Sunday, celebrating the mystery of God as three Persons, the divine Life and Love in which we all live and which lives within each of us, concludes this season.

Continuation—the Season of the Year (or Ordinary Time): twenty-four to twenty-eight weeks, through summer and fall (green vestments). Here we continue the Sundays in Ordinary Time that led up to Lent. During these months, guided by the Holy Spirit, we seek to grow in the love and practice of our faith. We are imitating Jesus Christ and looking forward to his second coming. This season ends with the celebration of the feast of Christ the King, the Lord of the Cosmos. Then we begin the liturgical year over again with the Advent Season, our preparation for Christmas.

There is also the Proper of the Saints, the liturgical cycle of lesser importance. In using this we derive inspiration, creativity, and strength from the example of the saints, the outstanding personages of the Church. Often, the date is the day of the saint's death, his "birthday" into eternal life. The Proper of the Mass changes on that day, according to the particular saint; a "Common" is a Proper for a particular type of saint and may be used for a number of similar saints. By bringing before our minds these different saints, the Church wants to teach us that we can imitate Christ's suffering and glorification as they did.

There are ranks of feasts in the Church's liturgy, the most important taking precedence. Sometimes a lesser feast is commemorated by adding some of its prayers to the Proper used that day. Any missal gives the rank of feasts, and includes a calendar telling what Proper is to be used on a particular day. The Proper of the Saints is also in the process of simplification today.

The Divine Office (or the Liturgy of the Hours) is the daily prayer of the Church by which we follow Christ's example and exhortation to "pray," "ask," "seek" during each day (Cf. Matthew 5, 44; Mark 13, 33; Luke 6, 28; John 14, 13ff.). It helps us enter into and prolongs the spirit of the Mass. As Christ prayed continually and periodically through the day (and night), so does his Church. The office is composed mainly of psalms, other scripture readings, hymns, prayers, and outstanding writings from the Church's tradition. It is arranged according to the liturgical year, and is divided into various "hours" or prayers for different parts of the day. It is recited particularly by priests, and may be recited or chanted in choir by monks and other religious.

Today a growing number of lay people are saying part of this "Liturgy of the Hours" as their prayer in the morning and in the evening. The official book for the United States is called *Christian Prayer,* and more and more families are finding that saying it in the morning and evening (at least when they can) gives meaning, strength, and tranquility to their often very difficult workday.

CHRIST AMONG US IN THE EUCHARIST

Christ's presence among us in the eucharist has always been a key teaching of the Christian faith. It has been the constant teaching of the Church from the beginning; the clear belief found in early Christian documents is overwhelming (Cf., for instance, Palmer, *The Sources of Christian Theology,* Newman, 1955, Vol. 1). Through bread and wine Christ becomes present in the eucharistic celebration; somehow Christ himself is now truly present under this form of food as St. Paul says succinctly: **Read 1 Corinthians 11, 27–30.**

Theologians today stress a dynamic or existentialist view of Christ's presence in the eucharist, that he is present with a purpose. He is not just a passive presence in the host, but rather he is present doing something to the Christian communicant, meeting him person-to-person, bringing him life and love. And only one who meets Christ in the eucharist with faith and love derives something from this.

There can be degrees of one person's presence to another: one might vaguely notice a person across the street, or he might pass close to him, he might have a deep conversation with him, etc.—the more each gives of himself, the greater is his communication of himself to another in understanding and love. In the eucharist Christ comes to us in the fullest possible expression and communication of his love. The more we try to be aware of him and what he is doing for us, the more we try to give ourselves to him as we meet him in communion, the more intimate will be our union with him, the greater will be the love and grace we will receive, and the more we will be transformed into him by this experience.

Another way of looking at this is to see the eucharistic meal as a sign through which we meet Christ and by which he expresses or "signifies" his love for us. A man might best express himself and his feelings by playing a violin for us; we would more fully "meet" him by listening to him play than by merely having him present. As the violin is an extension of the violinist, so the consecrated bread and wine are an extension of Christ through which we meet him most fully and are changed by him. Sharing in food expresses refreshment, strength, and a sharing in love—so Christ expresses these things to us, in an infinitely greater way, through the eucharistic food. Through this food Christ expresses himself and his love for us in the most intimate way possible. The more we try to express our love as we take part in communion, the greater our love will grow through it.

We need not take part in the sacrament of reconciliation, or confession, before taking part in holy communion—unless we would be in the situation of being alienated from God and the community by serious sinfulness. To take part in communion before confessing one's alienated state of serious sin, and being reconciled, would be an act of fundamental hypocrisy; we would be publicly proclaiming our unity with the rest of the Church by taking part in this sacrament of unity, while all the time realizing that we are cut off from them by our unrepentant sinfulness. We will see that the purpose of the sacrament of reconciliation (penance or "confession") is particularly to restore us to loving union with the "whole Christ," with Jesus and with our fellow humans.

It might happen, however, that one conscious of being in a state of serious alienation would find it necessary to take part in communion—it might, for instance, be embarrassing not to—and one would not have the opportunity for confession. In this case we should express our sorrow as best we can out of whatever love we can muster, and then have no hesitation about taking part. Jesus' desire would surely be for us to come to him and to share in this healing sacrament.

> *Before "first communion" the sacrament of penance should be available to a child, but there is certainly no obligation* for children to confess unless they are in serious sin, any more than there is for an adult. Those skilled in child psychology, and parents as well, question the ability of a young child to be in a situation of serious sin. Young children are often introduced to this sacrament, and become accustomed to express their sorrow for their sins, through communal penitential rites, as we shall see in chapter 19.

We fast before taking part in holy communion, to help us prepare for it. We normally do not eat or drink for one hour before communion (water or medicine, however, may be taken at any time). Just as one would not spoil his appetite by eating before a special meal, so we sharpen our spiritual appetite for Christ by this bit of self-discipline.

Catholics of the Latin rite usually take communion only under the

appearance of bread. This became customary in the late Middle Ages when the meal aspect of the Mass was being largely overlooked. It is usually more convenient to take part in communion under one form, especially where large city congregations are involved; the whole living Christ is present either under the appearance of bread or that of wine, so it is only necessary to take part in one form.

However, taking part under both forms brings out more fully our sharing in the eucharistic meal as Christ instituted it, and Vatican Council II has once again revived this for special occasions in the Latin rite; the Eastern rites of Catholicism have always communicated under both forms.

Today Latin rite Catholics often take part in communion under both the form of bread and the form of wine. Though the whole living Christ is present under either appearance, bread or wine, taking part under both forms brings out fully our sharing in the eucharistic meal as Christ instituted it.

In most areas of the Church, including the United States, the custom is growing today of taking communion in one's hand. This has been approved by the American bishops, and is the way in which communion was received throughout most of the Church's history. For many this practice is a visible, reverent expression of their desire to feed themselves, as spirtually adult Christians, on the body of Christ.

Some people prefer to dip the consecrated bread in the cup of consecrated wine; it is their way of making this divine food mean more to them as the meal of the "whole Christ." Others today, mostly older people, still wish to have the host of bread placed on their tongue by the priest; their lifelong expression of reverent love in this way is a beautiful thing that should claim our respect.

A Catholic's "Easter duty" means that he must take part in communion once a year, during the Easter season, i.e., from the first Sunday of Lent until Trinity Sunday. Otherwise, while still a Catholic he would not be considered a practicing one, because he has refused to take part in the greatest thing the Church has for him—the help toward which all the other helps of his religion are directed. Christ said: "Truly, truly, I say to you, unless you eat the flesh of the Son of man and drink his blood, you have no life in you. . . ." (John 6, 53).

A good Catholic should take part in communion at least weekly—normally at Sunday Mass, our great Christian family meal. Unfortunately some, from faulty training or timidity, hold back from the eucharist when they could easily take part. They realize they are unworthy, but they should remember what Christ said: "Those who are well have no need of a physician, but those who are sick" (Luke 5, 3). Not to take part in communion is to expect God to accept our gift while refusing his gift.

What Christ does for us in holy communion is shown by this sacrament's sign: he comes to us in the form of a meal, of food. As we must eat to maintain life, to grow and remain strong, so this food is the great means of growing in the life of grace. A preview of this food was the manna by which God kept the Israelites alive in the desert; Christ refers to this and then tells us that he himself will be the food which sustains the infinitely greater and eternal life of grace. **Read Exodus 16, 4–21.**

Read John 6, 47–59. Christ in the eucharist, then, is our "living bread," our greatest way of growing in God's grace-presence, his life within us. As a good meal can have an immediate effect of contentment and satisfaction, so we may sometimes experience a certain spiritual peace and strength after taking part in communion. As food builds energy and strength for the future, so Christ here strengthens us for further temptations. As we are sometimes hungrier, perhaps from hard work, than at other times, so we sometimes need more spiritual strength and should receive Christ more often.

Food must be taken frequently; so our spiritual growth requires frequent reception of the eucharist. Paradoxically this food satisfies, but also increases our hunger: the more we receive Christ, the more we inevitably hunger for God.

Our eucharistic meal is above all our greatest way of being united to one another in the Church. The more we eat together with our family and friends, the more we get to know and understand one another, the stronger our love should grow. So too with this meal. Its greatest effect is the unity of Christ's body, his Church.

By frequently taking part in the eucharist we are gradually transformed into Christ. We share the very life and personality of the risen Christ. We gradually shed our weaknesses and assume something of his own strength. His outlook, his reactions bit by bit become ours. Because we have here a real contact with Christ's risen body, this sacrament is the most effective way of keeping our bodily passions under control; many Christians can testify that it is for them the best way of remedying abuses of sex, drinking, anger, etc.

The more of ourselves we put into celebrating the Mass and par-

taking of the eucharist, the more we will derive from it. Christ is present in the priest and in the people, as we read and listen, preach and sing, and as we offer the great eucharistic prayer of thanks. The better we try to do these things, the more consciously we join ourselves to him, the more we will receive from our union with him in holy communion. The eucharist can be the most intimate, personal, and meaningful union with Christ possible—if we prepare for it and generously give ourselves to him. He gives us himself totally. The rest is up to us.

The eucharist is the greatest way to grow in the Christian life. Each time we take part in the eucharist we repledge ourselves to our baptismal commitment to Christ. The eucharist is the greatest way we grow in faith, hope, and love, the greatest source of light and strength for our prayer, and the surest way to grow in appreciation of the world around us.

Through the eucharist we are already beginning the life of heaven. We are on our way to the final resurrection and our eternal glorification with the Father. Heaven is often referred to in scripture as a banquet, a wedding feast. Now, through this food that is Christ, we are already beginning to take part in it.

Christ's presence in the eucharist in the tabernacle of every Catholic church is a way in which God today dwells among his people with special closeness. This is why our churches are open daily, why people often drop in for a "visit" to share their joys and sorrows with Christ, or just to talk things over. We saw how God was present among the Israelites, invisibly hovering over the Ark of the Covenant in his tabernacle. Today we have God become man in our midst. "And my tabernacle shall be with them and I will be their God, and they shall be my people" (Ezekiel 37, 27).

Because of this presence of Christ, upon entering their churches Catholics sometimes genuflect (go down on the right knee) as an act of adoration before entering the pew. In some places, a bow of the head is made to the tabernacle. Also, the candle kept burning day and night near the altar, usually in a red glass container, signifies this eucharistic presence of Christ in our midst.

We honor Christ in the holy eucharist in many ways. On Holy Thursday each year we celebrate with special liturgical services the great feast of Christ's institution of the holy eucharist at the last supper. On the Sunday after Trinity Sunday we celebrate the feast of Corpus Christi (the body of Christ).

The "Forty Hours Devotion" is a special service of honor and reparation to Christ in the eucharist, held in many Catholic parishes each year; by special Masses, processions, prayers, and preaching we pay him homage. This devotion commemorates the forty hours during which Christ's body was in the tomb before Easter Sunday. During this time, the host is exposed in the monstrance on the altar.

The service of Benediction ("Blessing") consists of putting a large host in a gold monstrance; it is then put on the altar for all to adore, hymns of praise are sung, and the host is incensed; then the priest blesses the people by making the sign of the cross over them with the monstrance containing the host.

The vigil lights or votive candles which one sometimes sees in churches are there to "keep watch" with Christ in place of the people who must be elsewhere. They represent our desire to be with him.

DAILY LIVING: ONE BREAD MAKES US ONE BODY
(1 Corinthians 10, 17)

On the occasion of the first eucharist Christ said, "By this shall all men know that you are my disciples, if you have love for one another." The great thing we should get from the eucharist is a greater love—not only of God but of our neighbor. We prepare best for Mass by attempting to practice some kindness or forgiveness in our daily life—and we best prolong the Mass in our daily life by this same concrete love.

Sincerely and actively taking part in the Mass should make us dynamic, socially-minded Christians. If we are sharing in the Mass as we should, we will become aware of how we are joined with God's family throughout the world. Those who cry for social justice, who are deprived of racial equality, the underprivileged of our city, the poor of other nations, the billions who will never hear of Christ and his love—these needs become ours.

People sometimes remark on Christians who worship on Sunday, but live unchristian lives the rest of the week. All too often this is so. Sometimes it is the result of a wrong emphasis in one's religious upbringing, a stressing of external obligations to the neglect of their inner spirit. However, we should remember Christ's warning not to judge, "that you be not judged." Sometimes seemingly immoral people are struggling against tremendous odds of background, deprivation, strong passions—and at least they manage to worship God and reach out for his help. They might be much worse without Mass.

Also, some cheat themselves of much of Christ's help by not taking part in communion when they attend Mass. They realize their unworthiness, but forget Christ's loving mercy and his desire to come and be their strength. Then, too, those who do communicate regularly may show no striking improvement in their lives, but might be undergoing a gradual, almost imperceptible growth in holiness.

The way many people come to desire union with Christ's Church is by taking part in the Mass. The disciples at Emmaus recognized Christ only in the "breaking of the bread"; they then realized why their hearts were burning within them. So too, many today come to recognize Christ in his Church, and want to be an active part of it, by regularly taking part in the Mass.

SOME SUGGESTIONS FOR . . .

DISCUSSION

Can you understand how the Mass developed and why changes are taking place today?

Can you understand how the Mass and the eucharist are the center of our Catholic faith, and our great way of having Christ among us?

How might one deepen his appreciation of the Mass, and bring from it more love into his daily life?

FURTHER READING

* *The New Yet Old Mass,* Champlin (Ave Maria Press, 1977)—This book deepens our understanding of the Mass and discusses its history, present status, and possibilities for future development.
* *Jesus and the Eucharist,* Guzie (Paulist Press, 1974)—An excellent sourcebook for reflection on the theology of the eucharist, presented in a fresh and insightful way.
* *The Eucharist and the Hunger of the World,* Hellwig (Paulist Press, 1976)—This book is a superb presentation on the meaning of the eucharist, especially as it relates to those going hungry in our world. This is a challenging, conscience-prodding presentation.

* *St. Joseph Daily Missal* (2 vols., Catholic Book Publishing Co.)—A complete daily missal of all the Mass prayers and readings for each day; handy for those who prefer a book of "permanence," rather than the seasonal and disposable booklets in the pews of most parishes.
* *Modern Liturgy Handbook,* Mossi, ed. (Paulist Press, 1976)—An excellent, very imaginative book of creative ideas, suggestions, theological clarifications, and sample liturgies used successfully by congregations. It covers the field, from music and drama to children's liturgies and home celebrations.
* *An Important Office of Immense Love: A Handbook for Eucharistic Ministers,* Champlin (Paulist Press, 1981)—A fine relatively brief "must" for all concerned with their special role as ministers of the eucharist.

FURTHER VIEWING/LISTENING

Celebrate the Mass! (Teleketics, Franciscan Communications)—A series of four filmstrips/cassettes that cover interestingly and well the main aspects of the Mass and our personal involvement in it.

Worshipping Wilma (Teleketics, Franciscan Communications)—13 minutes—Part of "The Changing Sacraments" series. A fine filmstrip on the history of our eucharistic worship.

Bread and Wine (Teleketics, Franciscan Communications)—An excellent, five-minute film on the everyday materials of the eucharist, bread and wine.

PERSONAL REFLECTION

A **"communion of desire"** (less appropriately called a "spiritual communion") can be made by one who cannot take part sacramentally in the eucharistic meal. One does this simply by telling Christ that he believes in his presence in the eucharist, is sorry for his sins, and desires to be united with him. This can deepen one's intimate union with Christ and one's neighbor.

If I cannot be united with Christ sacramentally, I might resolve to do so by desire at Mass this Sunday.

I might also drop into some Catholic church during the week to make a "visit" with Christ in his eucharistic presence—perhaps just sitting there quietly, thinking, and talking things over with him.

16

The Inner Life of a Christian

How can one obtain faith, and why do some people have more faith than others? What sums up the whole of Christ's teaching? How can one get help from prayer?

We have seen how baptism is the climax of one's conversion and the beginning of a totally new life. God lives his own life within us—we share in his life. To live and grow in this life he gives us new powers.

The virtues are attitudes, powers, relationships that we have as a result of God's presence within us. The virtues help us to look at things differently, to act differently, to relate differently to others—to conform ourselves to Christ's way of thinking and acting. They are sometimes called habits, because they make it easier for us to act as Christians should.

The three fundamental virtues of a Christian are faith, hope, and charity or love. They make it easier for us to give ourselves to God, to trust him, and to love him and our neighbor. Those who are not Christians may also have these powers as a result of God's grace-presence within them, but the Christian should be more aware of them, better able to grow in them and thereby witness to Christ's life within himself.

These virtues are meant to grow stronger by our developing them, as any attitude or relationship should between those in love. The virtues are not static "things" but living ways in which we express the grace-life within us. Every time, for instance, that we express our faith by our words and actions, the attitude of faith grows within us and makes easier our next act of faith.

FAITH—ACCEPTANCE AND COMMITMENT

Faith is our saying "yes" to God as he reveals himself to us. It is our response to Christ—he invites us and faith is our acceptance of

256

his invitation. It is something lasting—an attitude, a relationship to God by which we can open ourselves to him.

Faith is the power, the ability to say "I believe" to God in whatever he teaches and to commit ourselves to live by his teachings. When people generally speak of "faith" they mean accepting something on the word of someone else. Daily we make countless acts of this sort of faith: that the food we eat is nourishing and not poisoned, that the car we drive is safe, etc. We do not test these things for ourselves, but take another's word. By the virtue of faith we take God's word for something we cannot prove for ourselves.

There are several aspects or steps to a person's faith: first, faith is a personal contact with Christ, an intimate "meeting" or "encounter" with him. This usually happens gradually, and one's awareness of it is vague, unrecognized. Perhaps one will never recognize it explicitly. But the experience is real, profound, and bit by bit we are changed by it. Through Christ we gradually come into contact with the Triune God.

Then, by faith we believe that what God tells us is true not because we see the evidence for ourselves, but simply because we realize that he is telling us. We become certain that what he has revealed is true, even though we cannot fully understand it. Yet, knowing with a certain degree of clarity that God has spoken is one thing; faith is something further . . .

Faith is ultimately a commitment, a free choice by which we give ourselves to Christ and begin living a whole new way of life. It is a free and personal decision to abandon ourselves to the living God. We are converted, we turn fully toward him, a changed person.

Faith is perhaps best looked at as a dynamic relationship, a living and continual encounter between God and oneself, by which we continually grow in knowledge of him and his will for us, and commit ourselves to live by this.

We have great need of faith because it is the basis of our life with God. Without it we cannot accept God's teachings, nor can we commit ourselves to live by them. Our minds are obviously limited, especially when faced with the mysteries of the infinite God, and our wills are weak.

Faith is like a microscope enabling us to see God's design in the smallest things—though by faith we do not see clearly, but rather "in a mirror dimly, but then (in heaven) face to face" (1 Corinthians 13,

12). It can be compared, also, to a powerful magnet that draws us to God.

There are degrees of this faith-relationship. One person might be able to believe only in God, another might be able to accept the divinity of Jesus Christ, and yet another might perceive the role of the Church—with all sorts of degrees in between.

One might have some faith before being baptized, responding to what he can accept of the truth. Upon becoming a Christian—and particularly upon becoming a Catholic—his faith is broadened, deepened. He is able to accept more of Christ's teachings and commit himself more fully to live them. He is now a conscious, contributing member of God's people and has the Christian community's help to grow in faith.

The faith necessary to be a Catholic Christian—the "gift of faith"—is the power to believe God in whatever he teaches us through his Church, and to commit ourselves to live by those teachings. It is our response to what we now see is the fullness of God's revelation to us. We see that this is much more than we have believed before, and we are determined to live by this new knowledge. We realize that we previously held many good things, but now we see that we are getting more. We feel, somehow, that God wants us to embrace this teaching and way of life. We feel that our spiritual "home" is now in the Catholic Church.

If we have faith, we will show it by a life of love, by good works. "In Christ Jesus," Paul says, the only thing that avails is "faith working through love" (Galatians 5, 6). The faith that would not result in works of love would be counterfeit, spurious, a hypocritical delusion on the part of the "believer": **Read James 2, 14–18.**

> This faith needs to prove its fruitfulness by penetrating the believer's entire life . . . and by activating him toward justice and love, especially regarding the needy (*Constitution on the Church in the Modern World,* no. 21).
>
> *Faith is not an assurance that we are already "saved" regardless of our actions.* If our faith is genuine, good works will follow—but one can always fall away from faith. "I chastise my body," says Paul, "and bring it into subjection, lest perhaps after preaching to others I myself should be rejected" (1 Corinthians 9, 27; cf. 1 Corinthians 10, 12; 13, 2; Philippians 2, 12; James 2, 14–26). On the other hand, we cannot "work" ourselves to heaven; God's gift of grace is necessary, initially

and continually, that we might freely cooperate with him, that we might have the encounter of faith.

Some "unbelievers" show that they have more faith than some who profess Christianity. Their works of mercy and their exemplary lives prove this. Often they put to shame their Christian neighbors. They live according to their conscience, responding to God's call, but without an explicit awareness of it. However, moral goodness is not always a sign of a sincere faith; it might come at least in part from a self-justifying pride.

> Sometimes an unbeliever's rejection of Christianity is ". . . in reality a protest against the evident lack of faith in his Christian surroundings, and an expression of his deeply rooted yearning for the genuine dedication of a lively faith. . . . It is also possible that his self-evident moral endeavors are subconscious pretenses which arise from his disturbed conscience whereby he justifies his defection from the faith" (Bernard Häring, *Christian Renewal in a Changing World,* p. 107).

On the other hand many believers reveal their weak faith by constantly failing in charity. They may attend Church services and keep most of the Church's "rules," but in time of testing they act primarily out of self-interest or they "follow the crowd." They might, for instance, oppose minorities in their neighborhood, object to basic aid to the underprivileged, or adopt as their major goal in life the achieving of a certain material status.

HOW ONE COMES TO FAITH

The way faith comes to an adult is a mysterious, individual, and awesome process. One must be careful here of preconceptions, of assuming that God would or would not act in a particular way. Both the one who is seeking a possible faith and the one who seeks to lead him to faith must hold themselves open to the infinitely free action of the Spirit.

Faith, we know, is a free gift of God which we cannot earn by ourselves. It is God who enables us to have the attitude of faith toward him. Others may help to bring one to faith, but only because God wills to use them for this. "For by grace you have been saved through faith; and this is not your own doing, it is the gift of God—not because of works, lest any man should boast" (Ephesians 2, 8–9).

But we can and must do our part to obtain faith by humbly praying to know the truth and be able to live by it. St. Paul assures us that God ". . . desires all men to be saved and to come to the knowledge of the truth" (1 Timothy 2, 4). St. Mark's gospel tells the story of the father who brought his boy possessed with convulsions to Jesus and asked: " '. . . if you can do anything, have pity on us and help us.' And Jesus said to him, 'If you can! All things are possible to him who believes.' At once the father of the boy cried out, and said with tears, 'I believe; help my unbelief!' " (Mark 9, 21–23). Jesus then cured the boy, showing us that a sincere plea for faith will not go unanswered.

> "Ask and you shall receive," said Christ—and humility is vitally necessary: "Truly, I say to you, whoever does not receive the kingdom of God like a child shall not enter it" (Luke 18, 17). ". . . I thank thee, Father, Lord of heaven and earth, that thou hast hidden these things from the wise and understanding and revealed them to babes" (Matthew 11, 25).

We must also study, sincerely and open-mindedly seeking the truth. In Christ's words, "Seek and you shall find. . . ." We must use our minds, and be always open to truth wherever it may be found. Some have preconceived notions, prejudices that blind them.

> Christ refused to work miracles in his own town of Nazareth, for the people there had the unshakable idea that he was nothing more than a carpenter. Herod was convinced that Christ was merely a great magician; no matter what miracle Christ worked, Herod would only be confirmed in his opinion; so Christ scornfully "made no answer" to his questioning (Luke 23, 6–9).

To obtain faith we must live up to what we already believe. People often cannot see the truth of the Church's teachings because they are clinging to habits of sin. The blatantly immoral Herod and the hypocritical Jewish leaders of Christ's time are examples of this. We must live up to what we see of God's will in order to grasp more: "If anyone desires to do his will, he will know of the teaching whether it is from God. . . ." (John 7, 17).

A person can reject the faith that God is offering him, perhaps because he is proud and unwilling to seek it sincerely, perhaps because he is unwilling to live as he knows he should. God always respects our free will, and never forces himself upon us.

An adult comes to faith in the Church usually gradually and often painfully. It means facing oneself honestly, critically, perhaps breaking old habits, overcoming the fear that one cannot live his new life. Like Christ, one struggles to do the Father's will. And like him, one must die—not physically, but interiorly and often as painfully—in order to live the new life of faith.

Our coming to faith might be like that of the Samaritan woman who met Christ, was upset and embarrassed by him, gradually accepted him, and ended by bringing others to him: **Read John 4, 1–30.**

Faith is a risk, a "leap." The evidence is never so clear that one is forced to believe. A natural explanation can always be given for any divine intervention. To believe is to take a risk—it is the risk, really, of giving oneself to another in total love. The truly convinced believer is willing to risk all that he is sure of, even life itself, for a new life of love with Christ.

Elements of doubt always remain to plague him, and so there is conflict, a struggle over this choice: On the one hand there is the attraction of Christ and the unseen life he promises. On the other, the visible reality and concrete allurements of life here and now.

Some expect a "sign," a special experience or good feeling to assure them of God's presence. But usually God does not work this way. Often he prepares one for faith by allowing one to feel a great need, a discontent, an irritation, a helplessness. Slowly, by humble prayer, by study, and by trying to live a good life, faith usually comes—when we are ready for it and can appreciate it.

Often the example of those who have given all for their belief helps to persuade the sincere seeker—those who give their lives to serve others, truly dedicated and unselfish missionaries, those who are living a day-by-day martyrdom with a self-centered and perhaps neurotic marriage partner, those who do not marry in order to better serve others, or those who commit themselves to working among the poor and uneducated.

Many have been helped in their search for faith by reading the experiences of others who sought and found faith. There are available a number of interesting biographies and reflections of converts and other seekers of the truth, many in paperback editions.

Often believing friends or loved ones can be a great help in arriving at faith. By their love, prayer and exemplary lives they win God's grace for the seeker, and show how to believe. They can make God's love real for the one who is seeking, sometimes supplying for an earlier lack of love that makes God seem remote, unreal. If there is any way to overcome deeply-rooted erroneous notions or previous unpleasant experiences, it is through close contact with a genuine believer, cleric or lay person.

DOUBTING, GROWING, RETURNING TO FAITH

The extent of one's faith depends on the circumstances of one's life, besides God's gift and one's own free response. Faith comes to anyone who is baptized, yet its growth depends on one's background, love relationships, education, etc. It may always remain stunted, through no fault of one's own. God only expects us to respond to the extent that we are able.

Faith is not something that is possessed once and for all, but rather must be constantly renewed. It is a personal relationship that must continually grow, or else it weakens, perhaps dies. It is each instant a free gift of God for which we must continually ask.

We grow in faith by praying for a stronger faith, by publicly expressing our beliefs when opportunities arise, and particularly by trying to live according to our beliefs. Faith is not a flight from a sinful world, nor a sentiment to be kept within our hearts. If it remains only interior, it will die within us. The true Christian realizes that he must freely and openly express his beliefs to others, hoping to bring them as well to a further faith, to love a bit more.

The Christian's commitment of faith is strengthened or weakened by whether or not he lives the Christian life of love. The immoral, uncharitable Christian will soon find that he cannot accept many things in the belief he professes.

The believer must continue to learn more about his beliefs, particularly in our age of rapid change, new knowledge, and consequent confusion. Learning more not only deepens our own faith, but enables us to communicate it to others. The humble and realistic Christian knows that he cannot be constantly concerned with material things and this-worldly knowledge, however good, and yet expect the unseen world of faith to mean much to him.

Uncertainty and doubt will always co-exist with our faith. Faith is not knowledge that frees us from the proddings of doubt. Faith rather gives a certain deep direction, a meaning, illumination, purposefulness to our life. God will never overwhelm us with proofs that will force us to believe. An unbeliever can always give a logical, rational explanation for any of God's actions in history. This is because God loves us—he seeks to persuade rather than compel our assent.

The believer bred in the Christian faith must often painfully discard the uncomplicated faith of childhood and adolescence, and form a new, adult, simpler, deeper, more mature and realistic belief. This means for many a "crisis of faith"—usually in the late teens or early twenties, though it can come earlier or later—often involving a rejection of many of the Church's "rules" and structures.

Believers for the first time then face a challenge to what they have always accepted. They see now that they must be personally involved in and committed to living what they profess. They examine their beliefs critically, testing their power and relevance in their life. They see the weaknesses of the Church, the mediocrity of many Christians, and the dedication of many unbelievers. They may find the Church's moral code difficult to live with and they may wonder if it is not largely unrealistic. They must now distinguish the core of Christian belief from what is peripheral, the teachings of Christ from the weak human instruments who propose them, the Christian faith as they may have been taught it from what it really is.

Mature persons will realize their own weakness and their critical need of guidance during this period of massive doubt. They will realize that they must now study their faith on an adult level, that they cannot solve the problems of a sophisticated adulthood with an adolescent's knowledge of religion. They will also face their own moral weaknesses and realize that they are open to the promptings of pride and sensuality and the enticements of material success. They will humbly pray ". . . help my unbelief!" (Mark 9, 23). Finally, hopefully, they will emerge from this period of crisis recommitted to a new, mature and realistic Christian faith.

Vatican Council II took note of modern conditions which are causing growing numbers of people to abandon religious practices, but pointed out that this also results in "a more critical ability to distinguish religion from a magical view of the world and from the superstitions which still circulate, purifies (religion), and exacts day by day a more personal and explicit adherence to faith. As a result many persons are achieving a more vivid sense of God" (*Constitution on the Church in the Modern World,* no. 7).

IN THE LITURGY

The Church provides many opportunities for publicly renewing our commitment of faith. The choice of faith made at baptism is reaffirmed by us whenever we take part in any of the sacraments, but particularly in confirmation and at Mass. A renewal of baptismal promises is part of the Easter Vigil service, the high point of the Church's yearly liturgy. Taking part in a parish mission, a retreat, or cursillo are other ways of renewing one's faith.

HOPE—A CONFIDENT EXPECTATION

Following from faith is the virtue of hope, an attitude of confident expectation or trust in God, joined to a deep yearning for him. Christian hope is not "hope" as we use the word in our everyday speech. It is not just wishing or yearning for something. It is, rather, based on what we have already experienced, what we have already had a "taste" of (however small)—that God is real, totally loving toward us, and faithful to his promises. Thus it is a confident looking-forward, an expectation or yearning for what we know is to come fully. Sometimes this confident knowing is subject to periods of confusion and even doubt, as with faith, but it remains deep within us.

God gives us this power. It is a deep desire for God and for the consummation of his plan that all mankind will be united in perfect love with him and with one another, without any more strife, injustice, or pain. But hope is also confidence that his plan will come about fully—and that God will give us all the help necessary to do our part to attain our eternal destiny and that of all humanity. It is also the day-by-day confidence that he will take care of all our needs and will never abandon us for an instant.

By our attitude of hope we put our lives into his hands, confident that he will forgive our sins, and will turn even misfortune and suffering to mankind's eternal advantage. Paul describes the effects of hope in his own life when he says, "Now may the God of hope fill you with joy and peace in believing. . . ." (Romans 15, 13).

Despair and presumption are the two attitudes by which people reject God's gift of hope. Despair is a loss of hope in God's mercy, the depressing conviction that one is rejected by God or that God is not interested in us. It is the most tragic of attitudes, because it forgets that God has revealed himself to be above all else a God of merciful love, willing to undergo a humiliating death to convince us that he cares for each of us.

A presumptuous person, on the other hand, counts on obtaining heaven while doing little or nothing to overcome his sins. He considers God the "man upstairs" who "understands" his unrepentant wrongdoing. Such a person acts like a spoiled child and must sooner or later mature and face the living God.

People especially need hope in today's world because of the tensions and insecurity, the crimes, wars, and suffering of the innocent which we see all around us. To avoid discouragement or bitterness, to realize that good will come from the evil about us we need the joyful trust that is hope. "Cast all your anxiety upon him, because he cares for you" (1 Peter 5, 7).

The way to grow in hope is to pray for it and confidently and expectantly to live according to our beliefs. We should pray for this attitude of confidence in God especially during times of temptation, when depressed, in mental or physical suffering. St. Paul suffered as few of us will, but he wrote from his imprisonment:

> ... no one took my part; all deserted me. May it not be charged against them! But the Lord stood by me and gave me strength to proclaim the Word fully, that all the Gentiles might hear it. So I was rescued from the lion's mouth. The Lord will rescue me from every evil and save me for his heavenly kingdom. To him be the glory forever and ever. Amen (2 Timothy 4, 16–18).

LOVE—THE ONE THING NECESSARY

The central point in Christ's teaching, the topic to which he returned again and again, is love. No religion or philosophy before or since has taught love as Christ did. It distinguishes his teaching from all others. Only Christianity presents a transcendent, all-powerful God who is yet so loving that he becomes one of us, is disgraced and dies for us, and sums up his whole teaching in love: **Read Matthew 22, 34–40.**

Again he said: "A new commandment I give to you, that you love one another; even as I have loved you, that you also love one another. By this all men will know that you are my disciples, if you have love for one another!" (John 13, 34–35).

The greatest virtue, then, is charity or love: the power given us by God to love him above all things, and to love our neighbors as ourselves. "So faith, hope, love abide, these three; but the greatest of these is love" (1 Corinthians 13, 13). Love is not merely an emotion or feeling; it is not only physical or sexual; it is primarily spiritual, something that comes from God himself. "God *is* love," says St. John. The more of him we have in our life, the more we truly love— and the more we have of true love in our life, the more of him we possess.

Love is concern for another's happiness. Consider human love; when we are truly in love, we are primarily concerned with making another happy. It is the very opposite of selfish concern for oneself. We want to please our beloved in every way possible.

When we love, we want to be united with the one we love. We gladly give ourselves, seeking to be united with our beloved. The more we give ourselves, the more we fulfill ourselves—this is the paradox of love. We give ourselves in order to make the one we love happy. Their happiness, in turn, brings us the greatest happiness.

By the virtue of love we give ourselves to God and our neighbor, to make them happy. We are primarily concerned with what God wants, and the happiness of our neighbor. We give ourselves to God, either directly or through our neighbor, in order to be united with him. And in this, paradoxically, we fulfill ourselves and attain limitless, eternal happiness.

God has shown us how to love by loving us first and totally. He has given us everything we have, our life, our talents, our destiny. Above all he has given us himself—the root meaning of "charity" is the total gift of oneself. When man was unfaithful to him, he became one of us and died to prove his love for us. "In this is love, not that we loved God but that he loved us and sent his Son to be the expiation for our sins" (1 John 4, 10).

Though he has no need of us whatever, he yet gives us a share in his own life. He is constantly concerned with our happiness, and wants us to be united with himself. His love knows no limits, for he is willing to forgive us again and again.

We love God above all things by making him the center of our life, by trying to please him in everything we do. As a man would love the one woman who really matters to him, and she him, so we should try to love God. We will think of him each morning, offering ourselves to him. We are united with him especially by worshipping him, showing our love before others, celebrating it at special times. We respect his name, as a man would tolerate no one speaking disrespectfully of the woman he loves.

We want to know more about him, his desires, his friends, his innermost life, as a boy and girl falling in love take joy in discovering more and more about each other; the bible particularly tells us about him. We know that love is tested, not in the initial glow of romance but in the long hours of suffering, and so we are willing to bear the cross with him. As the center of our life, God will always come first: our family, friends, work, recreation should never cause us to do anything that would lead us away from him. We should be able to face him honestly each night, ask his pardon for any unselfishness, and quietly, peacefully renew our profession of love.

If we truly love God, we will also love our neighbor, our fellow human beings. It is impossible to love God and not love our neighbor. "Beloved, if God so loves us, we also ought to love one another. . . . If anyone says, 'I love God,' and hates his brother, he is a liar . . ." (1 John 4, 11. 19). Everyone else has been created by God for heaven, just as we; they have the same dignity, are redeemed by Christ, and have God living within them.

Our neighbor is everyone, whatever his race, color, background, belief, or talents. Christ made this clear in the famous parable of the Good Samaritan: **Read Luke 10, 29–37.**

We should note that this story, Christ's great example of love of neighbor, concerns love between men of different racial and religious backgrounds. Christ's fellow Jews looked on the Samaritans as an inferior breed and as heretics. Christ told the Samaritan woman that "salvation is from the Jews," but he significantly chooses a Samaritan as his great example of brotherly love.

Any form of prejudice or discrimination is a rejection of Christian love: if we do not associate with our neighbor because of his race, his lack of social position, his past moral failings, Christ makes clear that at the end we will be judged by the way we treat our "least" brethren: **Read Matthew 25, 35–40.**

Everyone must consider his every neighbor without exception as another self. . . . In our times a special obligation binds us to make ourselves the neighbor of every person without exception, and to actively help him when he comes across our path, whether he be an old person abandoned by all, a foreign laborer unjustly looked down upon, a refugee, a child born of an unlawful union and wrongly suffering for a sin he did not commit, or a hungry person who disturbs our conscience by recalling the voice of the Lord, "As long as you did it for one of these the least of my brethren, you did it for me" (Matthew 25, 40) (*Constitution on the Church in the Modern World,* no. 27).

We fail to love our neighbor by not respecting him: by anger, by jealousy or envy of his good fortune, and particularly by hatred or desiring revenge. If we love our neighbor we will also respect his right to the truth and to his good name: lying, calumny, and detraction—we should, remember that we have no right to repeat something uncharitable, even if true—are thoroughly unchristian.

Our Christian love of our neighbor should manifest itself in certain ways, often called the four "moral virtues." These are four aspects our love of others should include: prudence, by which we form our right judgment as to what to do or not do; justice, by which we give everyone what is due him; fortitude, courageously facing opposition to our Christian ideals; and temperance, controlling our passions so as to use them more fully to truly love.

True love means that we respect the one we love, especially in the use of the power of sex. If we truly love one another, we do not ever want to treat that person as a "thing," as the outlet for our passions. True love cannot be forced, as for example a man demanding that a woman give in to him. Nor can it be bought, as a woman might confusedly try to do in giving herself to a man. Even a couple deeply in love, who experience how naturally sexual intimacies can express their love, must realize that a true and mature love requires discipline and sacrifice. They will fully express their love sexually only when the marriage commitment has been made.

The love of our enemies is the test of a truly committed follower of Christ. This is as difficult for us today as when Christ first proposed it. Sometimes we may have to defend ourselves or others against our enemies, but always and only to the extent that we must, never using immoral means, and always ready to forgive without exacting vengeance. Christ said simply that if almighty God puts up with their sins, so should we: **Read Matthew 5, 43–48.**

Christ as he hung dying at the hands of his enemies gave us a strong hint as to why we should forgive those who have hurt us: "Father, forgive them; for they know not what they do" (Luke 23, 34). People rarely, if ever, hurt us with full deliberation—and even then they may think their action is for our good. Usually people bring to their actions all sorts of personality traits, pressures, and drives from their background and daily environment. Only if we are fully aware of these can we judge them—and God alone knows all that is within us, driving us on. So Christ says, "Judge not, that you be not judged" (Matthew 7, 1).

> *A modern poet/monk/mystic gives this insight about love:* "All life is love.... Men love, whether they know it or not, and never cease loving.... Love is. All else is not, because in the same measure in which things partake of being, they partake of love. All that is not love, is not. ... The conflicts which beset our world are not caused by the absence of love, but by a love which refuses to acknowledge itself as such, a love which has become ill because it fails to recognize its true nature and has lost sight of its object.... Cruelty is misdirected love, and hate is frustrated love...." (Thomas Merton's introduction to Ernesto Cardenal's *To Live Is To Love*).

Last, but certainly not least, we must love ourselves. Christ implied this when he told us to "love your neighbor as you love *yourself.*" True self-love, as opposed to narcissistic self-centeredness, is a virtue to be cultivated. It means several things: accepting yourself, your whole self, good and bad (as God actually does), "liking yourself" and realizing that, despite your failings, you have rights and abilities to contribute to others and to the world (whatever your IQ, personality, looks, etc.). It means not being afraid of being alone, enjoying your own company, and not needing continual social "strokes," popularity, or the constant approval of others. Lastly, it is gradually developing a sense of self-worth, self-respect, an ever-growing sense of your own identity, of your ability to have intimate, enduring relationships.

CHRISTIAN PRAYER

By prayer we communicate with God, open ourselves to him, find out his will for us and obtain the strength to live as we should. In the first chapter we saw the vital necessity of praying. We can never know God or ourselves unless we pray. In its daily necessity prayer can be compared to eating: sometimes it is enjoyable, sometimes not; it is more enjoyable for some than for others, but a daily necessity for everyone; as physical nourishment is more pleasurable if prepared well, so will our prayer be if we prepare by reading and reflection.

The prayer of a Christian has a new meaning and new power. The Christian knows that his prayer is joined to Christ's prayer by the power of the lay priesthood he received in baptism. He knows that Christ's prayer is already answered, that it can never fail to bring about good. The more we are consciously united in prayer to Christ, the more God can communicate himself to us and spread love in the world.

A Christian's prayer is especially powerful when he is united with Christ's whole body in the prayers of the liturgy. Whenever one unites with other believers in prayer, Christ promises his special help: "Where two or three are gathered in my name, there am I in the midst of them" (Matthew 18, 20). But the private individual prayer of a Christian also has special power:

> The spiritual life . . . is not limited solely to participation in the liturgy. The Christian is called to pray with his brethren, but he must also enter into his chamber to pray to the Father in secret (Matthew 6, 6); further, according to the teaching of the apostle, he should pray without ceasing (1 Thessalonians 5, 17) (*Constitution on the Sacred Liturgy,* no. 12).

Prayer is the great way in which God allows us to work with him in saving ourselves and others, in spreading love in the world. We do not pray to ask God for something he does not know we need; nor is prayer a cringing before a whimsical deity, coaxing him into giving what we want; nor is it something we give to God, "bargaining" with him, that he might proportionately help us in return. Rather it is our small but real contribution to the love which runs the universe. God wills that we shall obtain certain things for ourselves and others if we do our part, contribute our love, by expressing our reliance on him in prayer. He treats us like adults, with dignity and even reverence, giving us a part in the working out of our salvation.

The most important moments of our life are the moments of prayer—and someday we may come to see this. We can learn more in one second of pure prayer than in all the books ever written. We can accomplish more by one fervent moment of prayer than we might otherwise in a lifetime of effort. "The man of prayer is a worker of miracles" (Léon Bloy).

> In the heart of Manhattan there is a convent of contemplative nuns whose lives are devoted to praying and doing penance for that vast city. Unnoticed, this little group of women have a sublime and joyous faith that God is using them to bring his love to others. In almost every metropolitan center of the free world a group like this lives a life of prayer and self-discipline to open the hearts of the rest of us to God's love.

When we pray we try to make contact with God, become aware of him, open ourselves to his love and his desires for us. We can never become aware of his will for us unless we pause to pray. This is our basic human need—to give ourselves to the will of the Father, who after all knows what is best for us. So underlying our every prayer must be Christ's prayer: "My Father . . . not as I will, but as thou wilt" (Matthew 26, 39).

How does prayer for others "work"? Here we are before a great mystery, so we cannot analyze prayer in a mechanistic way. But we can say this: When we pray for others, our love reaches out to them through God—when we speak to him about them, his all-powerful love is joined to our poor, stumbling love, and now our joint love enfolds them. Our prayer for others also changes ourselves, so that we are more open and loving toward those others and toward God.

We should not pray to God, however, to do what we should do ourselves. Sometimes, instead of asking him to help someone or remedy some situation, we should be doing something about it ourselves. Our prayer should normally thank him for making us such wonderful and capable human beings, who can do such great things in partnership with him, and a plea that we might use our talents in the best way possible. At times, however, our weakness overwhelms us and we can only beg for his all-powerful help.

It is often hard to pray, and we must discipline ourselves to do it. Our sins keep us from prayer and disturb us when we do pray. In praying we must learn humble, loving adoration before our infinite God; pride resists this, inciting us to rely on our own efforts. Our minds are usually undisciplined, at least in trying to contact the Infinite, and so distractions are natural. We must mobilize our divided faculties, and compel them to pay attention to what God is doing in us. Prayer usually does not develop spontaneously, but is learned by persevering practice.

Christ tells us how to pray: first, confidently and perseveringly. We must remind ourselves that God always answers, in some way, every sincere prayer. Christ's parable is plain: **Read Luke 18, 1–7.**

We must be humble and reverent as we pray. We are sinners putting ourselves in the presence of the infinite God. Moses took off his shoes to approach the burning bush; and the Church uses Jacob's cry to describe a house of prayer: "Terrible is this place!" We sign ourselves and take holy water to remind ourselves that we are coming into God's presence to pray. We often kneel when we pray, an ancient, spontaneous attitude of reverence. We realize our sinfulness, but we are like the child who knows it is loved and trusts in its Father's forgiveness: **Read Luke 18, 10–14.**

Christ also reminds us that our prayer should be simple and sincere—the best prayers are usually those in our own words. "And in praying do not heap up empty phrases as the Gentiles do, for they think that they will be heard for their many words" (Matthew 6, 7). We may say just a few simple, stumbling words—reaching out, to make contact, to realize his presence.

Perhaps we will form no words, but just have a quiet awareness of his presence. Prayer can be seeing God at work in the things that happen each day, a peaceful realization that he is intimately with us, concerned about us. "Be still, and know that I am God!" (Psalm 46, 10).

It is often good to have a spiritual guide (or "director"), usually a priest or religious, though it might be a gifted lay person—someone to whom we can talk freely about our personal spiritual life, our life of prayer, who seems to understand us, and who can make suggestions for our further growth. Sometimes a prayer group can also give one another some profitable spiritual direction.

The Church's pattern for prayer is an ancient one: to God the Father, through Jesus Christ, in union with the Holy Spirit within us. We are children weak but loved, coming before our all-powerful Father. We try to unite ourselves with Christ, our Brother—he is there leading us to the Father—and we realize that it is the Spirit within us who is actually praying, who gives form, power and meaning to our prayers—so we try to hold ourselves open to the Spirit.

The Church often prays by prepared formulas which are meant to help us. These are most often prayers that have helped billions of people throughout Christian history, and so might be helpful to us as well. Sometimes it is hard to become used to praying in set words, especially when the prayer is gone through rapidly. Anything done over and over tends to become hurried, but we should remember that the attention of the will is what is important, the attempt to make contact with God—just as a couple in love may talk for hours and later are unable to tell what they discussed.

We should pray often, several times a day if possible. Prayer should be habit but not routine. We read how Christ many times "withdrew ... and prayed" (Luke 5, 16; Matthew 14, 23; Mark 6, 46, etc.) and sometimes he spent the night in prayer. Our prayers need not be lengthy, as long as we try to have some sense of "making contact" with God. Nor should we feel obligated to say a particular formula of prayer which is no longer meaningful.

Some good times to pray are in the morning upon arising and in the evening before retiring; when in special need of help, as in time of temptation, or before making an important decision; also, before and after meals. The family might gather for a moment in the morning before going off to work or school, or particularly before supper. Some couples pray for a few moments before going out on a date.

We will get much more out of our prayer if we prepare for it by reading spiritual books, particularly the bible. It is only natural that prayer will be difficult if we put no spiritual thoughts into our minds. "Meditative reading" is an excellent way of doing this: reading a bit, thinking over what we have read, then speaking to God in our own words whatever comes to mind.

Many times we will get nothing out of our attempts to pray. Everyone who seriously tries to reach God experiences this. Our prayer has no fervor: it seems to be cold, mechanical repetition. Often God himself seems to have disappeared, and we may even wonder whether he exists at all. We should expect this: God "hides" from us, perhaps so that we realize how much we need him and so that we will reach out for him all the more. He wants us to mature spiritually, to grow in "naked faith," and so he takes away our feelings of fervor. We are sharing in Christ's desolation, in this worst of his sufferings—and as with hin, this is the very time when we are accomplishing the most to spread love in the world.

We should pray for everyone and anyone—for all mankind, especially those close to us, those for whom we have a responsibility, those who need it the most, sinners, those for whom God is not real, and for our enemies. Our prayer can also embrace all creatures, including those who may be on other planets, that they too will attain their destiny with God. Our prayer truly has no limits.

Often the greatest help we can give someone is to pray for him. A crippled person may need help in standing and we reach out and help him up, or someone may be in pain or sorrow and we comfort him with words of sympathy—or we extend to him the love-power of our prayer and we help him as much and perhaps more.

We should remember that worship is our highest form of prayer—adoring, praising, thanking God for his goodness, instead of constantly asking for help. The great "practitioners of prayer," the saints and mystics, prayed mostly by pouring out their gratitude, admiration, and awe before the Lord.

DAILY LIVING: LOVE IN OUR LIFE

Our life with God, with his grace-presence within us, gives us fantastic new powers. By the virtues we can live the very life of Christ—the life of heaven already is a part of us. The whole purpose of our life is to grow in grace and the virtues, especially in love.

To be a successful Christian there is only one thing we have to do: love. Faith is meant to end in love, and the whole purpose of prayer is to make us love more. Conversely, if a Christian does not truly love, his Christianity is in vain. We might profess our beliefs and keep all the Church's rules, but unless we honestly love it is all a sham.

We cannot prove our love of God except by loving our fellow man. Jesus Christ loved God precisely by loving his fellow man. In his act of dying he loved God perfectly, by loving us to the extent of giving his life for us.

We cannot love everyone at once. But perhaps we could try to commit ourselves to one other person who is unlike us in some way, someone to whom we normally would not be attracted, but who needs our help, and whom circumstances have brought into our life.

At the very least we can try to be aware of someone in our life who is in need of love, whom we can consistently treat with kindness: someone insecure, or hypersensitive, or narrow and unimaginative, or perhaps one who is moody or melancholy—someone whom we can say is "the least of my brethren" (Matthew 26, 40).

> What people can do with the help of God's grace brings to mind the highly-publicized trip to Europe some years ago of a woman who went there to have an abortion of her deformed thalidomide baby. A Catholic couple wrote her a letter at the time, which said in part: "We have read that you have been advised to kill this unborn child because it might not be normal. . . . We have eight children and feel that we are about due to care for one who is handicapped. If your baby is born with handicaps, we will be happy to take him and raise him as our own. He will have ten of us to love him. I told the older children of the situation, and asked them if they would be willing to give up something they might want, in order that this child be allowed to live and be loved and be given the care he'll need. . . . I asked them if they would love our little one less if he didn't have arms or legs, and the incredulous looks told me they couldn't understand how that would make any difference. . . . If you should decide to let us adopt your baby, please get in touch with us through. . . ." (*America* magazine, Dec. 15, 1962).
>
> Their letter went unanswered. The woman had her abortion. But the world was richer for the Christian love manifested by this family.

SOME SUGGESTIONS FOR . . .

DISCUSSION

> Can you understand why coming to faith, and growing in faith, are often painful?
> What aspect of loving one's neighbor do you find the most difficult?
> What particularly do you find the most helpful in your attempts to pray?

FURTHER READING

* *Teach Us to Pray,* Louf (Paulist Press, 1975)—A wonderfully incisive little book, in which the author starts from zero because "the props have suddenly collapsed . . . and now the Lord can build everything up again, from scratch." The author is a man of profound prayer with much indeed to say to us concerning "learning a little about God."

* *The Journey Inwards,* Happold (John Knox Press, 1968)—A short but "packed" book on meditation and contemplation, uniting the insights of the East with those of Christianity. A simple introduction, beautifully done, for the ordinary person.

* *The Inner Eye of Love,* Johnston (Harper & Row, 1978)—The author skillfully shows us how to pray more deeply, sharpen our mystical abilities and better open ourselves to God. He gives us much help from his background in Eastern religions.

* *Living Simply Through the Day: Spiritual Survival in a Complex Age,* Edwards (Paulist Press, 1977)—A superbly simple and practical handbook of ways to simplify our prayer and our lives; the author, an Episcopal priest, draws deeply on his knowledge of Eastern meditative techniques, presenting them with wonderful clarity. A more recent book by the same author is *Spiritual Friend (Paulist Press, 1979), an excellent, practical guide for anyone searching for the "special friendship" of support one Christian can give another—a new, imaginative approach to the ancient practice of spiritual direction.

* *The Hour of the Unexpected,* Shea (Argus Communications, 1977)—A wonderful book of poetic, prayerful, profound reflections on the most ordinary—and unexpected—things of life that show us God. By the same author is *Stories of Faith (Thomas More Press, 1980), an excellent book on discovering the meaning of our own life's story, our experience of relating to the mystery of God, the meaning of church, where we share our God-stories, and how we can and should retell for ourselves Jesus' story. Rich in incisively beautiful imagery, Fr. Shea again helps us discover what we can so easily miss.

* *New Seeds of Contemplation,* Merton (New Directions, 1972)—A spiritual classic by the famous Trappist monk who taught so many of us so much about the life of the spirit.

* *The Fire and the Cloud,* Fleming, ed. (Paulist Press, 1978)—An excellent selection of excerpts from the great Catholic spiritual writings from the first century to the twentieth.

* *The Other Side of Silence,* Kelsey (Paulist Press, 1976)—A fine, comprehensive study of religious experience by a fine psychologist. It includes helpful, practical, concrete "ways to go" in the last chapter.

* *Mysticism: A Study and an Anthology,* Happold (Penguin, 1970)—This is still probably the finest study of Eastern and Western mysticism in print today; easy to read and inspiring.

* *Daily We Touch Him,* Pennington (Doubleday, 1977)—A simple, practical book on praying and religious experience; very popular.

* *Why Am I Afraid To Tell You Who I Am?* Powell (Argus Communications, 1969)—An outstanding yet brief book that has sold over a million copies. Like all of Fr. Powell's books, this is sensitive, penetrating, practical, and never beyond the grasp—or the attention-span—of the average reader.

* *Life Maps,* Fowler and Keen (Winston Press, 1978)—A "breakthrough" work on the various stages of faith/moral development building on the work of Piaget, Kohlberg, etc. An excellent book, and a "must" for all interested in the development of faith.
* *Trajectories in Faith,* by Fowler & Lovin (Abingdon, 1980) takes five famous people and traces the developmental stages through their lives.

FURTHER VIEWING/LISTENING

The Stringbean (ROA Films)—17 minutes—A hauntingly wistful little masterpiece about an old woman, her faith, and her optimism.

Billy's Mime (Paulist Productions)—An award-winning poetic parable of a young boy's relationship with Jesus within.

With Just a Little Trust (Teleketics, Franciscan Communications)—A film of an urban ghetto widow with three children, feeling moving despair over keeping her family together on a very low income, and her mother, whose great faith and courage helps her surmount almost impossible obstacles.

The Flawed Magi (Paulist Productions)—A perceptive probe into human motivation, and how we learn to love: a successful entertainer does a charity show at a county jail and discovers that he is empty inside.

Stages of Faith, Fowler (NCR Cassettes)—Eight cassettes with study guide, dealing with the author's faith-development stages as outlined in the book, *Life Maps.*

PERSONAL REFLECTION

I should treat at least one other person with true Christian love. I might reread the story of the Good Samaritan (Luke 10, 29–37) and then pray that I might honestly put it into practice in the next few days.

17

Our Christian Presence in the World

What of Christians who are concerned only with getting themselves to heaven? What practical things can one do to show concern for others? What can the average Christian do about the glaring injustices in our world? What can one do to bring about peace in our world? What does the sacrament of confirmation do for us?

OUR CHRISTIAN PRESENCE OF SERVICE

A self-centered Christian is no Christian at all. We cannot attain heaven alone. Following Christ, our God who came to share what he had with us, Christians try to share their faith and love with others. Millions today are without any strong religious or moral convictions. Millions more suffer from a gross lack of love and concern, in conditions of hunger, destitution and hopelessness. The need of countless people for something to believe in, for a faith to give meaning to their life, or for someone to show a bit of caring concern over their poverty and powerlessness is painfully evident to anyone who looks honestly at our world today.

A Christian is a serving person, a ministering person, one who witnesses to his or her belief by loving words and actions. The original apostles had a unique role as witnesses of the resurrection and sharers in Christ's own, personal love. They were sent forth by him to serve their fellow human beings, as he had, by sharing their belief and their love. Each Christian today also shares in the privilege of being Christ's chosen representative, speaking about him in his name and loving others as truly parts of him, of his Body. In this loving service it is the Holy Spirit, the Spirit of Christ, who is working within one, using one in a special way to teach and help others.

The particular sign of a follower of Christ is concern for the neglected, the poor and underprivileged. Jesus simply says, "As long as you did it for one of these, the least of my brethren, you did it for me" (Matthew 25, 40). He identifies himself with those who are the "least." Any true follower of his will therefore see something of him, something of beauty and divinity, particularly in those who are lacking. **Read, and ponder, Matthew 25, 31ff.**

Groups, formal and informal, work in the Church today in many forms of Christian service. Teaching, caring for the elderly and for the disabled, helping the poor in various ways, "consciousness-raising," helping those who are not able to cope receive what is legally and rightfully theirs, improving the quality of a neighborhood, working for decent housing, political action and lobbying for those unable to help themselves, feeding and housing the poor, nursing services for the sick, child care, aiding children and adults with disabilities, etc.—these are just a few of the works that groups in the Church are undertaking today.

Some groups train lay people for service in foreign countries, some work among those in need here at home, and some groups do both. These "lay missionaries" may be either married or single, and they usually volunteer to serve for a few years. Examples of these are the Grail, the Glenmary Lay Volunteers, the Jesuit Volunteers, the Maryknoll Lay Missionaries, the Papal Volunteers for Latin America, the Association for International Development, the Lay Mission Helpers Association, the International Catholic Liaison, the Young Christian Workers, the Catholic Worker Houses of Hospitality, the Latin American Mission Program, and the Missionaries of Charity.

THE DIGNITY AND SACREDNESS OF EACH HUMAN LIFE

A basic teaching of the Church is that of an individual's most basic right, the right to life—and especially in recent times, a person's right to live with dignity and with a just share of the material necessities for a dignified life. Though sometimes observed more in the breach than in practice (e.g., the Wars of Religion, the Crusades and the Inquisition), yet when history is considered as a whole, the Church and church people most often emerge as the champions of this most fundamental human right. Today, particularly, Christians are becoming more and more conscious of this right. It is hard to ignore the fact that millions are being deprived of their right to live, and to live in freedom, justice, dignity and peace.

> *Unfortunately our culture often tends to shunt many old and "useless" people into retirement and nursing homes, into institutions that have often (realistically) been called "people bins."* Our prison system still too often makes only meager efforts at rehabilitating those who enter prison, despite proven successes in rehabilitating tens of thousands. Many mental institutions continue to routinely use inhumane treatments and unnecessarily incapacitating drugs to control patients' behavior.
>
> *A growing number of disabled people have been making truly astounding progress in recent years* in educating themselves and living productive (and often inspiring) lives. The government financial aid these truly "exceptional" people have gotten in the past several years amounts to $2.00 per year for each taxpayer. Yet half the U.S. population will be permanently or temporarily disabled during their lifetime.

Enlightened Christians and others today see the measureless value and dignity of each human life, from conception to death. Taking human life is always objectively evil—whether of an unborn infant, one disabled at birth, an innocent victim of crime, a condemned criminal, or a useless old person. The subjective evil of taking life, however, must be judged carefully in the light of moral principles.

> *Most of the developed nations of the world—as well as many not as technologically advanced—have abolished capital punishment, without any reservations.* The National Conference of Catholic Bishops went on record against capital punishment in 1974, and again in 1980. In the words of Archbishop John Quinn, formerly head of the Conference, "Capital punishment, like the crimes for which it is imposed, only serves to cheapen human life, and further perpetuates a 'chain of violence' as the means of guiding and protecting our society."
>
> *Despite the expressed will of the great majority of Americans for effective control of handguns, as shown in poll after poll, the "gun lobby" continues to defeat every effort toward this.* The American bishops have for years been asking for effective legislation for national controls on the use of handguns. In Christ's plain words to Peter, who used his sword to defend Christ from seizure by his enemies and eventual death: "He who lives by the sword will perish by the sword."
>
> *In the area of genetic research, developments are coming faster than almost anyone could predict, confronting us with many moral dilemmas and decisions.* Mankind must be courageous and dedicated in working to solve problems of infertility, as well as those of genetic defects that

cause abnormal children. But many scientists, as well as others, realize that we must also have the far-sighted courage to proceed with care and caution where human subjects and human life are concerned. The ultimate question here is the total good-over-evil of this for humanity as a whole, for generations yet unborn.

Regarding the bringing about of human life outside the womb, i.e., the producing of "test-tube babies" by "in vitro" fertilization, Catholic moral thinkers—along with many other moralists—have reservations. There can be here a manipulation of a human person at inception, and a practice that might have grave long-range results.

The patenting and marketing of new life forms, including marketing for financial profit of human genetic material—our own life-technology left in the hands of profit-making corporations—is of concern to many, scientists, religionists, and humanists alike. It certainly seems evident that the broadest possible public interest must now be involved. Future genetic-engineering can mean replacing defective genes that produce abnormalities—an evidently laudable, promising prospect. But it could also mean the attempted production of flawless or "perfect" human beings (positive eugenics). Pressing questions arise here: Once we begin manipulatively breeding human children—"baby-making"—where will we stop? What consititutes the most desirable human being? Who decides this? And what happens to the unfit, the undesirable, that are costly to maintain?

Abortion is wrong because it takes away an innocent infant's right to life. Today's genetic evidence indicates overwhelmingly that the embryo and fetus is a full human person. The best proof that it is human from conception is simply that it is the product of a *human* couple, both of whom have *human* genetic structures.

The unborn infant has a right to life, as does any human person, no matter what age, or in what condition. If we take innocent human life at its inception because this is judged to be for the good of others—even for the child's good—there is logically nothing to prevent society from one day doing away with anyone judged to be useless, incapacitated, a burden on society, or simply unwanted.

Obviously, an infant should, ideally, be wanted by the parent(s). But to give this as a reason for an abortion, particularly in the United States, is simply fallacious. Even babies of mixed racial background are wanted by numerous childless American couples—and in almost every area of the country, long adoptive procedures must be undergone to assure that the baby will have the best home possible.

Yet, responding to the very real need of (for example) an unwed, pregnant teenager and her need of understanding, counseling, and practical help, the organization called "Birthright" (with approximately 250 centers in the United States, and growing in other countries as well), offers free medical, psychological, and other support to anyone, both during pregnancy and after birth. Volunteers and professionals, including a growing number of doctors, are giving their services to Birthright centers.

OUR CHRISTIAN COMMITMENT TO JUSTICE

Our respect for others' dignity and our Christian love are most basically proved by our sense of justice, our willingness to share with those in need. To be treated with justice or fairness is something we desire and need from childhood. Our heavenly Father has given his human children enough resources—natural resources, and those of human talent and ingenuity—for all his children on earth to have a just share of what is necessary for a dignified human life: a sufficient diet, a decent place to live, humane working conditions and a just wage, the education of one's children and sufficient leisure.

Our planet's resources can easily give these basic necessities for a dignified human life to every person on earth—and to many more besides. This has been shown by numerous studies. The basic problem is distribution. A relatively few "have," while most by far are "have nots." Most of us in the United States—and in Western Europe, Japan, the OPEC countries, and most Iron Curtain countries—not only have what we need for a dignified human life, but have far more than we need. At the same time, the majority of our fellow humans lack proper nourishment, decent housing, sufficient clothing, productive work, and even minimally adequate education.

"Some people are needy because other people are greedy," is the way eight-year-old Marc summed it up when he was told to conceive of our world as a village of 100 people: 70 people of the 100 are unable to read, 50 of them are suffering from malnutrition, and 15 will die before they are 5 years old. Of the 100, 30 earn less than $200 yearly, and over 80 live in slum-type housing. Six of the 100 are Americans, and these six have 40% of the village's entire income.

In the United States itself today almost 30 million people live below poverty level. Fifteen percent suffer from some serious form of malnutrition. A quarter of our senior citizens must go without some necessities to pay their bills each month. Today many people are hard-pressed by inflation, yet the upper and upper-middle class of our society, taken together, throw away as garbage enough edible food to feed all our deprived people adequately—as well as tens of millions of hungry people in the third world.

Despite some advances in recent years, there is still the helpless "rage" of the people of our ghettos, urban and rural, black, brown, and white. These roughly 14,000,000 Americans live each day hungry, sometimes very hungry. Besides the malnutrition which weakens them mentally and physically, their housing conditions are filthy, their education is far below average, and joblessness is their constantly depressing companion. The temptation to violence, or to escape into drugs or alcohol, is constantly with them. Many simply have no hope.

Christian social justice works to change unjust "structures" and institutions of society—as well as individuals—to conform to Christ's teachings on simple justice and love. It works to overcome the "institutionalized greed" of many corporations and conglomerates, the excessive profits that accrue to a small minority—those who have more and more, while most of the world's people have less and less—and who feel little or no obligation to share with those in need. Christian social justice upholds the right of workers to organize to be paid a just wage and have decent working conditions. It also works to eradicate the corrupt practices of some labor unions and their officials. Christian social justice tries to stop the exploitation of the poor that often accompanies the development of the less developed countries where corrupt local officials, financed by a wealthy few, work hand in glove with the military, assuring stability for investments, but at the expense of the basic human rights of their own people. **Read Luke 16, 19–36**

> *Wealth is not wrong in itself, but it can easily be a detriment to following Christ and a continual temptation to pride, arrogance, greed, political corruption and injustice.* Jesus permitted no one to follow him without that person giving his accumulated wealth to the poor (Cf. Mark 10, 17–22), and he said that it is "easier for a camel to get through the eye of a needle than for a rich man to enter the kingdom of heaven" (Mark 10, 25). His parable of the rich man and Lazarus, given above, clearly says that those who indulge their affluence, while giving token "crumbs" to the poor, will simply not attain salvation. The early Christian Church took him seriously and practiced a communal shar-

ing of their possessions (Cf. Acts, chapters 2, 3, 4; 2 Corinthians 6, 10; 8).

Vatican Council II makes clear what everyone has a right to: "There must be made available to all everything necessary for leading a truly human life, such as food, clothing and shelter, the right to freely choose a state of life and to found a family, the right to education, to employment, to a good reputation, to respect, to be informed, to be able to act in accord with the upright norms of one's own conscience, to protection of privacy, and to rightful freedom in religious matters also" (*Constitution on the Church in the Modern World,* no. 26).

The Council speaks further regarding the traditionally affirmed right to private property, and it addresses those who think it is sufficient to occasionally give a bit of charity after all their other needs and wants have been satisfied:

"Persons should regard their lawful possessions not merely as their own but also as common property.... The right to have a share of earthly goods sufficient for oneself and one's family belongs to everyone.... People are obliged to come to the relief of the poor, and to do so not merely out of their superfluous goods. If a person is in extreme necessity, such a one has the right to take from the riches of others what he or she needs.... This Council urges all ... to remember the (early Christian) saying: 'Feed those dying of hunger, because if you have not fed them you have killed them' " (*Constitution on the Church in the Modern World,* no. 69).

Pope Paul VI's encyclical, "On the Development of Peoples" (1967), concerns the critical situation of the widening gap between the "have" and the "have not" nations of the world. It spells out practical norms for worldwide Christian social action, and should be studied in detail by one seriously wanting to live as a Christian in today's world.

The central message of the encyclical is a call for social and economic justice on a global scale. Then the pope summed up what is most inimical in the intrinsic greed-orientation of much of our economic thinking: "the baseless theory which considers profit the key motive for economic progress, competition as the supreme law of economics, and private ownership of the means of production as an absolute right that has no limits and carries no corresponding social responsibilities. This has led to dictatorships and the international imperialism of money."

Next Pope Paul challenged our well-fed complacency with some practical tests of our Christianity and humanity: "Let each man examine his conscience, a conscience that conveys a new message for our times. Is he prepared to support out of his own pocket works and undertakings organized in favor of the most destitute? Is he ready to pay higher taxes so that the public authorities can intensify their efforts in favor of development? Is he ready to pay a higher price for imported goods so that the producer may be more justly rewarded? . . . When so many people are hungry, when so many families suffer from destitution, when so many remain steeped in ignorance, when so many schools, hospitals and homes worthy of the name remain to be built, all public or private squandering of wealth, all expenditure prompted by motives of national personal ostentation, every exhausting armaments race, becomes an intolerable scandal. We are conscious of our duty to denounce it. Would that those in authority listen to our words before it is too late."

Pope John Paul II's encyclical, "Redeemer of Man," also sharply criticizes dehumanizing economic and political systems. He says that both Marxist determinism and Western consumerism exalt materialism at the expense of the spirit and undermine the dignity of the individual human being.

When Pope John Paul visited the United States and the United Nations, he said plainly:

"It is not right that the standard of living of the rich countries should seek to maintain itself by draining off a great part of the reserve of energy and raw materials that are meant to serve the whole of humanity. . . . Riches and freedom create a special obligation (toward those who lack them)."

A growing movement in the Church for social justice, particularly in Latin America, is based on "liberation theology" or the theology of the oppressed. As is well known, there is poverty, exploitation, and political oppression in many nations of Central and South America. Tens of millions suffer from poverty, malnutrition, and political oppression, while a very small number (usually of the traditionally wealthy families) control the economy and live luxuriously, allied often with ruthless military leaders who pay lip service to democracy.

The Latin American bishops' conference at Medellín in 1968 confronted this problem and the great majority spoke out in a now-famous statement signaling that the Church would henceforth be the main champion for social change in Latin America. The bishops said simply that Christians and their Churches cannot be silent, ignore their share of responsibility for change, or remain inactive. As a result, many bishops, clergy and laity have been confronting governments and institutions that oppress and dehumanize the poor and are destroying whole native cultures; there are today daily incidents of bishops, priests and lay people being imprisoned, tortured, killed, or simply "disappearing."

The third Latin American Bishops' Conference at Puebla, Mexico in 1979 reaffirmed this commitment to labor for the material betterment of their oppressed people, as well as for their spiritual needs. Following the lead of Pope John Paul II, who opened the conference, the bishops noted the dangers of both a simplistic Marxist solution to their countries' social problems, and the even more present danger of exploitive capitalism—particularly multinational corporations, (many controlled by U.S.-dominated corporate conglomerates) who are aligned with the oppressing elite of their own countries, i.e., military dictatorships, greedy landholders and exploitive industrialists.

Lay people, particularly, have been wonderfully and courageously active in movements for social reform in Latin America, as well as numerous bishops, priests and religious. "Conscientization" is the amazing phenomenon of largely uneducated and impoverished peasants coming gradually to realize their human (and divine) dignity, and their right to demand a more just share of what they produce.

A growing phenomenon in many Latin American countries is the "Christian base communities," in which small groups of lay people and clergy meet together regularly to pray and to reflect on their experiences—in the light of the scriptures—in trying daily to live dignified Christian lives amid exploitive, impoverished, and unjust living conditions. Often they meet secretly, in danger of death, torture, and imprisonment.

OUR CHRISTIAN COMMITMENT TO PEACE

Where there is no justice, there is violence—or, put another way, "Peace is the fruit of justice," as St. Augustine perceived centuries ago. If people live in conditions of injustice, violence will inevitably result. This was the meaning of Mother Teresa of Calcutta's receiving the Nobel Peace Prize for 1979. Why give a nun, who has spent most of her life working among the poorest of the world's poor, this most distinguished award for peace? In her own words, "Greed is the greatest obstacle to peace in the world today—greed for power, for money, and for fame." So the fact of injustice, that some people are needy because other people are greedy, is the greatest obstacle to peace in the world.

Thus Pope John Paul II warned Latin American leaders, during his trip to Brazil, to make "profound and courageous reforms" on behalf of the human dignity of the oppressed poor. Or else, he predicted, they will all "fall victim to the forces of violence." He concluded, "Each one of you must make his choice at this historic hour."

The Christian ideal is clearly set down in Christ's words and in the example of his own life. We must use only peaceful, non-violent means to achieve the purpose of his gospel, a just and loving world as a prelude to an eternity of peace, love, and joy. We saw previously Christ's uncompromising words to St. Peter, after Peter had used his sword to defend Christ against seizure by his enemies and eventual death: "Put your sword back into its place, for all who take up the sword will perish by the sword" (Matthew 26, 51–53). Then Christ set the example for his followers through the centuries allowing himself to be unjustly scourged, mocked, and put to death.

There are those who point out that this is an imperfect world, that violence is permitted as a last resort in a just war or just revolution against a tyrannical government. They point out that there would today be no United States of America unless a war had been used against injustice, or that Hitler, for instance, could have conquered the world unless force had been used to stop him. This does indeed pose a dilemma for most Christians, and thus the "just war" theory evolved over the centuries.

The traditional conditions under which a just war may be fought are: (1) there is a just cause, (2) every possible peaceful way of settling the conflict has been taken, (3) the war is declared by a legitimate authority, and (4) the means used to fight the war will not do more harm than the purpose sought in going to war. Especially with regard to this latter norm, the Vietnam War, for instance, had become immoral, in the view of the great number of theologians today.

Certain means of warfare are plainly unchristian and immoral. The fact that so-called Christian nations have used them in the past is all the more reason for plainly repudiating them now. Some are: attempted destruction of entire cities or of extensive areas along with their population, indiscriminate bombing of populated areas, bombing or terrorist tactics aimed at civilians to weaken the morale of the enemy, torture of prisoners, use of chemical or biological weapons excluded by international agreement, indiscriminate use of napalm, acts of reprisal against prisoners of war or civilians, depriving large numbers of the civilian population of food through crop destruction, demands of unconditional surrender which kill reasonable hopes of a negotiated settlement, and the use of nuclear weapons designed for mass destruction of whole populations. If an enemy uses these or other immoral means, it gives us no right to retaliate in kind. The test of a Christian is the willingness to act as one when others do not.

The Christian ideal and purpose is obviously the elimination of all warfare, the way of Jesus and his closest followers, as we have said. In modern times, the Church's position has been evolving—particularly since Pope John XXIII's encyclical "Peace on Earth" (1963)—from a kind of opposition to but pained acceptance of the inevitability of war (and the just war position) toward one of continual condemnation of the arms race, nuclear proliferation, and the strategy of deterrence, and toward a constant encouragement of every effort to achieve world peace, and a vindication of the rights of conscientious objectors and Christian pacifists.

> *Vatican Council II had said this in 1965 about war and the arms race:* "Any act of war aimed indiscriminately at the destruction of entire cities or extensive areas along with their population is a crime against God and man himself. It merits unequivocal and unhesitating condemnation. . . . The arms race is an utterly treacherous trap for humanity, and one which injures the poor to an intolerable degree. . . . It is our clear duty, then, to strain every muscle as we work for the time when all war can be completely outlawed by international consent. . . ." (*The Church in the Modern World,* nos. 80–82).

Perhaps one's conscience will lead him to be a conscientious objector. Such a person certainly deserves the support of the Christian community. More and more parishes and dioceses are offering draft counseling facilities to help young men be informed about their choices and about how to best form their conscience in this regard.

The American bishops have long called for at least a recognition of the principle of selective conscientious objection—men who, for instance, would have fought against Hitler, or in defense of the fifty states, found it hard to justify our continued presence in Vietnam. Unfortunately the government has not yet seen fit to recognize this principle. Of course, the true pacifist—Christian or not—believes that it is morally wrong for him to fight in *any* war. There are other Christians who opt for following their consciences as part of the armed forces. Encouragingly, a growing number of military-based parishes have active education programs on these questions of justice and peace.

CHRIST SENDS US THE HOLY SPIRIT
IN CONFIRMATION

At baptism we were united to Christ and born into the life of grace. We come forth as children of God from the "womb" of baptismal water. Yet, as we know from everyday life, children are self-centered, concerned primarily with taking care of themselves. Gradually they must mature and become adults. They must become concerned with others, more sharing and more responsible. So, too, we must mature spiritually. Christ through his Church gives us the way whereby we continue our spiritual growth, now as adults, aware of our responsibilities, sharing our spiritual life and values with others. This is the sacrament of confirmation.

Confirmation is the sacrament in which Christ sends the Holy Spirit to make us mature, adult Christians, completing the process of Christian initiation begun at baptism. "Confirmation" means a strengthening—this sacrament strengthens, increases and completes what we received at baptism. We are now empowered by the Holy Spirit to minister to others, in the fullest sense, for the rest of our lives. Confirmation is the public expression or celebration of this emerging spiritual maturity, marking our entrance into full-fledged adulthood in the Christian community.

At confirmation Christ sends the Holy Spirit in a fuller outpouring of his indwelling presence. At baptism we had received by grace the presence of the Trinity within us. Now we receive a great increase of God's grace-presence, and particularly an increase of the presence of the Holy Spirit.

Confirmation leads the Christian to a deeper life of the spirit. Prayer, contemplation and meditation are ways in which this life of the spirit manifests itself in the life of a Christian. The whole spiritual life is rooted in the coming of the Holy Spirit who dwells in the believer and who directs and guides each person who is attentive to that presence within. Preparation for receiving the sacrament of confirmation focuses on the qualities of the spiritual part of life so that we can come to experience the peace and joy of that rich inner life which flows from the coming of the Holy Spirit.

The Holy Spirit is especially associated with maturely and courageously "bearing witness" to our beliefs and moral convictions. The

Spirit often moved the Old Testament prophets to bear witness. Luke points out how the Spirit inspired those associated with Christ's coming: Mary, Elizabeth, Zachary, Simeon (chapters 1 and 2).

Christ himself is given the Spirit by his Father. When he goes forth to preach the gospel, the Spirit inspires him:

> Now ... when Jesus also had been baptized and was praying, heaven was opened, and the Holy Spirit descended upon him in bodily form, as a dove.... And Jesus, full of the Holy Spirit, returned from the Jordan, and was led by the Spirit for forty days in the wilderness.... (Luke 3, 21–22 and 4, 1).
>
> And Jesus returned in the power of the Spirit into Galilee; and a report concerning him went out through all the surrounding country. And he taught in their synagogues, being glorified by all. And he came to Nazareth ... and he went to the synagogue ... on the sabbath day. And he stood up to read ... the book of the prophet Isaiah.... "The Spirit of the Lord is upon me, because he has anointed me to preach good news to the poor...." (Luke 4, 14–18).

Christ promised to his Church the Holy Spirit that he had received from the Father. When Christ sent his apostles to carry on his mission, he predicted that they would be persecuted, but that the Spirit would sustain them and speak through them (Matthew 10, 16–22). Further, he told the apostles that "the Spirit of truth" would be with them forever (John 14, 16). After his resurrection the Spirit came in his fullness to Christ. Then, about to leave his apostles, he gave them the great promise:

> But you shall receive power when the Holy Spirit has come upon you, and you shall be my witness in Jerusalem and in all Judea and Samaria, and to the ends of the earth (Acts 1, 8).

We saw how Christ fulfilled his promise and sent the Holy Spirit on Pentecost, transforming the fearful and confused apostles into courageous and eloquent witnesses. Amid a violent wind and tongues of fire, they "were all filled with the Holy Spirit" (Acts 2, 4). This could indeed be called their confirmation. On another occasion after this "they were all filled with the Holy Spirit and spoke the Word of God with boldness" (Acts 4, 31). Threatened by the authorities, they answered, "... we cannot but speak of what we have seen and heard.... We must obey God rather than men!" (Acts 4, 20; 5, 29).

Scourged by the authorities, "they departed from the presence of the council, rejoicing that they were counted worthy to suffer dishonor for the name (of Jesus). And every day in the temple and at home they did not cease teaching and preaching Jesus as the Christ" (Acts 4, 41–42).

The incident of Stephen, the Church's first martyr, is typical. Courageously professing his faith in Christ, he underwent death by stoning, "being full of the Holy Spirit" (Acts 7, 55). Especially during the first three centuries, a time of almost continuous persecution and courageous witnessing, we read of the activity of the Holy Spirit. Today, too, there are many who are strengthened by the Holy Spirit as they suffer and die for their convictions, especially for justice and freedom for the world's deprived and oppressed people.

At our confirmation the Holy Spirit comes to us, giving us a special, deepened power to maturely understand and profess our faith. Confirmation is our personal Pentecost. As at baptism the mystery of Christ's passing from death to life becomes visible in our life, so by the ceremony of confirmation we can envision the event of Pentecost happening to us.

The apostles gave others the Holy Spirit by the ordinary ancient way of imposing hands on them. From time immemorial the laying on of hands had been connected with the gift of the Spirit among God's people. It was only natural, then, for the apostles to use this for what was to become confirmation. We see this, for instance, after some converts had been baptized in Samaria: **Read Acts 8, 14–17.**

The sign or ceremony of confirmation is the imposition of the bishop's hands and anointing of the forehead with chrism. This ceremony gradually developed over the centuries as the essential part of the sacrament, best expressing the interior coming of the Spirit with power and strength. As the apostles gave the Holy Spirit by imposing hands on those who were baptized, so today the bishop and priests present lay their hands on those to be confirmed. Then the bishop anoints the forehead of each with chrism (a perfumed oil blessed by the bishop), and says, "N., receive the seal of the Holy Spirit, the gift of the Father."

Oil symbolizes strength, and this oil particularly symbolizes the strength we are given to share in Christ's work as prophet, priest, and king. We are given the strength to teach in his name with greater power and maturity, to share more fully his priesthood, and to lead others to his kingdom. The name of this oil, "chrism," and the word Christ have the same root. Oil was used in ancient times by soldiers in preparation for battle, and by athletes, and today it is used by people to make their bodies limber and strong.

By confirmation we share particularly in the prophetic work of Christ—teaching and bearing witness as he did—so we should have confidence when we speak of our religious convictions. The Holy Spirit illumines our minds so that we may better understand and explain the things of God. He deepens our faith so that we can more clearly and intelligently tell of it to others. Whether we realize it or not, however poor our words seem, we have something of Christ's own power and forcefulness in our witnessing. **Read Matthew 10, 19–20; 1 Corinthians 2, 9–13.**

> *In today's Church many lay men and women are outstandingly using their prophetic gifts.* While the prophetic function of teaching truth belongs in the strict sense to the authorities of the Church, it belongs as well to the whole Church and particularly to those gifted with this charism. A modern theologian has written perceptively: Prophecy within the Church is a remedy against corruption on all levels. There are times when the officers of the Church fail to speak as they ought; those who utter the authentic voice of the Church in such moments are prophets. There are times when the hierarchy itself needs to be redeemed from corruption; those who rebuke it are prophets. Prophecy in such times of need can be either speech or action. Prophecy is not found in any class or level in the Church; and it is not limited to men. . . . However . . . there are true prophets and false prophets. . . . The true prophet is recognized not only by the criterion of concord with the traditional faith of the Church, but also by whether his message supports unity in faith and in love, or whether it makes for disunity (John L. McKenzie, *Authority in the Church*, New York: Sheed, Andrews and McMeel).

By confirmation we share more fully in Christ's priestly powers, deriving more from the Mass and sacraments. We can now particularly pray for those who do not have his truth and bring them his grace. We are changed interiorly, and this change within us is called the "character" of confirmation. By our baptismal character we received the power to take part in the Mass and other sacraments; by this character of confirmation we can take part in them as mature adults.

By confirmation the Holy Spirit inspires and aids us to help develop the society in which we live. It is the social sacrament. It makes us more aware of our opportunities and responsibilities as members of society. We develop the powers of our confirmation by trying to make the world a better place—by prayer, study, and by joining with others to bring this about. Vatican Council II comments succinctly about often-overlooked virtues that confirmed Christians should have in today's world: "They should also hold in high esteem professional skill, family and civic spirit, and the virtues relating to social behavior, namely, honesty, justice, sincerity, kindness, and courage. . . ." (*Decree on the Apostolate of the Laity*, no. 4).

Each person has special gifts that can—and should—be used for the good of all, for the whole Church. We spoke of these earlier in chapter 9: the Spirit inspires our efforts, unifies them, and makes them truly effective. "Now there are varieties of gifts, but the same Spirit . . . varieties of service . . . for the common good" (1 Corinthians 12, 4–7). Vatican Council II said succinctly and strongly: "Each believer has the right and duty to use them in the Church and in the world for the good of mankind and for the upbuilding of the Church" (*Decree on the Apostolate of the Laity*, no. 3).

St. Paul describes the special gifts evident among the first Christians: **Read 1 Corinthians 12, 8–11.** Today we may not be gifted in as extraordinary and clearly noticeable ways, but there are quiet, everyday miracles of love, the healing of battered egos, those truly knowledgeable in little but important things, the older and mature who often speak with tongues of true wisdom, etc. All we need do is pay attention, and we can gradually discern giftedness all about us.

In response to Vatican Council II, which stressed the vital need of lay people taking part in Church affairs, diocesan and parish councils of clergy and laity have been set up in most places. In this way the clergy and laity consult regularly with one another and with the bishop, and the gifts and talents of all can be used for the good of the parish, the diocese, and in the nation and world as well (Cf. also chapter 21).

We take part in confirmation only once, because it permanently changes us (like baptism). We take on for life new powers and social responsibilities. It can take a lifetime of Christian living to bring to completion the lifelong interior commitment of the Spirit to us, and vice versa, in our confirmation.

The bishop or a priest delegated by him ordinarily gives confirma-

tion. A pastor may confirm his parishioners in danger of death, as can hospital chaplains with their patients, or any priest if empowered. A priest receiving converts into the Church gives those persons confirmation as part of their Christian initiation, or their reception into full communion with the Catholic Church.

Since confirmation completes baptism, it was given in the ancient Church immediately after baptism, as part of the same rite or ceremony of Christian initiation. Gradually, in the West, the two sacraments became separated, and confirmation would usually be given when a child began to mature, about the age of puberty. Some, however, have kept the practice of infant confirmation: in the Eastern Rites and in some parts of the Latin Church it is still given with baptism.

It is up to the local bishop to determine the age for confirmation and some guidelines for deciding whether one has sufficient understanding and a mature Christian commitment to take part in it; the bishop usually consults with his priests' "senate," with his diocesan council, or with other groups of religious and lay people about these guidelines.

Adults who are being initiated into the Catholic Church as converts are confirmed along with their baptism or reception into the Church by the priest who receives them as part of the full rite of Christian initiation. Those who are already baptized Christians, of course, would not be rebaptized or need to take part in the full process of Christian initiation. They would take part in confirmation—which would be an especially mature commitment and reception of the Spirit—and for the first time fully partake of the eucharist, the great sacrament that above all makes us one Body.

If those who have already received confirmation in a Protestant Church should desire to become Catholics, they would take part in the Catholic sacrament of confirmation at their reception into the Catholic Church.

The whole parish community should be as much a part of the celebration of confirmation as possible. We saw earlier that the process of conversion, and the sacraments of Christian initiation, are mutual commitments of love. Converted, fully initiated Christians commit themselves to be a part of the worship and life particularly of their local church community—and the church community pledges its support along the rest of life's way. Thus, this sacrament—as ideally with all the others—normally takes place within the Mass, our great act of worship which makes us literally one within Christ's Body.

We use the name of a saint at confirmation. We may use our baptismal name, or we may take an additional name, of a favorite saint, as another patron and model to bring us closer to Christ. If we take an additional name, we should choose someone whose life inspires us in a committed and courageous way.

There is a sponsor at confirmation, representing the commitment to the young adult's spiritual growth of the whole Church community. One may use one's baptismal sponsor or may choose someone else. If one does choose another sponsor, that person should be a practicing Catholic, of mature age, of either sex, and, most importantly, a person who will help one develop in maturing, adult faith. Sometimes when a group is confirmed, a man and woman will sponsor the whole group; they symbolize the whole parish community.

DAILY LIVING: BEING OPEN TO THE SPIRIT, PEACEFUL AND PRODDING

The Spirit is the one who, in the practical situations of life, inspires our choices, our willing, our sensitivity, our acting—if we but let him. He moves us to see how we should best plan for and react to the events of our life, and he prompts us toward what is best to do in times of trouble, pain and confusion. He stirs within us the grace of continual conversion, of understanding, and of compassion, and he gives us mature, unselfish sensitivity, and also the courage to act as we know we should.

Pope John XXIII, the old man who brought new life to the Catholic Church, said that our day is a "new Pentecost," and he called our times the age of the Holy Spirit. Many today are becoming more open to the Spirit, moving toward a sensitive, sharing, adult faith—and away from a self-centered and childishly narrow and threatened view of life.

An adult, loving faith will help us see honestly the pressing needs of our time and inspire us to do something about them. They are summed up in this chapter: the need of each human person to have his or her dignity respected and the right of each to live in conditions of justice and basic human decency, sharing the earth's goods.

Mother Teresa of Calcutta says simply that we who think ourselves fortunate are in fact the unfortunate ones. We who have so many material things are so often driven by them to aggressivity, over-competitiveness, over-achievement, "me-ness," insensitivity, and just plain greed. But we also have so much more potential to act effectively, to use our co-creativity and technology, our comparative wealth and abilities to bring justice and peace to our own country and to the world.

Pope John Paul II challenged us from a Brazil slum: "Look around you a bit. Does it not hurt your heart? Do you not feel stings of conscience for your surplus and your abundance?" Some are looking around and are acting in truly effective ways:

> Instead of opting out of the political process, many are asking for accountability from their elected representatives, informing themselves about candidates' voting records and the Christian and human rights issues involved, and are joining together with others to see that their votes make a difference. Some are becoming aware of the power of consumer boycotts: they persevere, are willing to sacrifice their time and personal interests for a more just, more loving society, and are starting to make a difference. Every diocese has social justice and peace groups that welcome any help or interest, however small. Often people in business and politics are not aware of what they can do to correct injustices and help make a better world; more and more dioceses and parishes are conducting study and discussion sessions in which different viewpoints are heard and practical conscience-decisions are arrived at.

The hardest thing of all, of course, is to boycott our own inbuilt tendency toward "consumerism," toward succumbing to the temptation that we must have the latest and the best. Our technology (which has done so much good) can more and more subtly take over our lives. We can let machines and their products become our masters and overlook the things that cost little or nothing.

> There is the inexpensive gift that says "I love you" better than an expensive adult toy—the simple beauties of nature, of making do without gadgetry, the small creative joys of making things ourselves, of working together—and giving the money we save to those in need. Best of all, we can give some of our time—however little—to sharing ourselves with someone who needs a bit more faith, hope and love.

SOME SUGGESTIONS FOR ...

DISCUSSION

Can you see a priority among human rights, e.g., that the right to the food and basic goods needed for a decent life has precedence over the right to private property and to surplus profits? Do you see a difference between consumerism and the Christian ideal of caring and sharing?

What do you think of "tithing," i.e., setting aside ten percent of your income for persons and groups who lovingly care for those in need worldwide?

Can you see the connection between greed and war—between the clinging selfishness of the "haves" and the eventual, and often violent, uprisings of the "have nots" to obtain what they need?

What does the purpose of confirmation—becoming a mature, adult Christian—mean to you at this point in your life?

FURTHER READING

* *Cry Justice, The Bible on Hunger and Poverty,* Sider (Paulist Press, 1980)—This small book shows striking parallels between what the bible says we should do and what we today are (or are not) doing, simply by quoting—in context—the pertinent biblical passages.
* *Toward a Human World Order: Beyond the National Security Straitjacket,* Mische (Paulist Press, 1977) presents a quietly objective framework for helping us understand the crises and opportunities of today's interdependent world.
* *Bread for the World,* Simon (Paulist Press and Eerdmans Publishing Co., 1975) is a factual presentation of the world's distribution of food resources, and what we can do to help the millions who are—literally—starving to death.
* *Something Beautiful for God,* Muggeridge (Doubleday Image Book, 1977) is the original work on Mother Teresa of Calcutta, the saintly nun and Nobel Prize winner who has captured the hearts of the world by her work among the poorest of the poor. If you read no other book recommended here, at least read this.
* *Meditations,* Dorothy Day (Paulist Press, also available from "The Catholic Worker," 36 E. 1st St., New York, N.Y. 10003)—A collection of her ponderings before her God, by the late, universally admired, and saintly co-founder of the Catholic worker movement.
* *Pacem in Terris (Peace on Earth),* Pope John XXIII (Paulist Press) is the late, great pope's "breakthrough" encyclical of 1963, saying simply that there can be no world peace without world justice; this encyclical, together with his *Mater et Magistra (Mother and Teacher),* and Pope Paul VI's *Populorum Progressio (On the Development of Peoples)* are the three great basic papal writings of our time on peace and justice concerning the Church and today's nuclear arms race.

* *Business Ethics,* Stevens (Paulist Press, 1980) is an especially useful book for business people, and their families, attempting to objectively help them evaluate their values and priorities.

FURTHER VIEWING/LISTENING

Happiness (Catholic Education Center)—A wonderful videotape experience that takes one into the world of Mother Teresa of Calcutta. An unforgettable 60 minutes. Bread for the World has a three-unit filmstrip series on world hunger and what can be done about it (Paulist Press, 1980). This is superbly done.

Cargoes (Paulist Productions) is a very relevant drama on moral dilemmas in Latin America. *The Eyes of the Camel* is another by Paulist Productions, telling of how the Church becomes committed to the liberation of the poor in a South American city. Finally, *Attention Must Be Paid* is another very good Paulist production, funny but provocative, about Christian caring among the aged. All these films are 26–28 minutes.

A World Hungry (Franciscan Communications) is an excellent five-unit filmstrip series which studies the world hunger situation and proposes a Christian solution. Each filmstrip averages 10 minutes.

18

Sin and What It Can Do to Us

SIN IN OUR LIFE

What is sin? How does it affect us? Why do we sin? How can we overcome our sins? Everyone at one time or another asks himself these things. To understand sin we must try to appreciate God's love which it rejects.

Read Luke 19, 41–44. The gospel picture of Christ weeping over Jerusalem is striking. He loved this city and its people, but he foresaw that because of their rejection of his warnings the city would be utterly destroyed. It was in 70 A.D. with the slaughter of a million people. Here is strikingly shown the effect of sin, of rejecting God's love.

We are the most fortunate beings in creation, for we are loved by the limitless God. He has given us life, an eternal destiny with him, and has himself come to save us. By baptism, we become his specially adopted children. In return, we should constantly desire to please him and to respond to his love. Yet often we do not. We sin against him and against our fellow humans he also loves.

Sin is a rejection of God's love, a refusal of an opportunity to accept his love and pass it on to others. All day long he gives us opportunities to respond to his love by our love—sin is a knowing neglect of these. It is as if God says, "Here is an opportunity to spread love in the world, to grow yourself in love and happiness"—and we refuse, we reject his loving guidance. Ultimately sin is a personal rebuff to our loving Father, to Christ our Brother and Savior, to the Spirit who is love within us. Incredibly, the infinite God is concerned with our rejection of his love. Christ tells us, also, ". . . as you did it to one of these, the least of my brethren, you did it to me" (Matthew 25, 40).

People today generally feel guilty about their moral failings. A poll of modern American adults by a national newsmagazine revealed that most people worry about personal failings, e.g., not going to church regularly, overeating, inconsiderateness, wasting time, not being active in the community, not contributing to charity, etc. The pollsters concluded that "worries about such personal failings beset some of us almost all of the time, and all of us some of the time."

But people are often fearful of facing their sins, of honestly acknowledging their sinfulness. Christ longs to help them if only they would humbly turn to him. His entire life and teaching divides people into two classes: those who admit they are sinners—and these he goes out of his way to forgive, again and again—and those who refuse to acknowledge their sins—and these he castigates, "Woe to you, scribes and Pharisees, hypocrites. . . ."

Sin is immaturity, destroys our personality, leads to ultimate frustration. By sinning, we yield to selfish, primitive urges. We refuse to recognize our personal relationship with God, our dependence on him, and we form an unreal concept of ourselves, making ourselves and our desires the supreme guide for our actions. Ironically, when we reject the demands of God's love, we spurn the one thing that can perfect our own personality and fulfill our aspirations.

Sin, then, is a failure to fulfill ourselves, to grow, to develop, to realize our potential. We fail to fulfill our capacity for good, for love, for lasting self-achievement in this particular situation. We miss a chance to achieve what we could. **Read Genesis 3, 1–5.**

Pride is at the root of all sin—and pride, if unchecked, is the one thing that might cut us off from God forever. As Lucifer had said, "I will ascend above the height of the clouds, I will be like the Most High," so in the story of the first human sin the devil promised Adam and Eve, "You shall be like God. . . ." Pride rejects the love that would bring us out of our egotistical little world, into union with God and his other children.

We should remember, incidentally, that a thought or desire can be sinful, as well as neglecting to do something we should. Christ says of lustful thoughts: ". . . whoever looks with lust at a woman has already committed adultery with her in his heart" (Matthew 5, 28). Sinful, too, would be a desire to harm someone, have revenge on him, bearing a grudge, etc. Many people sin by neglecting to do what they should—parents, for example, who neglect to guide their children, those who have no concern for the poor, who deliberately refuse to worship the God they know they should.

One who continually and deliberately indulges in the same sin finds it harder and harder to stop, and gradually becomes the slave of sin. Bit by bit he can blind himself to God's truth and deafen himself to the promptings of grace. His sin becomes a habit, a vice. Scripture says of such: "For what the true proverb says has happened to them—a dog returns to his vomit, and a sow even after washing wallows in the filth" (2 Peter 2, 22).

JUDGING THE SERIOUSNESS OF SIN

Read Matthew 26, 20–24. Some sins are obviously worse than others. We recognize the terrible malice of Judas' betrayal of Christ. So, too, hatred of another is worse than an impatient word and embezzling millions is more serious than stealing a few dollars. Some sins more deeply reject God.

As in human love, there are slight offenses—a man might be carelessly late in picking up his fiancée. Or the offense can be a more serious rejection of her love—he might begin dating another woman behind her back. Ultimately, the love relationship might be destroyed altogether.

> Facing the fact of our human weakness and sinfulness, and our tendency to become discouraged at keeping moral laws, there developed over the centuries in Catholic theology the legally-based notions of mortal and venial sin. Inadequate as is this categorizing of sin, these notions can yet provide us with some basis for making realistic judgments about our moral faults.

A mortal sin is a fundamental rejection of God's love. By it we drive his grace-presence from us. "Mortal" means "death-dealing"—this sin kills God's life and love within us. "Then desire when it has conceived gives birth to sin; and sin when it is full-grown brings forth death. . . . All wrongdoing is sin, but there is sin which is not mortal" (James 1, 15; 1 John 5, 16).

To sin mortally, our offense must be seriously wrong, we must fully realize it is seriously wrong, and we must fully want to choose our way over God's. In sinning mortally we make a basic choice of our own way over God's, and are willing to repudiate our friendship with God over this choice. We thus want this thing or person more than God. Such a choice must engage one's whole person to the depths of one's being.

Not all serious wrongs are mortal sins. Many people do seriously wrong things without fully realizing they are such, e.g., the millions who have had little or no education regarding Christ's moral teachings, the many nominal Catholics who do not sufficiently know their religion, or some converts before studying Catholicism. Some do seriously wrong things, but do not fully want to do them; people often act under pressing mental strain, or from deeply-rooted bad habits. Most would rarely, if ever, make a fundamental and lasting choice of their way over God's.

Mortal sin, then, is a fundamental choice of oneself over God that engages us to the depths of our being. Rather than thinking of mortal sin as a particular action, we should see it as a fundamental option, an attitude, a state of living contrary to God, that we knowingly and deliberately choose.

> Some might conclude that it is impossible to choose to live in mortal sin—to fully and deliberately reject God's will for us—so that even serious sins need not be taken too seriously. But mortal sin is an attitude that is built up by continual sinning. Each sinful act turns us further from God and hardens us in our growing attitude of rejection. Therefore each must be taken seriously. Otherwise we may become so hardened, bit by bit, that we will not recognize the point of ultimate rejection.

Mortal sin is the one real evil of our universe. Those in mortal sin cut themselves off from God's love, reject Christ, and are a detriment to others and a source of disruption in the universe. While in this state, they are rejecting love and rendering useless for themselves Christ's sufferings and death. They paralyze the power of their own acts of love, their prayers, good works, acts of worship, sacraments, etc. God's love—actual graces—still surround them, but they are interiorly self-centered, spiritually starving individuals.

The vast majority of sins are less serious rejections of God's love, called venial ("easily forgiven") sins. The offense is not serious, or the person does not fully know or fully want to do a serious wrong. A venial sin weakens our love for God and our neighbor. It is like a spiritual sickness or wound which hurts but does not kill or lessen God's grace-presence within us. A venial sin can be lesser or greater, as a sickness can, according as we realize its evil more clearly or consent more willingly.

> *Even our less serious sins should not be taken lightly.* Deliberate. continual venial sin, like a virus, can leave us prey to the deadly infection of mortal sin. People who try only to avoid mortal sin and are unconcerned about venial sins have a relationship with God like that of a married couple who, though living together, argue ceaselessly. Their love is weak and stunted.

Each person must follow his or her own conscience in judging whether an action is sinful, and how serious it might be. One's personality, moral awareness, and other circumstances surrounding his sinful acts have a bearing on their seriousness. One's conscience usually considers these things. Our conscience, however, is influenced by many things—environment, passion, lack of knowledge, etc.—so that we obviously need guidance in forming a true conscience about sin.

Christ through his Church helps us form a true conscience, to best express our love and arrive at heaven. Like anyone in love, we want to know how best to express our love, and how to avoid anything that might disrupt our love. We can look at the Church's moral teachings like a road map and set of directions given us for an auto trip; they may seem negative, restrictive, warning us to avoid certain things—but only to bring us and our fellow travelers more easily and safely to our destination.

Christ's Church points out some actions that are normally considered seriously wrong. Long study by the teachers of the Church and the basic moral norms of Christian believers over the centuries, reflecting on Christ's teaching given in the scriptures, show that these things—or, better, attitudes—most often are serious rejections of God's love:

> Deliberately refusing to worship the God one believes in; blasphemy; hating or seriously injuring the reputation of another; refusing to help someone in serious need: adultery, or sexual intercourse outside of a marriage commitment; serious scandal; stealing, cheating, lying or making unjust profits; drunkenness or drug abuse (note that alcoholism is considered a disease); racial, religious and sexual discrimination

when these do serious harm; lustful or hateful thoughts that are deliberately prolonged and fully wanted; seriously neglecting one's duties to
family, job, country, the underprivileged, etc.

**Those who judge themselves to be in a state of mortal sin must
confess their sinfulness and be reconciled to Christ and the Church
before they can take part in the eucharist.** It would be a living lie to
proclaim our union with Christ and our brethren by taking part in
communion, if all the while we were cut off from them by an unrepentant attitude of serious sin. The purpose of the sacrament of penance or reconciliation is to reconcile us to our brothers and sisters in
the Church, as well as to God.

**God will forgive any sin again and again—even the most serious—
as long as we are truly sorry.** ". . . if your sins be like scarlet, they
shall be made white as snow; and if they be red as crimson, they shall
be white as wool" (Isaiah 1, 18). We shall see that Christ has given
us the sacrament of penance within his Church, by which he forgives
our sins.

God never punishes us for our sins—rather we do that ourselves.
Or perhaps others afflict us—punishment we bring on ourselves from
others—but punishment does not come from God. This is difficult
for many to accept, raised as most of us have been with the concept
of a just God who, naturally, punishes the wrongdoer. But this is
judging that God acts as we would act. We cannot shake the idea
that God treats us as erring children who must expect to be disciplined by him when we have done wrong. We have seen in previous
chapters another concept of God, the unconditionally loving Father
of Christ's revelation. He treats us not as children, but as adults who
are no longer in need of constant parental interventions.

*Sometimes unconscious or semi-conscious emotional drives carry people
toward sin, inhibiting free will and reducing responsibility. Many com-
pulsively reach out for what they can get here and now. Though their
action is objectively sinful, they may have little or no guilt in God's
eyes. St. Paul experienced this: "I do not understand my own actions.
For I do not do what I want, but I do the very thing I hate. . . . So then
it is no longer I that do it, but sin which dwells within me. . . . I can
will what is right but I cannot do it. For I do not do the good I want,
but the evil I do not want is what I do" (Romans 8, 15–19).*

*Some people have an overdeveloped sense of sin. They are scrupu-
lous—judging things to be sins that are not, exaggerating their guilt,*

constantly fearful of offending God, hounded by guilt feelings. They have an emotional problem, in need of counseling and often professional treatment. From childhood they have never been loved properly, so they find it hard to believe in God's love and mercy. Usually they can grasp the fact of God's love only through others who accept and love them.

Many people today, however, have an underdeveloped sense of sin: they do not consider things to be sinful that actually are. Some may not be subjectively guilty before God, but they injure their fellow man and hinder the spread of God's love in the world. Some are guilty of insincerely preferring to remain in ignorance, rather than trying to find God's will. The saints who loved God most perfectly had a most profound awareness of their sinfulness.

THE CONCEPT OF HELL

"If thy hand is an occasion of sin to thee, cut it off! . . . And if thy eye is an occasion of sin to thee, pluck it out! It is better for thee to enter the kingdom of God with one eye, than, having two eyes, to be cast into hellfire"—these harsh words of the usually gentle Christ emphasize the Church's teaching on hell: **Read Mark 9, 42–47.**

Hell, in Christian tradition, is the eternal state or situation of those who die totally turned away from God, in which they continue to reject him forever, in unimaginable pain, deprived of all happiness. The concept of an eternal, personal punishment after death took many centuries to develop. Israel had no clear notion of this. It came when men were ready and might better appreciate what totally rejecting his love could mean. Christ spoke of it in the primitive imagery of his time, for instance, as a place "where the worm dies not" and "the fire is not quenched" (Cf. Matthew 13, 36ff; Matthew 25, 41ff; 2 Thessalonians 1, 7–9; Revelation 14, 11). Reflecting on Christ's words, and spurred by an early novel opinion (of Origen) that hell was not eternal, the early Christian Church came to teach its eternity.

Reflecting on the concept of hell, its greatest suffering is the realization that one has forever cut himself off from God for whom he longs with his whole being. Christ most often speaks of hell, not in terms of bodily torment but as rejection, eternal isolation: "Then he will say to those on his left hand, 'Depart from me, accursed ones, into the everlasting fire which was prepared for the devil and his angels' " (Matthew 25, 41). The damned soul reaches out for God with his whole being and at the same time must reject God, for he has chosen himself over God.

One might now glimpse hell, in a sense, if he deliberately cuts himself off from God by continually living in a state of serious sin, clinging to some sinful situation while realizing fully that he is choosing it over God. Then, if God had been at all real in his life, he is not able to talk with him any longer. Prayer becomes an impossible situation. He wants God, loves him, but can't reach him—and the torment of this state can be the beginning of hell.

One in hell is seen as eternally alone. It is complete alienation. There is no love, no sympathy, no sense of companionship, only emptiness and hatred—of oneself, of the other damned, of all creation, of God. One ceaselessly turns within himself, finding only emptiness and an endless, frustrating restlessness. He fully realizes that he is utterly rejected by the good God. A faint image of this might be the anguish of a child told repeatedly by his parents that they wish he had not been born.

Some wonder how a merciful God could send anyone to hell eternally. It would seem that, if anyone is in hell, he has put himself there, and God only respects his free choice. One who has made himself totally the center of his world, who refuses to love anything beyond and greater than himself, could not be happy in heaven, for heaven is giving totally in love and being loved. God would not force such a one to love, since love cannot be forced. At death he would have for all eternity what he wanted—himself and only himself—and this would be hell.

We should not fear hell in a morbid way, nor make this fear the motive for living a Christian life. "God who wishes all men to be saved" assures us over and over that he loves us and will give us a superabundance of graces to attain heaven. He gives us many chances, warnings, proddings, to accept his love. His whole revelation of himself as a loving God makes it clear that no one will go to hell except one who, with full awareness, fundamentally and permanently rejects God with his total being.

It is perhaps significant that while the Church proclaims a large number of saints to have attained heaven, she has never declared anyone damned. Guilt-ridden people, particularly, with an image from childhood of a stern and punishing God, should put aside thoughts of hell and try to learn of God's love.

Even the very possibility of hell should make us realize how much we crave to be united with God. There must be good reason for God's bringing the concept of hell to our attention. Perhaps even its possibility, of what it could mean to be rejected by God, will make us realize how terrible is any separation from him by sin. For those who truly love, the thought of losing their beloved, however remote, will spur them on to greater appreciation and love.

Theology has no complete answer as to how, or even whether anyone may be damned forever. Many scholars, and ordinary people as well, feel that no one is damned; they cannot conceive of a person choosing with full knowledge and deliberation to be cut off from God forever. Nor can they conceive of a loving God damning anyone forever. Some people believe they make their hell here on earth, through their alienation from God, others and even themselves. Two things God has revealed: his loving will is that we all be with him forever, and there is a state of hell for any who reject him. How to reconcile these is a mystery we may never be able to resolve. This we can be sure of: if any are damned, it is fully their own fault, and God's love surrounds each of us with countless helps toward heaven.

MAKING UP FOR SIN

Read Luke 7, 36–50. The penitent prostitute fell at Christ's feet, bathed them with her tears, and anointed them with the most expensive ointments. She tried to show her gratitude for Christ's forgiveness of her sins by making up for them in this touching way. So our love should impel us to do something to make up for the sins God forgives us.

When God forgives us, he forgives thoroughly and asks nothing in return. He is not like a judge imposing a sentence for a crime. He "blots out" our sins, "forgets" them, "hurls them into the sea." When the scriptures picture him threatening punishment for sin, it is a way of saying that his people are bringing punishment on themselves—"Salvation is mine, O Israel, destruction is thy own." **Read Psalm 103, 8–14.**

Though God does not demand that we make up for our sins, there is a necessity within ourselves to do so, to rebuild the love between us. When one has offended someone he truly loves—and especially when he realizes his beloved is so much more loving than himself—he cannot be happy until he has made up for his offenses.

We make up for our sins by uniting ourselves to Christ who has made up for them. We particularly join ourselves to Christ's great act of healing love, his death and resurrection. By this we simply express our sincere willingness to let ourselves again be loved by him.

United with Christ, we can make up for our sins in many ways: by acts of worship, particularly the Mass, by the sacraments, deep sorrow in confession, prayer, offering up our sufferings, doing "penance" for our sins by any good action, and by helping our fellow humans whom we have hurt.

An *"indulgence"* has reference to a practice that began in the early Church: the bishop would lessen a sinner's public penance if a martyr would offer his sufferings to help make up for the penitent's sins. Gradually the Church declared that certain prayers or good works could gain an "indulgence," usually stated as the equivalent of a certain period of penance in the early Church. With the very long penances of the medieval Church, indulgences became a practical necessity to make them livable; with the token penances of recent times, this is no longer the case. Indulgences were never considered "automatic" ways of making up for sin—one had to be in the state of grace and sorry for his sins to gain them, and their effectiveness ultimately depended on God and one's own faith and love—but they were greatly abused and even sold by some medieval preachers, occasioning Luther's original and rightful protest.

Today indulgences are seen as of minor importance in Catholicism. At Vatican Council II new, more meaningful interpretations of indulgences were proposed, but the question was not declared upon. The whole practice has been simplified by new regulations—but the relevance of indulgences to modern Christians is highly questionable. In practice, indulgences can be viewed simply as the Church's recommendation of a particular prayer or good work.

If at our death we have not yet made up for our sins, we must make up for them in the next life, by passing through the state called purgatory. Our love may still be too weak for us to be taken up into

God's all-consuming love. In the view of some, this is our shattering meeting with God in the experience of death. We shall see this in more detail in the last chapter.

IN THE LITURGY

The Mass prayers several times remind us of our sinfulness: the opening confession of our sins, the Lord's Prayer, the "Lamb of God, have mercy on us," etc.

Besides the use of the sacrament of penance, the Church sets aside certain seasons to particularly make up for our sins: Advent, Lent, the Ember Days, and the devotion of the "First Fridays."

DAILY LIVING: OVERCOMING SIN

Read Matthew 4, 1-11. At the beginning of Christ's public life, the devil was there to tempt him—to an empty display of power by turning stones to bread, to challenge his Father's providence by hurling himself from the temple, to throw in his lot with the devil and thereby receive power over the whole world. He was tempted as each of us is, continually, but far more excruciatingly.

So strong was this initial temptation of Christ that "angels came and ministered to him." During the agony before his death, Luke tells us, he underwent a bloody sweat. On the cross he cried out from a terrible sense of abandonment: "My God, my God, why have you forsaken me?"

Temptations—attractions or enticements to sin—are inevitable. God permits us to have these, not that we might sin, but that by overcoming them we might be strengthened spiritually. Soldiers are toughened by obstacle courses; cars are tested on rough roads, not to weaken them, but to make them stronger. Temptations also humble us, making us realize how much we need God's help. When St. Paul complained of a constant temptation, Christ told him, "My grace is sufficient for you, for my power is made perfect in weakness" (2 Corinthians 12, 9). **Read 1 Peter 5, 8-10.**

We are attracted to sin by the pleasures of the material world, the weakness of our own flesh, and the influence of the devil. We must recognize our weakness: inclined by original sin, we are further weakened by our past personal sins. We may also be trying to compensate for a lack of love in our life; God may not be very real, and sinful human loves are.

The devil, the mysterious power of evil among us, exploits these weaknesses. Many sinful acts do bring a certain happiness. But eventually sin leaves only a deep uneasiness within us. We may try to ignore the "still, small voice" of conscience, or attempt to drown it out, but it persists.

When we are tempted, a good rule is to pray quickly for help, and then calmly turn our attention to doing something else that engages us. God is always there, giving us the strength to overcome temptation. "God is faithful and he will not let you be tempted beyond your strength, but with the temptation will also provide the way to escape that you may be able to endure it" (1 Corinthians 10, 13).

Even when we fall into sinful acts again and again, God's grace is always there to save us from sinning with full deliberation, inspiring us to start over again and again—perhaps until our deathbed.

To overcome sin, we must obviously avoid situations that might normally lead us to sin. It is seriously wrong to put ourselves in situations where we would probably commit serious sin. Such might be: a married man going out with another woman, an alcoholic going to a bar, a morally weak young couple parking together, or one's gossiping with another who consistently encourages serious uncharitableness.

The mature Christian, however, concentrates on doing good, rather than merely avoiding sin. If one flies from New York to Chicago, looking forward to seeing someone he loves, what motivates his travel is the positive desire to be in Chicago, not merely an urge to leave New York. So we should desire to show our love for God and our neighbors in our actions, instead of merely trying to avoid hurting them.

The life of a Christian should be a personal, free, loving response to God's love—doing good out of love, not because we feel forced to. In Exodus, before God lists the commandments that his people are to observe, he reminds them of how he has shown his love for them:

"I, the Lord, am your God, who brought you out of the land of Egypt, that place of slavery. . . ." Realizing how much God has loved us, even to dying for us, we spontaneously want to please him, like anyone in love.

We should never become discouraged about overcoming even the worst habit of sin. It was not Judas' betrayal of Christ that ruined him, but his despair: **Read Matthew 27, 3–5.**

Here we see the one lasting tragedy of sin—the conviction that it is no use trying any longer. God does not ask that we succeed, but only that we sincerely try. It may take years, even a lifetime of struggle, but God's grace will always sustain our efforts.

> At a meeting of Alcoholics Anonymous in New York, a man told how he had battled alcoholism for thirty years, losing job after job, taking a "cure" three times, in and out of A.A., alienating his family and friends. But now, with perseverance in using the sacraments and returning to A.A., he has been "dry" for several years, with a job he is capable of, happy amid his children and grandchildren. He may possibly fall again, but he has already achieved more than he once even hoped for.

Often the hardest battle is the initial decision to renounce one's sin, to start over. Countless people over the past 1,500 years have echoed St. Augustine's classic description of the clinging power of sin:

> The very toys of toys, the vanities of vanities, my old mistresses, still held me; they plucked my fleshy garment, and whispered softly, "Do you cast me off? And from this moment shall we no more be with thee forever?" . . . I hesitated to break away and shake myself free from them, and to lean over to where I was called. A violent habit said to me, "Thinkest thou, that thou canst live without them?" (*Confessions,* Bk. 8).

Our sins can be turned to profit. Through sorrow and repentance, the experience of sinning can teach us much: humility, our weakness and need of God's helping grace, understanding and tolerance of others, gratitude for God's love which receives us back again and again.

SOME SUGGESTIONS FOR ...

DISCUSSION

Why do you think people are reluctant to face their sins and try
to do something about them?
Can you understand how some sins are worse than others?
Have you found an effective way of dealing with temptations?

FURTHER READING

* *Sense of Sin, Sense of Life,* Kennedy (Doubleday Image Book, 1977)—A
  positive plan to achieve self-knowledge and a mature moral outlook, very
  well-written by a psychologist with priestly insights.
* *Beyond Guilt,* Stein (Fortress Press, 1972) is a brief, excellent book on the
  pervading human problem of guilt.
* *Whatever Became of Sin?* Menninger (Bantam Books, 1978) contains a
  world-famous psychiatrist's observations that we are increasingly denying
  responsibility for our acts, and that mental health without moral health,
  and moral health without responsibility, is a delusion.
* *Don't Let Your Conscience Be Your Guide,* Nelson (Paulist Press, 1978)—
  A small, well-written, insightful book; despite the paradoxical title, the
  book really tells us how to develop a well-formed, growth-producing conscience.

FURTHER VIEWING/LISTENING

Night and Fog (Contemporary Films)—30 minutes—A powerful documentary on the concentration and extermination camps of World War II,
   showing the results of sin at its worst.
All Out (Paulist Productions)—27 minutes—An excellent satire on the dehumanizing effects of greed, using a TV game show as a setting.
The Secret (Paulist Productions)—A striking story about assuming responsibility for one's moral failings.
Excuse Me, America (A.C.C. Productions)—15 minutes—A superb film
   about Archbishop Helder Camara of Brazil, documenting the poverty
   there, and what we can—and must—do about it. This powerful little
   film is perhaps the best examination of conscience for Americans now
   in circulation.

PERSONAL REFLECTION

Since Adam and Eve, sin has weakend our whole race and brought the fearfulness of death, endless pain and inhumanity to our world. Serious sin can cut me off from God and turn me against my fellow human beings. I should meditate frequently on how God has shown his love for me in my life, and consider what I can do to show my love for him—and others—in return. Such thoughts are the best way to defeat temptations to sin.

To appreciate what our sins can do, I might also reread in chapter 8 "What This Cost and Why." Christ took on our sins and suffered and died to show us sin's ultimate absurdity.

Before retiring I might examine my conscience, concluding with an expression of sincere sorrow and a firm resolution to turn away from at least any serious sin.

19

The Christian's
Continuing Conversion

What can we do when we have sinned, and we also know that we will surely sin again? How can we be helped by confessing to a priest? What does a Catholic do in confession?

OUR NEED OF CONTINUAL CONVERSION

Read Luke 15, 1–24. Christ recognized that the life of the average Christian would be a humiliating process of falling and rising and falling again—of sinning and continual reconversion. By this parable of the sinful son's return, Christ brings home to us God's immense love and joy at our return from sin. We plunge into sin, like going down into the grave, but Christ is always there to raise us up again. All God asks is that we sincerely continue to try, to be converted again, and never despair.

"Then Peter came up to him and said, 'Lord, how often shall my brother sin against me, and I forgive him? Up to seven times?'" (Matthew 18, 21). In Peter's question "seven times" means an indefinite number. Christ's answer is even more emphatic: "seventy times seven"—that is, we should never cease to forgive. Why? Because God never ceases to forgive us.

GOD WANTS TO FORGIVE OUR SINS

The assurance of forgiveness and reconciliation is a vital part of love. Couples in love often experience the wonder of mutual forgiveness after an argument; in fact, some of the deepest moments of love come after making up. On the other hand, a refusal to forgive can be a terrible thing. A recent news story told of a woman on her deathbed refusing to forgive her unfaithful husband, though he knelt tearfully beside her begging forgiveness. Ancient peoples often thought that the gods would not forgive men's offenses, and throughout history men have considered themselves damned by an implacable deity or rejected by a blind, unfeeling fate.

Many sincere people today, realizing their moral failings, feel that they ought to do something about them. They know that they have been selfish, insincere, immoderate, and have hurt others, even those they love. They vaguely wish for a chance to acknowledge their guilt, to be assured of understanding and forgiveness, and the strength to make a "fresh start." They may not realize it, but they are looking for God's forgiveness, for his understanding acceptance, and an assurance of his help to do better.

God has revealed himself to be, above all, understanding, merciful, and forgiving. Centuries ago his inspired psalmist proclaimed, "Not according to our sins does he deal with us, nor does he requite us according to our crimes." The prophet Hosea, from the example of his own life, portrays God as a husband who loves his wife and forgives her even when she degrades herself by prostitution. The book of Jonah describes in a delightfully human way how this prophet was scandalized because God did not destroy the sinful Ninevites, but allowed them to repent.

Micah says God "delights in mercy . . . he will put away our iniquities, and he will cast all our sins into the bottom of the sea" (7, 18–19). And the Lord bade Ezekiel to answer the sinful Israelites:

> You people say, "Our crimes and our sins weigh us down; we are rotting because of them. How can we survive?" Answer them: "As I live, says the Lord God, I swear I take no pleasure in the death of the wicked man, but rather in his conversion, that he may live" (Ezekiel 33, 10–11).

Read Luke 7, 36–50. Christ above all revealed God's merciful, forgiving love, by associating with sinners, and particularly by forgiving their sins. He welcomed this sinful woman who came weeping to him in Simon's house, and silenced his host's objections: " '. . . her sins, many as they are, shall be forgiven her, because she has loved much.'

And he said to her, 'Thy sins are forgiven.' " He often proclaimed that he was sent particularly to sinners, the "lost sheep." He scandalized the influential leaders of his people by his continual association with sinners.

Read Luke 5, 18–26. As an assurance that he could forgive sins, he cured the paralytic, ". . . that you may know that the Son of Man has power on earth to forgive sins . . . I say to thee, arise, take up thy pallet and go to thy house." This same assurance of forgiveness and reconciliation can be ours today when we submit ourselves to his merciful forgiveness.

CHRIST FORGIVES AND RECONCILES THROUGH HIS CHURCH

Christ continues to forgive our sins today through the sacrament of penance. John describes how Christ passed on to his apostles, the first bishops of his Church, the power of forgiving sins in his name: **Read John 20, 19–23.**

The apostles passed their power of forgiving on to others, the bishops and priests of Christ's Church. When a man is ordained a priest he receives this power of acting as Christ's instrument, giving his assurance of forgiveness to men.

Penance—or the rite of reconciliation—often called "confession"—is the sacrament in which Christ forgives our sins and reconciles us to our fellow Christians. Its sign or ceremony is the sinner's showing his sorrow by acknowledging his sins and the priest's words of forgiveness and reconciliation in Christ's name. While Christ is no longer visibly among us to assure us, "Thy sins are forgiven thee," he is with us in this sacrament, speaking through the priest, giving us his loving assurance of forgiveness.

The sinner confesses to the priest, the representative of the Church, because he has offended the whole Church by his sins, and comes to be reconciled to his fellow Christians. Sin, we saw, is essentially selfish and alienating. Even one's secret sins deprive his fellow Christians of love and helps toward heaven, and serious sin may cut one off from them. So the ceremony which restores our full love-union with them is public and social: our confession may be private, but we appear in church, before our fellow Christians, to acknowledge that our sins have affected them as well as us and that we wish to be reconciled to them.

An acknowledgment of one's guilt before others has usually been the first step in receiving God's forgiveness. Those who came for forgiveness to John the Baptist, Christ's precursor, "were baptized by him in the river Jordan, confessing their sins" (Matthew 3, 6). Over and over again sinners came to Christ himself, acknowledged their sinfulness, and received his forgiveness. When Paul preached Christ at Ephesus, "many also of those who were now believers came, confessing and divulging their practices" (Acts 19, 18). And St. James exhorts, "Confess, therefore, your sins to one another, and pray for one another, that you may be saved" (James 5, 16).

We can acknowledge our guilt, ask forgiveness, and be reconciled either privately or publicly. We might come and acknowledge our sins to the priest in secret, in the confessional, or some private room, or publicly, in a penitential service. When we go to confession privately, we confess our sins in confidence and receive forgiveness and reconciliation, but we come to the priest as the representative of the Christian community to acknowledge that our sins have upset our relationship of love to the other members of the community. If we take part in a public penitential service, we show before all that we are sinners and that our sins have affected them.

From the earliest days of Christianity the Church has had a ceremony of reconciliation by which sins were forgiven. Confession was generally public, infrequent, and only for the most serious sins, with long penances before forgiveness. A Christian guilty of serious sin, when publicly known, was excluded from communion with the Church. Then, after a long period of public penance, he was reconciled to the community. These ceremonies were usually done by the bishop, as spiritual father, before the assembled community. Today, incidentally, a priest must normally have "faculties" from the bishop to exercise his power of forgiving. Along with this was the secret confession of secret sins, a private forgiveness, and a private penance.

Pope Clement at the end of the 1st century urges those who had instigated a schism in the Corinthian church to "submit to the presbyters and be corrected unto repentance." The 2nd century Church leaders, Ignatius of Antioch, Irenaeus of Lyons, and Polycarp of Smyrna, speak of sinners confessing before the Church and receiving forgiveness and reconciliation from the bishop. The 3rd century scholar, Origen, speaks of private confessions and penance which was then beginning to replace the public form, and urges sinners to seek out an understanding confessor as they would a competent physician.

In the 4th century the Spanish Church leader, Pacian, answered the objection that the Church could not forgive certain sins: ". . . this, you say, only God can do. This is true; but what he does through his priest is the exercise of his own power. For what else is the meaning of that which he says to the apostles: 'Whatever you shall loose on earth shall be loosed in heaven,' and 'whatever you shall bind on earth shall be bound in heaven'? Why this, if it was not permitted to men to bind and loose?" (Cf. *Sources of Christian Theology,* Palmer, Vol. II).

Read Luke 22, 54–62. In each act of penance, the one we really come to meet is Christ. Though he is invisible, we encounter his look of love, and like Peter after his denial, we are penetrated by sorrow for our sins. Then through the assuring words of the priest we know that Christ is forgiving us. There is the silent and wonderful realization that he joyfully welcomes us back as he did Peter: "When they had finished breakfast, Jesus said to Simon Peter, 'Simon, son of John, do you love me more than these?' He said to him, 'Yes, Lord, you know that I love you.' He said to him, 'Feed my lambs' " (John 21, 15).

In penance Jesus Christ forgives us, restores God's grace-presence if we have lost it by mortal sin, and strengthens us to avoid future sins. Each confession also helps us to make up for our sins, to renew the bond of love between ourselves and Christ and our fellow man. Of course, all this depends on how sorry we are and how determined to avoid sin in the future. Each confession should bring home to us our selfish ingratitude in sinning, and our need of God's constant help, besides reminding us again of Christ's love in dying for our sins.

Confession of our sins makes us face our sins and helps us do something definite about them. Rather than forgetting them, we are made conscious of them, of our weakness and need of God's help. The trained and experienced priest can help us face our sins without equivocation, make us see that we must do something about them, and perhaps give suggestions for overcoming them.

Penance gives us, above all, the assurance that our sins are actually forgiven. If we have tried to make a sincere confession, the priest's words of forgiveness give us the same assurance as if we heard them from the lips of Christ himself: "Thy sins are forgiven thee."

The urge to confess one's wrongdoings to a trusted and helpful friend is natural. There can be psychological benefits in confessing—but these should not be exaggerated. Confession can relieve the natural sense of guilt that follows sin, and might temporarily decrease some neurotic guilt feelings. But the functions of confessor and psychiatrist should not be confused: the psychiatrist deals with unconscious, neurotic guilt, while the confessor is concerned with conscious guilt.

Confession particularly gives one a special sense of personal contact with God. One can express his personal sorrow in his own way for the sins that are his particular burden, and his personal need of God's help. Many a priest—and many a Catholic—can testify that this can be an extraordinary, penetrating experience. Perhaps this is why many Christian churches today are again making confession available for their people.

To safeguard this sacrament no priest is ever allowed to reveal, directly or indirectly, anything he has heard in confession. It is a remarkable fact of history how few instances there have been of the violation of this confessional "seal," despite priests' human weakness, persecution, etc.

> In the history of the Church certain priests have had an extraordinary influence as confessors. During the mid-1800's hundreds of thousands of people flocked to Ars, a village in southern France, to confess to the parish priest, John Vianney. An extraordinary ascetic whose daily diet was often only a few potatoes, he would sometimes hear confessions for seventeen or eighteen hours per day, amazing all by his wisdom and insights. Awarded the Legion of Honor before his death, and afterward declared a saint of the Church, he is credited with renewing the morals of much of France of his day.

SORROW, THE ONE THING NECESSARY

Read Luke 8, 9–14. Our Lord's parable is a glimpse into the life of the Pharisee and publican. Undoubtedly there were many times when their real life counterparts played out this scene—the Pharisee proudly enumerating his good works, while the publican could only acknowledge sorrowfully that he was a sinner—yet it was the publican who merited God's loving approbation.

**When we ask God's forgiveness, the first and most important thing
we must have is sorrow or contrition**—as in any breach of human
love. Without true sorrow there can be no forgiveness, and any ceremony of reconciliation would be a mockery.

True sorrow need not be felt. It is basically the will to be sorry. A
feeling of sadness, tears, etc., is an emotional reaction that may accompany some people's sorrow, but sorrow is essentially one's willing or wanting to be sorry.

The test of true sorrow is our determination not to sin again. We
must be determined to avoid at least all serious sins and the situations that lead to them, to seek more help from prayer, the sacraments, etc.

We should try to be sorry primarily because of our love for God.
We call this " perfect" sorrow. We may have other motives as well,
but we are sorry most of all because we have offended one who is so
good, who deserves all our love—simply because we want to love
him and know that he loves us.

**When we are sorry primarily because of love, our sins are forgiven
immediately, and God's grace-presence is restored if we have lost it.**
This is the way most people's sins are forgiven. So if we realize that
we are in a state of serious sin, we should try to express our sorrow
out of love as soon as possible.

For a Catholic this perfect sorrow includes a determination to take
part in the sacrament of penance as soon as normally possible. He
realizes that his sin has offended the whole Church, that he is alienated, and he must therefore come to be reconciled.

**Those who are sure they are in a state of serious alienation should
confess before taking part in holy communion.** It would be a living
lie to take part in this greatest sign of our unity while yet cut off from
one's fellow Christians by a state of serious sin.

**But otherwise we need not confess before taking part in holy com-
munion.** We need do so only if we are sure of being in the state of
serious alienating sin. If normally conscientious Catholics doubt
whether they are in serious sin, they can simply express their sorrow
out of love of God, and then take part in the eucharist without confessing. They may mention their doubtful state in their next confession, but need not do so.

**We might be sorry primarily because of what our sins have done
to us**—a wholesome fear of losing heaven and going to hell, a sorrow

because of the punishment we are inflicting on ourselves by our sin. This relatively selfish sorrow is sometimes the most a poor sinner can arouse.

Though we should try to be sorry from a motive of love when confessing, this less perfect sorrow is sufficient to obtain forgiveness. The sacramental grace Christ gives us makes up for our deficient sorrow and raises it to a perfect sorrow. This is a great advantage of penance—a sinner who could arouse only imperfect sorrow could still be assured of forgiveness because of his special meeting with the merciful Christ in this sacrament.

THE RITE OF RECONCILIATION

There are today three ways in which one may be reconciled: Privately, by coming alone to the priest in a confessional room, or publicly, by taking part in a group celebration of penance. This latter includes individual confession and absolution. Finally, in extraordinary circumstances there may be a general absolution for the community without confession.

The rite for private reconciliation of one penitent is usually now done in a "confessional room," where the priest and penitent may sit comfortably face to face—though there should also be a "screen" of some kind in case the penitent wishes to remain anonymous.

The rite of reconciliation or confession should first be prepared for. Before entering the confessional room we should examine our conscience. We ask the Holy Spirit particularly to help us be sensitive to our state of sinfulness and to be truly sorry. Then we run through in our mind our Christian duties, considering particularly any sinful attitudes we may have acquired, our *particular* weakness especially. We might consider some of the things mentioned in chapter 25 of this book, "Living Daily the Christian Life." One who has any sort of sensitive Christian conscience is usually quite aware of his or her main sinful attitudes and need not review every possible sin.

We should note particularly any seriously sinful attitudes and how often we give in to these in our daily lives—any action or neglect that deeply alienates us from God and from others. The purpose of this sacrament is especially to assure us of forgiveness for these and to effect our reconciliation to the Christian community.

Most people who come to this sacrament are aware of a less serious or venial state of sin—one that disrupts our relationships of love rather than deeply alienating them. This sacrament gives us a chance to acknowledge and talk about even our less serious sinful attitudes—but we should bear in mind that they are also forgiven, and we are reconciled for these in many other ways: for example, by taking part in any of the sacraments, particularly the eucharist, or by an act of sorrow or a work of charity.

The priest, too, should prepare for the confessional encounter by considering his own state of soul and what he is doing about his sinful attitudes—and then pray, if only briefly, that he will be an enlightened and loving instrument of the Holy Spirit in this confessional encounter.

> *The rite for the reconciliation of an individual* begins with a welcome by the priest, and if you, the penitent, are unknown to the priest, you might indicate your state in life, the time of your last confession, and your age.
>
> Then you and the priest, or both together, may read an appropriate passage from scripture, particularly one relating to conversion, God's mercy, love, and forgiveness.
>
> You then confess your sinful attitudes to the priest. This best takes the form of a dialogue between you and the priest, in which you "talk a bit" about your sins, why you think you have done them, what could be done to correct them, etc. To be particularly avoided is the "grocery list" type of confession in which you recite every possible fault you can think of, with no attempt at assessing your really basic sinful attitude(s) and what you can do about these. The priest, for his part, will, hopefully, sensitively counsel you, often questioning you and trying to discover your expectations, fears, and hopes. The priest should sense, and usually does, when you want to talk about something and when you wish to say very little.
>
> Then the priest asks you to do some "penance" as a sign of your sorrow and your renewed way of life. This penance should correspond to the seriousness and nature of your sins. It might be the saying of some prayer, an act of charity or self-denial—or perhaps to ask the forgiveness of a person you have hurt. Sometimes the priest may ask you to suggest a penance of your own choosing—or the two of you might discuss this together. The penance, of course, is only a token, a small start on what should be a renewed Christian way of life.
>
> Next you pray for God's pardon, perhaps by some formalized prayer, perhaps in your own words. On occasion, you and the priest might pray together.
>
> Then the priest extends his hand(s) over your head and says the for-

mula of absolution (forgiveness and reconciliation). The essential words of this are: "I absolve you from your sins in the name of the Father and of the Son and of the Holy Spirit." In this the priest acts as God's instrument, himself sinful, but the one chosen to thus reconcile the penitent.

There is often a short final prayer, perhaps together, and the priest bids you in your newly-renewed state to go in peace. It is, indeed, as if you are a new person, anxious to obey the Lord's command: "Go, now, and sin no more."

Then there is the rite of reconciliation for a group of penitents, usually called a penance service or a communal penance service. This has become particularly popular today in many places and brings out the fact that we are a community of sinners, that our sins affect one another, and that we are willing to forgive and be reconciled to one another.

The rite may begin with a hymn, after which the priest invites all to pray in silence, and then says the opening prayer.

There is a reading from scripture, or perhaps more than one reading, followed by the priest's homily to the congregation (which ideally takes its theme from the scripture text), usually dealing with interior repentance, God's mercy, the effect of our sins on others, our duty of making satisfaction for our sins, and suggestions for living a better Christian life.

Next there is a period for each to examine his or her conscience, usually in silence, though the priest may suggest some particularly pertinent things about which all should examine themselves. As said above for private confession, we should run over in our mind our sinful attitudes, noting particularly those that seriously affect our relationship with God and others, and then considering what, in a practical way, we can do to change.

Next, all together say some prayer asking forgiveness and reconciliation. They may then join in a litany or suitable song to express their attitude of sorrow and yet hope and trust in God's mercy. The Lord's Prayer is usually said together at this point.

Then those who wish to confess their sins go to the priest of their choice (there are usually several priests present for this), and they usually mention some particular sin or sinful attitude for which they are particularly sorry. All seriously sinful attitudes must be confessed. The priest then gives each some suitable penance, after which he says over the penitent the form of absolution, acting as God's instrument in reconciling him or her.

There may be a closing prayer or hymn, and then all may leave, renewed and reconciled, to try to live out more perfectly their Christian way of life.

Finally there is the rite of reconciliation for a group, with a "general" absolution said by the priest over the group. This is the same as the reconciliation ceremony for a group described above, with the exception that there is no individual confession, and the priest says the words of forgiveness and reconciliation over the whole group.

An act of penance is proposed by the priest for all, and they also say together some prayer indicating their sorrow for their sins and their intention to improve in the future.

This form is used only in an "emergency" situation, when there is a large number of penitents and insufficient priests present to hear the sins of each and give each individual absolution.

Also, according to Church law, those who are conscious of being in a state of serious sin, truly alienated from God and their neighbors, should confess this state of sin individually to a priest when they reasonably can.

In the liturgy at the beginning of the Mass there is usually a brief penitential service, during which all silently examine their conscience and then together express sorrow for their sins as a preparation for their worship of God.

Confessions are heard at these times in the average Catholic parish: during the afternoon and evening each Saturday, and where possible on weekdays—perhaps before or after daily Mass. One should check one's local parish schedule.

How often one should come to be reconciled depends on one's individual need. There are special circumstances and special times. One might have committed some upsetting sin or series of sins and want to express sorrow and be reconciled; one might feel a particular need for Christ's special help to do something about some sinful attitude, or one might feel the need to again recommit oneself to a fervent Christian life. Or there might be a special occasion for which one wishes to prepare by confessing and reconciliation: a birthday, anniversary, special feast or some other important event in one's life.

Most today are making use of private confession much less frequently than formerly—they may attend communal penitential services regularly—but are making their private confessions much more meaningfully when they do come. They confess perhaps once or twice yearly, but it is often a deeply renewing experience, during which they examine themselves extensively and show a profound intention of changing their life.

A person who feels sure of being in a state of serious sin should, of course, be reconciled as soon as possible, so he can return to the eucharist with a clear conscience. If such a one did not go to the eucharist for a year, he would no longer be considered a practicing Catholic.

It is natural to be somewhat nervous and ashamed when confessing, particularly when one is not used to it. This, however, is a sign that our sinful pride is being lessened. In a very rare case a person might, through shame, deliberately conceal a serious wrong in confession; the whole confession is then useless, as are any future confessions until he confesses the concealment.

If, however, one forgets to mention some serious wrongdoing it is still forgiven: he need not return to the sacrament, nor refrain from communion; he should try to remember it when next he takes part in the sacrament.

To get the most out of each confessional-encounter with Christ, we should prepare well, but not indulge in anxious soul searching. We should try to arouse in ourselves a deep, true sorrow for our sins, realizing the sufferings they have caused God who loves us infinitely, and how they have hurt our fellow men who so need our help. On the other hand, we should not try to ferret out each and every sin—serious attitudes of sin will usually come to mind immediately. Nor should we waste time in useless regrets, but rather make a confident, thought-out resolution to avoid whatever might lead to future sin.

Many find it helpful to confess regularly to the same priest, his or her "confessor," perhaps one's "spiritual director," with whom a particular appointment is usually made for the confession. One should try to find a priest with whom one can identify and carry on a "relaxed" but profitable dialogue in depth about one's spiritual state and the relevant conditions of one's state of life: doubts, pains, and hopes, family life or job—anything for which Christ's peace and help are needed.

DAILY LIVING: DOING PENANCE FOR OUR SINS

The test of our sincere desire to recommit ourselves is our willingness to "do penance" for our sins—by the sacraments, prayer, works of love, and self-discipline. If we are truly sorry for offending a loved one, we go out of our way to be kind to him in the future. We try, in this way, to repair the damage to our relationship. St. Paul unequivocally states his need of bodily penance: "I chastise my body and bring it into subjection, lest perhaps after preaching to others I myself should be rejected" (1 Corinthians 9, 27).

Since the penance given us is usually only a token atonement for our sins, it is necessary for us to do more, especially if we have sinned seriously. Love will impel us to do further penance for the harm we have done—if not in this life, then in a purgatory-state after death.

A particular way of doing penance is to fast and abstain. Fasting means eating less at mealtime and not eating between meals; abstinence is refraining from eating meat. In the United States, Ash Wednesday and Good Friday are days of fast and abstinence for those from 21 to 60 years of age; the Fridays of Lent are also days of abstinence for those 14 and over. Many people realize their need of voluntarily fasting on occasion, particularly during Lent.

The best way of doing penance, of course, is to perform some act of charity or kindness to another. We cannot make up to Christ, for he has totally forgiven and forgotten our sin, but we can make up to him in other people who need our love and kindness—often almost desperately. A kind word, a bit of sincere interest, a favor done for someone, even just patiently listening to someone—these can often go a long, long way.

To summarize, the one great lesson for us all is that we should never become discouraged about our sins. We may fall into sin again and again, and there seems no way of stopping. We are harassed by past falls, and perhaps our present situation demands of us heroism of which we are incapable. We are tempted to despair, to turn from God, saying like Peter, "Depart from me, for I am a sinful man, O Lord!" But God's purpose in all this is to make us nakedly face our sinfulness, our nothingness.

The only possible solution, then, is to flee to him in a supreme act of trust, to tell him that we are so sure of his love that we dare to come to him even as unfaithful as we are, that we know he loves even our worst weakness. We accept our sinful selves and throw ourselves on his love, determined to keep trying, though we may never cease falling—we know that at every moment, including our last, we can always return home to him. He is our Father who will always be waiting.

SOME SUGGESTIONS FOR ...

DISCUSSION

What is the most important thing to do when one recognizes that he or she is a sinner?
Can you see the value and/or necessity of confession?
Can you understand how "doing penance" can help to restore our love?

FURTHER READING

** *Renewal of the Sacrament of Penance,* Osborne (Catholic Society of America, 1975)—Various aspects of the renewed sacrament of penance or reconciliation, with a bibliography that is very helpful for priests, teachers, etc.

 * *Together in Peace,* Champlin (Ave Maria Press, 1975)—The penitent's edition is an excellent, widely-used help for one taking part in the sacrament of reconciliation. An edition for priests is also excellent.

FURTHER VIEWING/LISTENING

Penance, Sacrament of Reconciliation (Thomas Klise)—An excellent filmstrip that concentrates on the three penance parables in the fifteenth chapter of Luke's gospel; it develops the biblical concept of repentance and stresses confession as reconciliation with the community.

My Main Man (Paulist Productions)—A moving story of a black father and son's struggle to relate to each other, and their reconciliation; this is a well-done modern parable of the prodigal son.

Sinner Sam (Teleketics, Franciscan Communications)—A filmstrip that covers, in excellent and interesting fashion, the history of the sacrament of reconciliation. *Penance, Sacrament of Peace* (Franciscan Communications) tells of a man who injures a child in a traffic accident and, after seeking forgiveness from the child, finds the inner peace that had been denied him.

PERSONAL REFLECTION

The only thing in life that really matters is to strive continually to have God's grace-presence with us, to grow in his love. Unrepented mortal sin is the one thing that can ruin us.

A brief daily examination of my conscience, and a sincere expression of sorrow and recommitment to Christ by a specific resolution, can be the most realistic thing I do all day.

If I am truly penetrated by sorrow I will want to do something—preferably some act of love or kindness—to make up for the harm of my sins.

20

When Illness Comes to a Christian

Why is there so much sickness in the world, and what purpose can it serve? What of those who are disabled, perhaps for life? What help does God give us in sickness or in disability? How can one have a more profoundly Christian and growth-ful attitude toward sickness and disability?

THE POWER OF SICKNESS OVER US

Read John 9, 1-3. Sickness, particularly when serious and debilitating, is often regarded as evidence that God is not really loving and forgiving after all. Many people cannot understand why a good God would allow sickness in his universe, particularly the sufferings of the innocent, and because of this they sometimes reject the existence of a personal and loving God.

Public opinion in Israel in Christ's time—and of many people since—held that sickness always comes upon us because of our sins. It is God's way of punishing us. Job's friends remonstrated with him because of his afflictions, and Christ's disciples spontaneously asked whether the blind man's condition was due to his sin or that of his parents. Christ rejected this overly simple solution. We might bring suffering on ourselves by some sins, such as intemperance or stubborn pride—but the good can also suffer, as exemplified above all by Christ himself.

Sickness shows the influence of the power of evil in the world. In the gospels the cures of diabolic possession and of disease were considered the same—defeats for Satan and for the demonic in the world.

When our body is weak we can be tempted to despair or unbelief. Satan's influence always appears, not in vitality and joy and peace, but in misery, boredom and pain. Sickness, therefore, should be looked on like any temptation—it can be an occasion for growing in love, but it is basically bad and to be avoided as far as possible. Every cure of sickness is a setback for the power of evil. A Christian should never be dumbly resigned to sickness or disability but should do all he reasonably can to be cured.

CHRIST'S POWER OVER SICKNESS

Read Luke 7, 20-23. Christ's life was unceasingly devoted to curing the sick. Such cures were to be a sign to the Jews of the messianic age, and Christ pointed to his cures as proof of his divine mission: "Go and report to John what you have heard and seen: the blind see, the lame walk, the lepers are cleansed, the deaf hear, the dead rise. . . ." By his touch or by a simple command, he performed all sorts of healings.

Christ sent out his apostles with power to heal the sick: ". . . He gave them power and authority over all demons, with the power to heal diseases. And he sent them to proclaim the kingdom of God and to heal. . . ." (Luke 9, 1-2). These cures were done in two ways: the apostles laid on hands, and they "anointed many sick persons with oil, and healed them" (Mark 6, 13). Among the Christians of the first few centuries, particularly, special powers of healing appeared quite often.

Above all, Christ conquered the power of sickness over us, so that we can now use it to bring ourselves and others to heaven. Most of the sick he did not cure, and he did not abolish sickness, death, or drudgery. But far more important, these can now be "offered up" in union with his sacrifice to accomplish great good. We can overcome Satan in the very misery of sickness.

THE ANOINTING OF THE SICK

From the beginning Christ's followers used the power he had given them over sickness, anointing the sick with oil to heal the body and forgive sins: Read James 5, 13-16.

The presbyters (priests, bishops) were to pray over the sick person "after anointing him with oil in the name of the Lord," and this would "raise up" the sufferer and forgive his sins. The description shows this to be the ordinary sacramental rite for the sick, distinct from the extraordinary and miraculous gift of healing that some had in the early Church.

In the sacrament of the anointing and pastoral care of the sick, Christ uses the anointing and prayers of the priest to give comfort and strength to the soul and sometimes to the body of one seriously ill. We meet Christ here to receive his healing comfort, strength, and pardon. Anyone who is seriously ill, mentally or physically, may take part in it—or one who is weak from old age.

The rite of anointing the sick today is this: the priest prays over the sick person, lays hands on him, and then anoints with oil his forehead and hands, saying, "Through this holy anointing and his great love for you, may the Lord help you by the power of his Holy Spirit. R. Amen. May the Lord who freed you from sin heal you and extend his saving grace to you. R. Amen."

The full ceremony of anointing is designed to comfort and inspire: the priest blesses with holy water the one to be anointed; together they pray that God will have mercy and forgive our sins; comforting passages from Scripture may be read, after which the priest may give a short exhortation and then pray over the sick person. Then follow the laying on of hands, the anointing with oil, and a final prayer.

Ideally the ceremony is celebrated before the whole community, preferably at the Sunday eucharist, so that the prayers of all might aid the sick in their midst. The oil used, incidentally, is a special oil of the sick blessed by the bishop at the chrism Mass.

In this sacrament Christ's power may help to heal the sick—if it is for their good and they have sufficient faith—and it always strengthens and comforts them to bear their illness. The oil signifies what it produces—a soothing, comforting healing— in the way that we might use sunburn oil or certain liniments. The sick person will be healed to the extent that God sees it is for his spiritual good; and also, as one gospel of anointing says, "It shall be done in answer to your faith." But more importantly it gives one peace, strength to offer up this illness, to put aside fear and bitterness and entrust himself to God.

By this anointing Christ forgives the sick person's sins if he cannot confess but is interiorly sorry—as when unconscious or unable to respond. Even if his sorrow is mostly out of fear, Christ's power in this sacrament raises it to the sorrow out of love that unites him with God. If he is able, however, he makes his confession, since this is the particular sacrament of forgiveness and recommitment.

This sacrament is the prayer of the Church-family, represented by the priest, that the sick person will soon return to his place among them as they worship and work together. It assures him of the healing love of Christ and his fellow Christians. It should help him have the will to live, to be back with his friends who miss him, joined with them again in the eucharist. The priest prays, "In your mercy give him health . . . that he may once more be able to take up his work . . . and give him back to your holy Church, with all that is needed for his welfare."

But if the sickness is our last, this sacrament will help us toward the great family of heaven. It should never be delayed—otherwise we may be deprived of the strength, resignation, and purifying love Christ wishes to give through it. It helps us die as a totally committed Christian. It gives us the prayers of our friends, joined with Christ, making easier our passage into eternity.

This is primarily Christ's sacrament for the healing of sickness, more than a help for the dying, and should be given as soon as possible in any serious illness—so that Christ's loving grace can help our attitude and determination to get well, which is so often, as any doctor can testify, the determining factor as to whether people recover or not. Like all the sacraments, the more we can put into it of faith and love, the more benefit we will receive from it. Though it has a special power to help the dying, it is primarily Christ's rite of healing, meant to help us overcome and profit from our illness or disability.

Holy viaticum is meant to be the sacrament of the dying. Thus people should take part in it as soon as they are deemed to be in any close danger of death. To wait until people are dying—and are most likely unconscious—before calling a priest is to deprive them of their last eucharistic meal, the divine food for their journey into eternity. Even if one is not in immediate danger of dying, the priest should be called so that the person can more consciously and more fully benefit from it.

Anyone can take part in this sacrament who is sick from mental or physical illness, old age, or accident. A person may be anointed before surgery. The elderly and those weakened in health may be anointed even if no dangerous illness is present. Those who have lost consciousness or the use of their reason may be anointed if, when they were in possession of their faculties, they would have asked for it. Children may be anointed if they are sufficiently mature to be comforted by the sacrament. This sacrament may also be repeated during the same illness if the sick person's condition becomes more serious. Non-Catholics may also be given this sacrament if they request it and have some grasp of its meaning.

This sacrament is also given to the sick at the parish Mass. In fact, this is the ideal setting for it. Those who are ill gather before the priest and he lays his hands on them, while the congregation prays silently for their recovery. Then the priest anoints each with oil. There may be other prayers, songs, and scripture readings to show that the community cares for those who are sick among them and wishes them to be restored to the health that God wants us all to have.

Through this sacrament, then, Christ gives us the power not only to overcome the evil in our sickness, but to grow spiritually, to reflect on and make up for our past sins, and often on the course of our life and the things that are ultimately important. It can give us new insight, new quiet strength to overcome sin's power now and in the future.

Some Christians have a special "charism" or gift for healing those who are sick. While most of these are priests, some are lay people or religious. The use of this gift is not meant to supplant needed medical care, but to supplement it. The attitude of sick persons, as everyone knows, is usually crucial as to whether or not they recover. If certain individuals can help induce an attitude of faith in God and a desire to be well in order to better and longer serve the needs of others, then their "healing" power can be a true gift in the Church today, as it was among the first Christians.

In each parish community, there should be a ministry to the sick, a caring for their needs, of which the priest's anointing is only a part. Christians more and more seem inclined to take responsibility for the sick among them today, whether or not they are personally acquainted with those who are ill. The appreciation of those who are ill can often astound us. Those who are old or in rest or convalescent homes are particularly grateful for even the slightest attention given to them.

DAILY LIVING: OUR ATTITUDE TOWARD SICKNESS

Read 2 Corinthians 12, 7-10. Our sickness or disability when "offered up" makes us more like Christ. When St. Paul complained of his sickness, the "messenger of Satan," Christ reminded him, "My strength is made perfect in your weakness." We should try to overcome sickness, but when it must come, our attitude should be more than mere resignation. Our sickness should be looked upon as an opportunity for Christ to gradually take over our life.

"We bear at all times in our body the sufferings of the death of Jesus, that the life of Jesus also may be manifested in our body." Suffering like him and with him, we die to selfish egotism, become aware of our utter need for the Father's help, and are also made more understanding toward others' weaknesses.

Sickness can be a power given to us to spread love in the world, to help others toward heaven, to make up for their sins, and open them to God's love. Realizing this, Paul could say: "I rejoice now in the sufferings I bear for your sake; and what is lacking of the sufferings of Christ, I fill up in my flesh for his body which is the Church" (Colossians 1, 24).

A stirring example of the use of suffering is the electronics company on Long Island, New York, founded by a man born without legs, and employing only disabled persons. Here each makes his contribution, motivated by love, knowing that he is accepted. "Love," says the founder, "gives our incredible, wonderful crew a right to share—to know what is going on in the work of which they are part, to understand its problems, to learn new ways in which to do better. . . ."

A great opportunity for genuine Christian living is to help others in their illness, caring for them, visiting them, consoling them and their families. The sick are especially in need of our loving attention, and few people are more appreciative. Christ assures us, "As long as you did it for one of these, the least of my brethren, you did it for me" (Matthew 25, 40).

A particular need of our time is to recognize the human and Christian dignity of disabled people. Most of us view the physically and emotionally handicapped as difficult to deal with, and we tend to avoid them in our daily lives. Perhaps we are uncomfortable in their presence because of our own inability to perceive the simple dignity and spiritual depth which often lie beneath their "different" appearance.

An especially pressing need today is sincere interest in the mentally ill. So often we avoid emotionally disturbed people, when what they need is a bit of friendship, someone to be concerned about them. Love is the best therapy, and one we can all give.

SOME SUGGESTIONS FOR . . .

DISCUSSION

What, in your opinion and experience, is the best attitude of Christians when serious illness or disability afflicts them?

Does it make sense to you that most still tend to shy away from one who is disabled—and especially from one who is retarded or perhaps mentally unable to cope in some way?

Do you believe that some people may have a genuine charism or gift of healing?

Can you understand how the anointing of the sick can help one who is ill in the Christian community?

FURTHER READING

* *Healing,* MacNutt (Ave Maria Press, 1974)—A good discussion of healing in the sacraments of reconciliation and the anointing of the sick, and the practice of prayer for healing.
* *Healing Life's Hurts,* Linn and Linn (Paulist Press, 1977)—A warm, readable, and insightful book about the healing process. It is a common sense integration of psychology, medicine, and religion.
* *Healing of Memories,* by the same authors (Paulist Press, 1975) is a small book on how prayer and confession can help one's inner healing.
* *Healing and Wholeness,* Sanford (Paulist Press, 1966)—An excellent book about what persons can do to help themselves, written by an Episco-

pal priest and Jungian analyst with two decades of experience in this ministry.

FURTHER VIEWING/LISTENING

Blessed Be (Insight Films)—8 minutes—A wonderful series of vignettes in which retarded children dramatize the meaning of the beatitudes. A true masterpiece.

Ailing Annie (Teleketics, Franciscan Productions)—An excellent filmstrip that deals with the history of the sacrament of the anointing of the sick.

PERSONAL REFLECTION

Christ accomplished the greatest deed of history, our salvation, through suffering. Offering up my sufferings and frustrations with his may be the greatest thing I will accomplish in my life. Christ, I know, lives particularly in those who are sick. I might visit someone who is ill, mentally or physically, or one who is neglected or isolated because of a disability.

21

Christ Joins a Man and Woman in Marriage

What is unique about Christian marriage? How can one have a happy marriage? How can one best raise a Christian family? What about divorce? Planning a family? Can mixed marriages work?

WHY MARRIAGE?

God originated marriage as the basic way of giving and growing in love and together attaining salvation. He created us in such a way that we would find happiness in each other. We are not meant to live in isolation, but to find and fulfill ourselves through the love of others. The figurative story of Genesis conveys how close was the union of the first man and wife: **Read Genesis 2, 18 and 21–25.**

Marriage is God's way of joining two people in love and fidelity and of bringing new human persons into existence. Genesis pictures God saying to the first man and woman, "Be fruitful and multiply, and fill the earth and subdue it. . . ." (1, 28). Through the union of marriage, God's human creatures come to be, grow in knowledge and love and eventually attain perfect union with him forever. Marriage is thus a continuing living sign of God's love for human beings.

A loving family, then, is God's purpose in originating marriage and should be the reason why a couple marry. Love and fidelity are part of but are not the fullness of the ideal of marital love. Neither is the desire for children sufficient, unless the couple have a true and mature love for one another. The loving fidelity and the co-creation of children obviously take time to achieve—and sometimes both cannot be achieved. What is important is that the couple desire both these ideals, see how they go together, and do their best, then, to attain a loving family.

Throughout the history of his dealings with men, God shows his constant regard for the marriage union. The nuptial theme is woven throughout scripture: Israel is the spouse of God, he pledges her his unending love by the covenant-bond, and even when Israel is unfaithful he takes her back again and again. Scripture often speaks of the nobility and joys of marriage: "Happy the husband of a good wife, twice lengthened are his days; a worthy wife brings joy to her husband, peaceful and full is his life" (Sirach 26, 1-2).

Marriage is a covenant, of its nature monogamous and permanent. Two people pledge themselves to each other for life. Polygamy, polyandry, divorce and remarriage appear as exceptions to God's desires for marriage: "A man cleaves to his wife and they become as one flesh" (Genesis 2, 24). When questioned about divorce Christ said, "For the hardness of your heart Moses allowed you to divorce your wives, but from the beginning it was not so" (Matthew 19, 8).

> Throughout most of history, marriages were arranged by the family or society in which the couple lived, the bride especially having little to say about it. In recent times, since prospective partners are better educated and presumably more capable, the commitment to each other is made by the couple themselves. Thus their great responsibility to prepare themselves well; the choice is ultimately theirs alone.

WHAT IS CHRISTIAN MARRIAGE?

It is significant that Christ's first miracle was performed—before he was ready to begin his ministry, it seems—to help a young couple on their wedding day. **Read John 2, 1-11.**

Christ made marriage a sacrament in that he gave it a new meaning, a new power and new beauty. Though he left it up to his Church to develop over the centuries, he yet made marriage one of the great ways of encountering him and receiving abundantly his grace and help. When two people take one another in marriage, they are uniting themselves not only to one another, but to Christ. Further, by this they become a living microcosm of Christ's love-union with his Church. Their relationship is *the* example, in miniature, of Christ's bond with his Church.

St. Paul uses the imagery of his day and culture (when wives were considered their husband's property) to express this as beautifully as he could: The husband should love his wife and even die for her as Christ, our Savior, did for us; and the wife should love her husband as we are to love Christ. **Now read Ephesians 5, 21-33.**

Marriage is the sacrament by which Christ joins a Christian man and woman in a grace-giving, lifelong union of mutual growth and creativity. Any two baptized people capable of marriage, when they are freely and legally married, thereby take part in the sacrament of marriage. Even when one of the parties is not baptized as a Christian, Christ comes to join them by his sacramental presence, "invited" formally by the Christian partner—and hopefully, too, by the non-Christian who would at least want to bring Christ's ideals of love into the marriage.

> *Christ joins the couple together and guarantees them all the love and help they need to make their union a success*—provided they do their part, using their intelligence to prepare well, and to seek assistance not only for difficulties in their life together, but for positive growth. This help is always waiting for them from God, their third partner. But, like any true lover, he will never force himself upon them. They must open themselves to his guidance by their prayer, their intimacies and sharing, worshipping together, and seeing themselves in their children.

Marriage is in a special way a sacrament of the Church community, the "whole Christ" uniting the couple by their communal love, and pledging the couple their lifelong support. The couple, in turn, pledge themselves to the community, to help it grow, particularly by the new life and creativity they will bring to it. This is why the sacrament of marriage is celebrated before the Church-community—ideally with the couple and the community taking part together in the eucharist, the greatest sign and builder of union we have on this earth. Also, this is why there must always be two witnesses to the marriage: they are the very minimum of the community taking part in the sacrament with the couple.

The couple gives the sacrament of marriage to each other in what is probably the most important exercise of their priesthood. As the ordained priest is Christ's instrument in bringing about the eucharist or in giving Christ's forgiveness in confession, so the husband gives this sacrament to his wife, and she to him. The priest acts as the official witness of the Church to their union, and brings to the marriage the Church's blessing.

The power of Christ's action in this sacrament comes fully when the couple are joined by their mutual "I do." His grace continues to strengthen them each day and hour of their married life as they continue to give this sacrament to each other. Each sacrifice, each act of love, each bit of work for their common good is used by Christ to communicate more of his love. As they give themselves more and more to each other, he can give himself more fully to them.

Christian marriage is not only a goal in itself, but the way in which a couple will attain their ultimate goal of eternal life. This is their vocation, their call from God, the state by which they will attain heaven; they enter marriage just as a priest or nun would enter his or her state of life, as their vocation, as the most important part of God's plan for their salvation. As a couple work at their marriage they grow in love of God as well as one another.

A Christian marriage is a sign to the world of Christ's presence among us. Marriage partners accept the responsibility not only for their own salvation, but for that of their mate and for each member of their family. The family, in turn, is responsible for showing the world that total and enduring love is possible in this life. In this way the Christian couple take on at marriage a lifelong commitment to be a missionary of Christ's love in the world.

The Christian family, which springs from marriage as a reflection of the loving covenant uniting Christ with the Church, and as a participation in that covenant, will manifest to all men Christ's living presence in the world and the genuine nature of the Church *(Church in the Modern World,* no. 48).

Permanence is of the very nature of Christian marriage. We saw that each Christian marriage is a miniature of Christ's union with his Church. Just as there is no divorce between Christ and his Church, so there should be none between the Christian husband and wife. "Is Christ divided?" says St. Paul. This is a lifelong commitment, requiring one's best efforts for years— which emphasizes the need of care in choosing one's partner.

In order to raise a family properly a marriage must have the assurance of being lifelong—and in order that a couple's mutual love may continue to grow throughout their lives, they must naturally be determined to have a permanent union. Marriage needs to be a permanent commitment in order that the couple can give themselves fully to one another in love, without the undermining possibility that one or the other will leave when the going gets difficult. One reason why so many marriages break up today—one out of three in the United States—is because many couples enter the marriage without any reservations about divorce; these obviously will not give themselves as fully and perseveringly as those for whom divorce and remarriage is not a consideration. People are free to enter into this covenant or not, but once decided, the choice should be for life. "Until death do us part" should mean just that.

The Catholic Church has taught for centuries that there could be no divorce and remarriage for Christians. Read Matthew 19, 3-11. Here Christ is evidently changing the Mosaic law which allowed divorce, restoring it to what it was "from the beginning."

> Though debated by some, the phrase, "except for unchastity" (v. 9), is taken by most Catholic scholars today to mean the legal uncleanness of marrying within the degrees of kinship forbidden by Jewish law (Cf. 1 Corinthians 5, 1). Such a marriage would not be a real and valid marriage, and therefore one could separate and remarry. There is no exception mentioned in the earlier version of Mark (10, 2–12), in Luke (16, 18), or in St. Paul (1 Corinthians 7, 10–11 and 39).

It should be noted, however, that Jesus is laying down the basic **principle of** Christian married life when he excludes divorce—but he is not specifying the exact marital laws which would be appropriate for his followers in attempting to carry out that principle in practice.

But some couples must face the agony of divorce—they realize they are destroying themselves and perhaps their children and have no alternative but to separate and begin a new life. Particularly today, in our unstable society, this is often the decision—painful but courageous—that many people will have to make.

Separation and divorce without remarriage is sometimes allowed by the Church for a serious reason. The local bishop is the judge of this. Catholics may be allowed to go through the formality of a civil divorce (or separation) to settle custody of children, property, support, alimony, etc.—but not to remarry. And since separation is against the very nature of marriage, this can be done only for a very serious reason. St. Paul says:

> To the married I give charge, not I but the Lord, that the wife should not separate from her husband (but if she does, let her remain single or

else be reconciled to her husband)—and that the husband should not divorce his wife (1 Corinthians 7, 10–11).

Divorce and remarriage is also not allowed in the Eastern Churches united with Rome, but it was (and is) tolerated by the Eastern Christian Churches during the several centuries that these churches (now mostly Orthodox) were in union with Rome; vindicating reasons were "moral death," e.g., long separation, incurable disease, or adultery; and remarried persons had to undergo a period of penance before they would be readmitted to the sacraments. There are also instances of this in the Western Church.

Some bishops at Vatican Council II and some prominent canon lawyers today, as well as many couples, are urging that the Church reconsider its position on remarriage in cases of desertion, lack of mental as well as physical consummation, where the bond of love and therefore the marriage is "dead," etc.

To many in the Church, it may seem inhuman to require that divorced people, except for the few exceptions remain unmarried for the rest of their lives. However the Church must clearly teach the permanence of marriage as a real demand and not merely an unattainable ideal. This teaching is necessary for the common good.

It is estimated that today a third of all married Catholics in the United States will divorce or permanently separate. Many, unfortunately, abandon the practice of their religion altogether, while a minority join other churches which recognize a second marriage as valid. A relatively small number remain single, while most remarry "outside" the Catholic Church. Today, however, broadened "annulment" requirements enable many to remarry with the blessing of the Church, as shall be discussed shortly. For others, various possibilities have arisen, enabling them to take part in the Church's sacramental life while yet not being remarried in the Church.

One solution proposed by some theologians today is that if one has remarried "outside" the Church, has been living for some time in this second marriage, and it seems that the union is a good thing morally and spiritually, and one wishes to fully practice the Catholic faith (and particularly if there are children), a priest in a confessional situation might allow that person to once again take part in the sacraments (providing that no public scandal would be caused). It should be noted that those who favor this solution argue for it as a private step. It is not an approach officially and publically recognized by the Church.

There are divorced Catholic groups in many places throughout the country today and their numbers are growing. They offer the support and understanding that is so often desperately needed by one who has been through a divorce—counteracting the deep feelings of failure, guilt, insecurity, etc., that haunt so many people who have been divorced. Often these people give moving, personal testimony to their need of another marital relationship that hopefully will prove to be successful.

As far as Catholic teaching is concerned, the marriages of non-Catholics are real marriages and are valid until death (on condition, obviously, that they were free to marry—not married before, etc.—and did so freely and legally, intending to enter a permanent union). Obviously the Church cannot judge the conscience before God of a divorced and remarried person, Catholic or non-Catholic.

The Church may dissolve a valid marriage when one (or both) of the parties is not baptized as a Christian. This practice dates from the early Church. (Paul mentions it in 1 Corinthians 7, 12–15—hence the name "Pauline Privilege" given to some of these cases), and is predicated upon one of the parties sincerely wanting to become a Catholic and marry a Catholic. This second marriage is allowed because of the advantage to the partners and their children of Christians being married to other Christians rather than to persons who do not share their faith. Much investigation is usually required for this, and hence a priest should be consulted early in the relationship if one thinks this may apply to his or her situation.

An annulment is a declaration that, in the eyes of the Church, no marriage bond existed in the first place. It says nothing about the legal or social status of the marriage, that children born of the marriage are illegitimate, etc. An annulment might be given if the partners never intended to enter a permanent union or intended absolutely never to have any children; if one partner substantially deceived the other in relation to the marriage ("lack of moral rectitude"), or had significant psychological problems that would interfere with giving true, i.e., sufficiently mature, consent, or was an alcoholic, homosexual, or impotent; if a couple married only to legitimize a baby; if a Catholic were to marry without permission before a judge or non-Catholic minister—or for a number of other causes that might affect one's capacity to consent to a lifelong marriage, i.e., one's ability to fulfill the requirements of marriage.

Today annulments may be given for a wider number of reasons than ever before, as should be evident from what was said above—particularly with regard to medical or psychological problems that existed from the beginning, but came to the surface perhaps years later. Therefore persons whose marriages have permanently broken up should not hesi-

tate to talk to a priest about their situation—an annulment might be possible in their case. More and more competent, trained, and sensitive priests, deacons, religious, and lay people are now available to investigate and pass judgment on the validity of a marriage.

It is wise to consult a priest before judging whether someone's marriage—including one's own—is valid and permanent, or not, in the eyes of the Catholic Church. Often an understanding can be a great help to those trying to work out their marriage situation. Though greatly simplified today, the Church's marriage laws can be complicated; often help can be given to a couple where it seemed nothing could be done. Marriage is society's basic institution and all sorts of possible situations can arise. The Church has its own system of marriage courts, staffed by trained and sensitive priests and lay people, whose work it is to investigate and judge these situations. The Church's investigation is always confidential, and in most countries (including the United States) it has no legal effect, so one should not hesitate to seek advice.

Today a married couple must undergo new, confusing, and painful stresses and strains upon their mutual relationship—and upon their family life with their children. Thus, it is vitally important that couples be sufficiently prepared for marriage by re-examining and deepening commitments to their religious beliefs, their maturity and their ability to relate for life to one another, to raise a family, and to mesh this with their career/job plans. With the majority of married women working outside the home at least sometime in the marriage—and many for most of the marriage—there are inevitable husband-wife stresses, misunderstandings, and confusion about their roles.

BEFORE MARRIAGE

A couple should be mature—ready and able to assume the responsibilities of married life, the daily struggles as well as the joys, and the financial and social obligations that will come.

A couple should pray each day for a happy marriage and frequently take part in communion, asking for God's insights and blessings upon their union. "God is love," says St. John, and the more of God they have in their union, the more love there will be.

A wise couple will seek out some sort of premarital instruction or counseling, to prepare them for this greatest venture of their lives. They should particularly examine their religious convictions, especially if they are entering an interfaith marriage—this is often the most open time of their lives—and in most places competent adult religious instruction or discussion is available today. Many places have a series of lectures or discussions to prepare couples regarding the different aspects of marriage: spiritual, psychological, sexual, financial, etc. Some places have pre-marriage "encounters" in which a group of people spend a weekend together in prayer and practical preparation for their marriage. In fact more and more dioceses require an average six-month period for this beginning phase of thorough preparation.

> *A couple should especially be mature enough to seek advice* of an understanding and competently trained priest, minister, or marriage counselor if there is some continual, upsetting difficulty which they are not resolving—deep conflicts with either's family, inability to attain the proper sexual discipline, doubts about financial capabilities, or anything else that is causing either of them to worry.
>
> True and lasting intimacy can only be had between two people who are firm in their own sense of identity (a "comfortableness" with oneself and a mature sense of one's self-worth). Countless marriages end in divorce because the partners enter this relationship of intimacy to find out who they really are— in effect, each one using the other to try to get a secure sense of one's identity, one's true needs, abilities, and limitations. It is primarily saying, "I need you," rather than primarily, "I *want* you."

In their developing relationship with one another, a mature couple grow to respect the individuality of each other. They try to learn about one another—likes and dislikes, hopes and fears, strengths and weaknesses—and then each tries by loving respect to encourage and foster what is best in the other, and never tries to basically change the other. It often comes as hard to face that one's partner has convictions and personality traits quite different, and even opposed to one's own—and yet still deeply loves the partner.

They respect and show mature love for one another, as well, in the difficult and beautiful area of sex. They realize that sex is a powerful thing, reflective of their deepest attitudes toward one another, and the power that produces new human life. In this matter, particularly, the wise couple respects one another's ideals.

> Premarital chastity has been the Christian norm throughout the centuries. This norm was reaffirmed by the Sacred Congregation for the Doctrine of the Faith in its *Declaration on Sexual Ethics* in 1975. Pre-

marital chastity is the Christian norm not because sexual intercourse is something "dirty," but because it is the symbol and expression of a permanent union, of a lifelong commitment to one's partner. There is the type of young man who tries to "get what he can" from the girls he dates and who is usually quite boastful of his conquests, and there is the girl who clutches at whatever affection she can get, who is starved for true love, who wants someone to commit himself to her, and who therefore gives herself to anyone.

These young men and women are running from the real-life, permanent commitment to another that true love involves; they flit from one affair to another, trying to convince themselves that they are involved in loving—or seeking a true, lifelong love— but actually they are avoiding truly deep and mature human relationships. They usually have been rejected in their own childhood attempts to love, and so ever after they are fearful deep within themselves of being ultimately rejected by one to whom they would give themselves totally. The bottom line is that they cannot really conceive of themselves as truly lovable—as one who could be intimately known and yet cared about by someone else, day after day and year after year.

However, there are those who are capable of loving maturely, who are truly in love and intend to enter a permanent union and who therefore want to express their love, meaningfully and totally, by intercourse. Here, too, premarital chastity is expected because the public, lifelong communal commitment of the marriage ceremony has not yet been made. God, who surely has been in the relationship before, comes in this ceremony in a special and fuller way, as the couple make their commitment public before the Christian community and the world. In this ceremony they pledge themselves to this community, and to the world, no longer as two, but as one—and this permanently. They are announcing publicly that they belong solely to each other—they are now celebrating this with the community of those who know and love them most. The community, in turn, pledges them its support and strength for the rest of their lives.

Thus the marriage ceremony is far more than a mere giving of a "piece of paper" which says that the couple is legally and sacramentally married. It is a sacred occasion, perhaps the most sacred of the couple's lives. By this ceremony the couple express and celebrate the commitment they have made to give and accept one another totally for life, taking on all the day-to-day consequences with no longer any possibility of its ending. It is at this point that the total covenant commitment of the couple takes place; here it is that God gives them his special blessing and peace.

The act of intercourse is the fullest possible physical expression of the couple's total giving to each other. The Christian teaching then, is that it should take place when there has been the public, total and final commitment of one to the other in the marriage ceremony. The partners save for one another, in a sense, their wedding gift to each other—

this fullest expression of their love. Many couples have found by experience that it is deeply worth waiting until marriage before engaging in sexual intercourse because it makes the marriage that much more special.

Some couples feel that they have a deep, mature and permanent commitment to one another before the marriage ceremony—and often it has its consummation in the sexual union—and in the judgment of the couples this is not wrong. Their permanent, unconditional commitment (not the instability of trial or companionate marriage) draws them to a fuller expression of their love. Priests who are counselling couples, while they must present the Church's teaching regarding this, also realize that this teaching will be difficult for some couples to accept. The priest must challenge the couple; he must also be pastorally sensitive to them. Each couple, in dialogue with God, will have to do what they are capable of. Discipline is always necessary, and the realization that there will always be difficulty in attaining the values present in sexual restraint. Yet, we must face the fact that individuals and their moral capacities do differ; while there are objective moral norms to guide us, not everyone can follow these equally.

Sex can be a beautiful experience; it can express and deepen one's growing together with another, the developing, expanding, deepening that are what life is all about. Accepting one's sexuality—being regarded fully as a woman or a man—can be a great experience. It implies commitment and growth together, not something passing or merely fulfilling of one's physical or emotional needs. It means there must be love—enduring, growing daily, experiencing together the grime as well as the glory—in other words a permanent commitment to one another.

Sometimes living together sexually is a stumbling, questing experience in which two people seek to discover one another—and each his or her own identity as well. The couple should bear in mind that this is a powerful thing that brings them together; if it comes to be regarded lightly (as can happen in our "pill" oriented society), they will have destroyed the meaning of one of the most beautiful and fulfilling experiences in life.

Sinfulness enters into sexuality when one uses it to take advantage of another, or uses another for one's own selfish ends, as an object of one's lust, hostility, or the need to build one's own ego. This exploitation of another through sex is the root meaning of the "adultery" forbidden by the commandment of Judaism and by Christ himself.

There can also be a sinful *mutual* exploitation by a couple engaging in sexual actions; they might use one another as objects, to simply gratify one another's passions, escaping from life's responsibilities in one another's arms, seizing this passing sexual pleasure without reference to the future. They are indulging in the immature and sinful "luxury of suspended commitment." This is a great temptation in today's confused world, to ". . . be merry, for tomorrow we die"—it is sex without hope, choosing death in an act whose meaning is life.

One thing is certain: A truly authentic act of sexual intercourse will be expressive of a love that is totally self-giving, a final, permanent, and exclusive commitment.

The love of a couple, if it is genuine, will be expansive. It will not only stay within themselves but reach out to others. The couple will see beauty everywhere, especially in other people. They will find themselves more concerned with others, more understanding, tolerant, sympathetic. They will want to share the happiness of their love with all.

The couple must realize that they are still part of the human family, and have relationships to others of love, friendship, concern. Their own love should help, should deepen their bonds with others—and in turn, by the mysterious chemistry of charity, their love will be deepened by these other human involvements.

The deep sharing and intimacy of love can involve risks for the couple, but the risks, if the love is genuine, are worth it. A test might be this: Does their relationship make them turn out toward others in understanding and concern—even though they may at times fail—or does their relationship cause them primarily to turn in on themselves, feel sorry for themselves, be disturbed, not at peace, or resentful of others?

HOW TO GET MARRIED

A Catholic is normally married before a priest and two witnesses. Marriage is a sacrament of the Catholic Church. Just as other important religious actions are celebrated by Catholics in the presence of the Catholic community, with a priestly representative presiding—for example, confession or holy communion—so is marriage normally solemnized this way.

However, for good reason the bishop may allow an interfaith couple to be married before a non-Catholic minister. This might be more deeply meaningful to a couple, or at least to the family of the non-Catholic. In some cases a couple may wish a priest to be present also and offer some prayers or a blessing after the minister has officiated at the exchange of vows. Each couple should work this out for themselves, respecting each other's religious sensibilities.

These are some of the things necessary for a valid Catholic marriage: A man and woman must be of age, never before validly married, unless one's previous spouse has died, capable of sexual intercourse, freely intending to live together until death and to raise a family (if physically possible), not closely related by blood or marriage, and otherwise legally capable of marrying. The Church, incidentally, sees no obstacle to marriage in the fact that prospective partners are of different races.

> What was mentioned above covers most of the impediments or "blocks" which the Church has set up to safeguard marriage. The most common of these are grave fear or violence, lack of sufficient age, close blood or marriage relationship, a previous marriage by either party, lack of intention to live together and have children, certain mental or physical defects, and the common impediment of one party not being a Catholic. When there is sufficient reason to do so, the bishop may grant a dispensation which nullifies certain impediments.

To arrange for a marriage, the couple should see a priest in the parish of the bride at least a few months before their intended marriage, to fill out the necessary papers and to take part in whatever instruction he judges necessary. In the case of an interfaith marriage, the couple should see a priest in the parish of the Catholic party, and should allow an additional month or two for instructions. Permission can be obtained to have the marriage elsewhere than in the parish of the bride, or of the Catholic party to a mixed marriage.

The "banns" of marriage are usually announced for the marriage of two Catholics on the three Sundays before the marriage, usually at the principal Mass, in the respective parishes of the bride and groom; sometimes the banns are printed in the parish announcements. The banns may be dispensed with for any good reason.

Catholic marriage is normally celebrated at a nuptial Mass, although a couple could be married outside of Mass. (The nuptial Mass is briefly described in the section "IN THE LITURGY.") Interfaith marriages may also take place at a nuptial Mass if the couple so desires.

There should normally be two Catholic witnesses to the marriage, but one may have a non-Catholic as best man or maid of honor. Other attendants may also be non-Catholic.

CREATIVE, RESPONSIBLE MARRIED LOVE

True married love shares in the love of God for man, the love of Christ for his Church. By the total giving of one's self to another, asking nothing in return, the married couple participate in the nature of God, which is love. And likewise, both receive the tremendous support that comes with having their love accepted by their spouse. One can abandon oneself in complete trust to the other. Christ's example of love is his death, his abandonment of self, and his resurrection. For the married couple, sexual intercourse is the highest expression of total, unselfish, trusting love, of the giving of body, intellect, and spirit.

Like the love of God for us, true married love is meant to be creative. As the resurrection followed Christ's death, so new life follows the gift of selves between married couples. This life is shown in a deeper love between the couple themselves and the more encompassing love that they extend beyond themselves to include others. The unique extension of total love expressed by sexual intercourse—the living symbol and embodiment of their love—is another human being, their child. Married people, then, have this great privilege: "to be ready with stout hearts to cooperate with the love of the Creator and the Savior who through them will enlarge and enrich his own family day by day" *(Church in the Modern World,* no. 50).

A couple's sexual expression of their love, therefore, is a wonderful privilege given them by God. The married man and woman celebrate each other's beauty and goodness, with truly creative interaction, sharing intimate knowledge of each other. "With my body I thee worship," runs the mutual pledge in the form used by English Catholics. In an earlier period in the Church, the priest would often bless the wedding bed of the newly married couple; it is for them a sacred place where they find God in each other. Indeed, there is no such thing as immodesty when they are alone together. There is a call to complete trust in the hands of the other. The body of each is sacrament: "This is my body which is for you."

Sexual intimacy is a profound communication of one partner to the other, sometimes revealing God himself. Couples testify to this: in the heights of sexual union, they soar beyond themselves and experience a sense of belonging to what can only be God. Some compare this to the experience of the mystics in prayer—profound, surpassingly beautiful, indescribable.

This can also be vastly revealing of oneself, and therefore cries out for a fully open and honest commitment. This profound discovery of God and each other in sexual intimacy, this most beautiful experience, means that it must never be abused, but must be used with deep consideration, foresight, and honesty as God meant it from the beginning.

Sexual intimacy is meant to be used according to reason and God's plan. Humans alone can use this power according to judgments of mind and will, as well as instinctual attraction, simply because its use has such deep and lasting effects. This power can be compared to a beautiful lake formed above a dam: properly channeled, the water provides life and beauty; but if uncontrolled, havoc and hurt will follow.

> Because this is such a complex power, reflecting the depths of a person's being, it takes time for a couple to adjust sexually to one another. A mistaken modern notion is that sexual compatibility can be achieved almost immediately, or that its near-perfect "achievement" is necessary to the success of a marriage. There will be intercourse of the mind and heart between a couple a hundred times more often than that of the body. Each couple has special communications—words, touches, even looks—that can be as meaningful as the act of intercourse, and sometimes more so.

The deliberate abuse of one's sexual powers is seriously wrong, and often can contribute to the destruction of a couple's happiness, if not their marriage. Adultery, manipulatively refusing intercourse to one's partner, and sometimes masturbation are ways by which people abuse their sexual powers.

Adultery (sexual intercourse with someone other than one's marriage partner) is a perversion of the basic meaning of the act of intercourse. It makes of this fullest sexual expression, not a giving of oneself to fulfill one's covenant of love, but rather a means of self-gratification, or a confused seeking of intimacy and love elsewhere. Adulterous relationships are signs that something is seriously wrong in the marriage and that help should be sought by the couple.

> *Also it is a sign of something seriously wrong in the marriage when one partner continually has problems with sexual intimacies that are reason-*

ably desired by the other. The act of sex is an expression of mutual love, of union, of total giving. At times the expression may be hard, but to our partner it says that we love. Each should try to be responsive and/or not be afraid to tell our partner we aren't up to it. One should not expect perfection from oneself and the other. However, when sex is continually used as a weapon, a reward for good behavior or a way of manipulating one's partner, the marriage is in trouble. In these situations, each should be honest with the other about one's feelings, and together they should seek competent help.

Obviously there will be times when love requires that partners restrain themselves or put up with some manipulative use of sex that vents frustration from other areas of life. Often a person's temporary impotency or frigidity—or inability to fully enter into what the other desires—directly reflects one's feelings of impotency or unfulfillment in areas one cannot control, e.g., some period of change or crisis in one's life, one's work, etc. Wise, mature partners are sensitive to and usually become accustomed to each other's feelings, needs, and abilities.

Homosexuality, too, has been considered through the centuries as a perversion of the natural order of the sexes, and often as a threat to human society. This teaching was reaffirmed by the *Declaration on Sexual Ethics* in 1975. Modern studies and pastoral experience, however, show that there are types and degrees of homosexuality, some evidently morally culpable and some not, and that many homosexuals have made notable contributions to human society.

The sin in a homosexual relationship, as with all sexuality, comes when it is a stunting process, a lustful or mutually narcissistic escape from the responsibility of human growth. Most confessors today would urge their actively homosexual penitents to do what is possible for them, to realize their human dignity and talents, to avoid self-castigation, and to never lose hope for deep and stable friendships, consider themselves pariahs, or give up the eucharist because of this.

Anyone who has worked with pastoral sensitivity among homosexuals knows of the self-contempt, loneliness, and fear of disclosure that have haunted so many of them. Their sad history of abuse and discrimination is fortunately gradually changing. The 1973 paper addressed to confessors by the American Catholic bishops discerningly recognizes several things:

There is nothing evil in being homosexual. Homosexuals do not will to become such. But there is a wrongness attached to homosexual "acts." Further, confessors should not insist that homosexuals seek psychiatric treatment when it is clear that their sexual orientation is "fixed" or irreversible. Homosexuals are urged to practice sexual abstinence; they need deep and stable friendships among both heterosexuals and other homosexuals (the same need for human intimacy we all have, and a necessity for mature growth as a person, psychologically as well as spiritually).

Also, the bishops state, homosexuals have the same human and civil rights as anyone, including the right to jobs for which they are qualified. Finally, the bishops encourage homosexuals to be active members of their local church communities.

More is becoming known about homosexuality today, and much more needs to be known. Continuing theological reflection is needed in the light of our broadening knowledge. As Christians, we do know that each homosexual person is an individual of dignity and lovableness, and, as with anyone, has particular talents and gifts to contribute to the Christian community and to the world. Especially among Christians, homosexual people should find sensitivity, appreciation, caring, and opportunities for mutual growth. The *Declaration on Sexual Ethics* calls on us to treat homosexual persons with understanding.

It seems clear that there are "true" homosexuals, i.e., those who are comfortable within themselves regarding their basic homosexual orientation. And there are those who are not, who may have had homosexual encounters (even over a period of years), but who are yet unsure of their basic sexual orientation and are unhappy or confused.

Particularly during one's teenage years of psychosexual development, one can regard oneself as a true homosexual when in reality one is not. Thus, most respected college counselors generally advise students against openly declaring themselves homosexual during this period. Often, homosexual or bisexual inclinations of young people who are forming their initial adult identity disappear once they have a more mature sense of their total identity, of who they are, what they want and are capable of in life. On the other hand, true homosexuals may be confirmed in their sexual orientation during this time, and can better integrate it with their total sense of their adult self and be persons as lovable in God's eyes as anyone. People who experience ambiguity about this can often be greatly helped by competent counseling.

Masturbation also has been considered wrong through the centuries as a perversion of the sexual act which of its nature is social, meant to be generative and expressive of love, and not solitary. This was reaffirmed in the *Declaration on Sexual Ethics.* Priests and others who are counseling with regard to this today find that masturbation is sometimes described as a satisfying release from tension, frustration, etc., and is an almost inevitable experience of adolescent boys—and contemporary studies bear this out. Habitual masturbation in adulthood might also be a symbol of a deeper problem which requires attention. The sin here is in using this as an escape, a stunting of one's heterosexual and interpersonal growth. To be avoided is worrying over masturbation as a great, serious wrong, on the one hand, and on the other, taking it too lightly with little or no attempt at personal discipline. The *Declaration on Sexual Ethics'* statement that in sexual matters full consent of the person may not always be given, would seem to apply to some cases of masturbation.

Parents should have "human and Christian responsibility" in the raising of their family *(The Church in the Modern World,* no. 50). Procreation involves not only having but also raising children. God does not demand that a couple have as many children as possible. Parents must return to God mature Christian adults, not babies. Responsible parenthood goes on for years and demands the best talents, the fullest response a couple are able to give. Each couple must look conscientiously at themselves and at the generosity of their life service—and generosity is not always measured in numbers, though the sacrifice of couples in raising large families and the wholesome love evident in many of them is beyond question a wonderful thing.

> *How many children a couple should have is something that only they, in dialogue with God and one another, can determine.* This is sometimes not easy to decide. Some couples need to plan their family more than others, and for many it can become a positive obligation. Couples can differ greatly—some have difficulty raising a few children, while others can successfully raise a dozen. Capabilities, temperament, circumstances of finances, health, and ability to live up to the Christian ideal can vary a good deal.

> Let them thoughtfully take into account both their own welfare and that of their children, those already born and those which the future will bring. For this they need to reckon with both the material and the spiritual conditions of the times, as well as of their state in life . . . (and) they should consult the interests of the family group, of temporal society, and of the Church herself. The parents themselves, and no one else, would ultimately make this judgment in the sight of God (*Church in the Modern World,* no. 50).

> *The several "natural" methods of family planning—the best-known of which is the "Billings Method" (also called "Natural Family Planning")—are definitely approved* by the Church. These (and their predecessor, the "rhythm" method) are considered natural, and therefore morally unobjectionable, since nothing mechanical (condoms, diaphragms, intrauterine devices or IUDs), nothing chemical (the "pill") or "artificial" is used to prevent conception. Direct sterilization—at present America's most-used method of birth control—is considered

unnatural because it deprives a person of his or her ability to reproduce, one of the two purposes of marriage. This teaching was upheld in a letter from the Vatican to the American Bishops in 1975.

Contraceptive birth control as a means of preventing the generation of children has been considered wrong in the Church's teaching. The Church has held to this through the centuries because of its regard for marriage and the sacredness of human life, including the way in which it is brought about. It has been pointed out that one of the great purposes of the sex act is to bring into existence new human beings who will live forever; to interfere with this act unnaturally is to prevent life in an act meant to give life. Further, artificial birth control can frustrate the total physical self-surrender which is vital to married love. Pope Pius XI, Pius XII, Paul VI, and John Paul II have all condemned contraceptive birth control.

However, as is generally known, there has been much discussion within the Church about this question. Many point out that now that a consideration of what is "natural" involves not only the physical sex act, but its meaning to the human persons involved and the total context in which it is done (the family the couple already have, their physical, mental and material capabilities, the society in which they live, etc.); as with any action, the circumstances and purpose of the sex act must be considered in determining its morality. The intentions of some couples seem to be purely selfish, while others are trying their best to live a truly Christian marriage. However, this does not mean that each couple can decide the morality of this solely by themselves, however well-intentioned they may be; while their conscience is always their ultimate guide, they must also consider the objective standards of morality given them by the Church (Cf. *Church in the Modern World,* no. 51).

We must recognize that within recent years our understanding of human problems has increased rapidly. New cultural outlooks, social conditions and pressures are now upon us—the problem of overpopulation, for example, is becoming crucial. Our understanding of human nature and of marriage is blossoming, as articulate Catholic laypeople, particularly, give their views. In this matter, as in anything, the Church has not spoken the final word, and a development of its teaching in view of changed modern conditions is quite possible. No question of infallibility is involved.

Some leading cardinals and bishops on the floor of Vatican Council II publicly questioned the Church's traditional teaching on birth control and asked for a new look at the problem. The Council did not give any concrete solution. Pope John XXIII and then Pope Paul VI in June 1964 formed a special commission of bishops, theologians, medical doctors, psychologists, sociologists, population experts, married couples, and others to study the problem and recommend possible solutions. The Commission members recommended by a ratio of four to one that the Church liberalize its teaching on contraception. Then, in July, 1968, Pope Paul VI in the encyclical "Humanae Vitae" reiterated the traditional ban on any form of contraception: He said that the Church teaches "that each and every marriage act must remain open to the transmission of life." Reaction to the encyclical was swift: Many priests and laypeople dissented from the pope's statement, including 172 American teaching theologians who asserted that for grave reasons Catholics may follow their conscience on this even though the pope had spoken. Others, mostly bishops, backed the pope and said his teaching was binding on all.

In practice there are circumstances in which couples feel that they cannot now comply with the pope's teaching. These couples may be rightly motivated, trying to lead a good Christian married life, willing to practice self-denial; but they feel that their present situation is such that for grave physical, financial, or psychological reasons they cannot use periodic abstinence. Their conscience tells them that great damage would be done to their marital love and perhaps to the children they already have if a child were to come at this time. For some couples, usually under heavy financial and other pressures, the choice of contraception can present itself to them as the only alternative to a possible abortion, obviously a far greater evil. In effect, today many Catholic couples feel justified in conscience in using contraceptives. Vatican Council II recognized their situation:

> This Council realizes that certain conditions often keep couples from arranging their married lives harmoniously, and that they find themselves in circumstances where at least temporarily the size of their families should not be increased. As a result, the faithful exercise of love and the full intimacy of their marriage is hard to maintain. But where the intimacy of married life is broken off, its faithfulness can sometimes be imperiled and its quality of fruitfulness ruined, for then the upbringing of children and the courage to accept new ones are both endangered (*Church in the Modern World,* no. 51).

As various national conferences of bishops met in 1968 and 1969, they affirmed the pope's right to speak authoritatively in this matter. But many of them recognized the difficulties for couples in adhering to the pope's teaching. The Belgian bishops, for instance, said: "We cannot assume that those who do not see the convincing value of (the pope's) reasons are acting out of selfish or hedonistic motives. . . .We must recognize, according to the traditional teaching, that the ultimate practical norm of action is conscience which has been duly enlightened. . . ."

The German bishops recognized that "no encyclical of the last decades has aroused so much opposition as this one. . . . Many priests and laypeople who want to remain loyal to the Church are greatly perplexed. . . ." Recognizing that many cannot accept the encyclical's statement on the methods of regulating births, they add: "Pastors will respect in their work, especially in the administration of sacraments, the decisions of conscience of the believers made in the awareness of their responsibility." The bishops of Austria speak of the "uneasiness which has gripped so many of our Catholics" and say that if someone should go against the teaching of this encyclical, "he must not feel cut off from God's love in every case, and may then receive Holy Communion without first going to confession." The U.S. bishops, after affirming the objective evil of artificial contraception, "urge those who have resorted to this never to lose heart but to continue to take full advantage of the strength which comes from the sacrament of Penance and the grace, healing, and peace in the Eucharist."

The Canadian bishops recognized that on this matter "many Catholics face a grave problem of conscience." They quote Vatican II: "In all his activity a man is bound to follow his conscience faithfully . . . according to truly Christian values and principles. . . . They state that "the confessor or counselor must show sympathetic understanding and reverence for the sincere good faith of those who fail in their effort to accept some point of the (pope's) encyclical," and then they say that there are some who, "accepting the teaching of the Holy Father, find that because of particular circumstances they are involved in what seems to them a clear conflict of duties, e.g., the reconciling of conjugal love and responsible parenthood with the education of children already born or with the health of the mother. In accord with the accepted principles of moral theology, if these persons have tried sincerely but without success to pursue a line of conduct in keeping with the given directives, they may be safely assured that whoever honestly chooses that course which seems right to him does so in good conscience."

In more recent years some authors have softened these early criticisms of "Humanae Vitae" by noting the presence in our society of a destructive contraceptive or anti-child mentality, and by noting that, while we must respect persons' consciences, false or erroneous decisions can sometimes be made by those who follow their consciences. Priests and counselors, therefore, will need to explain clearly and fairly the Church's teaching and be respectful of the difficulties couples can face and the decisions they honestly make.

CHRISTIAN FAMILY LIFE DAY BY DAY

A Christian marriage is a public expression of a deep, personal and spiritual commitment—much more than a license from society or an agreement to live together. It is a lifelong commitment of two persons to merge their two lives into one. It is an awesome commitment and an awesome responsibility—possible only because of God's help.

God is the third partner in every successful marriage. A Christian couple prays regularly for their marriage and for their family. Many spend some "quiet time," or solitude, periodically, in prayerful reflection before God, considering the course of their life and marriage, as well as the needs and wants of their partner. Then, on occasion, they spontaneously share what has come to each in solitude with God. Some may set aside a time regularly to share their solitudes. Some very happy couples pray together regularly or read and reflect on some of the scriptures with one another.

Success in marriage requires much more than a romantic feeling of loving and being loved. True marital love consists of a fundamental choice made from the depth of one's being, a decision to give oneself totally and unconditionally to one's partner, and a living out of this when the glow of romance goes.

A Christian marriage is a commitment of a man and woman to learn to love ever more perfectly. It is a promise to grow in love, including a pledge to cooperate actively in providing nourishment to the budding relationship. Marriage is not an "end" but rather a "means"—and thus only the beginning of an ever-deepening love relationship which will require a great deal of effort, patience, and grace. It requires a strong, total commitment to the basic marriage commitment—and to its permanence. When times of conflict arise, this "commitment to the commitment" can provide the determination necessary to refuse to abandon a troubled marriage and to work together through the difficult times toward a more rewarding marriage relationship.

Christian marriage is also a commitment to life—to becoming fully alive. A mature Christian marriage provides a secure setting in which the partners have the time and freedom to become more truly themselves, more creative, more productive, more nourished by the spouse's love and support, and more mature. Guided and strengthened by one's faith, marital love thrives in an atmosphere of freedom and trust, where each is allowed and encouraged to grow, individually and together. In the absence of this, the marriage commitment can become a stifling bond which hinders rather than aids the partners' development and which can eventually suffocate the love relationship.

> The partners, then, should be free to develop their own interests, while at the same time being sensitive to their mutual need to share common interests and goals. It is vitally important that basic long-range goals be similar and that each one's expectations be discussed honestly and regularly, so that the partners are working in the same direction, rather than one or both being (often silently) frustrated, confused, and resentful.

A mature Christian married couple will realize that they are an integral part of the human community which surrounds them in their daily living. They reach out in love to others who come into their lives, as much as is practicable, rather than becoming selfishly absorbed in only their own happiness. They develop relationships of love, friendship, and concern with those around them, according to each one's ability to do so. These relationships can contribute to the growth of the couple, individually and jointly.

> Each partner most often has some personal friendships which the other does not share. Even cross-sexual friendships need not be a threat to fidelity, but can contribute to a deeper appreciation of one's partner, and to a growth in fidelity unpoisoned by possessiveness and jealousy. One's mature sense of "territoriality" will tell one if one's partner is overdoing this, and it should be discussed frankly, or advice should be sought from a counselor.

Mature couples realize that there will be inevitable stresses and conflicts because of the changing nature of marriage and family life today. With most married women working full- or part-time—to make ends meet financially and/or for their own personal development—there are usually "role reversal" problems—insecurity, identity-confusion, feelings that one's partner "does not understand," and often serious communication breakdowns. Partners must work at trying to appreciate the other's viewpoint, vital interests and needs, and keep trying to mutually communicate.

Partners in a successful marriage learn to develop a sensitive imaginativeness and spontaneity. They make every effort to be aware of the little things which especially bring joy and pleasure to their spouse; one of them may be better at this, by nature and temperament, than the other. They express the often unpredictable excitement of real loving, discovering new depths and resources within each other. A good spouse is like the Holy Spirit, peaceful but also prodding (that we might be our best self). Often this requires a conscious effort to plan for special times together, away from the kids, etc.

The sexual expression of their love is usually each one's most precious gift to his or her beloved. Each should be sensitive to the partner's needs and desires and try to approach their love-making in a spirit of loving cooperation, imagination, creativity, discovery, and fun. The sexual act is meant—and is used—by God to be literally love-making, i.e., to bring about new, deepening, more binding bonds of love between each other and with God himself.

Good communication is an absolutely essential ingredient of a successful marriage. If the partners are able to express themselves freely, and if each has learned to really listen to what the other is trying to say, almost any problem that arises can eventually be resolved. Truly honest communication can be delightfully satisfying, and painfully disrupting, with many variations in between. But for real knowledge and true understanding of one's partner, honest communication is absolutely necessary.

To maintain open and intimate emotional contact, it is essential to share verbally one's honest likes and dislikes, compliments and complaints, hopes and fears—though perhaps not as the first thing in the morning, or immediately after coming home from work. Partners who continually avoid the discomfort that honest interchanges can bring usually wind up with a superficial, frustrating, unfulfilling relationship—a mere living together for social acceptance, personal security or occasional sexual strokes, instead of a deep, truly sharing, truly mature Christian union.

Financial difficulties are a cause of many marital problems. Some people allow themselves to be slowly and subtly enslaved by an ever-increasing desire for material things, for the comforts and status that money can bring, by a feeling that they should have what neighbors, relatives, business associates, and friends have. One day they may find that they have all the material things they want, but have no marriage. In their struggle to have, they have forgotten how to be—how to love. Many couples suddenly find that spending more than they can afford—the so-easy use of credit cards, for instance—causes much anxiety and affects every area of their marriage.

A couple must be truly wise to resist the bombardment of modern "consumeristic" advertising (especially from television) which makes luxuries seem like necessities, the badgerings from their children, and the temptation to give material gifts as a substitute for one's time or one's self. Often the pressure (and/or inner psychic need) to succeed, and the constant competitiveness that is endemic to our society, can make one a quasi—or full blown—workaholic, and perhaps one day the wealthiest person in the divorce court.

Disagreement over having, and especially over the raising of, children is another large problem. Here, as in all areas, wise partners must continually communicate, openly and sensitively, sharing their most honest feelings and opinions, in order to achieve a unified method of parenting—firm but always flexible. Methods of child-raising will vary from family to family, and degrees of firmness or permissiveness differ, but good guidance and many good books on the subject are available. Cf. FURTHER READING.

WHAT OF INTERFAITH MARRIAGES?

The Catholic Church, like most other faiths, wants marriage partners to be of the same religion, but allows interfaith marriages because of the circumstances of our society. A couple who disagree on the basic points of religion usually cannot expect to have the perfect union and total sharing of interests and ideals that those of the same religion should have. Serious differences often arise over prayer, church attendance, the children's education, etc. Religion is often pushed into the background because it is a point of conflict, and both parties and their children can end up with no religion.

However, some interfaith marriages have a greater chance of succeeding than others. There is, first of all, a crucial distinction between a marriage of two Christians, one of whom is a Roman Catholic, and a marriage of a Christian to one who is not. Further, if a couple is compatible in other things, well-adjusted and mature, their interfaith marriage obviously has a better chance of succeeding than one in which there are other major differences as well. If both can genuinely agree on the religious upbringing of the children, they have far more in their favor than if one only reluctantly agrees to raise the children in another faith. If each has a thorough understanding of the other's religious belief, the chances for a successful marriage are greater.

The Catholic in an interfaith marriage is asked to promise: "to do all in my power to share the faith I have received with our children by having them baptized and reared as Catholics." This simply means that Catholics will do all that, according to their grasp of and degree of faith, they feel is necessary and feasible for the children's religious upbringing. What is able to be done by one parent in one marriage may not be possible for another in another marriage. The couple must respect one another's conscience and religious sensibilities. A Catholic upbringing means a pledging of the child to this Christian community in baptism and the other sacraments; it does not necessarily mean attending Catholic schooling, nor that other religious beliefs should not be taught, but that the child's basic orientation is Catholic. It is a choice made for the child, as parents will do in many areas they consider important; later in life he may feel in conscience that he wishes to change his religious commitment.

The Church has asked this promise because it honestly believes it can present the children with the truth that God gives us in Christ and that any good Catholic who knows his faith would want his children to share that faith. Any responsible parent wants his child to have the best training and upbringing possible; in this most important area of all, our relationship with God and attainment of heaven, the Catholic parent normally wants his child to have all the helps he has, to share most completely in God's plan of salvation.

A problem which might arise is that the partners may not be able to agree on the religious upbringing of their children. Couples should definitely discuss this before marriage. Sometimes the inability of a couple to agree beforehand on this is a sign, however painful it is to face, that their marriage might not work out. They may simply be too far apart on what, for each, is a fundamental conviction in their lives. They may need the maturity and courage to break off their relationship. One person may "give in" to the other, but as the children arrive and grow, there may develop a smoldering resentment that can destroy or paralyze the marriage. Couples who must maturely face the need of breaking off a relationship should realize that the experience has not been a total loss, that each has received much from the other, that they both have matured toward even better future relationships—however remote this may seem at present.

It seems, however, that today the religious question can usually be resolved by the couple, particularly if they are in agreement on other aspects of their future relationship. But occasionally a deep disagreement over religion by the couple is a telltale clue that there are other fundamental incompatibilities that they are unaware of or are ignoring. Sometimes it is in reality a signal that there is already under way a "power struggle" for dominance in the relationship. Here, of course, perceptive and unhurried premarital counseling is needed.

The Church's attitude toward interfaith marriages has changed in recent years from grudging approval to recognition; now it tries to give as much spiritual help as possible to the union. The nuptial Mass and blessing may be used to celebrate interfaith marriages, if the couple so desire. Local bishops may allow the couple to ask a minister to say some prayers and give a blessing and exhortation to the couple after the Catholic wedding ceremony. Also the local bishop may allow the couple to have a non-Catholic minister perform the whole marriage ceremony—usually with a priest present as the Catholic Church's official witness—if there is some good reason for doing so (e.g., it would ameliorate the feelings of the non-Catholic family) and providing there is no scandal by doing it.

With intelligent cooperation and the help of God, an interfaith marriage can enjoy a good deal of success—and sometimes have more of God's love than one between those who have the same faith but are lukewarm in their practice of it and their love. The couple must respect one another's belief, and should try to discuss their religious convictions frankly, calmly, and with a sincere desire to learn.

In some cases, especially after adequate previous instruction, the points of agreement will be found to far outweigh those of disagreement. Above all, religious discussion and practices should never be pushed into the background simply because of differences.

The common religious beliefs of a couple should be sought out and emphasized, particularly in raising the family. Both partners should take an active part in the religious upbringing of the children, for each has insights, ideals and practices to communicate; a situation should never develop where one party feels "left out." Although the children are being raised basically in one belief, the convictions of the other partner should also be honestly and tactfully presented.

Some further suggestions: If both parents are believers, they can pray together and with the children—prayers of any faith, or "made up" by the parents or children. The bible can usually be a common source of religious inspiration, stories and teachings for the children in which both parents can take part. Teachings and stories about God, his love for us, our moral obligations, etc., are things both can share in.

If both parents are Christians they can share even more: They pray to the same Triune God, profess their faith in the same Apostles' Creed, take their teachings from the bible, believe in Christ as Savior, acknowledge their Christian unity by baptism, know the importance of some sort of confession and forgiveness of sin, share basically the same moral code, celebrate the same feasts, and often follow the same liturgical cycle of scripture readings.

IN THE LITURGY

The Catholic marriage ceremony takes place after the gospel of the nuptial Mass. The priest usually gives the couple an instruction on marriage. Then the bridegroom and bride exchange vows. The wedding rings are blessed, and exchanged by the couple. The priest asks God's blessing upon the couple and the Mass continues: the couple offer themselves through Christ, with Christ, and in Christ to the Father; after the Lord's Prayer the priest reads over them the nuptial blessing; at communion they are joined in the most intimate way possible with Christ and through Christ with one another. After communion there is a final blessing, and they go forth as husband and wife.

Many couples now plan their wedding service, to reflect themselves and the role of their families, friends, and the Christian community closest to them. They can choose meaningful scripture readings and prayers and can write their own wedding vows (keeping, of course, the essential element of a lifelong commitment of fidelity). They can include family and friends in the readings, prayers and other little ceremonials that they will talk over with the priest as they plan their marriage. The service should be a joyous, personal, and shared event of culminated love. Cf. FURTHER READING for books and booklets to help the couple prepare spiritually, and in other ways, for their ceremony.

The feast of the Holy Family—Jesus and his human family, Mary and Joseph—is celebrated on the Sunday after Christmas. The great feast of the Incarnation, Christmas, is immediately followed by this feast, thus proclaiming that God truly became a man, truly one of us, because he came among us as part of a very ordinary human family—and he was nourished and loved, and he grew in wisdom and learning in his human family, just as any of us did.

> Parishes may have a renewal of marriage vows on this day. A Christ-conscious parish will be sensitive to all its married members on this day: those who are living out their marriage vows in pain, those who are separated or divorced, and those who are remarried.

SOME SUGGESTIONS FOR ...

DISCUSSION

What expectations should one have—and not have—when entering upon a Christian marriage?

What, for you, are the most essential ingredients for a successful Christian marriage?

Can you understand the creative place of sex in marriage, physically, psychically, and also for spiritual growth together?

What do you think are some of the liabilities and possibilities of an interfaith marriage?

What are the most important aspects of a truly Christian family, in your experience?

FURTHER READING

* *Together for Life,* Champlin (Ave Maria Press, 1979). A widely-used, very good book for couples planning marriage. Especially useful are the suggestions for planning a wedding ceremony.
* *Preparing for the Sacrament of Marriage.* DelVecchio (Ave Maria Press, 1980). A psychologically-oriented book for testing compatibility.
* *The Premarital Inventory* (Bess Associates). A widely-used indicator of how a couple are communicating.
* *Marriage Preparation Resource Book* (National Institute for the Family, 3015 4th St. N.E., Washington, D.C. 20017). An updated publication of the U.S. Catholic Conference offering a compendium of material and resources for marriage preparation programs.
* *Creative Marriage,* Barbeau (Seabury, 1976). Excellent for couples who have been married for some time.
* *Living Happily Ever After,* Hart (Paulist Press, 1979). A useful book on the theology of marriage.
* *Declaration on Sexual Ethics,* (U.S. Catholic Conference, 1975). A statement of the Sacred Congregation for the Doctrine of the Faith.
* *Sexual Morality, A Catholic Perspective,* Keane (Paulist Press, 1977). A balanced and realistic appraisal of sexual morality. Contemporary in spirit, but using traditional moral norms.
* *Growing Through Divorce,* Young (Paulist Press, 1979). A pastoral and compassionate look at divorce in the Catholic Church.

FURTHER VIEWING/LISTENING

Roommates on a Rainy Day (Paulist Productions)—A warm, insightful probe into the commitment of marriage that many young couples are hesitant to make today. 26 minutes.

A Small Statistic (Paulist Productions)—A moving story of a sophisticated young couple who find God in the death of their baby. 29 minutes.

Celebration in Fresh Power (Paulist Productions)—A timely, sensitive story of a young couple's confrontation with the morality of abortion.

PERSONAL REFLECTION

Christ promises a couple all the graces they need to make their marriage a success—but he will never force himself upon them. The couple must come and receive these graces, especially by acts of mutual love and caring, by prayer and taking part in the Church's worship and sacraments. In the sacrament of reconciliation the couple should concentrate on overcoming the faults that interfere with their union and their role as parents; when taking part in communion they should particularly ask to grow in love for one another and their children. Each of us should pray daily for our own marriage, for those close to us who are experiencing problems and pain in their relationships.

22
The Family That Is the Church

How can the Church be a meaningful community of love in today's world? What place do laypeople have in the Church? Why are priests and nuns particular groups within the Church, and what are their basic functions? What emerging role do women have in the Church? What is the role of the bishop?

GOD'S GIFTED PEOPLE

The Church is a family in which all the members should love and serve one another and all men. We are "one body and one Spirit. . . ." We have "one Lord, one faith, one baptism: one God and Father of all, who is above all and throughout all, and in us all" (Ephesians 4, 4–6). What affects one, affects the others. We must love one another and work together for the good of all. Christ tells us clearly, "By this all men will know that you are my disciples, if you have love for one another" (John 13, 35).

Our Christian family love extends to all men, for all have God as their Father and Christ as their brother. Race, creed, color, sex, age, talents or social status should make no difference. Christ reminds us again, ". . . as you did it to one of the least of these my brethren, you did it to me" (Matthew 25, 40).

No one is essentially holier or better than anyone else in the Church. Christ said to all his followers, "You, therefore, must be perfect, as your heavenly Father is perfect" (Matthew 5, 48). The Church today emphasizes his words: ". . . All the faithful of Christ, of whatever rank or status, are called to the fullness of the Christian life and to the perfection of charity. . . ." *(Constitution on the Church,* no. 40). Some seek this holiness as priests, others as nuns or brothers, others in the married state, and yet others in the single state, or by their labor.

Everyone in the Church, clergy and laity, is to share in its work, each using his or her particular gifts. We saw how all the members of the Church have particular charisms, or gifts of the Spirit, to be used for the good of all. Vatican Council II reminds bishops and pastors that "the right and duty to exercise the apostolate is common to all the faithful, both clergy and laity, and . . . the laity also have their proper roles in building up the Church. . . ." *(Decree on the Apostolate of the Laity,* no. 25).

> *The laity are "sometimes even obliged" to express their opinion* on what concerns the good of the Church. The Council envisions that this will be done "through the organs erected by the Church for this purpose." Pastors are exhorted to give the laity responsibilities, to allow them freedom of action, and listen to their advice (Cf. *Constitution on the Church,* no. 37; *Decree on the Apostolate of the Laity,* no. 3).
>
> . . . Let it be recognized that all the faithful, clerical and lay, possess a lawful freedom of inquiry and of thought, and the freedom to express their minds humbly and courageously about those matters in which they enjoy competence (*The Church in the Modern World,* no. 62).

We saw that every Christian layperson shares in Christ's priesthood and is a special mediator between God and man. All Christians by the power of baptism, and again by confirmation, can offer Christ at Mass in a special, powerful way, and can bring down grace upon mankind by their prayer and partaking of the sacraments. **Reread 1 Peter 2, 9.**

Every Christian also teaches and bears witness to his faith as one specially chosen by Christ. "Christ . . . continually fulfills his prophetic office . . . not only through the hierarchy who teach in his name and with his authority, but also through the laity whom . . . he made his witness and instructed by an understanding of the faith . . . and the grace of the Word. . . ." (*Constitution on the Church,* no. 35). All persons have the understanding, power and grace to be an instrument of the Spirit in bearing witness in their own way. All should ask the Spirit to help them fulfill their role.

PRIESTS, GOD'S INSTRUMENTS
AT THE SERVICE OF MEN

Men have always had need of mediators, those who can give assurance, particularly from the witness of their own lives, that they are "in touch" with the beyond. They are those who struggle as anyone does, but they show by their example, by the inspiration, learning, discipline and service of their lives that they know of a power beyond. People want the testimony of someone they can trust, particularly if that person is learned, not prejudiced or narrow, in touch with human realities and concerned about people. People seem to intuit the divine presence behind one's words, that one is the instrument, however poor and stumbling, of this power.

There have always been priests among us, mediators between God and humanity. Ancient pagan tribes had priests to offer sacrifice. In Israel as in other societies the oldest member, or patriarch, of the family or tribe offered sacrifice and acted as mediator between God and his people. Then Aaron and his sons were chosen as priests, to offer sacrifice; they were to be made "holy to the Lord," specially consecrated, clothed in sacred vestments and anointed with oil: **Read Exodus 40, 12–15.**

Jesus Christ is the one priest of the new covenant, the great and only necessary mediator between God and us. He offered himself in sacrifice, shedding his own blood, to seal the new covenant for all time.

> The former priests were many in number, because they were prevented by death from continuing in office; but he holds his priesthood permanently, because he continues forever. Consequently, he is able for all time to save those who draw near to God through him, since he always lives to make intercession for them . . . he has no need . . . to offer sacrifice daily, first for his own sins and then for those of the people; he did this once for all when he offered up himself (Hebrews 5, 23–27).

Christ made his apostles his first priests. He sent them out early in his ministry to preach the kingdom of God, to exhort the people to conversion, to cast out devils and heal the sick (Cf. Mark 6, 7–13). Then, at the last supper he gave them the central priestly power of continuing his eucharistic meal: "Do this in remembrance of me"

(Cf. 1 Corinthians 11, 23–26). When he appeared to them on Easter evening he gave them the power of forgiving sins (John 20, 21–23).

In the New Testament the term "priest" is used almost exclusively of the Jewish priesthood; it is sometimes applied to Christ (in the Epistle to the Hebrews) and to the whole Christian people who are a "royal priesthood" (1 Peter 2, 5 and 9). Yet it is evident that the apostles were specially chosen by Christ to do what ordained priests do: to sacrifice, teach authoritatively, and bring men his saving helps.

From the beginning in the Church certain men were ordained by laying on of hands and prayer, to minister to the spiritual needs of the community. In the account of the ordination of the Seven who would serve at table (undoubtedly often the Lord's supper or eucharist) and who later preached and baptized, we read, "These they set before the apostles, and they prayed and laid their hands upon them" (Acts 6, 1–6).

We saw (chapter 10) that the organization of the early Church was formed only gradually—Christ left it to his followers to work out—and that New Testament terms do not necessarily mean what they do later. But the terms "presbyter" (elder) and "bishop" refer to those who had some office in ruling over the local churches (Acts 14, 23; 20–28, etc.). The ordination ceremony of Timothy, chosen by Paul to lead a local church, is clear: Paul writes, "Do not neglect the gift you have, which was given you by prophetic utterance when the elders laid their hands upon you. . . . I remind you to rekindle the gift of God that is within you through the laying on of my hands. . . ." (1 Timothy 4, 14; 2 Timothy 6).

While the New Testament stresses the pastoral work of the apostles and their successors, the bishops, early Christian tradition shows that they also presided over the eucharistic sacrifice-meal. Clement of Rome writes near the end of the 1st century: "It will be no small sin for us if we eject men who have irreproachably and piously offered the sacrifices proper to the episcopate" (Epistle to the Corinthians, 42, 44). These sacrifices are "the bread and the cup," the eucharistic sacrifice. In an early 3rd century Roman liturgy, the newly ordained bishop consecrates the bread and chalice and then addresses God with the remembrance prayer or "anamnesis": "Doing therefore the anamnesis of his death and resurrection, we offer to thee the bread and the cup, making eucharist to thee because thou hast bidden us to stand before thee and minister as priests to thee" (*Apostolic Tradition of Hippolytus* 4, 11).

From the 1st century there has been a hierarchy of orders in the Church—bishops, priests (presbyters), and deacons (Cf. chapter 10). For the first eight centuries the rite of ordination to these offices was simply an imposition of the bishop's hands and an invocation of the Holy Spirit. In the Middle Ages the rite was expanded to include an anointing of the hands, bestowal of chalice and paten, etc., but the heart of the ceremony remained what it was from the early centuries.

> The earliest detailed rite is given in the *Apostolic Tradition of Hippolytus* referred to above, a Roman bishop's book compiled about 215 A.D. In this we find the hierarchy of bishops, presbyters, and deacons, each ordained by a laying on of hands. There are other, lesser offices, but these are merely appointed, not ordained by a laying on of hands. The bishop is chosen by all the people, and is ordained by the imposition of hands of his fellow bishops alone; the presbyter is ordained by an imposition of the bishop's hands with "the presbyters also touching him."

Men become priests today as always—by the sacrament of holy orders—the laying on of the bishop's hands and prayer. Through this sacrament Christ changes one interiorly, giving one the powers of the priesthood, a great increase of his grace-presence, and a promise of all the actual graces and helps he needs to carry out his priesthood.

Holy orders is received only once, like baptism and confirmation. By it a man is changed permanently; he is a priest forever. Even if he stops practicing the priesthood, or is released from his priestly vows, he still is a priest in God's eyes. He is established for all time in this permanent function for God and men.

There are different orders or degrees in the priesthood:

A bishop has the fullness of Christ's priesthood. He is a successor of the apostles, in that he carries on what they received from Christ himself. He acts as Christ's instrument in giving all the sacraments, is the only one who can administer holy orders, and is normally the one to give confirmation.

A priest has the power of presiding at Mass, leading the people and acting as Christ's special instrument re-presenting his sacrifice. He also acts as Christ's instrument in giving the sacraments (except holy orders and normally confirmation), in preaching and teaching, and in asking God's blessing upon people and things.

A deacon's ministry is to baptize, distribute communion, read the scriptures and preach, conduct marriages and funerals, give sacramentals, and give himself to works of charity and administration;

these works are done to the extent the local hierarchy sees fit. A deacon is also ordained by a bishop. A permanent diaconate has been revived by Vatican Council II, and can include married men "of more mature age" as well as celibate young men.

> According to the Apostolic Letter of Pope Paul VI, *Ministeria Quaedam*, the following changes in regard to major and minor orders are to be noted:
> 1. Minor orders are henceforth called "ministries." They are no longer seen as steps to the priesthood, but they are also open to lay Christians who have no intentions of going on for the priesthood.
> 2. First tonsure is no longer conferred; entrance into the clerical state is joined to the diaconate.
> 3. Only the ministries of *reader* and *acolyte* have been retained.
> 4. The *subdiaconate* has been suppressed.

> A *"monsignor"* (as the term is used in America) is a priest who reeives this honorary title from the pope, at the request of his bishop, because of some outstanding work he has done or some position of importance he holds. There is some discussion today about the meaningfulness of such titles in the Church.

"Priests, as co-workers with their bishops, have as their primary duty the proclamation of the gospel of God to all. In this way they fulfill the Lord's command: 'Go into the whole world and preach the gospel to every creature' (Mark 16, 15). Thus they establish and build up the people of God" (*Decree on the Ministry and Life of Priests,* no. 4). Preaching the Word leads to faith, to conversion, to holiness. If we are to take part profitably in the sacraments and the Mass we must listen openly to this preaching, allowing faith to grow in us and our heart to be converted. God speaks even through the dullest sermon; his Word always does something to us if we but let it.

The celebration of the eucharist, the Mass, is the high point of a priest's work, ". . . the source and the apex of the whole work of preaching the gospel. . . . The other sacraments, as well as every ministry of the Church and every work of the apostolate, are linked with the holy eucharist and are directed toward it . . . (as) the very heartbeat of the congregation of the faithful over which the priest presides" (*Decree on the Ministry and Life of Priests,* no. 5).

For a further glimpse into how the Church views the mission of her priests, we have this summary of Vatican Council II:

For the sick and penitents among the faithful, they exercise the ministry of alleviation and reconciliation, and they present the needs and the prayers of the faithful to God the Father.... They gather together God's family as a brotherhood, all of one mind, and lead them in the Spirit through Christ to God the Father. In the midst of the flock they adore him in spirit and in truth.... They labor in word and doctrine ... believing what they have read and meditated upon in the law of God, teaching what they have believed, and putting in practice in their own lives what they have taught (*Constitution on the Church,* no. 21).

This, too, is an apt summary of a priest's calling: "The heart of the vocation of the priesthood is to minister to the deepest needs of man: man's need for meaning in life, man's need for encouragement in despair, for support in crisis, for forgiveness of guilt and return to God...." (Kennedy and D'Arcy, *The Genius of the Apostolate,* Sheed & Ward, 1965, p. 7).

Priests are called "Father" because they give the life of grace to their spiritual children and teach them God's Word—just as a natural father gives physical life and instructs his children. "... I became your father in Christ Jesus through the gospel," says St. Paul (1 Corinthians 4, 15).

Priests are chosen from among God's people to serve the people. They are first of all Christians, and then priests. They live a special life in order that they may be better instruments of Christ in serving the whole Church. They are not necessarily holier, nor are they of a higher class in the Church's structure; whatever authority they have, or respect they are given, comes to them only because they visibly represent Christ—as deference to an ambassador is meant for the country he represents. Laypeople may often be gifted by God to accomplish far more for the Church and the world.

Vatican Council II says that while priests are "set apart" among God's people, "this is so, not that they may be separated from this people or from any man, but that they may be totally dedicated to the work for which the Lord has raised them up. They cannot be ministers of Christ unless they are witnesses and dispensers of a life other than this earthly one. But they cannot be of service to men if they remain strangers to the life and conditions of men" (*The Ministry and Life of Priests,* no. 3).

Today in the Church there is stress on the priesthood of service, on the ministerial as well as the cultic priesthood. The modern priest sees that he follows one who "came not to be served, but to serve" (Mark 10, 45), and who gave a striking example of service by washing the feet of his first priests, the apostles, when he "ordained" them at the last supper.

Priests also have different charisms or gifts for different works. One is talented at a certain type of work, while another may be a failure at it. In today's age of specialization, particularly, it is almost impossible for priests to be "all things to all men"—and yet this is required of many, especially parish priests. Catholic people, however, are usually wonderfully understanding of the inadequacies of their priests.

To become a priest one studies and prepares from four to five years after completing college. Usually he does his graduate work in theology, scripture studies, and pastoral practice in a seminary with other candidates for the priesthood. He must not only have the continuing and free desire to be a priest, but must be judged suitable (by his bishop or religious superior) in learning, character, and health.

Priests of the Latin rite bind themselves to celibacy, not to marry. This custom began to grow from the 4th century and was made a general law of the Western Church in the 12th century. Priests of the Eastern rites may marry, usually before the diaconate. The basic reason for celibacy is that the priest might better be a living sign or witness to the reality of Christ among us. In giving up the fundamental and deepest human love relationship, marriage, the priest expresses his total attachment to the divine. He is staking all on the reality of God among us. The loneliness that is his gives him a kinship with all who are alone or who are neglected in their pain, and can propel him into a deep intimacy with Christ. Christ alone is at the core of his being, and no one else.

The celibate priest can often have a greater independence, be more totally at the service of others. St. Paul expresses it: "The unmarried man is anxious about the affairs of the Lord, how to please the Lord; but the married man is anxious about worldly affairs, how to please his wife, and his interests are divided" (1 Corinthians 7, 32–34).

As to why they are celibate, however, many today in the priesthood, religious life, or among the laity would probably echo these perceptive words of one who has been an influential celibate of our time:

"Today, the Christian who renounces marriage and children for the kingdom's sake seeks no abstract or concrete *reason* for his decision. His choice is pure risk in faith, the result of the intimate and mysterious experience of his heart. He chooses to live *now* the absolute poverty every Christian hopes to experience at the hour of death. His life does not *prove* God's transcendence; rather, his whole being expresses faith in it. His decision to renounce a spouse is as intimate and incommunicable as another's decision to prefer *his* spouse over all others" (Ivan Illich, in *"The Critic,"* June–July, 1967).

A modern poet/priest writes: "In love we desire to possess a human body, but the body of the beloved can never be wholly possessed. Only God can be totally possessed. Only God can be truly embraced, because the arms of the human soul were created for the infinite, for nothing more and nothing less. Thus neither the world nor the woman we love can be truly and wholly embraced and possessed, and neither the world nor a woman can fully satisfy human desire, for only God can do that" (Ernesto Cardenal, in *To Live Is To Love*).

However, many in the Church today recognize that there is no necessary connection, historically or pastorally, between the priesthood and celibacy. Pope Paul VI in his encyclical reaffirming celibacy allows for further study of the question. Many today recognize that among priests, as among all Christians, there are different charisms. Some are called to work and witness as celibates, others as married. Many feel that good men are being eliminated from the priesthood because of celibacy. Among Eastern rite Catholics and among Orthodox Christians both forms of the priestly life have always been recognized. Countless Protestant ministers have effectively served the Lord and their flocks while married, while celibacy too is practiced among them by individuals and by small but significant groups. Most who advocate optional celibacy in the priesthood do not wish to abolish celibacy, but to make it what they feel is a freer choice. In the Church of the future, many predict, religious communities will be celibate, while diocesan priests will embrace either state of life.

There are two general types of priests: diocesan or secular, and religious. While the work of the priesthood is basically the same, these two general types of priests have developed over the centuries to better carry out this work. The diocesan priest works under the bishop of a particular diocese, is bound by the law of celibacy (not to marry, in the Latin rite), and provides for his own support from a small salary, offerings, etc. The average parish priest is a diocesan priest, though these may also specialize in particular works. Bishops are usually chosen from among these.

Religious priests belong to a religious community, and take vows or solemn promises of poverty (in some way restricting their ownership of things), of celibacy or chastity, and of obedience to their religious superior whom they usually elect. Each religious community has a particular spirit and work, and strives to have a "common life," praying and working together as a group and ready to move from diocese to diocese or even to other countries to carry out their particular priestly work.

> *Priests are human instruments of Christ, often sinful and defective, and in need of the support and prayers of the people.* Eleven of the first twelve priests deserted Christ, their leader denied him and one of them betrayed him—so we should expect to find weaknesses among his priests today. People often do not realize how much their priests need the constant support of their prayers. No one realizes his inadequacies, limitations, and sinfulness more than a priest. St. Paul expresses every priest's feelings when he writes: **Read 1 Corinthians 1, 26–31.**
>
> Vatican Council II also poignantly expresses the mind of every priest: ". . . the ministers of the Church and even, at times, the faithful themselves feel like strangers in the world, anxiously looking for appropriate ways and words with which to communicate with it. . . . The modern obstacles which block faith, the seeming sterility of their past labors, and the bitter loneliness they experience can lead them to the danger of becoming depressed in spirit. . . . Priests should remember that in performing their tasks they are never alone. . . ." *(Decree on the Ministry and Life of Priests,* no. 22).

Christ, then, shows himself among us today in a particular way in his priests. One of Christ's first and greatest priests, St. Paul, describes all priests when he says, ". . . we are ambassadors for Christ, God making his appeal through us" (1 Corinthians 5, 20). Through the priesthood Christ makes himself available to all in a special, organized, human way. The priesthood witnesses to God's loving reality among us by serving all men—making God's love real to people as best we poor humans can.

The priest is there at the high points and critical moments of people's lives: when men come before God in worship, when they come to express repentance, at the moment of their lifelong commitment in marriage, in sickness, and when they are facing the conclusion of it all in death—and with advice and guidance in many little ways along the path of life.

> Every priest also has insights, like that of the fictional Pope Kiril I, in Morris West's novel, *The Shoes of the Fisherman:* "Once more I

have been brought to see vividly that the real battleground of the Church is not in politics or in diplomacy or finance or material extension. It is the secret landscape of the individual spirit. To enter into this hidden place the pastor needs tact and understanding, and the very particular grace bestowed by the sacrament of holy orders. . . ."

The great modern priest-paleontologist, Teilhard de Chardin, expressed his priestly vocation in this way: "To the full extent of my power, because I am a priest, I wish from now on to be the first to become conscious of all that the world loves, pursues and suffers; I want to be the first to seek, to sympathize and to suffer; the first to unfold and sacrifice myself . . . to become more widely human and more nobly of the earth than any of the world's servants."

Today it is seen more and more that the Church is a community in which different people have different gifts, all of which are necessary and important. The once clear distinction between priestly leaders and people whose role was mainly to follow has been disappearing. We are coming to realize that each member has something to contribute, and often the contribution of a lay person in a particular matter is more vital than that of a priest or religious. We are coming to see that the Spirit speaks and acts through all, particularly where "two or three are gathered together" as a group in his name. It is also becoming clear that sometimes the special way of dress, titles, separate living facilities, etc., which are generally part of a priest's lifestyle today, while often helpful, need not be necessary to the priest's role in the community, and sometimes may in fact be a hindrance in his work.

There is much discussion today about the priesthood—particularly when the Church is seen both as a hierarchical community and as one of people with different gifts. One way of viewing the priesthood is to see the priest as the one who particularly shows forth, and brings about, the unity and order of the community—and this especially when he leads the community in liturgy. Though others may have gifts that are more important to a particular community, the priest is the unifier and the one who assures that gifts of all are recognized and used effectively.

Some today also see the priesthood as an office within the community to which one is called by God either for life or for a time—though the role of the priest as the unifier and stabilizer of the community would seem to usually call for a long-term commitment.

THE ROLE OF RELIGIOUS

The religious life is that by which priests, nuns, or brothers join together in a particular religious community, with a particular spirit and "rule" or way of life, to do particular works in the Church. Religious life is found in all the world religions, in Islam, Buddhism, Hinduism, among Catholics and Orthodox Christians, and it is a small but growing movement in Protestant Christianity. In the Catholic Church there are several hundred religious communities, each with its particular spirit and functions.

"Religious," that is, men and women in religious communities, have a "common life." They usually live together, have some daily pattern of prayer and work, and to a greater or lesser extent share what they own with one another.

Each community has some distinctive "habit" or garb worn by the members; this might be thought of as a sort of uniform signifying their profession. Many religious habits, particularly of nuns, have been modified today to conform to the realities of life in the modern world. Some religious live in their homes, wear ordinary clothing and may have regular jobs or professions; these come together periodically for study and spiritual renewal.

Religious take vows, or solemn promises, of poverty, chastity, and obedience. By these they seek more fully to imitate Christ, and serve the Christian community.

By poverty they restrict their ownership of things and depend for their support upon their religious community; this detachment from material things enables them to give themselves more fully to God and to others. By chastity they witness to the reality of God among us, and can give themselves fully to the service of all in the Christian community. Obedience puts them at the service of the Christian community in that they better use their talents in the cooperative effort of all. In some newer religious groups, nuns write their own expressions of dedication which retain the essence of the three vows.

These vows do not mean that religious are in a state of life higher than the other people of the Church, nor that they are holier. Rather they join together with others in the stable life of a religious community, and bind themselves by vows, to better attain the perfection to which all Christians are called, and by their lives to be "a sign that can and ought to attract all the members of the Church to an effective and prompt fulfillment of the duties of their Christian vocation" (*Constitution on the Church,* no. 45). They are living reminders to all Christians that Christ is now among us and that shortly we will be with him forever.

> *Many "contemplative" communities,* focused mainly on the worship of God and union with him, share their insights and wisdom with those who come to their "guest houses" for retreats and other spiritual guidance.

A nun or "sister" is a woman who belongs to a particular religious community. Nuns serve the Church and the world as educators, doing hospital and social work, by working in the missions, in the business world, in the sciences, etc. Others live relatively secluded lives of prayer and penance, doing a minimum of outside work, in contemplative orders; these might be compared to unnoticed but vitally necessary powerhouses—they bring God's grace and love into all our lives, especially by being models of total dedication and detachment.

A brother is a man who lives the religious life in a state other than the priesthood. As with nuns, some brothers are teachers; others do hospital, social or missionary work, or any work for which they are suitable. Some, too, are in contemplative communities.

> *To become a nun or brother,* as in becoming a priest, one must have a desire for this life, undertake several years of study and training, and be judged suitable in character, learning, and health. After taking temporary vows or promises for several years, perpetual vows are taken, committing one for life to this vocation; but even after this one could leave and return to a lay Christian life.
>
> *All religious communities today have updated themselves,* changing the rules under which they function, according to the principles of Vatican Council II. The process of change has been often painful and stress-filled for those concerned, but it has gone forward wonderfully. There is discussion today about the role of religious communities in the future Church. Some foresee the emergence of smaller, less structured, more specialized and homogeneous groups in which the talents of the individual members will be used more effectively for particular works of service. Some older communities are already doing this, as well as the newer communities that have more recently emerged. Lay people, often married, are becoming "co-members" of some of these groups.

Religious and priests might be compared to signposts—standing somewhat apart, often lonely, but at the service of men as they point the way to God; others may pass them on the way to holiness, but without them the others would have a much harder time finding their way.

OUR BISHOP AND OUR DIOCESE

A bishop has the highest degree of holy orders, the greatest share in Christ's priesthood. We saw (chapter 10) that the bishops occupy the same place in the Church as the apostles chosen by Christ—that they are ordained, as they have been for two thousand years, by the laying on of hands of another bishop (usually three bishops take part)—and that bishops are chosen by the pope usually upon the recommendation of the other bishops of the area, and, finally, that many today favor the practice of giving the local clergy and laity once again a voice in the selection of their bishops.

The bishops of the Church are responsible for the welfare of the whole Church. They have a responsiblity of teaching and governing all the parts of the Church, and at present they are exercising this through elected representative-bishops who tri-annually meet to advise the pope in a World Synod (Cf. chapter 10). They are particularly responsible for their own region or country—for this, regional or national conferences of bishops have been established. Each bishop should especially be concerned to provide clergy, lay people, and material help to the deprived parts of the Church.

The bishop is the leader of the local church or diocese—in a sense, its spiritual father. If the diocese is large, he may be assisted by auxiliary bishops. Dioceses are grouped into provinces centered around an archdiocese (usually the largest diocese of the area) presided over by an archbishop. Each bishop in his diocese is independent, subject only to the pope and in some matters to the national conference of bishops.

A *"cardinal"* is a bishop who is the leader of a particularly large archdiocese or has some high administrative position in the Church. This is essentially an honorary function, dating from the Middle Ages. The cardinals come together when a pope dies to elect a new one, chosen for the last several centuries from their own number—in this they are the successors of the ancient clergy of Rome who from the earliest days came together to elect their bishop, who was therefore the pope. The pope chooses the members of the "college of cardinals" which in recent years has been made a more international and representative group. There is speculation today as to the future status of this group, since their function of advising the pope and setting Church policy, and perhaps the election of the pope, may be in the future more and more taken over by or shared with the synod of bishops.

The bishop is the chief preacher and teacher of his diocese, its chief priest and pastor. He should make Christ's doctrine relevant to the needs of the time, bring forth holiness in people, and should himself give an example of holiness "in charity, humility and simplicity of life." The liturgy celebrated with the bishop is the high point of the worship of the diocese. The bishop is also to "seek out various people and both request and promote dialogue with them" and should "deal lovingly with our separated brethren . . . and foster ecumenism. . . ." (*Decree on the Pastoral Office of Bishops,* nos. 12, 13, 16).

"In exercising his office of father and pastor, a bishop should stand in the midst of his people as one who serves." A bishop is not above the Church, nor is the Church his private domain. He is to be a servant of the people of God, in imitation of the servant of all, Jesus. He should know his people and they should know him. He is to be "a true father who excels in the spirit of love and solicitude for all." He should "so gather and mold the whole family of the flock that everyone, conscious of his own duties, may live and work in the communion of love" (*Decree on the Pastoral Office of Bishops,* no. 16).

The people of a diocese, in turn, should give respect to their bishop, assisting and working with him in whatever way they can. The people realize that bishops are only human, that in fact the twelve apostles themselves could even betray, deny and desert Christ. They know, too, that only so much can be expected of some older bishops in today's rapidly changing world. They realize that their bishop is given a special gift to guide them. They should remember particularly that he is in need of their prayers because of his great responsibilities.

The priests and people of a diocese should be in continual commu-

nication with their bishop, giving him "active cooperation rather than passive obedience." They should try to use their particular gifts for the service of the diocese, realizing that the Holy Spirit also acts through them. Almost all dioceses now have a senate of priests set up as a consultive body to assist the bishop in governing the diocese. This was a reform decreed by Vatican Council II *(Decree on the Pastoral Office of Bishops).*

All the people of the diocese are to share in the work of the diocese, contributing not only their talents and money, but also opinions that would be helpful in its administration. Vatican Council II recommends that "in each diocese a pastoral council be established over which the diocesan bishop himself will preside and in which specially chosen clergy, religious, and lay people will participate . . . to investigate and to weigh matters which bear on pastoral activity, and to formulate practical conclusions regarding them." Some dioceses have had "little councils," and others are gradually incorporating more clerical and lay representatives into their administrative structures.

Where the regular channels of communication and common effort envisioned by the Council are not fully set up, lay people should write their bishops when they feel they have something to contribute so that the bishops can more easily get to know their views.

> Some suggest today that in our rapidly changing world the Church would be better served if bishops were elected for a certain term of office, long enough to give stability and yet limited enough to make those selected sensitive and responsive to the needs of the times. Some see this as a partial solution to the evident credibility gap that now exists in some dioceses between hierarchy and people. Some dioceses now have begun appointing parish pastors for a limited tenure of office; religious communities have long had this practice in their parishes.

Dioceses are divided into parishes, each of which has a pastor and, if needed, assistant or associate pastors. The pastor and priests are to serve the people of the parish, teaching them and leading them in the liturgy and in lives of practical charity. The people should cooperate with them, contributing their talents in whatever way they can. There is usually some parish organization of which one can be an active part. If there is no suitable group in your own parish, you should seek out one in a neighboring parish, or perhaps a diocesan or informal interparochial group.

Vatican Council II recommended regular meetings of the clergy, religious, and lay people of the parish, and also interparochial meetings (*Decree on the Apostolate of the Laity,* no. 26). Much of the administrative and pastoral work of a parish can be taken over by competent lay people; various types of lay boards are successfully operating in some places. We can learn much from our Protestant brethren about this.

Where diocesan and parish councils are functioning in the Church, getting them under way and keeping them operating effectively has often been a difficult and yet deeply rewarding process. Gradually clerical authorities and people come to know and trust one another, and also to trust the democratic process, and real progress can emerge. Catholicism is now experiencing what our Protestant brothers have long been struggling with; it is a slow but vitally necessary process, requiring patience, openness, mutual respect, and charity of all involved.

The parish, with the church as its center, is the place where the Christian people gain strength and go forth continually into the world to witness to Christ. From the local Christian community grace goes forth into the whole neighborhood—and the more truly Christian they are, the more their influence will radiate to everyone, to the whole world. The parish priest is the living sign of the unity of those who are a part of their little community; he must do the best he can to represent Christ by his service to all who come to him.

However, in today's increasingly urban, mobile society, large city parishes particularly are less and less able to produce an effective contact, or a real sense of community, among the people within their boundaries. Different solutions have been tried: smaller parishes that are not burdened with the upkeep of a large "plant"; "sub-parishes," ideally with a priest over each, within the structure of the larger unit; or special services given to specialized groups, using whatever facilities are available.

In today's changing Church, a number of people, especially those who are younger, are seeking out parishes other than their own where the style of worship and activities are compatible with their religious needs. While we might wish that every parish could be "all things to all men," it is evidently not possible, particularly in this age of change and fragmentation.

Mutual aid among parishes of a diocese—and of the world— should be practiced more and more, with the wealthier in terms of

money, talent, and stable population helping the less well off. Interparochial structures are also being used more today, particularly for
effective religious education, social action, etc.

THE EMERGING ROLE OF WOMEN IN THE CHURCH

**Today more and more women are emerging into new, more equal
and more creative roles in the Church, as in all of society.** There is
no doubt that, despite the dignity given women in Christianity (in
part due to the cult of the Virgin Mary), women have often been ex-
ploited and reduced to an inferior status by male celibates who may
have been unconsciously anti-feminist. This is changing, slowly but
steadily, as women's roles in all of society are changing. Today's sexual revolution, quietly in preparation for centuries, is now fully with
us—especially during the past decade—and is perhaps the most far-
reaching in history.

**The ideal Christian (and human) community, toward which the
Church is committed to strive, was simply stated by St. Paul almost
two thousand years ago:** "There is neither Jew nor Greek, there is
neither slave nor free, there is neither male nor female, for you are all
one in Christ Jesus" (Galatians 3, 28). Though it may seem to some
that women have advanced little since Vatican Council II, they ha
been growing in numbers and importance as competent, innovative
theologians, writers, pastoral workers, and in many other ministries;
they are more and more the articulators of family values, of business
and professional ethical norms, and defenders of the victims of our
highly competitive, often "macho," society. They are finding new
creative strengths and talents, as well as imaginatively expanding
their traditional role as homemakers (with the sharing help of
spouses).

All growth is painful—especially rapid growth in a relatively short
time—and so there is often confusion and conflict about roles, defen-
siveness on the one hand, and impatience with delay on the other.
Women often disagree (as do many men) about their future roles in the
Church, but their influence is expanding in every aspect of the
Church's life. Their greatest need—and right—is a more effective voice
in decision-making processes, especially beyond the local level. One
thing is certain: the clock cannot be turned back, and women's seeking

of more effective participation and the "intrinsic equality" stressed by Vatican II can only go forward.

The priesthood has been limited to men from the beginning of the Church. In view of the low social status of most ancient women in Israel and elsewhere, it is not surprising that women were not among the twelve chosen by Christ. However, modern scholarship has shown that women were prominent among Jesus' disciples, and that they shared in ministries of hitherto unrecognized importance in the early Church. For instance, respected New Testament scholar Fr. Raymond Brown has shown that women and men shared equally in the essential function of discipleship in the early Johannine communities. In several communities founded by St. Paul the same evidently was true.

In medieval times, influential abbesses often took an active part in local and ecumenical Church councils. St. Teresa of Avila and St. Catherine had decisive influences on the course of Church history. During the nineteenth and early twentieth century, women religious helped powerfully in shaping the growing American Church, as typified by St. Elizabeth Ann Seton, the first native-born United States citizen canonized a saint.

The Church's traditional restriction of ordination to men was restated by Pope Paul VI in 1977 (and also in the statements of Pope John Paul II). The core of the 1977 papal decree is that men "more perfectly show forth the image of Christ." Polls show, incidentally, that a majority of American Catholics, of both sexes, do not at present favor the ordination of women—but the percentage in favor of their ordination is steadily increasing. The large majority of theologians agree that the ordination of women is not a matter of doctrine, but—as with priestly celibacy—a matter of Church discipline. Masculinity is not intrinsic to the theology of the priesthood. Therefore this requirement might one day be changed without the relatively long process of doctrinal development.

Seen in worldwide perspective, all the major world religions—except for most of Protestant Christianity and a fraction of Judaism—do not allow the ordination of women (or its equivalent). The growing movement favoring the ordination of Catholic women is taking place in Western Europe and particularly in the United States and Canada. Many here feel that social, cultural, and educational differences in the universal Church should be taken into account—that women in our culture, for instance, might be ordained as deaconesses. These—men as well as women—view the denial of any participation in the sacrament of holy orders to women as a continuing symbol of their *de facto* inequality. Interestingly, many women do not want to simply follow the traditional male model of the priesthood, but rather are gradually and creatively developing their own models of ministry. Equality does not mean sameness, and while deriving much from males in ministry (and vice versa), many women want to contribute their own unique insights and strengths.

Finally, well worth reading is the statement from the National Conference of Catholic Bishops in the United States on "The Changing Roles of Men and Women." The bishops draw some very relevant conclusions that, if taken seriously, should go far to reduce traditional stereotyping of the roles and functions of sexes.

IN THE LITURGY

At Mass in the Prayer of the Faithful we pray particularly for those who are associated with us in the Church—for those who are sick, deceased, or in any need, as well as for our bishop, priests, and religious. During the eucharistic prayer of the Mass we pray for all the types of people in the Church, clergy and lay, living and dead, and ask the intercession of those who have gone on ahead of us into eternity.

DAILY LIVING: THE MATTER OF VOCATION

People are gifted and inspired by God to live a particular form of life. This is their vocation. Most are called to be in the married state, others are called to be priests or religious, and yet others are attracted to remain in the single life. An indication of one's vocation is an attraction to that particular state plus the capability of living it. All persons should ask for guidance in choosing or in living the vocation that they feel God wants them to have.

We should also recognize the single life—aside from the priesthood or religious life—as a true vocation, and one that can be fruitful and joyful. Some can be single involuntarily, or have a divided mind about marriage, and their lives might be filled with sadness and frustration. But others accept their single state, try to center their lives on others, and often show great creativity in helping others and the world in general. Some of the best people in the Church are living this sort of life.

If one's son or daughter feels an attraction to the priesthood or religious life, he or she should be encouraged to follow this up freely and intelligently (Cf. Hebrews 8, 4). Good counseling is available today in the Church. No seminary or religious community wants to carry along those who would be misfits in such a life. More and more, too, it is seen that this choice must be made when young people are more mature, if they are to persevere in this life.

SOME SUGGESTIONS FOR ...

DISCUSSION

Is it evident to you how the Church is a family, a community in which all should have a part?

How do you think the Church locally, as you know it, might more effectively use the gifts of all to serve all?

What do you think are the most notable problems, and possibilities, of the priesthood today? Of the religious life?

FURTHER READING

* *Why Priests?* Küng (Doubleday, 1972)—A creative consideration of the priest's role in today's world.
* *The Second Journey, Spiritual Awareness and the Mid-Life Crisis,* O'Collins (Paulist Press, 1978) is a discussion, good especially for priests and religious, of this widespread developmental problem; worth noting is that some seem to go through this several times, and some not at all.
* *Followers of Christ,* Metz (Paulist Press, 1978): An excellent, brief book on the religious life and the meaning of poverty, chastity, and obedience in today's context.
* *The Silent Life,* Merton (Farrar, Straus & Cudahy, 1957) is a fine look into monastic life, from the least to the most "detached" from the world.
** *Women Priests: A Catholic Commentary on the Vatican Declaration,* Swidler & Swidler (Paulist Press, 1977)—A comprehensive, broad-based and very good collection of writings on all aspects of women and the priesthood.
** *Women in New Testament Ministry,* Tetlow (Paulist Press, 1980) is a fine scholarly study on this significant question.

FURTHER VIEWING/LISTENING

A Slight Change in Plans (Paulist Productions)—27 minutes—is a pointed story of a young man's search for something more in his life; quite thought-provoking.

PERSONAL REFLECTION

God has given each of us particular talents—gifts to help carry out his plan. I might ask myself how well I am using the gifts I have—particularly in working with others in the Church family, or with other men of good will.

23

The Greater Family to Which We Belong

Why do Catholics pray to saints? Why is such honor particularly paid to Mary, the mother of Christ? Is prayer to Mary or the saints essential for a Catholic? Can these and other dedicated Christians help us to lead better lives?

THE SAINTS: OUR MODELS AND INTERCESSORS

To be a Christian is to realize that we are joined with one another on the way to heaven. One does not go alone, as if sealed by oneself in a sort of space capsule. We must help and be helped by others. Unfortunately the religion of some is narrowly individualistic, a "God-and-me" relationship. The Church, however, is a family in which we are concerned for one another: "If one member suffers, all suffer together; if one member is honored, all rejoice together" (1 Corinthians 12, 26).

Besides our Church family on earth, we belong to a larger family of God, the Communion of Saints. We are united with those who have gone before us—those in heaven and in the preparatory state of purgatory (these latter we will discuss in the last chapter). We call this the Communion of Saints, that is, the union of all who share in the life of Christ, whether on earth or in the next world; this is why the early Christians used the term "saint" for one another. Later the word came to mean primarily a person in heaven.

From the beginning Christians have believed that our love and help for one another could extend beyond death (except, of course, to the damned). Early inscriptions, as in the Roman catacombs, show that the first Christians prayed for those who had died, and also asked their prayers. Those who had died were still part of the Christian family, loving and being loved, only temporarily hidden from the sight of those yet here below.

We honor and imitate the saints—those in heaven—as we would anyone we love, particularly if he or she is outstanding. The saints are the outstanding members of our Christian family, our Christian heroes. They are the truly great lovers of history. Each one shows some particular aspect of Christ, and in imitating them we are trying to imitate Christ; thus St. Paul could tell his converts, "I urge you, then, be imitators of me" (1 Corinthians 4, 16).

There are saints from every class, every occupation, with every type of temperament and background. They show us how Christ can be imitated in anyone's life including our own. As we tend to follow models in medicine, business, science, homemaking, etc., so here. Statues, pictures, relics (things which belonged to the saint) are reminders of them and their holiness; such things have no power of themselves, and to believe such would be superstition.

The Church is careful about who is declared to be a saint. For the past several centuries they have had to undergo the long process of "canonization," a scrupulous investigation for several decades of every aspect of their lives including the scrutiny of a "devil's advocate" whose sworn duty it is to try to disprove their holiness, and usually the requirement of miracles (cures with no known physical or psychic explanation) through their intercession. Despite this, several thousands have been canonized for their heroic sanctity, declared to be with God in heaven.

In earlier centuries saints often became such through popular acclamation or continued veneration. During those more credulous centuries some were venerated as saints about whom little or nothing was known, and others have been shown by modern research to have little claim to our veneration. A group of historical researchers called the Bollandists have been at work for the past few centuries systematically and painstakingly separating fact from fiction about the saints. No claim is made that the canonized saints are more than a tiny fraction of those who are with God in heaven. They are simply the ones that God has brought to our attention in the Church, to spur us on to imitate them. Undoubtedly there are other and holier people in heaven, but the saints are proof that holiness and heaven are attainable, that it *can* be done, and they show us how to do it amidst the same circumstances of life as our own. The great Swedish Lutheran Bishop Söderblom put it precisely: "The saints make clear to us that God lives."

We ask the saints to pray for us, as we might ask someone here on earth for his prayers. Since we are all one family, if we are attracted to certain saints and ask for their help, their love can help us as it might have if we had known them on earth. This is only natural; if love and interest toward our neighbor sums up the way we should live on earth, we would not expect that those in heaven would suddenly forget us here on earth and have no more interest in us.

For those not used to asking others to pray for them, this practice will seem especially strange. Sometimes Catholics are little help when they speak of "praying to Saint So-and-So"—actually a prayer can end only with God, and to believe differently would be idolatry; we should rather speak of asking a saint to pray with us, or for us, to Christ and the Father. The Church's liturgy always asks the saints to pray for us, through Christ to the Father.

A patron saint is chosen for an infant at baptism, and if the baptized later wishes, at confirmation. This should be someone with whom we can feel particularly close—in modern terms, a role model. Most churches are named in honor of saints, and there are patrons for various professions, trades, etc., usually because of some connection that the saint had with that work.

Devotion to the saints is one of the more familiar practices of Catholicism which often helps people in their faith and prayer life. As was pointed out at Vatican Council II, some ninety percent of the saints venerated by the Church until that time came from the three major Latin countries of Europe. In the history of Catholicism there has been a good deal of exaggeration in the veneration of the saints: abuses regarding this were reprimanded by the Council, and significantly at the particular behest of the Latin American bishops. Today, more cultures and more lay people—with whom the average person can more easily identify—are being canonized as saints. Also, the number of saints' feast days in the Church's worldwide liturgy has been sharply reduced. Many saints have a local cultural symbolism that is quite meaningful to the people of a country or an area, and their feast days are times of celebration for everyone.

Reading some well-written, modern life of a saint—or one of the good collections now available—can be a great help and spur to the better practice of one's own faith, especially when we feel the need of understanding support from one who has "been there."

GOD'S MOTHER AND OURS

We particularly honor Mary, the mother of Christ, because of her great role in God's plan of salvation. She was closer to Christ than anyone else, particularly by her virginal conception and sinlessness— and it was he who chose her for the great honor of being his mother. If she were the mother merely of a great man we would have some reason for honoring her, but not for paying her the honor we do— but if one believes that her son is divine, then it is only natural to honor her greatly. The fact that she is the Mother of God is the basis of our veneration of her.

Mary is God's masterpiece. To honor her is to honor God who made her what she is. Luke depicts her saying this: "For behold, henceforth all generations will call me blessed, for he who is mighty has done great things for me. . . ." (Luke 1, 48-49). If we are sincere in our praise of an artist, for example, we will praise his paintings without hesitation. Mary is God's creature, infinitely distant from him, as are any of us—but she is unique among us in that she was totally centered on God.

Mary shows what God could do with any of us, if we but fully opened ourselves to him. She gave herself wholly to doing God's will—this was the purpose of her Son's mission and therefore of her life. One day a woman cried out to Christ, "Blessed is the womb that bore you, and the breasts that you sucked!" His answer shows the real source of Mary's holiness: "Blessed rather are those who hear the word of God and keep it!"

> *Because of Mary's great role she was conceived without sin, remained sinless throughout her life, and was perpetually a virgin.* We saw (chapter 6) the continuous belief of the Church in Mary's sinlessness and life-long virginity. These privileges of Mary, however, should not obscure the fact that she was totally human, tempted like any of us, sometimes lacking in understanding of her Son's mission and pained by it (Luke 2, 48–49). But she clung to God's will in great faith, as we must often do.

We believe in Mary's assumption, that "she was taken into heaven body and soul at the end of her earthly life." Here again Mary imitated her Son who was "taken to heaven" when his work was finished. What happened to her is meant to encourage the rest of us who are also merely human. As she was taken to heaven and glorified, we have the assurance that one day we also will be. She was taken in a special way because it was not fitting that the body from which the Son of God had taken his human body should undergo corruption.

Mary's assumption is celebrated on August 15th as a holyday in the United States. The assumption was declared solemnly to be an infallible teaching of the Church in 1950, but belief in it goes back to the early Church; a tomb of Mary was venerated, but there were no relics of her body, unlike the apostles and other early Christian heroes; when Christian writers and the liturgy became concerned with Mary's assumption in the 6th and 7th centuries, it was accepted throughout the Church.

But what does the assumption literally mean? Here popular imagery and art, and the use of symbolic language, can obscure what is meant. We certainly should not think of Mary's being "taken up" through the clouds and earth's atmosphere to some "place" in outer space. It simply means that Mary upon "leaving this earth" was in the state we call "heaven"—that she "went the way we will all go, but in some extraordinary, undefined way, more lovingly, more strikingly. Mary, like Christ himself, has disappeared from physical contact with us, and is with God, but in a real sense she is also among us and present to us. She is thus seen as the "first among Christians," the model for all followers of Christ. What we all look forward to one day, our total transformation in God, happened to her in the most loving way possible for a human.

Viewed positively, Mary's assumption strikingly points out that it was a woman who was most intimately associated with God-come-among-us, even to the end of her life. The assumption can thus be seen as the Church's way of proclaiming the extraordinary dignity and holiness of a woman—something sorely needed today as women strive for the recognition of their equal rights and dignity with men.

We give special place to Mary's intercession and sometimes consider her our spiritual "mother." Scripture shows her interceding with Christ for a young couple on their wedding day, and despite his seeming reluctance he worked his first miracle to fulfill her request (Cf. John 2, 1–11). Many of the early Church fathers saw a special significance in Christ's giving his mother to John as he was dying on the cross—she was to be a mother to all his followers, by her love and tenderness bringing them to him, as she had once brought him to the world (Cf. John 19, 26–27). So many today, as through the centuries, ask her intercession.

Mary's intercession must not be misunderstood. Vatican Council II tells us: "There is but one mediator as we know from the words of the apostles, 'for there is one God and one mediator of God and men, the man Christ Jesus, who gave himself as redemption for all' (1 Timothy 2, 5–6). The maternal duty of Mary toward men in no way obscures or diminishes this unique mediation of Christ, but rather shows his power. For all the salvific influence of the Blessed Virgin on men originates, not from some inner necessity, but from divine pleasure and from the superabundance of the merits of Christ. It rests on his mediation, depends entirely on it and draws all its power from it. In no way does it impede, but rather does it foster the immediate union of the faithful with Christ" (*Constitution on the Church,* no. 60).

How, then, can we speak of Mary's intercession or mediation? The more perfectly our will is aligned with God's, the more we ask for whatever he wants to give mankind, the more grace and love we can have a share in spreading in the world. Thus St. Paul said, " . . . I complete what is lacking in Christ's afflictions for the sake of his body, that is, the Church. . . ." (Colossians 1, 24).

Mary's will was perfectly open to God's will. She cooperated with Christ's work of salvation as fully as she knew how, more fully than anyone before or since. Not only did she give him birth and lovingly raise him, she watched the progress of his preaching, his final rejection, and then as he hung dying she freely and painfully offered him back to the Father. Her faith and obedience to God's will was total. In heaven now, she continues to totally desire God's will, asking for whatever he wills to give to men.

It is in this light that we must understand such terms as "spiritual mother," "mediatrix," "co-redemptrix," and "Queen." By her special closeness to Christ and openness to God's will she does for all what the rest of us do for some. She leads us in our intercession and mediation.

MARY, FIRST AMONG CHRISTIANS

Mary is the model Christian, the preeminent member of the Church. She is a model for us all, particularly in her faith and love. She is the "humble virgin," not noted in scripture for any great deeds, and therefore one whom we all can imitate. Her life consisted simply in being totally committed to God's will. She is the "fully redeemed one"—she shows how Christ's saving power can transform the entire personal existence of the humblest human being.

Mary is the perfect image and model of the Church itself. She is unique in that no other person has the Church so fully concentrated in herself. From the early Christian centuries the same titles are again and again given to Mary and to the Church: for instance, both are referred to as the Woman who is the enemy of the serpent (Genesis 3, 15), as the Virgin Mother, the Bride of Christ, the great sign that appeared in heaven (Revelation 12), and as the "New Eve" who undid the damage of the first by her cooperation with Christ, the New Adam.

Mary was the embodiment of the Church of the Old Testament, the "daughter of Sion" who personified the people of the promise (Cf. Isaiah 66, 7ff). She was the climax of the Old Covenant, the one who was perfectly faithful, who alone could fully welcome the Messiah and be the dwelling of God among men.

From what Mary is, the Church sees what it should become; by her virginity Mary shows the total dedication to God and to Christ that the Church too must have. As Mary, the Church must be the "handmaid of the Lord" in her trusting faith and love and service. As Mary was the Mother of Christ, so the Church is the mother of Christians—we often speak of "Mother Church." Mary particularly shows the patience, gentleness, and understanding the Church must have to balance its organizational and legalistic aspects.

Mary is particularly the model of our worship. We could say she is in the first pew, leading us by her example, directing us to her Son and our Brother as together we worship the Father. "But standing by the cross of Jesus were his mother. . . . " (John 19, 25)—as she was there on the first Good Friday, so she above all will help us to sacrifice ourselves totally with him at each Mass. Her whole life and purpose are simply to bring us to him.

Mary's influence in the history of the Church has been great. At first little attention was paid to Mary because of the necessary concern with who and what Jesus Christ was. Then she came to the fore particularly as the "Mother of God," a title which was meant to safeguard the true nature of Christ. The medieval veneration of the virgin-mother did much to give woman a dignity which was unthought of in the ancient world.

The devotion of the rosary has had a tremendous influence in helping hundreds of millions of Christians to pray. Among Orthodox Christians an even greater regard for Mary has developed than among Catholics. The shrines of Mary have also had a great influence, particularly places like Lourdes in southern France where each year a few million people come to strengthen their faith in the supernatural—or Czestochowa in Poland which is the center of that nation's resistance to political godlessness.

There have been, and are, exaggerations in the honor paid to Mary. Some, particularly among the less educated, have tended to regard her in isolation from the Church, as one who grants favors in her own right; perhaps much of this is inevitable, particularly among those for whom Christ is more divine than human, who would therefore turn to another whom they could more easily think of as human like themselves.

As we saw (chapter 17) when Christ's divinity was overstressed in the medieval liturgy, the cult of Mary and the saints developed in order to bridge the gap with the divine. Also some prayers and devotions, even of recent times, have been exaggerated, or could easily be misunderstood like the "Salve Regina" which speaks of Mary as "our life, our sweetness, and our hope." On the other hand, we should not expect the language of poetry and popular piety to be theologically exact. An Anglican priest writes of this: "Prayer should always be theological, but not nervously so. Always to be stopping short in praises of the Virgin lest we might overstep the bounds of exact truth is like the man who is terrified lest he might say something extravagant about his mother. A good mother would not mind if he did; still less, if I may use a daring, yet I hope not irreverent, analogy, would a good father overhearing" (*Ways of Worship,* WCC, 1948).

Today many non-Catholics recognize the rightful place of Mary in the Christian Church, just as Catholics recognize a frequent overemphasis on her role. Many theologians in Protestantism are urging that a proper honor be paid to Mary and the saints as a way of bringing us closer to Christ.

IN THE LITURGY

At Mass we commemorate Mary and the saints during the official eucharistic prayers, asking their intercession, that we may be admitted to their eternal fellowship. The various feasts of Mary and the saints during the year are meant to spur us on to imitate Christ's passion and glorification as they did.

The rosary is the devotion by which we meditate on Christ's life and ask Mary to bring us closer to him. The months of May and October are those in which devotions to Mary are held in some places.

DAILY LIVING: THE SPUR OF SANCTITY

The example of what others have done can often spur us on to do good. Considering how others have overcome their weaknesses can help us to overcome self-pity and do something concrete about our faults. Sometimes, when we realize what others have suffered for God and their fellow men, we can be very ashamed of our complaints.

We should read the life of some dedicated Christian, some saint, or some truly committed person—Christian or not.

In asking the help of those who have gone before us, we need not be concerned only with the Christian saints. Perhaps we might feel a kinship with other outstanding and dedicated men of our own era who are in the next life, such as Dr. Tom Dooley, the great Indian leader Gandhi, Dag Hammarskjöld, or some friend or relative whom we greatly admired during life.

There are many kinds of saints, today as in times past, both canonized and unrecognized. The heroic Dr. Tom Dooley who himself died of cancer while helping the natives of Laos, describes some contemporary Christian martyrs: an old priest there was hung by his heels and beaten throughout the night with stout bamboo rods; another had nails driven into his skull (*Deliver Us From Evil,* New American Library paperback).

Several years ago 22 young men were canonized as saints and martyrs of the Church in Uganda. They were lay catechists who had been tortured and killed by a fanatical anti-Christian king because they would not renounce their new faith. One had his limbs amputated, first at the ankles and wrists, then at the knees and elbows, strips of flesh were taken from his body and roasted before his eyes, and finally after three days of agony he died. Another was lashed to a tree to be torn apart while alive by savage dogs, while others were burnt alive.

A current candidate for canonization, Father Titus Brandsma, a Dutch Carmelite, defied the Nazi occupation authorities and saved many of their intended victims. He was imprisoned in Holland, and for leading prayers and preaching in the prison barracks was transferred to the infamous Dachau. There he was continually beaten, though broken in health—and finally a beating by a guard killed him.

Several years ago in Hayneville, Alabama an Episcopal seminarian was killed by a shotgun blast outside a grocery store, and a Catholic priest was seriously wounded with him. A girl civil rights worker testified that she was pushed to the ground by the seminarian just before the shooting, thus saving her life.

There are also those who are living daily lives of heroic sanctity, like the slum mother abandoned by her husband who works twelve hours daily to keep together her family of three children; the possibility of giving up, of turning her children over to the welfare authorities has never occurred to her; she has a face worn beyond her years, but her tough, bright spirit shines through.

SOME SUGGESTIONS FOR ...

DISCUSSION

Does it seem logical that our love for one another should extend beyond the grave?

Does the notion of Mary as the model Christian have meaning for you?

Is there some outstanding person now dead, Christian or non-Christian, for whom you feel a particular attachment and whose example is of help to you?

FURTHER READING

* *Saints in a Time of Turmoil,* Sheridan (Paulist Press, 1977)—A collection of the lives of twelve saints relevant to today, from Jerome and Augustine to our recently-canonized American saints.
* *Elizabeth Seton,* Hindeman (Srena Lettres, 1976) is a very simple and moving biography of our first American native-born saint, a woman who followed her conscience and changed the Church in America.
* *Harvester of Souls,* Langon (Our Sunday Visitor, 1976) is a very good biography of the saint, Bishop John Neumann, called "the father of American parochial schools."
* *Give Joy to My Youth,* Gallagher (Farrar, Straus and Giroux, 1965) is the biography of Dr. Tom Dooley, the heroic medic of Southeast Asia, whom many consider a model of modern, serving sanctity.
* *A Woman Wrapped in Silence,* Lynch (Paulist Press, 1968): A beautiful work, in blank verse, expanding the scriptural passages concerning Mary; this is an older classic that once again has become popular.
* *Mary, Womb of God,* Maloney (Dimension Press, 1976) sensitively shows Mary as a woman of prayer.

FURTHER VIEWING/LISTENING

Bloodstrike (Paulist Productions)—28 minutes—The story of a modern attempt at sainthood, this film movingly shows the principal of a suburban school seeking God among the poorest of those on skid row.

They Are My People (Franciscan Communications)—A filmstrip telling the story of the saintly Mother Teresa of Calcutta.

Something Beautiful for God (B.B.C.)—55 minutes—A superb documentary on the work of Mother Teresa. Usually available through one's diocesan communications or audio/visual people.

Mary, The Mother of Jesus (Teleketics, Franciscan Communications): A fine, four-filmstrip set on the role of Mary in the life-history of the Church.

PERSONAL REFLECTION   •

I might try asking for the help of someone I believe is now with God in heaven. Perhaps it will help me to better imitate Christ.

24

Christ's Church in the World Today

What does Christ's Church have to offer the world today? How does one know whether or not to join the Church? What of the scandals and weaknesses within the Church? What of the scandal of disunity among Christians?

CHRIST'S CHURCH IS DIVINE

Vatican Council II "yearns to explain" to all men the Church's work in the world today. The Church is at the service of mankind, particularly to make all men brothers. "Inspired by no earthly ambition, the Church seeks but a solitary goal: to carry forward the work of Christ . . . (who) entered this world to give witness to the truth, to rescue and not to sit in judgment, to serve and not to be served" (*The Church in the Modern World,* nos. 2 and 3).

Christ's Church is himself and us—divine and holy, and yet human and imperfect. We have seen how Christ is among us in the Church, uniting us with himself, using human instruments to bring us to heaven. He teaches us with authority and certainty through the pope and bishops. He communicates his grace primarily through men chosen by him as his instruments.

The Church is divine and holy because she has Christ as her head, is guided by the Holy Spirit, and has all the helps necessary for us to live a holy life. Obviously not all Christians are holy, but the Church has all the means to make them so. These we have seen: the Mass and the sacraments, the great ways we meet Christ at the critical moments of life, and by which we can be certain of making contact with God; and all sorts of devotions and sacramentals to bring God into our daily life. The Church's laws provide that we perform regular acts of worship and reparation for our sins. It has many groups to help us and millions of people whose lives are totally dedicated to God and others.

The Church has produced thousands of saints, extraordinarily holy people. It is hard to find any group in history that compares with them. The Anglican author Evelyn Underhill says in her classic work, *Mysticism*, that it is an historical fact that mysticism is at its best in Christianity and that the greatest mystics have been the Catholic saints.

The Church through its history has worked to take care of the poor, uneducated, and underprivileged, laying the foundation for the education and philanthropy of our Western civilization and influencing other cultures as well. The hospitals, old age homes, orphanages, schools, etc. that have become a part of our way of life were originally sponsored by the Church. The Church civilized and Christianized the pagans, brought to the world a new respect for women, marriage, and virginity, and taught men to take care of the poor, the sick, and the aged, all the while continually upholding the dignity of the individual person.

Today many have noted that the Catholic Church has a particularly universal appeal while yet maintaining a striking unity—that it seems to have more to offer for more people of diverse cultures and social classes. In this it is trying to earn its title of "catholic." Vance Packard has remarked in *The Status Seekers* that religion in America tends to stratify according to social status and wealth—certain groups gravitating toward certain churches—with but two notable exceptions: in the area of desegregation, the Congregational Church, and, in general, the Roman Catholic Church.

The survival and influence of the Church after almost twenty centuries of opposition and persecution and scandal seems to Catholics to show that it is uniquely guided by God. The Church began with a dozen simple men—one a traitor, another a perjurer, and the rest cowards—and the wildly improbable story that a man put to death by his own people as a criminal was God himself. They started out preaching a way of life that challenged almost every standard of the world around them. Christ had predicted, "They have persecuted me; they will persecute you also. . . ." (John 15, 20). And so they were. First they were persecuted by the leaders of the Jews, their own people; then under the Roman emperors the Church endured three centuries of persistent harassment, torture, imprisonment, and death.

The official attitude was, "Non licet esse vos!"—"It is not permitted you to exist!" The Roman emperor Diocletian confidently built himself a column bearing the inscription: "To Diocletian, who destroyed the very name Christian." Yet the Church did not change its principles in the face of this. Unlike other kingdoms and empires of history, it spread simply by sanctity and suffering.

Scarcely had the Church gained recognition in the Empire, when there came the barbarian invasions and the gradual collapse of civilization. The Church converted and civilized the barbarians, and became the center of stability and learning, the heart of Western civilization in the Middle Ages. But then scandals, quarrels, and apostasies disrupted her from within. Often those within the Church who paid her lip-service—Catholic princes, her own officials—were her greatest enemies because of their greed and corruption.

By all human rules, the Church should have died many times. There were scandals in high places, even in the highest—Dante put two popes in his Inferno. Then came the Reformation which rent the Church, the "Enlightenment" with its rejection of religion (and vice versa), the age of reason, and the modern "isms." There has been no period, except briefly in the Middle Ages, when the Church was in tune with the prevailing intellectual atmosphere. Yet today those who considered the Church backward and dying are themselves dead and largely forgotten, and the Church continues to influence hundreds of millions.

> The Church has been persecuted in almost every modern nation. It has survived Nazism, and Communism has been waging against it a relentless war of suppression, wherever possible closing churches and schools, harassing, imprisoning, and killing believers who speak out for human rights or too vigorously practice their faith. Pope John Paul II lived all his adult life first under the Nazi tyranny in Poland, and then for thirty-five years in a constant war of nerves with a Communist state that would dearly love to eliminate Catholic Christianity altogether (this is nothing new to the Poles who have had to fight for their Christian beliefs and identity for a thousand years). In Latin America today, military dictatorships and greedy economic imperialists (some of them North American "multinationals") are daily trying to destroy or negate the Church's influence because it is the only effective defense of the poor and oppressed. Therefore, for many millions, the only possible explanation for the survival and influence today of the Catholic Church

is that it is uniquely guided by God—despite being composed of weak, sometimes unenlightened and often sinful men and women.

Catholics conclude that in their Church Jesus Christ makes available to them in a unique way his truth and grace. The Church can trace itself back to Christ and the apostles, under the authority of the pope and bishops, with the same basic teachings of the apostles. It is united throughout the world in its basic doctrines, fundamental moral principles, and liturgy, with the same authority guiding all. It embraces all types of people, of every race, nation, and social class. Its countless people who are sincerely striving for holiness, and its survival and influence for nearly two thousand years, show it to have a unique role in the world. For Catholics, then, it is the Church founded by Jesus Christ to give a special fullness of his teaching and grace to the world.

What many Catholics see as "special" for them about their Church is its extraordinary unity-in-catholicity, a worldwide community of tremendously diverse people who yet have a sense of oneness in their spiritual outlook and ideals. They know too that they are part of an immense group that has been committed to trying to live lives of love, in imitation of Jesus Christ, for two thousand years. The pope's role is something like that of the spiritual leader or symbol of mankind's highest strivings for unity, peace, and love. Though some, on occasion, disagree with him on matters outside of basic doctrine, they (and others) still take seriously the moral issues he raises. This is a visible sign for Catholics of their commitment to try to bring about a better world in which this is taking place, now and forever.

The Church, however, is not a privileged, exclusive club for those who have a sure way to salvation, as opposed to those who have not. The attitude of a Catholic can never be one of smugness or pride. It is only through God's goodness that he possesses what he does. If he does not live up to his belief, he, too, can be lost. If he knows more of the truth, he also has a greater responsibility for living up to it. Often those who are not Catholics put us to shame by their holiness and love.

To say that the Church has a special fullness of Christ's truth is not to imply that we have all the truth and no one else has any. Nor is it to say that there have been no theological errors held by those even in high position within the Church; the Church's infallibility, as we said earlier, is quite limited. Nor can the Church give us the truth in the sense of answering our every question or solving every moral problem. "The teaching office of the Church is not commissioned to tell people what to do, but to make it possible for people to decide what to do" (Father John McKenzie, in *The Catholic World*).

While in the Catholic view there is available in Catholicism all that God has revealed to man, the fullness of his grace and truth, yet the expression of this truth may not be the best, and the communication of grace might be hindered by human weakness. For various reasons Catholics might not use, or might be unable to use, what is available. The Church known by an individual Catholic might be much more human than divine. Then, too, a Catholic might deliberately turn away from the Church's truth and grace. Others who are not Catholic might use better the truth and grace they have—and many have a great deal—and thus be closer in faith and love to God and their fellow man.

God is present through all of creation, and uses many ways to communicate his truth and grace. He works especially through those who are baptized—"Where two or three are gathered in my name, there am I in the midst of them" (Matthew 18, 20). All men, however, can have access to his truth and grace. To be saved we must be united with Christ, but most of mankind does not realize their union with him. Other leaders, prophets, "gurus," have been God's instruments to bring them truth and grace. Christ is humanity's unique, divine savior and teacher, but others too show forth aspects of God.

The Church's purpose in the world is to bear witness in a special way to God's love among men. By its beliefs it wants to tell men that God has come among us and saved us, that he loves us infinitely and wants us to love one another. It is the way of salvation not for all of humanity, but for those chosen to work more closely in a visible, communal way for the salvation of all—the minority whose purpose is to serve the majority by trying to show God's love in the world. Its members are to proclaim—however inadequately—that the world has been saved and is filled with God's love.

The Church, therefore, is a sign set among the world's people to give them hope, to assure them that God and his love are ever with us, so that all in the world will continue to strive together to grow in love, and not resort to unloving ways. The Church is there to tell us that none of our efforts—even the slightest—is ever in vain, but is helping to bring about an eternal, perfect universe.

CATHOLIC CHRISTIAN EDUCATION— SHARING THE GOOD NEWS AND A WAY OF LIFE

Catholics have maintained their own educational system because they wish to share the good news of their faith and pass on as well as possible a Christian way of life. Parochial schools try to communicate a Christian way of living as a day-by-day part of the students' lives. Parochial schools came into being, for the most part, to preserve and develop the religion of a largely immigrant people in an often anti-Catholic atmosphere, and to help these people better integrate themselves into the American way of life. Over the years they have done a remarkable job, and in the past few decades they have been swamped by children—often as many non-Catholic as Catholic—whose parents want them to receive an education based on firm values, loving discipline and motivation, and care for each child as a unique creation of God.

Most Catholic education, however, takes place in programs like the Confraternity of Christian Doctrine, where children come for a few hours a week to be educated by religious-education professionals, priests, religious, and lay people—aided by numerous volunteer laymen and laywomen. The C.C.D. educates at least two-thirds of America's elementary school children whose parents want them to have some systematic training in their faith and in moral values; there is an even greater proportion of high school students enrolled in this. Considering that the C.C.D. receives, on a national average, approximately one-fourth to one-fifth of a typical parish's financial outlay for education, this program has over the years done an amazingly outstanding job of religious educating.

Today, parents are more involved than ever in their children's education-process under this program—in fact, in most cases active parent participation is a "must." But many parents feel ill-equipped in religious education matters, or uneasy about taking part in what they have traditionally felt is the work of professional religious educators—

though Vatican Council II, and countless documents since, stress again and again that parents are the primary educators of their children.

Today, in what is probably the most promising and challenging time in the Church's history, programs in adult/parent (and clergy) education are our greatest need. This is the view of the most experienced educators in the Church. The American Catholic Church's National Catechetical Directory of 1977—the product of eight years' work, including consultation with tens of thousands of people—says clearly that adult education is our primary need today. In most parishes, we have a large number of lay people who are better educated than ever before—except that most are still woefully equipped in the matter of religious education. Most have only a minimal grasp of the reforms, the whole new worldview, and the immense opportunities for growth—for themselves as well as their children—that have emerged from Vatican Council II. The opportunities in this area are immense.

WHETHER OR NOT TO JOIN THE CHURCH

If one comes to know and believe in the Catholic Church, he should become a Catholic. If he comes to believe that this is the Church founded by Jesus Christ with his complete truth for the salvation of men, and refuses to join it, he would be refusing to follow what his conscience tells him is true. Christ said of a person like this, ". . . He who does not believe will be condemned" (Mark 16, 17).

But if one has doubts about the truth of one or another of the Church's basic doctrines, or if he is satisfied with his present belief, he should not become a Catholic. Some are able to accept the Church's teachings, and others of equally good faith are not. The ability to believe, as we said earlier, comes ultimately from God. All one can and must do is try to live up to his conscience.

Our belief must always be a free response to God, with our conscience our supreme guide. If we have tried to inform ourselves about what God wants, and sincerely try to live up to our conscience, we can rest content. In finding God's will for us, we must "enjoy immunity from external coercion, as well as psychological freedom" (*Declaration on Religious Freedom,* no. 2).

. . . Every man has the duty, and therefore the right, to seek the truth in religious matters, in order that he may with prudence form for himself right and true judgments of conscience. . . . However . . . the inquiry is to be free. . . . In all his activity a man is bound to follow his conscience faithfully ... he is not to be forced to act in a manner contrary to his conscience. Nor, on the other hand, is he to be restrained from acting in accordance with his conscience, especially in matters religious (*Declaration on Religious Freedom,* no. 3).

One should never become a Catholic solely to have the same religion in a marriage, or to please someone else. He may have come to investigate the Church because he intended marrying a Catholic (as most do), and he sees that sharing the same faith will be a great thing for the marriage and for the children—but now, to become a Catholic, he must believe on his own. He must now feel that there is something more in Catholicism than what he already believes, something that he wants and feels he should have in his life—that Catholicism has become one's spiritual home. He may know that the help of a Catholic spouse will be needed to live his new belief, but he can sincerely say that he is not becoming a Catholic for the other but rather on his own.

If one is undecided, it is good to consider whether he has true doubts or only difficulties. If one doubts the truth of one or another of the Church's basic doctrines, or if one is simply not sure, he or she should not become a Catholic. One should remember, however, that one does not have to accept, or practice, every Catholic belief with equal attention or enthusiasm. One might, for example, accept the Church's Marian doctrines, but realize that they probably will never be very meaningful in one's life. This would be a difficulty—something hard to accept. Or it might be something one is not able to understand, for example, how Christ's presence can be in the wafer of the eucharist, or how three Persons are one God, or something intellectually or emotionally repugnant—such as some Catholic devotions or some clerical attitudes.

There may be family opposition to one's becoming a Catholic. (**Read Luke 12, 51–53, and Matthew 23, 34.**) This can be particularly difficult. Usually later, when the family sees the convert is happy in his new faith, opposition is replaced by acceptance. Then, too, one should realize that after twenty or thirty years in another religious background, or with perhaps no religious background, it is only natural that he should take time to adjust to Catholicism. There may be little or no emotional enthusiasm about this step. The famous English convert, Cardinal Newman, summed up such feelings: "A thousand difficulties do not make a single doubt."

If one wonders whether there are doubts or only difficulties, he might consider whether or not he wants to live the life of a good Catholic. Despite the fact that some of the teachings may not yet be fully accepted intellectually, or he is simply not sure, is there the interior desire to live a Catholic life? One might also ask himself: Do I feel at home, comfortable at worship here in this Catholic community? Do I feel that Catholicism is helping me find God and do his will? Do I think that I am a better person because of my Catholic experience? Obviously, too, one who is thinking about this should consult a priest.

Finally, the way to the Catholic Church for any individual is a two-way street. One usually brings to it as much as he receives. The Church needs and profits by the things the convert has acquired from a background in another religion, from his or her own religious insights and moral strivings. The convert must try to be aware of what he or she can contribute, and patiently but perseveringly try to use one's special gifts within the Church. Many of the Church's best people are those who found their way to it as adults.

CHRIST'S CHURCH IS HUMAN

The human beings Christ uses in his Church remain truly human, weak, and subject to sin. This is why he guides his Church through infallibility, to make sure it will never teach error because of human weakness. There have been bad popes, bishops, priests, and people throughout the Church's history. Christ warned us that this would happen. He compared the kingdom to a net containing good and bad fishes, a flock from which some sheep stray, a field containing both good and bad growths: **Read Matthew 13, 24–30.**

Of Christ's chosen apostles, Peter denied him, Judas betrayed him, and all but one deserted him in his most crucial hour. If these who were close to him could act so scandalously, we should expect scandals among their successors centuries later—". . . it must be that scandals come, but woe to the man through whom scandal does come!" (Matthew 18, 7). It is significant that the gospels tie in a personal reprimand of Peter with each conferral of power on him; this clearly shows the distinction between the man, who would be weak and sinful, and the office which would be divinely protected. Unworthy men are then to be expected in Christ's Church in all ages; they should not cause us to have doubts about the truth of the Church, any more than one would have doubts about mathematics because some professors are poor teachers.

The Church is "very well aware that among her members, both clerical and lay, some have been unfaithful to the Spirit of God during the course of many centuries; in the present age, too, it does not escape the Church how great a distance lies between the message she offers and the human failings of those to whom the gospel is entrusted. . . . The Church also realizes that in working out her relationship with the world she always has great need of the ripening which comes with the experience of the centuries. Led by the Holy Spirit, Mother Church unceasingly exhorts her sons to purify and renew themselves so that the sign of Christ can shine more brightly on the face of the Church" (*The Church in the Modern World,* no. 43).

Many of the institutional elements of the Church particularly scandalize people, and must be unrelentingly reformed. There are many things in the Church's human organization which cause the best people both within and without the Church to draw back from it. The best people within the Church are facing these realistically, and are determinedly working to improve them:

There is bureaucracy, over-centralization, and legalism in many of the Church's structures and procedures. Some wonder why the Church cannot have the gospel simplicity of Christ's band of followers—but any human organization must grow in complexity as it grows in size. Yet it is all too true that churchmen often have become "frozen" in bureaucratic methods, that there is too much legalism in the Church's procedures. But here again the Council has spurred a movement of adaptability, decentralization and simplification that hopefully will continue to gain momentum. Many scandalous procedures—silencing of scholars, arbitrary censorship, political involvements, excessive secrecy—are slowly being reformed as a result of stinging conciliar and lay criticism.

There is a lack of sufficient communication between people in various local churches, between local church authorities and people, and between various national churches and the central authorities of the Church. Sometimes people in a particular nation, culture, or group of nations may find that a universal, non-infallible ideal or norm, especially regarding morality, conflicts with their grasp of the total gospel preached by the Church, and with their own consciences. Here continual communication, listening to one another, sincere attempts at discussion and prayerful reflection are called for. Those in authority must be sensitive to the pastoral situation and theological reflection of those in particular cultures and nations—or their own credibility suffers in the long run. In turn, people of various cultures must try to understand the fundamental intent of the universal teaching, that the Church is truly varied in its makeup, and that what is a problem for them might be quite the opposite elsewhere. The mature Christian knows that unity in a universal Church will not mean uniformity, but it should mean understanding and mutually open, sensitive love. The Church has a long memory, and its mature members know that patient love always wins out.

In all this Catholics remember that the twelve apostles chosen by Christ himself were far from outstanding. They realize, too, that many of today's issues are complex, and that bishops trained and skilled in administration cannot usually be expected to speak expertly on these things. They look for improvement to the implementation of the Council's recommendation that bishops regularly consult with their clergy and people, and with one another, in a more organized way, and they look also to a more representative way of selecting bishops in the future. The potentially articulate voice of a better-and-better educated laity will, hopefully, help immensely in forming the Church of the future.

The Church, then, is in need of continual reformation and renewal. "While Christ, holy, innocent and undefiled, knew nothing of sin . . . the Church, embracing sinners in her bosom, at the same time holy and always in need of being purified, follows the endless way of penance and renewal. Christ summons the Church to continual reformation as she goes her pilgrim way. . . ." (*Constitution on the Church,* no. 8; *Decree on Ecumenism,* no. 6). God afflicts the Church so that it will never forget it is a pilgrim here below; he hammers and chisels at it so that it will remain a useful tool.

As a member of the Church one is a part of its structure, with its strengths and its weaknesses, its certitude and formalism, its love and legalism. Many have suffered much in remaining loyal to the Church. When the French worker priests, for instance, were suppressed by insensitive Roman authorities, one of them, Father de Lorgeril, literally died of sorrow. The great Teilhard de Chardin also suffered much from the same narrowness and short-sightedness, yet he wrote:

> Blessed are they who suffer at not seeing the Church so fair as they would wish, and are only the more submissive and prayerful for it. It is a profound grief, but of high spiritual value. It can never be repeated too often: the Catholic is the man who is sure of the existence of Jesus-Christ-God, for a number of reasons and in spite of many stumbling-blocks. Why is it that so many minds see nothing but the stumbling-blocks and wait until they are removed before they look at

the reasons? (Teilhard de Chardin, *Making of a Mind,* Harper and Row, 1965, p. 59).

Franz Jagerstatter was an Austrian peasant who was beheaded in 1943 because he refused to serve in Hitler's army. A loyal Catholic to the end, he went against the advice of his compromising bishop, priest-friends, and family, and died like St. Thomas More. *In Solitary Witness* is the title of the inspiring book about his life and martyr's death. Like Joan of Arc he is now being proposed for canonization by some of the very churchmen who acquiesced in his death. Countless others have helped fulfill the Church's mission of redemption while yet suffering deeply from her inadequacies.

Our current age particularly is a time of crisis and change in which the Church is becoming less an institution and more a community—less a structure and more a place where truly human persons encounter Christ and one another—less a judge of the world and more a servant of the world. The work of renewal begun by Pope John and Vatican Council II is continuing, and this means critical re-examination, development, creativity—and also confusion, reaction, uncertainty.

Today, since Vatican Council II, the Church has come into difficult times, in the opinion of many. The hopeful, halcyon days that followed Vatican II are over, and the Church in many places is divided and confused. Conservative Catholics are unhappy with many of the changes that have taken place; it has been very difficult for many to see cherished practices discarded and old certitudes universally questioned. Progressives, on the other hand, feel that the brakes have been put on the reforms begun by the Council, by a frightened, tired, and conservative hierarchy which is very often incapable of real leadership. Young people are clearly not taking the Church as seriously as they once did, and uncounted numbers of them have abandoned it altogether, "turned off" by irrelevant liturgies, negative sermons, by proscriptions against birth control, divorce and remarriage, etc., and by a general dissatisfaction with the inadequacies of institutional religion.

Many of the Church's current difficulties are due to the era of rapid change in every field, and the consequent confusion and conflict through which we are now living. It was inevitable that the Church should suffer from the same stresses as the other institutions of our society. The Church particularly, as the great stabilizing influence of Western civilization for almost two thousand years, could not be expected to cope to everyone's satisfaction with the change that is all about us. It was inevitable that many people in the Church would be hurt and alienated.

But there are hopeful signs as well: In many, many places the reforms of Vatican II are slowly and quietly going forward; aging obstructionists are gradually disappearing from the scene, and in many parish councils, for example, conservatives and progressives are learning to dialogue and to work together. Many people are learning a new tolerance, an appreciation of other world religions, the fact that there are many theologies within the Church, that one can submit to the Church's guidance without giving up the inviolability of his conscience. Many detect an increased moral awareness and sensitivity today, particularly in social matters, by comparison with only a few decades ago. In many places, new, imaginative liturgical forms are slowly emerging and often stir young and old alike. The "people of God" are more and more realizing that the Spirit is stirring among them, and that they need not wait for official leadership to act. Change usually begins from below and then is gradually accepted above—the "peace movement" within the Church comes immediately to mind. A new and deep interest in spirituality (charismatic sharing, private or otherwise) is manifesting itself. New theological insights, often upsetting at first sight, are bit by bit revealing a profound and staggering vision of God, man, and the universe undreamed of before. Today the Church can no longer be triumphalistic—it must be humbler, poorer, simpler, and more honest—more like the way Jesus Christ himself envisioned it.

Today particularly it seems to take maturity to be an active member of the Church. It is no longer as simple and unchallenging as it once was. Each of us is challenged to examine his faith and find God for himself within the Church, instead of having him spoon-fed to us. The most authentic religious act of some will be to reject the caricatured God of the institution, the comfortable, narrow God that was once given them.

In all this we recognize that the structures of the institutional Church, however inadequate and in need of continual reform, are necessary. Those who know the Church realize that Christ's message would have been lost to history had the institution not been there—

however it obscured his message at times. They know that the institution is basically meant to be a ministry to serve the Christian people and all humanity, that it can never do this adequately, and that even when it fails Christ goes on accomplishing his work in mankind. He brings success out of our human failures. This should not surprise us, for it is ultimately Christ who is working among us.

The Church reproduces the weakness and humiliation of Christ. Christ was sinless but accounted a sinner and traitor to his people. The Church is sinners who are trying to bring Christ to all people. The Church must reproduce in itself the whole mystery of Christ, especially that of his cross—and no cross is greater for those who love Christ than the weaknesses of his Church. "Christ lives on in the Church, but he lives as crucified. . . . The imperfections of the Church are the cross of Christ" (Guardini).

A modern theologian has written perceptively:

> . . . *Let us love the Church of weakness.* . . . We are not ashamed of her because there are so many shameful things about her. We take it for one of the most overwhelming proofs of her unity and holiness that she has always had to suffer from the disdain of human refinement. . . . We tremble for her when we see her excessively honored by the world. Rather—wherever in the world it is a disgrace or a ridiculously old-fashioned thing to be a Catholic, there we know in the pure joy of our faith that the kingdom is near. . . . We must cherish the Church as Christ does. We must fill her with warm love . . . and behold, precisely through this love, the transformation of the Church from weakness to power, from crippled ugliness to immortal beauty, is taking place, silently and irresistibly until the end of time. . . . (Hugo Rahner, *The Church*, Kenedy, 1963).

RECONCILING THE DIVIDED CHURCH AND A DIVIDED WORLD

Due to human weakness through the centuries the unity of Christ's Church has been upset by individuals and groups. These splits within the Church have usually been caused, on the one hand, by the shortsightedness and sinfulness of the Church's members, particularly those in authority, and, on the other, by the understandable but divisive impatience of those who wanted to reform the Church.

Among those who split from the Church, a heresy is a denial of an infallible teaching of the Church, while a schism is a denial of the Church's authority. Both have existed from the beginning in the Church. John wrote the fourth gospel with those in mind who were even then denying the true nature of Christ. St. Paul was constantly harassed by those he calls "deceitful workers, disguising themselves as apostles of Christ" (2 Corinthians 11, 13). 1 John 2, 19 and 2 Peter 2 also refer to those who broke away from the teaching of the apostles. In the early centuries and into the Middle Ages there were many heresies, great and small; most of them have long since passed into history and a few continue today in a weak form.

The Eastern Orthodox Churches came about when certain ancient Christian Churches, mostly of the Middle East, finally separated themselves in the 11th century from the authority of the pope. The background of this split (touched on briefly in chapter 10) shows that the causes were more cultural and political than religious.

As the Christian Church developed, the four great patriarchates, particularly Rome and Constantinople, became the leading churches and centers of unity. In the East, the local churches gradually found a common unity—geographical, political, social, and cultural—under the same emperor, who came to consider himself the ultimate representative of Christ on earth. In the West, however, the unity of the Church was to be independent of all secular power, including that of the emperor. We saw that while the Eastern Churches had little recourse to Rome during the first four centuries, their recognition of Rome's teaching as the criterion of orthodoxy became more frequent from the 5th century on; they were thus originally united with the Roman Church.

However, with the rising political power of Constantinople, an inevitable rivalry developed between it and Rome. The pope assumed a central role in uniting the Western world that was becoming more and more opposed to the Byzantine Empire. The Eastern emperors tried to browbeat the popes and sometimes imprisoned them, and the popes in turn showed a disdain for the legitimate leadership among the Eastern Churches of the patriarch of Constantinople. Then a 9th century pope, who was particularly insensitive to the Eastern tradition of autonomy among the patriarchates, tried to impose upon them a strongly centralized papal authority. They reacted and eventually, in 1054, split with Rome.

A few times during the succeeding centuries these Churches were again united with Rome, but the positions against one another gradually hardened: the Latins would not recognize the legitimate basis of the powers of the Oriental bishops and saw the uniformity of Western Catholics as the only ideal (positions reversed by Vatican Council II, incidentally). On the other hand, the Orthodox came to look on every development of dogma in the Western Church as a betrayal of apostolic tradition, and the Churches often became isolated nationalistic enclaves.

The causes of this schism were as much political and cultural as doctrinal—the Greek reality versus the Roman, the isolation caused by Islam, etc.—furthered by a good deal of pride and lack of understanding on both sides. Today an ecumenical "thaw" has been developing between the Churches, culminating in the moving meetings of Pope Paul VI and Patriarch Athenagoras of Constantinople in the Holy Land in 1964 and again in Istanbul, from which have come regular theological discussions with the hopeful ultimate goal of unity. The Rhodes Conference of the Orthodox Churches also attempted to achieve more unity for this dialogue with the West. Pope John Paul II has encouraged and deepened the discussions taking place, with unity today seemingly closer than ever. He went to Istanbul shortly after his installation and met with the new Patriarch and encouraged anew the dialogue.

The Orthodox Churches have the same basic doctrines, moral code, Mass, sacraments, devotion to Mary and the saints, etc., as the Roman Catholic Church. They are the same as the Eastern Rites of the Roman Catholic Church in almost every respect, except that they do not recognize the universal authority and infallibility of the pope. They have suffered heroically for their Christianity, especially from the Turks, and in recent years from atheistic communism. They are gradually attaining a closer working unity among themselves, and their recently deceased titular leader ("first among equals"), Athenagoras, was a holy and heroic man who was harassed by the Turkish authorities, as has been his successor, and as have been countless Orthodox Christians in Russia and in several other countries of Eastern Europe.

The Eastern Rites of the Catholic Church are the groups among the Eastern Churches that are united with Rome. A "rite" is not just a particular way of worship, but a whole unique, yet Catholic tradition, including schools of theology, devotions, spirituality, church discipline, art, architecture, music, etc.—in other words, a particular Catholic culture. We of the West must remember that the Christian Church was born in the East and that its life during the early centuries was centered in the East. From there originally came its basic theology, monasticism, and liturgy, and its greatest Fathers and Doctors.

The liturgies of the Eastern Christian Church—those united with Rome and those that are not yet—have many local differences, but this is what largely preserved their cultures and national unity during centuries of oppression. While the West developed an "incarnational" spirit, involved in present problems of Christian life on earth, Eastern Christianity expressed itself in a more mystical, "otherworldly" point of view; the institutional and juridical aspects of the Church were relegated to the emperor. The extreme autonomy of the Eastern Churches and their attitude of detachment from institutional concerns have obviously had both good and bad effects, as history shows. The same, of course, can be said of the West's more pragmatic approach.

> *Most people notice the obvious differences of the Eastern Churches from the West in discipline and ceremonies.* They baptize by immersion, confirm infants at the time of their baptism, have a more elaborate Mass ritual, make greater use of sacred images (ikons), etc.—and their priests, unless they are monks, can marry. Eastern liturgies have a great sense of sacredness and mystery, and they emphasize man's openness in worship to God's majestic action, rather than our own action; they are less simple and orderly than those of the West, but are usually participated in more fully and continually by the whole congregation. More and more, their liturgies are gradually undergoing a needed simplification.
>
> For a further appreciation of the riches of the Eastern Churches and the possibilities of reunion, cf. Vatican Council II's *Decree on Ecumenism,* nos. 14–18.

The Protestant Reformation was the split in the Western Church in the 16th century. It is seen today that its effects were both bad and good. It was inevitable, we realize today, so many and so deep were its causes.

> By the 16th century there had been for some time widespread evils in the Church. There was corruption and scandal in the lives of many churchmen. The prestige of the popes was seriously impaired by scandals and political maneuverings; during the great schism, two and even three men claimed to be pope. In many places, there was a superstitious overemphasis on externals and neglect of an inner religious spirit. At this time also the spirit of nationalism was growing and with it a spirit of political rebellion against any authority higher than a local one. A pagan spirit left from the Renaissance and a breakdown of the

Church's scholastic scholarship contributed to the immorality and confusion.

However, the evils with the Church, bad as they were, should not be exaggerated. The basic doctrines of the Church were still there, though some churchmen were greatly distorting some of them. Historians today testify that there was no general breakdown in the Church's works of charity and mercy and in its care for people, and that there were many holy men and women all over the Catholic world who had been working and praying for reform. Much of what happened was due to the fact that this period was a transitional one in history, much like our own, but the Church's leaders then were too blind, too ensconced in their positions, to see this and change their ways.

Martin Luther, a Catholic priest, joined others in protesting against some of the more flagrant abuses. He did not at first intend to break with the Catholic Church. His early teaching is a return to genuinely Catholic beliefs that were being largely overlooked. But, caught up in this crucial period of history, faced with the intransigence of the papal court, and encouraged by some of the German princes for their own purposes, he was pushed to some extreme views of his own. Today we recognize that he had genuine and much needed insights into the nature of Christianity and that his views were not as un-Catholic as was once thought.

But anathemas and counter-anathemas had been hurled by both sides, and the split became an irreparable fact. Martin Luther was the first of the reformers. After Luther, others broke away—John Calvin in Switzerland, Henry VIII in England, John Knox in Scotland, etc. Generally, as in Scandinavia, most people did not realize what was happening, but simply followed their rulers, whether Catholic or Protestant.

The result of the Reformation was that Christ's Church was split, dividing millions of Christians in the West, as the Eastern schism had done earlier. Within a short time numerous rival Christian groups sprang up. There was much religious anarchy, as even Luther deplored in his day. It led to much of the confusion we find in Christianity today with rival Christian Churches disputing among themselves. Then a significant start toward unity was made early in the 20th century, leading to the formation of the World Council of Churches. Most of the "mainline" Protestant Churches and Orthodox Churches joined this group, which aimed at doctrinal dialogue and at joint social action. Intercommunion or "open communion" gradually became the practice among most Protestant Churches. Finally, today, four hundred years later, the movement for unity has been truly progressing since Vatican Council II, with the entrance of the Roman Catholic Church into the dialogue and into cooperative efforts on every level.

The splitting of the Church at the Reformation was the fault of both "sides," as Popes John, Paul and John Paul II and many at Vatican Council II declared. If the reformers were sometimes extreme, Catholic leaders on the other hand had blinded themselves to how bad things were. As Cardinal Pole, the pope's representative at the reform Council of Trent, admitted:

> Before the tribunal of God's mercy we, the shepherds, should make ourselves responsible for all the evils now burdening the flock of Christ. The sins of all we should take upon ourselves, not in generosity but in justice; because the truth is that of these evils we are in great part the cause, and therefore we should implore the divine mercy through Jesus Christ (Henry S. John, *Essays on Christian Unity,* p. 20).

One crucial question posed by the Reformation is that of the visible as well as invisible unity of Christ's Church. The Reformers rightly emphasized the inner nature of the Church as against an exaggerated external authoritarian structure. But by emphasizing the spiritual union of the Church at the expense of the united, visible organization, many people today believe they went too far in the opposite direction. This was natural, in view of the circumstances of the time—and, as Pope John XXIII said, "We do not intend to conduct a trial of the past; we do not want to prove who was right and who was wrong." But the succession of an external and uniting hierarchical authority from the time of the apostles had been broken.

The Reformation spurred the Catholic Church to reform itself. History has shown that it was de facto necessary so that certain theological insights and other aspects of the Church might emerge, and that abuses be shunted aside. While we feel that some teachings of Christianity have been neglected by our separated brethren, other aspects of Christ's teaching have been well developed and many new insights gained among them. They have "many elements of sanctification and truth" (*Constitution on the Church,* no. 8). We can learn much from each other, as we seek together to know Christ's will more fully and follow it (*Decree on Ecumenism,* no. 3). (For a further description of the good and needed things held and developed by our Protestant brethren, Cf. Vatican Council II's *Decree on Ecumenism,* nos. 19–23.)

We cannot see clearly why God has permitted divisions among Christians. But one thing seems obvious: They were brought about originally by the evil lives of Christians. When God's people of the Old Testament were unfaithful to him, Israel was split. So too among us. Hopefully, the confusion and pain of division will make us realize that unity must be earned by the good lives of us all.

Today we see that we deeply need one another. To Catholics, other Christians are our brothers who come from the same family as we do. There was a tragic family quarrel and we have split up. Today we see once again that our family, the Christian religion, is not what it should be because of our separateness. While, therefore, avoiding a "false irenicism" which pretends that there are no real differences between us, we are trying to patiently explain our teachings to one another, discuss our differences, and work to understand and share one another's insights. We should cooperate wherever we can, trying never to do separately what we can do together. Even though our communion is imperfect we are united in the most important things.

Vatican Council II stresses particularly our cooperation in social action:

> Cooperation among Christians vividly expresses the relationship which in fact already unites them, and sets in clearer relief the features of Christ the Servant. Such cooperation . . . should be developed more and more, particularly . . . where a social and technical evolution is taking place. It should contribute to a just evaluation of the dignity of the human person, to peace, the application of the gospel principles to social life, and the advancement of the arts and sciences in a truly Christian spirit. It should also be intensified in the use of every possible means to relieve the afflictions of our times, such as famine and natural disasters, illiteracy and poverty, lack of housing and the unequal distribution of wealth. . . . (*Decree on Ecumenism,* no. 12).

Today the great movement for Christian unity, called ecumenism or the ecumenical movement, is well under way among almost all Christian Churches. The "siege mentality" that had developed during the centuries after the Reformation has finally been almost wholly dissipated, and a new appreciation of Christian Churches for one another has come about. Christian unity grew more in the four years of Vatican Council II than in the previous four hundred. Since the Council, despite occasional setbacks, it has been moving steadily forward.

To contribute in a practical and greater way to Christian unity, Catholics, first of all, are taking part in their own, often painful renewal, to which the Council gave such an impetus. "Their primary duty is to take a careful and honest appraisal of whatever needs to be renewed and done in the Catholic household itself" (*Decree on Ecumenism,* no. 4).

We must continue to pray for unity, particularly with our fellow Christians. There is simply no substitute for praying together to make us realize the unity we have, and to spur us to work for further closeness. Pope Paul and Pope John Paul II have led the way in this on numerous occasions.

We should continually ask for a humble, open appreciation and love of our brethren. "There can be no ecumenism worthy of the name without interior conversion. For it is from newness of attitudes of mind (Cf. Ephesians 4, 23), from self-denial and unstinted love, that desires of unity take their rise and develop in a mature way. We should therefore pray to the Holy Spirit for the grace to be genuinely self-denying, humble, and gentle in the service of others, and to have an attitude of brotherly generosity toward them.... This change of heart and holiness of life, along with public and private prayer for the unity of Christians, should be regarded as the soul of the whole ecumenical movement...." (*Decree on Ecumenism,* nos. 7 and 8).

Prayer and a gradual, interior change of heart are causing concerned Christians to be genuinely pained at our division, which "openly contradicts the will of Christ, scandalizes the world, and damages that most holy cause, the preaching of the gospel to every creature" (*Decree on Ecumenism,* no. 1). In many places, unfortunately, people have come to accept the presence of different Christian religions as they accept competing grocery chains or gas stations. Often it is only when one becomes personally involved, as for example when facing a possible interfaith marriage, that one realizes the true pain of division. Division hurts us all. It makes the faith and Christian life of all of us that much poorer, that much less truly catholic.

We are getting to know the outlook of our separated brethren. "Study is absolutely required for this.... Catholics ... need to acquire a more adequate understanding of the respective doctrines of our separated brethren, their history, their spiritual and liturgical life, their religious psychology, and cultural background" (*Decree on*

Ecumenism, no. 9). Christians now are quietly experiencing the riches of dialogue—getting to know one another, respecting one another, listening, communicating, praying, and mutually growing through one another's insights and ministering together in practical ways.

Quietly progressing today are the "official" dialogues, periodic meetings among the scholars and theologians of the major Christian faiths. Amazing strides in understanding and agreement have been made, and some of these have been published as Documents on Anglican–Roman Catholic Relations, Lutheran–Roman Catholic Relations, and others.

Students for the priesthood and for the ministry of various denominations often study together in theological "unions" or "consortiums." Here all can take advantage of the scholarship and insights of professors of other faiths, of different theologies, etc., thus broadening them all, and producing practical results of cooperation in ministries to the poor, to students, business people, etc.

In a number of places, "sister parishes" are coming together, sharing in their common Christian ministerial concerns for social justice, and for spreading the gospel message—in a word, working together to more effectively bring Christian love to their particular neighborhood. The "sister parishes" may be Catholic-Episcopalian, Catholic-Lutheran, etc. Their common Christian concerns draw them to pray and worship together periodically, opening themselves to the power of the one Spirit, anticipating the day when they can share together in the one eucharistic Body of Christ.

Honest dialogue with one another can be difficult, rewarding, and sometimes painfully self-confronting. Some experience "the agony of communication." Gradually we learn of shared experiences and common problems. We learn what is meant by each other's theological terminology. Different, seemingly contradictory theological formulations can mask actual agreement, or at least views that are "complementary rather than conflicting"—this because of our "different methods and approaches in understanding and confessing divine things," especially between the Eastern and Western traditions. (Cf. *Decree on Ecumenism,* no. 17). Pope John XXIII said, "The substance of the old doctrine of the deposit of faith is one thing, the formulation of its presentation another."

We should remember especially that the Church's dogmas, while infallible and therefore irrevocable, can never express everything about their subjects, nor even begin to exhaust the fullness of truth that is in the mystery of Christianity. No formulation can ever adequately express the reality that we come to know in Christ. There is a wide and ever-open field for discussion, explanation, and development in clarifying even infallible definitions. We should also keep in mind that there is a "hierarchy of truths" in Catholic doctrine, that beliefs vary in their relationship to the foundation of the Christian faith, and therefore in their importance in the lives of Catholics.

Appreciation, cooperation and love must also be shown to those of some Christian religions, and of no formal religion, who so often have good will and seek to carry out their humanitarian ideals. Sometimes non-Christians and secular humanists shame us by the goodness and dedication of their lives; as St. Augustine said, "There are many outside who seem to be inside, and many inside who seem to be outside." There are aspects of truth and love which we can learn from one another; the Church has set up at Rome a Secretariat for Non-Christians and also one to dialogue with atheists.

Vatican Council II exhorts us:

Prudently and lovingly, through dialogue and collaboration with the followers of other religions and in witness of Christian faith and life (we should) acknowledge, preserve and promote the spiritual and moral goods found among these men, as well as the values in their society and culture (*Declaration of Non-Christian Religions*, no. 2).

While rejecting atheism, root and branch, the Church sincerely professes that all men, believers and unbelievers alike, ought to work for the rightful betterment of this world in which all alike live; such an ideal cannot be realized, however, apart from sincere and prudent dialogue. . . . Respect and love ought to be extended also to those who think or act differently than we do in social, political, and even religious matters . . . to understand their ways of thinking through courtesy and love. . . . (*The Church in the Modern World*, nos. 21 and 28).

Finally we must remember that the Church is a mystery—it is continually developing, unfolding, growing in its understanding of itself. It is not just a static institution. It is a love relationship with Christ, the Trinity and one another—and like any love relationship it is continually growing, sometimes painfully, revealing new depths and richness. This relationship, however, is unique because it is the mystery of Christ, God communicating himself to men—and this has no bounds whatever.

This is why there will always be changes in the Church, new insights from various sources into its basic truths, new ways of expressing our beliefs, i.e., new ways of bringing God to men and

women. The content, the "core" truths, of our faith remain the same, but what we understand of these grows and deepens. We can better understand and profit today from what was given us two thousand years ago if we are imaginatively open and can see how some truths can sometimes be better expressed in terms more understandable, more "living" for us today. If we are open, we let the Spirit expand our consciousness and give us new understanding, new insights, and renewed commitment to love, particularly when we gather to hear God's Word and share the eucharist.

Growth, however, comes not only from those within the visible structure of the Church and from the insights of other Christians, but also from other world religions and from non-believers. The Church must look at these in the light of Christ's revelation that comes to us from the Church, but also must be truly and constantly open to the Spirit who breathes where he will and can use anyone as his prophet. The Spirit brings to light hitherto latent or unnoticed aspects of God's revelation of himself in Jesus Christ. Thus there must be among Christians, especially, a common and continual searching into the "unfathomable riches of Christ."

Today Christians are coming to appreciate the religions of the East—Hinduism, Buddhism, Taoism—just as many Easterners are coming to appreciate more fully the teachings of Christ and the "active charity" of Western Christianity. We can learn much from the authentic religious teachers of the East—methods of meditation, self-discipline, detachment or "letting go" of material concerns, a "quieting" of one's inner self, a oneness with nature, an appreciation of intuitive or non-rational ways of arriving at truth, etc. Often, through contact with Eastern religions, Christians come to appreciate more fully the deeply spiritual nature of their own tradition—just as Gandhi, for instance, was helped in formulating his history-changing way of non-violent resistance by studying the teachings of Christ.

There are problems for Christians in many of these Eastern traditions—pantheism, polytheism, reincarnation, a tendency to denigrate the material world and the eternal uniqueness of each individual person—but as the dialogue between East and West continues, more similarities are coming to light.

Progressing more slowly, but nevertheless making some progress, is the dialogue with Islam, the world's third great monotheistic religion (along with Christianity and Judaism) which also looks to the bible as the basis of many of the teachings contained in its sacred book, the Koran. Islam strongly emphasizes the transcendence of God, his total "otherness" and utter holiness. Islam also stresses God's compassion; however, in the Christian view, because Islam does not believe that God has come among us as a man, in Jesus Christ, it could profit from the Christian revelation of God as closely caring and understanding, as one who has become one of us. Pope John Paul II has appealed that the request of Vatican Council II for dialogue and better understanding be accelerated on all levels, and that we put behind us the enmities of the past and work toward a future world of love and peace under our common Father.

Changes in the Church call for openness, patience and charity among all. They also call for a deep faith. Some will tend to resist almost any change, others will want everything changed almost at once. The change that is growth is always painful and confusing, but to refuse to suffer this pain is to remain underdeveloped, immature. The willingness to endure uncertainty is a sign of maturity.

The Council recognized the problems involved, that Church members will disagree with one another—but ". . . they should always try to enlighten one another through honest discussion, preserving mutual charity and caring above all for the common good" (*The Church in the Modern World,* no. 43).

In Morris West's famous novel of the papacy, the hero, Pope Kiril I, comments: "The Church is a family. Like every family, it has its homebodies and its adventurers. It has its critics and its conformists; those who are jealous of its least important traditions; those who wish to thrust it forward, a bright lamp into a glorious future" (*The Shoes of the Fisherman*).

THE CHURCH'S MISSION OF LOVING SERVICE IN TODAY'S WORLD

The Church rejoices in the world's accomplishments, not only in its own small successes. Every achievement toward making this a better world helps carry out the plan of God, and the Church encourages its members to be a part of this.

Christians, on pilgrimage toward the heavenly city, should seek and think of the things which are above. But this duty in no way decreases, rather it increases, the importance of their obligation to work with all men in the building of a more human world. Indeed the mystery of the Christian faith furnishes them with an excellent stimulant and aid to fulfill this duty more courageously and especially to uncover the full meaning of this activity. ... When man develops the earth by the work of his hands or with the aid of technology ... he carries out the design of God manifested at the beginning of time, that he should subdue the earth, perfect creation and develop himself. At the same time he obeys the commandment of Christ that he place himself at the service of his brethren (*The Church in the Modern World,* no. 57).

When we work we are carrying out God's plan, as surely as when we pray. There should be no dichotomy though there will always be a "tension" between one's spiritual life and his human accomplishments. Usually an integration is difficult to achieve, but as long as we try, whatever we do is used by God to fulfill his plan for the world's salvation:

> ... Whoever labors to penetrate the secrets of reality with a humble and steady mind, even though he is unaware of the fact, is nevertheless being led by the hand of God. ... By his labor a man ordinarily supports himself and his family, is joined to his fellow men and serves them, can exercise genuine charity, and be a partner in the work of bringing divine creation to perfection. Indeed, we hold that through labor offered to God, many are associated with the redemptive work of Jesus Christ, who conferred an eminent dignity on labor when at Nazareth he worked with his own hands (*The Church in the Modern World,* nos. 36 and 67).

The Church wants to work with all mankind to make our world a better place, to end war, poverty, and discrimination, to develop the resources of the earth and give all men a share in them. "... The world is becoming unified and ... we have a duty to build a better world based upon truth and justice. ... We are witnesses of the birth of a new humanism" (*The Church in the Modern World,* no. 55).

One great and pressing need of our world is that of peace. The Church's concern was epitomized by Pope Paul's trip to the United Nations in late 1965 when he pleaded: "No more war—war never again!" Almost everyone knows of the Vatican's constant attempts to bring about a ceasefire, negotiations, and a just peace.

Vatican Council II said this, in part, about war and the arms race:

Any act of war aimed indiscriminately at the destruction of entire cities or extensive areas along with their population is a crime against God and man himself. It merits unequivocal and unhesitating condemnation. . . . The arms race is an utterly treacherous trap for humanity, and one which injures the poor to an intolerable degree. It is much to be feared that if this race persists, it will eventually spawn all the lethal ruin whose path it is now making ready. . . . *It is our clear duty, then, to strain every muscle as we work for the time when all war can be completely outlawed* by international consent. This goal undoubtedly requires the establishment of some universal public authority acknowledged as such by all. . . . The highest existing international centers must devote themselves vigorously to the pursuit of better means for obtaining common security . . . to put aside national selfishness and ambition to dominate other nations. . . . International meetings . . . (and) studies . . . should be promoted with even greater urgency. . . . Those who are dedicated to the work of education, particularly of the young, or who mold public opinion, should regard as their most weighty task the effort to instruct all in fresh sentiments of peace. Indeed, every one of us should have a change of heart. . . ." (*The Church in the Modern World,* nos. 80–82).

The Church is willing to work with anyone of good will to achieve peace and to better our world. ". . . All men, believers and unbelievers alike, ought to work for the rightful betterment of this world in which all alike live. . . ." Sincere men will disagree on the best means to peace, and it often seems that we have no choice but the lesser of two evils. Unsatisfactory and often agonizing as this may be, it is better than "opting out" and doing nothing to bring about peace. Here again, in our modern world, we must learn to live with uncertainty and doubt, to do what little we can rather than nothing at all.

If Christians must take part in war, they should assure themselves that it is a just war, that is, a last resort, an act of defense against unjust demands backed by aggressive force, with a reasonable hope of victory without doing more harm than good to the people involved—and the military tactics and objectives of the war must discriminate between soldiers and civilians. Some question whether in today's atomic age it is possible to have a just war. Perhaps one's conscience will lead him to be a conscientious objector—providing he serves the human community in some other way. He deserves the support of the Christian community. On the other hand, Christians realize also that they must do what they can to deter unjust aggression and secure peace with justice for all men.

Certain means of warfare are plainly unchristian and immoral. The fact that so-called Christian nations have used them in the past is all the more reason for plainly repudiating them now: attempted destruction of entire cities or of extensive areas along with their population, indiscriminate bombing of populated areas, bombing or terrorist tactics aimed at civilians to weaken the morale of the enemy, torture of prisoners, use of chemical or biological weapons excluded by international agreement, indiscriminate use of napalm, acts of reprisal against prisoners of war or civilians, depriving large numbers of the civilian population of food through crop destruction, demands of unconditional surrender which kill reasonable hopes of a negotiated settlement, and the use of nuclear weapons designed for "overkill" which would very probably lead to nuclear war.

If an enemy uses these or other immoral means, it gives us no right to retaliate in kind. The test of a Christian is his willingness to act as one when others do not.

DAILY LIVING: THE COMPASSIONATE CHURCH

The Church's mission, and that of every Christian, must first of all be to the poor, underprivileged, and oppressed. We must desire for all men what we desire for ourselves: civil rights, health, adequate education, development, civilization, and culture. Over half the world is deprived of some major need. Yet our American contribution to the economies of backward and starving nations is one-half of one percent—less than what we spend annually on cigarettes and chewing gum.

In our own country forty million people are poor or deprived. 12,000 of the world's people die each day from some form of starvation. In India six million babies die each year because of malnutrition, and a third of the children in Africa will not live into adolescence. Several million families in Latin America must survive on the equivalent of a dollar a week. As we consider these facts we should also consider Christ's clear words about how we will be judged at the end: **Reread Matthew 25, 35–40.**

Vatican Council II speaks plainly of the scandal of so-called Christians who are unconcerned with the poor and deprived of the world: "Some nations with a majority of citizens who are counted as Christians have an abundance of this world's goods, while others are deprived of the necessities of life and are tormented with hunger, disease, and every kind of misery. This situation must not be allowed to continue, to the scandal of humanity. For the spirit of poverty and of charity is the glory and authentication of the Church of Christ" (*The Church in the Modern World,* no. 88).

> The Council reiterates that the Church must above all imitate the poor and persecuted Christ in carrying out its mission:
> "Just as Christ carried out the work of redemption in poverty and oppression, so the Church is called to follow the same route. . . . Christ Jesus though he was by nature God . . . emptied himself, taking the nature of a slave, and 'being rich became poor' for our sakes. Thus the Church, although it needs human resources to carry out its mission, is not set up to seek earthly glory but to proclaim, even by its own example, humility and self-sacrifice.
> "Christ was sent by the Father 'to bring good news to the poor, to heal the contrite of heart' and 'to seek and to save what was lost.' . . . Similarly, the Church encompasses with love all those who are poor and who suffer in the image of its poor and suffering founder. It does all it can to relieve their need and in them it strives to serve Christ" (*Constitution on the Church,* no. 8).

But quite simply, the Church is on the side of the poor, the oppressed, and the neglected. Those who are poor, underprivileged, and wayward are the truly special members of the Church. They are "united with the suffering Christ in a special way for the salvation of the world" (*Constitution on the Church,* no. 41). They are the Church's real power—not its great universities or soaring cathedrals or well-scrubbed suburban multitudes.

Pope John XXIII once scandalized his entourage by insisting on visiting the worst prisoners in one of Rome's prisons, among them two murderers. After listening to the pope's brief talk, one of them said, "These words of hope that you have just given us—do they also apply to me, such a great sinner?" Pope John's only answer was to open his arms and clasp him to his heart.

SOME SUGGESTIONS FOR ...

DISCUSSION

Can you understand how there must be both divine and human elements in the Church?

Can you see evidences of renewal—or lack of it—in the Church today?

What, in your experience, has been most helpful to unite Christians?

How do you think Christians might best contribute to making the world a better place for all today?

FURTHER READING

* *An Introduction to the Faith of Catholics,* Chilson (Paulist Press, 1975) is an excellent, imaginative book, and good reading to complement this one; it is popular and pertinent.
* *To Be a Catholic,* Gallagher (Paulist Press) is a simple presentation of Catholic teaching in the old question-and-answer format; brief and yet stimulating, it is available in both English and Spanish editions.
** *Catholicism,* McBrien (Winston Press, 1980) is an excellent two-volume compendium of the Catholic faith that is both traditional and modern. It is a "must" investment for anyone seriously interested in theology today.
** *On Being a Christian,* Küng (Doubleday, 1976) and its briefer summary, ** *Signposts for the Future, Contemporary Issues Facing The Church* (Doubleday, 1978) are excellent presentations of Catholic Christianity.
* *The Communal Catholic: A Personal Manifesto,* Greeley (Seabury, 1976) is a well-written, realistic book for those today who are alienated by the organizational Church, showing how they are and can be further linked with the worldwide Catholic Christian community.
** *The Community of the Beloved Disciple,* Brown (Paulist Press, 1979) is a superb book, the fruit of almost a lifetime of scholarly, prayerful work that tells of the early "Johannine" Christian communities—it is "must" reading, especially for those upset by divisions in today's Church.
* *Stories of God, An Unauthorized Biography,* Shea (Thomas More Press, 1980) is a truly creative, rewarding book about our understanding of God and our ongoing Christian story.
* *Turning, Reflections on the Experience of Conversion,* Griffin (Doubleday, 1980) is a frank, insightful, and fine book about her conversion to Catholicism, by a wife/mother/advertising executive.
* *Protestantism,* Marty (Doubleday Image Book, 1974) is an excellent pre-

sentation of Protestantism's "main line" churches, their culture, rituals, and doctrines, by the brilliant, insightful church historian who was recently voted by his peers the year's outstanding churchman.

* *Oriental Mysticism,* Stevens (Paulist Press, 1973) is a fine, concise introduction to this increasingly popular field.
* Return to the Center, Griffiths (Templegate, 1977) is an excellent, meditative book by a Catholic monk who has spent twenty years in his own Indian "ashram."
* *Aging: The Fulfillment of Life,* Nouwen and Gaffney (Doubleday Image Book, 1976) is a fine book about how to make one's later years a time of hope and the climax of our life's journey toward God.
* *Maggie Kuhn on Aging,* A dialogue edited by Dieter Hessel (Westminster Press, 1977) is another very wise, very wonderful book by the truly remarkable woman who brought together the "Gray Panthers."

PERSONAL REFLECTION

As a Christian, a human being, I must ask myself honestly: Do I desire for all men all that I have and enjoy? Am I doing something to bring what I have to at least one who is deprived?

I might renew my resolution to help some individual poor person or family, someone retarded, forgotten, discriminated against, or underprivileged. I might join a group that is combatting poverty or discrimination or working for peace—or I might regularly send help to some charity, mission, or peace project of which I know.

25

Living Daily the Christian Life

What should motivate a Christian to be "different" in his daily life? Should one do things out of fear, because he is forced to? What are some practical guidelines by which one can live daily a Christian life?

HOW DO WE KNOW HOW TO LIVE?

The way a Christian lives begins with a loving call from the Father. He invites us to share in a special way in his plan. We are free to respond or not. He reminds us, as he did the Israelites at Sinai, what he has done for us—and then he gives us commandments by which we can give him our response of love.

If we choose to accept the Father's loving invitation, we respond in and through Christ. The Christian life is an imitation of Christ, but it is more. It is being transformed into Christ, sharing his life, being here and now his hands and feet and eyes and ears. He lives in us and uses us to do now among men the things he did 2,000 years ago. ". . . It is no longer I who live, but Christ who lives in me" (Galatians 2, 20).

Each Christian, then, is Christ among us. Each is a new, special manifestation of Christ that will never exist again. Each of us in his own way must expect to undergo his "passover," his death and resurrection. We must struggle and suffer and die in order to be raised up to eternal happiness. It is not easy to live a life with Christ and in Christ. But once one tastes this life, nothing else can satisfy.

Christ guides us in living his life through his Spirit who is within us. It is the Spirit who conforms us to Christ, who shows us what to do and who inspires and strengthens us to do it. The Holy Spirit, we recall, is the Person who is love—and in guiding us to live the Christian life the Spirit is simply showing us how to love—or, rather, how to let ourselves be loved by God, and then love in return.

The Spirit has been sent by Christ to form us into a community, his Church, to show us how to love and be loved. The Church is Christ among us as he works through his Spirit to unite and guide us so that we can witness to his love among men. The Church is Christ among us doing the things he began to do two thousand years ago. The Church's role in the world is not to build itself as an institution of salvation, nor to enforce a series of moral laws, but always and only to help God's revelation of love reach people.

The Church has laws, norms and guides by which we live. (It should be evident by now that they are not nearly as numerous or as restrictive as might have been thought.) The purpose of the Church's laws is simply to show us how to let ourselves be loved by God, and how to love him in return, particularly through our neighbor. All the Church's rules, and its every exercise of authority, are meant only to help us open ourselves freely and maturely to God's love.

> Those in love want to know, often in detail, what will please their beloved. They want to be told how to avoid upsetting their love relationship, and how to grow in love day by day. They fear, with the wholesome fear of a lover, to hurt the one they love. And because they are mature, they know that if they hurt their beloved, if they upset their love relationship, they will not only bring unhappiness upon themselves. Their lovingness itself will punish them for what they have done, and they cannot be happy until they have righted the wrong they have done to their beloved.

Christians know, too, that because they are human, they will sometimes be blinded by emotion, greed, or pride—which can lead to the formation of an erroneous conscience. Sometimes people are simply bored with the whole process. People then may not want to show their love at all—they are faithful only from a sheer sense of duty—but they realize that faithfulness now is the real test of their love. To comply, to give up one's own way, to show one's love when it is hard, even very painful to do so, is the test of true love. So it is with our mature obedience to Christ in his Church. We know our weakness—that we will at times obey only reluctantly—but this can sometimes be the truest test of our love of God.

Of course, there is the ever-present temptation to legalism: to equate keeping the letter of the law with pleasing God. A servile fear or a comfortable, rationalized rule-keeping can take over our moral life. This is precisely what Christ came to dispel. He said, "Beware of the leaven of the Pharisees and Sadducees" (Matthew 16, 6); these had stressed the exact keeping of many observances to the detriment of the heart and spirit of the law which is love. Some Christians, unfortunately, cannot yet realize that "perfect love casts out fear" (1 John 4, 18).

As one progresses in the Christian life there is less and less need to consult the "rules." One gradually develops a Christian moral sense, comes to "think with the Church." We do not expect of the Church detailed answers which solve our moral dilemmas for us (although consultation with a spiritual guide may be sometimes necessary). Rather we try to grasp the Church's basic principles of morality, and with the guidance of the Spirit to apply them to our daily life. We take seriously the guidance of the Church in the formation of our conscience to avoid the danger of erroneous conscience.

> One realizes that many, perhaps most, moral situations are not clearly good or evil, that sometimes all one can do is choose what seems to be the lesser of two evils. But this is Christian maturity. As children must be given continual, explicit instructions when they are young, but have less and less need of guidance as they mature, so with maturing Christians in their moral development.

Here, then, are proposed not detailed rules of Christian morality but some general principles for daily living, suggestions as to how to follow the Spirit's guidance in everyday life. Four main areas of life are considered: our home life, our work or school life, our social life, and our religious life.

OUR HOME LIFE

—At home upon arising, Christians thank God for another day in which to live and to love, and ask his help, especially for some particular thing that they will have special need of that day. Realistically, some Christians, like a good proportion of humanity, will hardly feel alive, much less prayerful, when they arise; some would better delay their attempt at prayer until they are on the way to work, or later, as opportunities arise.

—**Our meals** have always been associated in human custom with an awareness that it is ultimately God who gives us "our daily bread." Hence we begin them with some sort of brief prayer. All in the family might take their turns asking a blessing, or each can express his or her particular thanks. Our best prayers are usually those we compose ourselves.

—**Parents remember that they are God-models to their children, and when they realize their own weaknesses, they try to remember that God gives them special strength and insights.** They *show* their love and affection toward their children, and they give example for their children's later life by expressing their love of one another—yet realizing that occasional inevitable conflicts also show their children that people can deeply love one another and yet be angry and at odds.

—**Parents remember that they are "by word and example . . . the first preachers of the faith to their children"** (*Constitution on the Church*). They try to make God real to their children, helping them express simple prayers, and praying with them (for example, at bedtime). To the extent they can, they regularly read with their children the bible and other stories which give examples of Christian living and attitudes the children can understand and relate to. Many good bibles and imaginative spiritually-based books are available today for children.

—**They try to give their children the vital sense of trust and security that can come only from showing mutual love, respect, and kindness.** To the extent that they can, they love "unconditionally," i.e., regardless of whether or not the children live up to their expectations. They try to give their children the "why" of anything they ask them to do, as this is possible. They know where their children are, and as best they can they try to make their home a center for the growing children's social life, a welcome place for them and their friends to come. They can and should talk things over with their children, e.g., the limited family budget, and let the children have a sense of shared responsibility for the family's decisions. They try to do things together with their children, as a family, and try to be imaginatively sensitive to their children's own growing preferences and skills. They help them make gradually more mature decisions on their own, letting them make choices as much as possible, but letting them know they are responsible and accountable for their choices.

—**Parents also are alert to helping their children prepare for the time when they will leave home,** and for their own marriage and/or job career. They correct their children's faults unhesitantly, but also praise them for their accomplishments, however small. They use firm but loving discipline, and "hang tough," especially during their children's teens against sometimes overwhelming peer pressure and other, perhaps inept, overly-permissive parents. They do not yield to the temptation to give in, and largely let their teenagers run their own lives. They use persistent love and continually try to consult, talk, and share enthusiasm and interests with their emerging adults.

—**Mature Christian parents remember that they are the "primary and principal educators"** of their children. "Parents moreover have the right to determine, in accordance with their own religious beliefs, the kind of religious education that their children are to receive" (*Declaration on Christian Education,* no. 3; Cf. *Decree on Religious Liberty,* no. 5). Theirs is the primary duty of teaching their children and choosing schools and programs that will promote the child's spiritual and moral growth, as well as their intellectual development. They take time to work with their child's teachers and demand accountability where education is inept or inefficient. The Catholic school, C.C.D., and other catechetical programs are only meant to help parents do *their* job more effectively. There is no duty of *both* parents more serious than this.

The Christian family will look beyond their immediate circle and try to be aware of the needs of others: the needs of their neighborhood, particularly people with few friends, children whose parents neglect them, the poor and underprivileged of their area—and of the world. Wise parents try to direct their children beyond the selfish and suffocating spiritual mediocrity that is often a danger (especially with materially well-off parents) and they give their children a broad, truly Christians world view.

OUR WORK OR SCHOOL LIFE

—**Christians go to their job or profession with the knowledge that their work is helping to carry out God's plan for the universe.** No act, however boring or seemingly fruitless, is ever wasted. They try to do their best because by their work they are spreading love and helping to bring the world to perfection.

—**Christians look for opportunities to help others** in their office, factory, or classroom. They expect friction and conflicts and try to see the beam in their own eye before the speck in their neighbor's. They try to be genuinely interested in even one other person who needs help in some way.

—**Christians give a full day's work for a full day's pay,** and try to take a constructive interest in their job. If they are employers, they provide safe and decent working conditions, give a living wage, avoid subtle perpetuations of sexual, racial, or age discrimination, and share profits and policy-making with employees to the extent that they can.

—**Christians in their business dealings practice honesty and justice.** They realize that some things are fundamentally wrong: cheating, false advertising, dishonest business agreements, or taking profits from corporate investments in places and countries that violate human rights in the name of productivity. Selfish and greedy lobbying for one's particular interest to the detriment of the common good, avoiding one's justly owed taxes or debts, bribery and "kickbacks" are plainly dishonest, avaricious and unchristian. They realize that if they have been dishonest, they owe restitution; if this cannot be made to those from whom it was stolen, it can be given to charity.

—**Christians give regularly, to the poor, disabled, aged, and underprivileged, of their money, and whatever is possible of their time** (and something, however small, always *is* possible, if we are honest with ourselves). They realize that they can quickly become caught up in the accumulation of material things that are not really necessary— while more than half the world is underfed, without decent clothing or housing, and with little or no education. Christians desire for all men the good things they themselves enjoy. They may come to realize that if they never refuse an appeal for help, they will themselves never be in want of anything essential.

—**Christians who are students** are grateful for the opportunities they have for an education. They try to develop their God-given talents. If they do not succeed in one field, they imaginatively try another; they realize that they have something vital to contribute, in God's plan, to the world's development. They are honest and avoid cheating or taking advantage of those who are helping them attain an education. They steadily and courageously seek truth, realizing that this may sometimes cause them problems of faith, or problems with those interested only in learning for the material success and/or status it may bring.

OUR SOCIAL LIFE

—**Here again the Christian's basic attitude is one of universal love:** "As you did it to one of the least of these my brethren you did it to me" (Matthew 25, 40). They try to reach out as Christ would to all men. They choose their friends and acquaintances not only from among those who are pleasant and personable, but also among those who are lonely, defensive, embittered.

—**Christians try to contribute to their country, their state, and their city** by being good neighbors, joining some civic group and voting for good candidates; perhaps they may feel qualified to run for office themselves. They realize that patriotism is a virtue, and they support their country when it needs them. If they feel that they must witness by being conscientious objectors in time of war, they know that they must "agree to serve the human community in some other way" (*The Church in the Modern World*, no. 79).

—**Christians try to take seriously the admonition of the council that we "strain every muscle" in working for world peace—built on justice**—realizing that this is the crucial need of our time. They realize that they are Christian citizens of the world, and they try to learn about and help those of other countries, particularly the needy emerging nations.

—**Christians appreciate their leisure time, but also realize that there are many things they can do to help others in their spare moments:** visiting the sick, particularly those old, neglected, or mentally ill; giving time to a social or civic group working to obtain better and fairer housing, job opportunities for those relatively unskilled, etc.

They are alert to speak out against immoral policies of government and demand accountability of elected officials. Better yet, they are alert to lawmakers' and other officials' achievements for the common good so that they can compliment and encourage them, even if only by dropping them a postcard.

—**Christians respect the person and dignity of their neighbor and their neighbor's right to his or her good reputation.** Our neighbor, of course, is everyone. Neighbors avoid injuring another in any way, except in self-defense; they keep to themselves information that, however true, would harm another's reputation. Christians realize that hatred, carrying a grudge, or injuring another's good name is usually seriously wrong. They recognize their neighbor's right to the truth, and particularly avoid lying that would do serious harm. They know, too, that they have an obligation in conscience to drive safely.

—**Christians remember their dignity** and avoid injuring themselves and giving scandal by drunkenness, taking drugs, or smoking that harms their health. They realize that alcoholism, particularly, can get a hold on one without one's realizing it, and they are humble and realistic enough to recognize its warning signs.

—**Christians respect their own dignity and that of the one they profess to love by controlling their sexual desires, having and enjoying sex only within the marriage commitment.** They recognize that they live in a sexually over-stimulated society, and realistically take safeguards to avoid what they know are occasions of sin, temptations to use another or let oneself be used. If they fail, no matter how often, they return to seek forgiveness, and start over again, realizing that they are thereby building a disciplined and faithful love.

—**Christians realize that one's attitude toward those who are "different" because of race, nationality, sex, or old age is usually the real test of the genuineness of their Christianity.** They recognize that an attitude of discrimination, segregation, or intrinsic superiority is seriously wrong; they try to do whatever they can to help bring about understanding and acceptance of all. Christians do not patronize a place, or live in housing, which excludes those of another race or ethnic background. They do what they can to obtain fair housing, education, and job opportunities for all. They do not let apathy, fear, or disillusionment take over.

—**Christians recognize that prejudices are deep within us all, and that overcoming these requires much perseverance and often great**

sacrifice. They may regard themselves as victims of "reverse discrimination," in, for example, an affirmative action program—but they are willing to endure some of this for the sake of a minority's long denied right to justice and equality. They try to look on all men and women as individuals, to get to know them and appreciate them as human beings with strengths and weaknesses like themselves.

—Christians expect that they will be mocked and sometimes harassed for living up to their beliefs. They remember Christ's words, "Behold, I send you as sheep in the midst of wolves. . . . If the world hates you, know that it has hated me before it hated you. . . ." (Matthew 10, 16; John 15, 18).

OUR RELIGIOUS LIFE

—Christians truly believe that they can find God daily in their neighbors and that in their efforts to make this world even a bit better, they are working hand in hand with God. But they know, too, that they must pause periodically, try to be aware of God's presence, and recollect and remotivate themselves. They know that this is particularly necessary in our modern, materialistic, secularistic world, where things of the spirit are so easily forgotten.

—Christians also pause to pray whenever they can, though it may be only once or twice during the day. They pray with confidence, no matter how sinful they have been, for they know that their poor prayer is joined with that of Christ and that it is the Spirit who is praying within them. Some sort of spiritual reading, particularly brief passages from the bible, can be the "food" that makes meaningful these brief prayer-pauses. Some Christians know they can get help from dropping into a church occasionally for a quiet "visit" with Christ in the eucharist.

—Christians who are truly serious about growing in God's love know that they must set aside a time to spiritually "take inventory," if possible for a few days or more, at least once during the year. They might make a weekend retreat or take part in a cursillo or parish renewal mission or at least a day of recollection.

—Christians also realize that they must join together with others in order to grow spiritually themselves and help others grow. They know that family prayer and religious discussion are only a start.

They can usually find a group that they can join, whether an organized parish group or an informal one, to learn more about their faith, to contribute their own insights, or to do some apostolic or ministering work. Some are not "joiners" by nature, but can take advantage of periodic classes and discussions.

—**Christians remember that a self-centered Christian is no Christian at all.** They try to respond to opportunities to tactfully share their religious and moral convictions, especially with those who seem to need something in which to believe. But Christians also know that loving concern, a sensitivity to helping those in need of personal or material support, is the best way to bring Christ to others.

—**Christians try to develop a sense of reverence, of worship, both personally and with others.** They respect the sacred things and places associated with their religion. They try to be active members of their parish, contributing their talents and suggestions, as well as financial support according to their means. They are humbly aware of the prevalent Christian sins: passivity, not wanting to get involved, and selfishness, even greediness, in not wanting to share one's talents and material things.

—**The weekly eucharistic family meal of their parish, the Mass, is the big spiritual event of the Christians' week.** They know that if they deliberately neglect it, they must ask themselves how seriously they love Christ, or whether they appreciate what the Mass is. Christians should usually look forward to Mass and perhaps prepare a bit by reading and/or recollection at home beforehand. They try to get at least one practical point out of the sermon, and above all take part in the communion meal as the great source of strength and ability to love during the coming week. As long as they are not sure of being alienated from God and others by a state of serious sin, they should never hesitate to take part in communion.

—**Christians periodically feel the need of seeking God's forgiveness,** of making up for what they have done to their fellow humans, of making a new start. Christians realize that their life will be one of continual conversion—and are not discouraged because of it.

—**Christians realize their weakness and take advantage of the Church's reminders to do penance.** They try to make Lent, for example, a time when they can do some positive good, particularly by way of self-discipline; they abstain willingly and fast if they can, but they try particularly to make up for their sins by acts of kindness, patience, and interest in others.

—**Christians know that sometimes doubts will come,** or the spiritual ennui in which they no longer seem to get anything out of their religion. They try to remember that God never forces himself upon us, but rather solicits our love in often hidden ways. They know that God's ways are not our ways.

—**Finally, Christians know that they must suffer and die with Christ** in order to rise with him. They expect pain, frustration, and hardships during the day. But Christians try to offer them up with Christ's sufferings, realizing that this may ultimately be their greatest contribution to spreading love in the world.

SOME SUGGESTIONS FOR ...

DISCUSSION

What should motivate a Christian's daily life?

Can you understand why one needs some "rules" and what part they should play in his daily life?

What do you think is your greatest need in living Christ's life daily?

FURTHER READING

* *Principles for a Catholic Morality,* O'Connell (Seabury, 1978). A good summary of Catholic moral teaching in a popular style for the student, seminarian, and lay person.
* *Making Moral Decisions,* Stevens (Paulist Press, 1981). A standard work on the process of Christian decision-making, recently updated. Also a useful book by the same author is *Business Ethics* (Paulist Press, 1979).
* *Newness of Life,* Gaffney (Paulist Press, 1979). A good one-volume summary of Christian ethics.
* *Education Toward Adulthood,* Moran (Paulist Press, 1979). An excellent, short work, covering almost every aspect of our life's striving for spiritual growth and maturity.
* *An Introduction to Bioethics,* Shannon and DiGiacomo (Paulist Press,

1979). For lay readers seeking information about recent developments in medicine, science, and technology.

* *Gospel and Law,* Dodd (Columbia, 1951) A noted scripture scholar comments on the law of love in the New Testament.
* *The Sermon on the Mount,* Jeremias (Fortress, 1963). Scholarly but insightful, by a New Testament expert.

PERSONAL REFLECTION

If I believe in Christ I am tremendously privileged. I can consciously live with him and in him each day, doing the things he did 2,000 years ago. The Spirit within me will help my poor weakness and gradually form me into another Christ.

I might pick one or two areas in which I am particularly unlike Christ and ask the Spirit's daily help with these.

26
Fulfillment Forever

Why do we say that death is the climax of a Christian life? What will happen to us after death? What is the meaning of purgatory? What do we mean by saying that Christians expect a new heaven and a new earth forever? What, ultimately, is the difference in being a Christian?

OUR MEETING WITH CHRIST AT DEATH

Death is the climactic experience of our life. It is more than just a moment of time; it is an experience. We awaken to full consciousness and full freedom, and encounter God himself. All our life has been lived for just this. But death usually has a fearfulness attached to it because of our sinfulness—men and women, even those otherwise strong, tend to shrink from it.

Christ by his death has changed the nature of our death. The Christian knows this: death is now our most meaningful act, the one to which we look forward as the climax and summation of our life. Someone has said, "The moment a man is born he begins to die." None of us can avoid death, but committed Christians look ahead to it and live their life in the realization of its coming.

Some scholars hold that in the experience of death (after death, as we humans look at it) a man makes his first completely personal, totally free act—his final decision about his eternal destiny. During life he has been too distracted to make this all-important choice. Now after death, with full freedom and his whole being he chooses for God or against him. This, however, does not mean that one gets a total "second chance" after death; all the free actions of his life have been preparing him for and pointing him toward this choice (Cf. Laudislaus Boros, *The Mystery of Death*, Herder & Herder, 1965).

It is Christ whom we encounter after death face to face, in the clearest, most intimate way possible. He whom we have been reaching for in our prayers, whom we have dimly encountered in the sacraments, is now before us in the overwhelming fullness of his light and love and power. Our whole life is present, summed up, in this experience. People sometimes testify how their life flashed before them as they faced death. This is but a taste of what will happen when we meet Christ.

We should often think of this moment. We know how we long to see someone whom we love and from whom we have been separated for some time—and on the other hand, how ashamed we are at meeting someone whom we have deeply offended. In these first moments of eternity, we shall be face to face with Christ whose love has always been with us, and for whom we should have been reaching all our life.

In this final moment there is no in-between. The time of probation is over; there are no more chances. We are either saved or damned. This is the ultimate and only important distinction between men: either they have God's grace-presence with them or they do not—either they choose him or they turn away. And we never know when this moment will come for us.

To prepare a person for death, the Church gives some or all of these sacraments:

The sacrament of penance or reconciliation (conditional absolution reconciliation if the person is unconscious).
The anointing of the sick.
Holy communion, here called "holy viaticum"—the Church's sacrament for the dying. This is followed by a special blessing for the dying.

During these rites those who are present should join in the prayers to the extent that they can.

A priest should be called as soon as it becomes apparent that an illness is serious. We mentioned before the mistaken charity of not calling the priest for fear of frightening the patient. The sooner in a serious illness one receives the anointing of the sick, the better may be his or her chance of recovery, or at least the better the sick person can prepare for this final, all-important meeting with Christ at death.

It should be remembered, too, that if someone dies suddenly or is fatally injured, the priest should be called immediately—even though to all appearances death has already taken place.

The Christian's attitude toward death should be one of confidence and expectation. We know that God wants all men to be saved, that he has surrounded us through life with the constant helps of his love. He will surely be with us at death. No matter what sins we have committed, if we are sorry he forgives them all.

As Jesus faced death confident that the Father would raise him to life, so should we. Jesus assures each of us: "... I go to prepare a place for you. I will come again and will take you to myself, that where I am you may be also" (John 14, 2–4).

PURGATORY: THE IDEA OF ACCOUNTABILITY

—We have seen that we are responsible and accountable for our sins, and have a need within ourselves to make up for them. If we do not do this in our present life, we will have to do so after death. This has traditionally been called "purgatory," an attempt to express our need of eventual "purification"—the growth in needed love we must undergo before attaining union with God, who is Limitless Love, forever in heaven. This is essentially a way of saying we are responsible beings, ultimately accountable for our free actions and choices.

Purgatory is perhaps best described as the painful state or experience of encountering God after death, when we see him as he really is "face to face" (1 Corinthians 13, 12), and, by contrast, ourselves as we really are, as sinful humans. An encounter with the living God always is painfully, totally upsetting. God's manifestations of himself in scripture show this:

Moses veiled his face when he beheld the burning bush, for he was afraid to look on God (Exodus 3, 6). Elijah performed the same symbolic gesture of veiling his face on Mount Sinai (1 Kings 19, 13). In the vision in which God called Isaiah, even the seraphim veil their faces and the prophet exclaims with the terror of any creature menaced by the divine: "Woe is me! For I am lost ... for my eyes have seen the King, the Lord of Hosts" (Isaiah 6, 5). Daniel saw God in a vision of fire and the proximity of God caused him to enter something like a mystical agony (Daniel 7, 9–10; 8, 17-18. 27). Ezekiel fell down before

God, stricken with a strange paralysis and with dumbness (Ezekiel 3, 23-26). At the transfiguration the disciples fell on their faces and were filled with awe (Matthew 17, 1-6).

We saw that we will meet Christ after death, and in and through him, God himself. Without any more rationalizations or equivocation, we now face the One who has loved us totally, unconditionally. We now clearly realize how often we have hurt him and our fellow humans, and yet did nothing about it.

In this experience of purgation we make up for our sins by growing in love. Christ has made up for our sins, and now accepts us totally, but we yet have the need of doing something about them ourselves, as when we hurt anyone we love. We experience this painful purgation because we have not loved enough. This is only reasonable. Most people realize that they have not made up for all their sins, that they still are clinging to some faults, and therefore could not expect to be perfectly happy immediately after death with the perfect, totally accepting Love we call God. On the other hand, they know that they are not evil enough to be damned. It is only logical, then, to believe in this experience, this situation or state of purgation.

Many scholars today do not accept the traditional notion of purgatory as a post-death state, but see it rather as something undergone in this life—unequivocal, painful times of facing and making up for our sins. Perhaps this takes place in the experience of dying. The concept of accountability after death, however, is an ancient one.

Parts of the Christian Church almost from the beginning believed in a state of purgation after death where the dead could not help themselves but could be helped by the prayers of those on earth. God's people of the Old Testament had only a vague notion of this, but a widespread Jewish tradition of the century before Christ held that it was a "holy and wholesome thought to pray for the dead that they may be loosed from their sins" (2 Maccabees 12, 46).

The concept of purgatory as a place of purification by "fire," before entering heaven, has been prevalent only since the thirteenth century. Archeology, however, shows that the earliest Christians prayed for their dead who were sometimes said to be in a "place of tears" or a "place of darkness." The ancient liturgies of both East and West contain prayers for the dead, as in our Mass today. Many early Christian writers mention prayers for the dead: Cyprian says (c. 245 A.D.) that such had been said in all churches since the time of the apostles. Tertullian also witnesses to the ancient practice of the Church: "The faithful wife will pray for the soul of her deceased husband, particularly on the anniversary of his falling asleep. And if she fails to do so, she has repudiated her husband as far as in her lies" (*De Monag.,* 10). In a touching passage of his *Confessions,* St. Augustine tells of his mother's dying request: "Lay this body anywhere at all; the care of it must not trouble you. This only I ask of you, that you remember me at the altar of the Lord wherever you are" (IX, chapter XI).

Those passing through this purgatory state know clearly that they are saved, God's love overwhelms them, and they have a joy far more intense than anything on earth. The imagery of purgatory as a "place" where we would go for a certain "time" to be purified by "fire" should not be misunderstood. Purgatory is certainly not hell for a short time, nor a vast torture chamber where God revenges himself upon trapped souls, nor is there time in our sense in this purgatory state. These metaphors attempt to describe the paradox of purgatory—a state of joy and yet of suffering.

What we are doing, as we said, is growing in love by submitting ourselves to the burning, penetrating, purifying power of God's love. We realize clearly our immature self-love, our ingratitude, sloth, and attachments to sinful habits. We "grow up" in love and break away from our childish self-centeredness. Our real self then emerges, perfected, totally absorbed in God, totally in love.

All our wayward habits and affections must be directed toward this one, true Love. One person at death may still cling to material possessions, another has an overly-sensitive pride, and another has never really disciplined his or her sex power. All these must be purified, "burnt up" in an all-absorbing divine love. God wants nothing to interfere with his filling us with limitless love.

There is pain in this purgatory-state. Any deep personality change is painful—and this is our final, perfect change for eternity. Growing in love can be particularly painful, especially when we contrast our imperfections with our beloved. For example, a man with a bad habit—alcoholism, a violent temper—might meet a wonderful woman. He realizes he must conquer this habit if there is to be any permanent love between them; if he loves enough, he will strive painfully until he overcomes it. In this purgation we come to love perfectly the perfect Lover.

Those in this purgatory-state, therefore, want to be with God, and yet do not want to be with him the way they are. We see clearly

God's infinite goodness and our own faults by contrast—like a piercing ray penetrating and revealing the depths of our being. Seeing our miserable state, we want to be purged, purified, and yet we ache and burn with desire to be with God. The pain is simply that we cannot be united with him quickly enough.

Those in the state of purgation cannot help themselves, but we can help them attain heaven by praying for them, offering Mass for them, offering our sufferings, good actions, etc. The power of love for one another within the Mystical Body goes on after death. We can help others, even as we will be helped. Sometimes people feel helpless at the death of a loved one, wishing there was more they could do for their beloved. Catholics know that the power of their love can help even after death.

We should remember that we need not go through this purgatory-state after death if we have loved sufficiently in this life. Some people by their great suffering surely seem to be going through their purgatory here.

IN THE LITURGY

The Church treats the dead body with reverence, a sign of our belief that we will rise to eternal life. The body is brought to the church where a Mass of Christian Burial is offered; afterward, it is incensed, blessed with holy water, and brought to the cemetery where after some final prayers it is buried, often in blessed ground.

The Church's liturgy for the dead emphasizes our confident hope of resurrection and eternal life. The prayers and songs speak of the fulfillment of life and eternal joy. A candle burns by the dead Christian's body, a sign of his or her eternal life with Christ, "the Light of the World" who came to lead us through the shadows and blackness of death, to the indescribably dazzling eternal Light, God himself.

At the weekly parish eucharist the priest usually leads the parish family during the Prayer of the Faithful in praying for those who are deceased. In the Mass liturgy, during some of the eucharistic prayers there is a commemoration of our dead: the priest may pause with his hands joined before him as we pray for our dead. Black vestments used to indicate that the priest was offering Mass for the dead (formerly called a Requiem Mass or Mass of eternal "rest"). White is now used—a sign of confident hope in our resurrection.

During the month of November we particularly pray for the "holy souls" in purgatory. November 2 is the Feast of All Souls, "All Souls Day," on which Catholics usually take part in Mass for their dead.

People sometimes have Masses celebrated for deceased relatives and friends: they usually give an offering, not to pay for the Mass, but to help the works of the Church.

AT THE END

When we speak of the end of the world we mean its completion, its consummation and transformation, not its destruction. Then the limitations of time and space, of disharmony and waste, will be over. A new order of things will begin.

We do not know when the end of the world is coming and we know little about how it will take place. Christ says ". . . of that day or that hour no one knows . . . only the Father" (Matthew 13, 32). The knowledge of this was not part of Christ's earthly mission, and we need not waste time uselessly speculating about it. There is too much to do with the wonderful world we have here and now.

There will be for all of us the "resurrection of the body," that is, we will be alive as full human beings and not just as spirits. In some sense, our world will be there too, only it will be transformed (Cf. the next section).

Christ will appear in judgment with all mankind before him: Read John 5, 25–30.

The sermon of Christ which is often taken as giving a detailed picture of the end uses images from Jewish apocalyptic literature. Many think that it is primarily concerned with the beginning of the messianic era, the "last days" (Cf. Mark 13, 3ff; Matthew 24, 3ff; Luke 21, 7ff; also Revelation 20, 11–13). At any rate, the Old Testament concept of the "Day of Yahweh," reflected in the New Testament in the above sermon and particularly in Revelation (the Apocalypse), is this apocalyptic style of writing. It dates back to the Maccabean persecution and is a kind of "religious underground resistance" literature; it has striking and mysterious visions, symbolic numbers, explanations given by an angel, etc.—all centering on the fact that though the powers hostile to God are triumphing for the moment, a new era will dawn and God and his people will strikingly triumph.

Christ will somehow be revealed as the Lord and Savior of all creation. All the universe will acknowledge him. He will lead those in his kingdom of love to his Father and eternal happiness.

Many today do not expect Christ's second coming (the parousia) to be an apocalyptic event in the future, but consider that it has already begun, that Christ's presence is gradually being realized in human history. The end of the world, rather than being passively awaited, is actively being brought about by the love and labor of man. Christ who is among us will be revealed at the end, at the culmination of this unfolding, for all to see in power and glory.

. . . Christ is now at work in the hearts of men through the energy of his Spirit, arousing not only a desire for the age to come, but by that very fact animating, purifying, and strengthening those noble longings by which the human family makes its life more human, and strives to render the whole earth submissive to his goal (*The Church in the Modern World*, no. 38).

When Christ comes to us in judgment the whole of human history will be revealed. Then we will understand the "why" of everything, that all has worked out for God's glory and man's happiness—even the crimes, wars, and countless cruelties throughout history. At present we are like someone with a few pieces of a jigsaw puzzle. Then we shall see the whole puzzle of history put together—and our faith tells us that it will be a picture of immense beauty and love.

Our existence immediately after death could already be something like that of the resurrected man. We will then be beyond time as we know it now. So we should not think of ourselves as separated spirits, having to "wait" until events on this earth have been completed before we begin our full human existence in eternity. There are unanswered questions, of course, about this new existence; however, "a biology of our future life is impossible; at the most only a very restrained anthropology can be outlined" (Schoonenberg, *op. cit.*, p. 199).

THE NEW UNIVERSE TOWARD WHICH WE WORK

**After the end there will be a new universe—a new heaven and a
new earth.** "But according to his promise we wait for a new heaven
and a new earth in which righteousness dwells" (2 Peter 13). Since
the material world has suffered from the disorder that has come from
man's sin, it is only fitting that it should share in man's final glory.
The universe is now "in labor" toward this better state (Cf. Romans
8, 20–22).

The new universe will be beautiful and perfect beyond imagining.
We do not know the exact nature of this perfect universe, but we do
know that nature will be in harmony with itself and with man; there
will be no more devastating storms, tornadoes, earthquakes, etc., and
the immense power we have begun to discover in the subatomic
world and throughout the universe will then be put to full use. There
will be a vast cosmic renewal and glorification, and God will be revealed in all things, present among us in undreamed of ways.

It is up to us now to bring about this new universe. We said before
that God has placed in our hands an unfinished universe, has entrusted to us the privilege of perfecting his work. Every step we take
toward harnessing nature, toward using the power of the universe,
continues creation and carries out God's plan of love. We are "co-
creators" with God—and the more conscious we are of this the more
we can contribute. Particularly whenever we spread truth or expend
pain and love for others, we help to bring about the perfection of all
things.

**Christians and all who realize this have an especially great respon-
sibility and privilege** toward helping perfect the universe. We can
never be satisfied with things as they are in their present state. We
must be driven on to advance truth and love—for every conquest of
the universe which does not help to spread love serves to strengthen
tyranny and holds back the perfection of all things.

Who then but the Christian—I mean the man authentically inspired by
the love of Christ (for there is no other, whether he bears officially the
name of Christian or whether he is one in fact without knowing it)—
who then but such a man is capable of placing the universe at the service of love and thus contributing, modestly but efficaciously, to the re-

demption of the universe, the object of his hope? (Lyonnet, in *The Church*).

By their labor they are unfolding the Creator's work . . . and are contributing by their personal industry to the realization in history of the divine plan. . . . Therefore while we are warned that it profits a man nothing if he gain the whole world and lose himself, the expectation of a new earth must not weaken but rather stimulate our concern for cultivating this one. For here grows the body of a new human family, a body which even now is able to give some kind of foreshadowing of the new age. . . . (*The Church in the Modern World*, nos. 34 and 39).

The writings of the scientist-mystic, Teilhard de Chardin, probably still best convey the insight adopted by Vatican Council II, that to do the work of the world is to contribute to the fulfillment and completion of Christ's redemption of the universe. The world of matter with which men work is "the divine milieu, charged with creative power . . . the ocean stirred by the Spirit . . . the clay molded and infused with life by the incarnate Word." As we work and love to perfect the world, we are helping to bring about the clear and full revelation of Christ as the center of all things. Then "the presence of Christ, which has been silently accruing in things, will suddenly be revealed—like a flash of light from pole to pole. Breaking through all the barriers with which the veil of matter and the water-tightness of souls have seemingly kept it confined, it will invade the face of the earth . . . (and) the attraction exerted by the Son of Man will lay hold of all the whirling elements in the universe so as to reunite them or subject them to his body. . . . Such will be the consummation of the divine milieu" (*The Divine Milieu*, pp. 7, 133–34).

HEAVEN, OUR DESTINY

Heaven is perfect union with God and one another forever. It is not a place, not "here" or "there," but a state in which, while yet retaining our individuality, we will be caught up into the infinite God. While we can deduce next to nothing about the next life from scripture, as today's scholars point out—it was not part of Christ's mission on earth to describe eternity, but rather to announce the good news of God's kingdom—yet the implications of Christ's teachings, the constant tradition of the Church, and the insights of the saints and mystics can tell us much.

We will love and be loved with an unimaginable, ever-increasing love. We will be fully possessed, continually overwhelmed by God's beauty and goodness, and yet we will go on thirsting for more—even as we are filled to perfect contentment—and yet seek and find still more and more.

God will be able to totally give *himself* to us. No longer shall we have to intuit or reason to him from his works, speculate about him, or catch fleeting, unsatisfying "glimpses." We shall see him as he is, his very self, "face to face" (1 Corinthians 13, 12). Each of us will know God and be loved by him in the most intimate way possible, in a way no one or nothing in creation is or ever will be.

This will be incredible, unimaginable happiness. One cannot now begin to describe it. St. Paul who was caught up into its "outer fringes" was helpless to describe it; he could only quote Isaiah who had also glimpsed it: "What no eye has seen, nor ear heard, nor the heart of man conceived, (that is) what God has prepared for those who love him. . . ." (1 Corinthians 2, 9).

In this heaven-state there will be no sorrow, no pain, no hardship, no struggle or temptation of any kind. We will understand everything we have ever wanted to—the secrets of the universe, the mysteries of our faith. We will have everything we want. And we will be secure in this eternal happiness, knowing that there is no possibility of ever losing it.

He will dwell with them, and they shall be his people, and God himself will be with them; he will wipe away every tear from their eyes, and death shall be no more, neither shall there be mourning nor crying nor pain any more, for the former things have passed away (Revelation 21, 3–4).

An insight coming to the fore today is that none of us will fully arrive until we all arrive. In some mysterious way, we are all bound together, dependent on one another, so that in helping another we are ultimately helping ourselves. This comes from many sources, some of which are the biblical, Teilhardian, process views of life, and the concept of Vatican Council II that we are one people journeying together toward our destiny, based on Paul's revelation that we are all the one interdependent Body of Christ. Strikingly, modern physical sciences and much of psychology, sociology, responsible politics and even economics see humanity as more and more interdependent on our "spaceship earth."

The liturgy calls this "eternal rest" to try to communicate to us its perfect peace, contentment, and security in knowing it will never be lost. For many people today, this security and peace has great meaning, because they have spent most of their lives coping with the almost frantic, often meaningless work and contrived "relaxations" of our modern life. It will be comforting just to know there are no more "obligations," no more threats of loss of job, of savings, and especially no more wrenching loss of loved ones—not to mention the inbuilt anxiety that most people today are not fully conscious of, but is a part of the ground of their anxieties: the threat of nuclear annihilation and total contamination.

Yet, paradoxically, this heaven-state is really living at last: a continual growth in knowledge and love, an endless expanding of our whole being, while in uttermost peace and contentment. Those who have had a brief glimpse of this state, the great mystics (including St. Paul, quoted above), universally tell us in their different ways when they come out of their experiencing that our present life is, by comparison, like a dream, a "shadow life," a tiny foothold on what life really is. Thus they are unwilling to try to describe even their brief glimpses. As St. Paul says in the passage above, we have no concepts to even begin to conceive it. Or as the Zen masters are fond of repeating regarding their tiny glimpses of Nirvana: "He who says does not know, and he who knows does not say."

The bible represents eternal life by images of activity and celebration of feasts, joyous worship and rewards for our service of God. We are to be the servants who because we have been faithful in little things during this life will enjoy not only the Lord's joy but all his goods (Luke 19, 17 and 19). Activity that is pained by anxiety and struggle will cease, and joyous celebration will go on forever. One modern author says, "If this sounds to us monotonous, it is because we need to rid ourselves of a neurotic over-esteem of reproductive work, and of a not yet integrated and personalized use of our free time" (Schoonenberg, *God's World in the Making,* Duquesne, 1964).

We will be ceaselessly growing in love and happiness, unendingly fulfilling our every power in the most intense activity imaginable. Even now we know how our consciousness can be expanded. Then we will have our full personality, alive to the depths of our being, fully ourselves, and have perfect love and friendship with others. We will be beyond time and space, able to transcend the whole universe in an instant, be wherever we want and do whatever we want. We will be glorified like the resurrected Christ who is "the first-fruits of those who have fallen asleep" (1 Corinthians 15, 20).

In our heavenly state we will also know all those we have known and loved in this world, the saints and all the great people of history—in fact we will be strangers to no one, and we will delight in one another's perfections and in our mutual love. There will be no distracted turning away from God to others, or vice versa—the problem that so often disturbs us now—but rather we will then clearly see God in them, acting through them, giving himself and revealing himself through them. Everything will then be sacred, for God will be "all in all."

There will be degrees of love and happiness in heaven: the more we have loved in this life, the more of God's grace-presence we have with us now, the greater will be our love and happiness forever. The great 16th century mystic, Teresa of Avila, said that she would remain on earth till the end of the world, suffering terribly, if she would love God just a bit more in heaven.

Christ's teaching assures us that heaven goes on forever (Cf. Matthew 25, 46; 1 Corinthians 15, 52). This, of course, we cannot imagine. But we can try to appreciate its astounding privilege: in return for a lifetime of faithfulness on earth, God might have given us a thousand years of happiness in heaven, and this would be a wonderful reward; or he might have given us ten thousand, a million or a billion years of happiness. But he does infinitely more, so great is his love: he gives us eternity, forever and ever and ever, with himself.

The only thing that can keep us from heaven is deliberately turning away from God. If we fully reject God by choosing a condition of mortal sin and die hardened in our sin, we have cut ourselves off from him, from love, from happiness, and have isolated ourselves forever in hell. However remote this possibility, it should make us better appreciate how much we need God's love, should make us work now with all our heart and strength to love him and our fellow human beings.

Above all, we should think often of being with God and Christ and one another in heaven, and have a great longing for this. The early Christians lived in constant expectation of Christ's reappearance, and were spurred to astounding deeds of love and sacrifice. This present life is but a brief bridge between nothingness and eternity; when the crossing becomes too difficult, we should think of our real destiny on the other side. We should not hesitate to cry out with St.

Paul, "Here indeed we groan and long to put on our heavenly dwelling" (2 Corinthians 5, 2). Or with John as he finished the last book of scripture, "Amen—Come, Lord Jesus!"

DAILY LIVING: THE DIFFERENCE IN BEING A CHRISTIAN

A special view of human history is what makes a Christian different. He believes that it has an author and a plot and a meaningful end. He believes that all things will one day be perfected in Christ. The Christian works and loves with confidence that nothing ultimately is wasted, that he is carrying out God's plan, that the world can and will be perfected. He can fail, hurt his fellow man, neglect to alleviate some of the pain of our existence, but he knows that the victory is on its way. He is convinced of what Christ said: ". . . He who hears my word and believes him who sent me, *has* eternal life . . . (and) has passed from death to life" (John 5, 24).

The Christian knows that his life is often no better than that of the unbeliever (and sometimes it is worse), that he is weak, a sinner, often confused, and even capable of monstrous misdeeds. He knows that only some Christians grasp and live their life with Christ at all fully. But he believes that somehow God uses his poor efforts, takes them and transfigures them into love that is changing the world. He believes that "he who has begun his work in you will complete it" (Philippians 1, 6). This is because he knows that God has come among men in Jesus Christ, that he himself is now joined to Christ, and that this gives even his poorest efforts a new power.

By his life the Christian tries to radiate Christ's love to the world. He tries to show, especially in the union with his fellow Christians that is the Church, the love that animates them all. He knows that he needs the Church—its Word and its sacraments, particularly the eucharist—as his daily strength. He tries not to expect visible results from his acts of love, and realizes that he must often live in a "dark night" where faith seems to be dead and God appears to have vanished.

He knows that he must suffer and die with Christ in order to rise with him—that he also has to undergo much mortification and suffering to make up for his sins and to open himself perfectly to the love God has in store for him. He knows that love must be more than a humanitarian service to one's fellows, that it must also express itself in humbly asking God's help, crying out in worship, in pure, human weakness, asking to know, to be able to do God's will—and not merely his own.

Committed Christians occasionally catch a glimpse of God, even in this age when God is often considered to have disappeared. They look at their fellow human beings and sometimes, perhaps only for an instant, see in them something divine. They look at nature, and on occasion it may cry out to them that there is a Creator. They occasionally have an insight, realize in retrospect how providence has watched over them, catch a bit of meaning behind it all—and perhaps they once may have personally experienced the great, shattering peace and joy that could only be God.

They hold the conviction, sometimes only mutely and obscurely, but with deep faith, "that neither death, nor life, nor angels, nor principalities, nor things present, nor things to come, nor powers, nor height nor depth, nor anything else in all creation, will be able to separate us from the love of God in Christ Jesus our Lord" (Romans 8, 38–39).

SOME SUGGESTIONS FOR ...

DISCUSSION

Why should the Christian, however much he may naturally fear it, and however full life may be here and now, nevertheless have an attitude of expectation toward death?

Can you understand something of what heaven must be like?

What do you think sums up the way a Christian should live?

FURTHER READING

** *What Are They Saying About Death and Christian Hope?* Hellwig (Paulist Press, 1978)—Brief and clearly-written, this book by one of today's best theologians updates us on death and what will and what may follow.

* *Good Grief,* Westberg (Fortress Press, 1971)—A helpful 51-page booklet

for those grieving for a loved one. Written by a Lutheran minister, whose ministry has been with the sick and dying, it has been of help to thousands.

* *The Hospice Movement: A Better Way of Caring for the Dying,* Stoddard (Vintage Books, 1978)—In this growing movement many are finding their vocation of caring for the terminally ill; this book tells how the sick need a caring community and how the community needs the dying to see things in an eternal perspective.

* *Life After Life,* Moody (Bantam Books, 1975) and *Life at Death,* Ring (Coward, McCann & Geoghegan, 1980)—These books tell of those who have been "brought back" from medical death, and the peace and well-being almost all experienced; Dr. Moody's book lacks verifiable data, but psychologist Ring provides some in his carefully-done, thought-provoking book.

* *The Everlasting Now,* Maloney (Ave Maria Press, 1980)—A series of meditative writings on the mystery of death and afterward, and how they can help us in our daily choices.

* *Afterlife: The Other Side of Dying,* Kelsey (Paulist Press, 1978)—In this book the widely-read Episcopal psychologist contrasts the beauty, joy, and unending growth of Christianity's beliefs about the afterlife with modern materialistic and Eastern views; he gives us a solidly-based, scholarly, and spiritually profound view of what awaits us all.

FURTHER VIEWING/LISTENING

This One for Dad (Paulist Productions)—An incisive story of how a young man turns off all his emotions to escape the reality of his father's death, but slowly comes to realize that he must face his grief and his world.

Ultimate Questions (Teleketics, Franciscan Communications)—A fine series of six filmstrips on life's ultimate questions. Each averages twelve minutes.

A FINAL REFLECTION

The story of Christ among us is now concluded. If you have been using this book regularly, during the past weeks you have been drawing closer to God, to Christ. In the gospels those who drew close to Christ were always changed—deeply changed.

Peter was an ordinary, simple fisherman—and he became the first leader of God's Church on earth. Mary Magdalene was a prostitute known far and wide—and she became a great saint. Judas was an ordinary businessman, and became the prototype of all traitors.

If you have been following this story faithfully, you too are changed. You have had an open mind and heart, and have been willing to risk this encounter with God. Whether you now classify yourself as a believer, an unbeliever, or one wavering between, you can be sure that you have been profoundly changed for the better—and the world has also, because of you.

May you be blessed for your generous effort!

Index

A

Abortion, morality of, 281–282
Abraham (or Abram), God's covenant with, 45–47; outstanding faith of, 45
Absolution, God's forgiveness during reconciliation, 322–323
Acts of the Apostles, 173
Adam and Eve, 36–38
Adultery, morality of, 350–351
Advent, season of, 62
Afterlife, see "immortality"
"Agape," or eucharist, 232
All Souls Day, November 2, 449
Angels, as traditionally conceived, 27; relevance of today, 27
Annulment, of marriage, 342–343
Anointing of the sick, as part of last rites, 444; sacrament of, 329–332
Anti-Semitism, see "Jews"
Apocrypha, or deutero-canonical books, 166–168
Apostles, appointed leaders of Christ's Church, 75, 136–138; original twelve, 121–124, 136–137
Apostles Creed, ancient Christian profession of faith, 157
Ascension Thursday, 116
Ash Wednesday, 25
Assumption of Mary, 392–393
Atheists, dialogue with, 422
Authority, and primacy of one's conscience, 155; of apostles in Church, 137–138; of bishops, 150; of pope in Church, 143–144, 150; of service within Christ's Church, 147; our attitude toward, 154–156

B

Baptism, infants, 197–198; renewal of baptismal conversion, 208, 212; and Rite of Christian Initiation of Adults (RCIA), 204–207; sacrament of, 194–202; the majority who are not baptized, 209–212
Belief, 11; doubts inevitable, 12; need to grow and deepen, 212
Benediction, service of, 253
Bible, aids for study of, 176–177; as interpreted by tradition, 168–171; and Vatican Council II, 158; basis of Church's teachings, 158–159; biblical story of creation, 22–23; canon of, 164; daily use of, 177; great force for Christian unity, 165; historical reliability of basic story, 20–21, 160–162; inspired record, 159–160; meditative reading of, 175–176; New Testament, 21; Old Testament, 21; origin and development of, 162–164; outline of, 171–174; particular type of book, 19–21; relation to sacraments, 191; relation to science, 22; use by Catholic Church, 163–165; use in liturgy, 174–175; various translations, 165–166; "Word" of God, 159; work of men, 159
Birth control, morality of, 353–356
Bishops, at service of Christian community, 147; college of, 140–143, 145; leaders of local

churches, 141–142, 380; ordinary ministers of confirmation, 293; responsibility of toward the whole Church, 142–143; synod of, 146; within the Church and the diocese, 142, 380–384

Blessed Trinity, 13–14; indwelling presence, 98; and respect for our bodies, 98–99; in the liturgy, 97–98; mystery of, 94–97; our relationship to, 96–97

Body, Christ's among us in glory, 112–113; dignity of, 98–99; resurrection of our bodies, 449

"Born again" Christians, 210–212

Brotherhood of all humanity, 25–26

Brothers, men religious, 379

Business dealings, Christian attitude toward, 436

C

Canon, of the Mass, or eucharistic prayer, 226–227

"Canonization," of saints, 390

Capital punishment, morality of, 280

Cardinals, 358–359

Catechumenate, in RCIA, 205–206

Catholic, whether or not to become, 406–408

Catholic or universal, Church of Christ, 126–128

Catholicity, of Christ's Church, 127–129, 403; still an ideal, 129

Celibacy, of Latin rite priests, 374–375

Charisms, gifts of service for all, 148–149; use by people of particular gifts, 293

Charity, see "love," virtue of

Chastity, vow of, 378

Children, parents primary educators of, 405–406, 435; parents' responsibilities toward, 434–435

Christ, see "Jesus Christ"

"Christening," 194; also see "baptism"

Christian life, and that of unbeliever, 259; as lived in marriage, 357–360; as lived in single life, 386; living daily of, 433–441

Christians, and scandal of poor, 427–428; concern with world's problems, 283–284; dignity of, 134; divisions among, 413–424; as special manifestation of Christ among us, 431; involvement in political and social affairs, 284–286; responsibility and privilege to bring about new universe, 451–452; the difference in being a Christian, 456–457

Christmas Day, 71; liturgy of the Christmas season, 245–246

Church, and the world today, 278–288, 400–428; and the work for world peace, 286–288; as Christ among us, 129–130; catholicity or universality of, 127–129; catholicity, missionary aspect, 127–129; changes within always necessary, 422–423; Christ's body, 131–133; community of people with different gifts of service, 147–149, 404; criteria for joining, 406–408; divineness and holiness of, 400–405; divisions among Christians, 413–424; Eastern Orthodox Churches, history of and relation to Roman Catholicism, 414–416; and ecumenical movement, 419–422; and the eucharist, 240; as God's gifted people, 367–368; humanness of, need of continual reformation and renewal, 408–413; not exclusive club, 403; of the Old Testament, 49; organization of early Christian Church, 141–142; persecutions of, 401–402; purpose is to serve God and world, 149; purpose of laws within, 432–433; scriptural descriptions of 130–131; as sign of hope, 404; some teachings more important than others, 153–154; stabilizing influence of, 411–412; the compassionate Church, 427–428; unfolding mystery of, 422; unity of, 125–127

Circumcision, sign of the covenant, 46

Collegiality, or co-responsibility of bishops and pope, 145–146

Communion, see "Holy Communion"

Communion of the Saints, 389

Community life, of Religious, 378–380

"Confession," see "reconciliation"

Confirmation, 202; coming of Holy Spirit, 290–291; sign or ceremony of, 291–295

Conscience, 39; and the practice of birth control, 355–356; Church helps in forming, 433; daily examination of, 321–322; in judging sinfulness of our actions, 303; ultimate authority of, 155, 406

Conscientious objection, 288

Consecration, center of eucharistic prayer, 226–227

Contraception, see "birth control"

Conversion, before baptism, 202–203; our need for continual conversion, 212, 314; preached by Christ, 74

Councils, ecumenical, 145–146; also see Vatican Council II

Covenant, meal of the New Testament, the Mass, 219–220; new and unending through Christ, 106–108; with Abraham, 45–46; with Israel, 49

Creation, biblical story of, 22–23; continuing today, 26; people as co-creators with God, 26

Crucifix, personal meaning of, 120; reminder of Christ's death, 117

Cursillo, 439

D

Deacons, sharers of bishops' work, 143; within the Church today, 372–373

Dead Sea Scrolls, 61, 160–161

Death, condition of our existence after, 443; Christian attitude toward, 443–445; meeting with Christ at, 444; new liturgy for dead, 448

Despair, rejection of hope, 264–265

Devils, as traditionally conceived, 27; possession by, 27

Diocese, local church and its bishop, 142, 380–384; roles of all the people within, 381–382

Discrimination, see "prejudice"

Divine Office, 184, 247–248

Divorce, and Christian marriage, 340–342

Doctrine, development of in Church, 151–152; limitations of, 403–404, 427

Dogmas, infallible teachings, 151–152

Doubt, inevitability of, 12, 262–263, 407, 441

Drinking, abusive excesses of, 99, 438

Drugs, abuse of, 99, 438

E

Easter, celebrated each Sunday, 116; "duty" of a Catholic, 250; liturgy of the Easter season, 246; Sunday, 77; vigil service, 52, 116, 207–208

Eastern religions (Buddhism, etc.), 423

Ecumenical councils, historical

development of, 145–146; teaching and guiding Church, 145–146

Ecumenism, movement for Christian unity, 127, 419–422

Education, religious, 405–406

Epistles, of New Testament, 173–174

Essenes, community of Qumran, 61–62

Eucharist, Christ among us in eucharist, 239–240; Christ among us under bread and wine, 219–220, 248–249; as food, 251; high point of priest's work, 372–373; reserved in tabernacle, 252; also see "Mass"

Eucharistic prayer, or canon of Mass, 226–227

Evolution, and human soul, 24; compatible with biblical account of creation, 22

Examination of conscience, 321–322

Exodus, 48

Exorcism, 27

F

Faith, "crisis of," 263; difficulties regarding Church, 407–408; "gift of," 259; of Old Testament people, 64; search for, 260–262; virtue of, 256–264; way to faith, 259–262

Family, what a Christian family should be, 433–435; of the Church, 367–388

Fasting, and abstinence as way of penance, 324; by Christ, 73; by Moses, 50; before Holy Communion, 249

Father, God's revelation of himself as, 13, 82–83

First Friday, meaning of, 117

"Forty Hours Devotion," 253

Friday, act of penance on each, 112

Fulfillment, purpose of life, 5; forever, 443–457

G

Genesis, and story of creation, 22–23; first book of the bible, 21; and covenant, 45–46; and original sin, 35–36

Genetic research, morality of, 280–281

Genuflection, act of adoration, 252

Gnostics, 161

God, always answers prayers, 16; demonstration of from reason, 7–8; and plan for our life, 6; and sufferings of innocent people, 14; believers fabricating "comfortable God," 12; greatest obstacle to belief in, 10–11; doubts about inevitable, 12; experience of, 7; grace as God's loving presence, 33–34; hiddenness of today, 9–10; how people arrive at, 7–8; inability to express belief in, 8; Jesus as revelation of God as Father, 13; Judaeo-Christian belief in revelation of, 13; knowledge of from universe, 12; knowledge of through love, 7–8; knowledge of through openness to truth, 8; need of faith to know, 8; Our Father, 82–83; personal, unique love for each of us, 13; "powerlessness" of God in this world, 110; prayer as our necessary contact with, 15–17; "process" view of, 14; recognizing his action today, 53; rejection of by young, 11; respector of our freedom, 14; search for faith in God, 260–262; suffering and rejoicing with us, 14; transcendence, mysteriousness of, 13–14; what is necessary to know, 8–12; why some people are unable to find, 10–11; worship of, natural and necessary, 28–30

Godparents, or sponsors at baptism, 199–200

Good Friday, liturgy of, 115–116

Gospels, brief description of each, 172–173; "Good News" about Christ, 68–69, 73

Grace, a living presence loving us, 33–34, 197; actual, 41–42; communicated through sacraments, 185–190; sanctifying, 33–34; transformation of ourselves by, 34–35

Guilt, people's sense of, 300

H

"Hail Mary," scriptural origin of, 69; words of, 92

Happiness, unending, 5–6, 453

Heaven, our destiny, what it is, 452–456

Hell, discussion of, 305–307

Heresy, nature of, 414

Hierarchy, see "bishops," "papacy"

History, special Christian view of, 456

Holy Communion, in the Mass, 228–229; uniting us with one another, 229; under two species, 250

Holy Days in the United States, 243

Holy Eucharist, see "eucharist" and "Mass"

Holy Orders, sacrament of, 371–372

Holy Spirit, and Jesus Christ, 93–95; being open to, 295–296; community of, 124–125; forms God's new people, 122–123; fuller coming of in confirmation, 289–291; giving power to bear witness, 289–292; Pope John XXIII and our age of, 295; successor of Jesus among us, 93–95, 114, 122

Holy Thursday, liturgy of, 115

Holy Saturday, night liturgy of, 116

"Holy Viaticum," or Holy Communion to dying, 444

Holy water, reminder of baptism, 208

Holy week, 115–116, 246

Home life, of a Christian, 433–435

Homosexuality, morality of, 351–352

Honesty, necessary for members of Christ, 134

Hope, today's particular need, 265; virtue of a confident yearning, 264–265

Hunger, in the world, 282–283

I

Illness, Christian attitude toward, 328–334

Immaculate Conception of Mary, 392

Immortality, Christ's teaching on, 25; mankind's belief in, 25; also see "heaven"

Incarnation, 91; and development of our earth, 99–100; in the liturgy, 98

Indulgences, 308

Infallibility, concerns Christ's revelation, 149; expressed by bishops as a group, 150; expressed by people's belief, 150; expressed by pope, 150–151; gift of in Christ's Church, 149–151; limitations of, 151; naturalness of, 154–155

Intercommunion, between Christians, 237–239

Interfaith marriages, 65, 360–363

Islam, 423–424

Israel, uniqueness of, 49–50

Israelites, God's chosen people, 44–62

J

Jacob (or Israel), covenant renewed with, 46–47

Jesus Christ, and purpose of life, 5–6; arriving at the historical Christ,

162; baptism of, 72; Church as
Christ's body, 131–132; birth of,
71; coming of, 67ff; death and
resurrection, 77–78, 102–105;
death and resurrection renewal at
Mass, 227–228; "descent into
hell," 105; divine Son, 85–93;
gradual realization of his divinity,
86–88; humanness of, 83–85;
imitation of his love in our lives,
78–79; King of the Universe, 113;
meeting with at death, 444; more
fully with us now than 2000
years ago, 114; new and unending
covenant through Christ,
106–108; New Testament record
of, 68–69; our mediator and
priest, 106; our Savior, 102–105;
overcoming sin for us, 103–105;
perfect sacrifice by, 105–106;
preaching of the kingdom, 73–75;
presentation of, February 2, 71;
real leader of the Church,
144–145; resurrection of, great
proof of his divinity, 88–90; the
"sacrament" of God, 186; Sacred
Heart of, 117; suffering for us,
108–111; the "new Adam," 91;
the "New Israel," 73; the one
who is totally for others, 110; two
natures of, 95; ultimate revelation
of God, 14; wonder-worker, 73,
76, 86

Jews, and anti-semitism, 64–66; and
death of Jesus, 111–112; God's
people, 44ff; dialogue with, 65

John the Baptist, 72

Judaeo-Christian revelation of God,
12–13

Judgement, at end of the world,
449–450

K

Kingdom of God, as announced by
Christ, 73–74

L

"Last rites," 444

Laws, necessity of within Church,
432–433; temptation to legalism,
432–433

Lay people, prophetic gifts of, 292,
368

Leisure time, Christian use of, 437

Lent, fasting by Christ, 72–73;
preparation for Easter, 246

Life, biblical account of human origin,
22–23; God's plan for, 5;
possibility of other rational life in
universe, 28; purpose of, 5;
sacredness of, 279–282

Life after death, see "immortality"
and "heaven"

Liturgical year, reliving great events
of Christ's life, 78, 244–248

Liturgy, Constitution on the Sacred
Liturgy, 234–235; of the Mass,
234–236; sacred signs or
ceremonies, 179–183

Lord's Prayer, expresses our attitude
toward God, 13

"Lord's Supper," the eucharist, 241

Love, central point of Christ's
teaching, 265–266; for God, 267;
for neighbor, 267–268; grace as
God's love transforming us, 35;
great rule of morality, 40;
greatest gift within Church, 149;
Jesus' teaching about, 78–79; of
enemies, 268; of God for us, 266;
of other Christians and all
people, 133–134; reason for
everything that exists, 26; virtue
of, 265–269

M

Magi, first gentiles to worship Christ,
71

Man, a unified being, 24; and other
rational creatures in universe, 28;

brotherhood of all humanity,
25–26; "co-creators" with God,
26, 451; composed of body and
soul, 23–24; peak of creation, 22;
personal responsibility for eternal
destiny, 25; sinfulness of from
origin, 36–38; transformation by
God's grace, 33–35
Marriage, Christian concept of,
337–343; before marriage,
343–347; creative, responsive
married love, 349–357; history of
in God's plan, 336–337; how to
get married, 347–348; liturgy of,
363–364; living a Christian
marriage day by day, 357–360
Mary, "annunciation" to, 69;
assumption of, 392–393;
immaculate conception,
celebrated on December 8, 92;
model Christian, 394–396;
"mother of God," 92; mother of
Jesus Christ, 69–70; proper honor
paid to, 396; role of in Church,
393–396; sinlessness of, 392;
virginity of, 69–70, 392
Mass, centered on Christ, 78, 81; and
Christian unity, 237–239; as
Christian meal, 224; as covenant
meal, 219–220, 230–231; as
gathering of Christians, 216–219;
history of, 232–235; meaning of,
216–230; order of Mass, 225–230;
meaning of, 216–230; order of
Mass, 225–230; as renewal of
Christ's sacrifice, 221–223;
weekly attendance at, 230, 243;
also see "eucharist"
Masturbation, morality of, 352–353
Materiality, our material aspect,
23–24
Messiah, Jesus Christ as Messiah,
75–78; messianic age, 59–62;
prophecies about, 59–61
Miracles, of Jesus, 73, 76, 86

Missionary, aspect of Christ's Church,
128–129
Mixed religion marriage, see
"interfaith marriage"
Monogenism, 23
"Monsignor," honorary title of priest,
372
Morality, forming mature Christian
moral sense, 431–433; general
principles for daily moral living,
433–441
Moses, and experience of God, 13;
God's covenant with, 49; Israelite
leader, 47–50; and story of
creation, 22
"Mother of God," see "Mary"
Myth, 20

N

Neighbor, Christ's great example
concerning love of, 267–268
New Testament, 21; composition of,
67–68; development of, 162–163;
interpretation of, 68; outline of,
172–174; record of early Church's
faith, 67–68
November, particular remembrance of
dead, 449
Novenas, origin of, 154
Nuns, or "sisters," 379
Nuptial Mass, 348, 363–364

O

Obedience, freely given to Church's
authority, 156; not blind, 156;
vow of, 378
Offertory of the Mass, 226
Old Testament, 21, 62; Abraham, first
of the patriarchs, 45; outline of,
171–172; priests, kings and
prophets, 56–63; story of creation
in, 22–23

On the Development of Peoples, encyclical of Pope Paul VI, 284–285

Original sin, 37–38; symbolic story of, 35–36

Orthodox Churches, of the East, 238, 414–416

P

Pain, meaning of, see "suffering"

Palm Sunday, 115

Papacy, the, 139, 143–147; conflict with Eastern Orthodox, 414–416

Parents, place of in Christian home, 434–435; primary educators of children, 405–406, 435

Parishes, in ecumenical service, 427; local centers of Christian community, 382–384

Parousia, Christ's second coming, 449–450

Paschal candle, representing risen Christ, 116

Passover, or Pasch, 48

Paul, Saint, apostle of the gentiles, 127–128, 136; epistles of, 174

"Pauline Privilege," 342

Peace, Christian need to work for, 286–288, 425–426, 437; also see "war"

Penance, "doing penance" for our sins, 325–326, 440; either public or private, 317–318; public penitential services, 323; also see "reconciliation"

Pentateuch, first five books of Old Testament, 171

Pentecost, Christian community begins to spread, 122; in the liturgy, 154, 246

People of God, 122–123

Peter, Saint, 136; leader of the early Christian Church, 138–140; leader of the apostles, 138

Pharisees, 61

Poor, the most special concern of the Church, 279, 401, 428

Pope, at service of all, 147–148; authority of, in early Church, 143–144; Peter's successor, 139, 143–144

Pope John XXIII, and modern social challenges, 288; and our age of the Holy Spirit, 295

Pope John Paul II, 402; and anti-semitism, 65; and social justice, 285–287, 296

Pope Paul VI, and modern social challenges, 284–285

Poverty, vow of, 378

Prayer, experiencing the living God in, 16; for others, 271; God always answers, 16; in daily Christian life, 439; of a Christian, 270; our contact with God, 15–17; power of, 270–271; reason for, 16; suggestions about how to pray, 16–17, 272–274; talking with God, 15; way of learning how to love, 79; worship as prayer, 28–30

Prejudice, or discrimination; rejection of Christian love, 134; totally unchristian, 425, 438–439

Pre-marital intercourse, 344–347

Pride, root of all sin, 300

Priesthood, history of, 369–371

"Priesthood of the laity," 368; at confirmation, 292; at Mass, 241; with baptism, 198

Priests, different types of, 375–376; at the service of humanity, 369–377; offerers of sacrifice, 221; ordination by Holy Orders, 371–372; in Old Testament, 57–58, 369; sharers in bishop's work, 141

Profession of faith, upon conversion, 201, 203

Prophets, God's spokesmen, 58–60; within Church today, 292

Protestant Churches, and relation to Roman Catholicism, 416–424

Psalms, 62

Purgatory, belief in throughout Christian history, 446–447

Purgation, experience of encountering God after death, 445; or purgatory-state, 445–447; our ability to help those in this state, 448

Q

Qumran, community of Essenes, 61–62, 160–161

R

Race relations, today's test of being a Christian, 134, 425; rage of ghetto people, 283; also see "prejudice"

Reconciliation, sacrament of, explained, 316–324; continuing need to seek reconciliation, 440; history of, 317–318; and penance, 325–326; and the place of sorrow, 319–321; preparing for confession, 325; the rite of reconciliation, 321–325

Reformation, Protestant, 416–419

Religious, priests, nuns and brothers living in community, 378–380

"Remnant," of Israel, 59, 63

Requiem Mass, for the dead, 448–449

Resurrection, and our resurrection, 113, 449–450; as proof of Christ's divinity, 88–90; key truth of Christian faith, 112–114; Mass of for dead, 448; of Jesus Christ, 88–90

Retreats, in a Christian's life, 439

Revelation, 12–13; continuing today, 170; in bible, 19, 159–160; in tradition, 168–171; or Apocalypse of bible, 174

"Rhythm," method of family planning, 353

Rite of Christian Initiation of Adults (RCIA), 204–207; stages of, 205–207

Rome, bishop successor of Peter, 139–140; leadership of Church by, 139, 143–144

Rosary, Catholic devotion, 78, 117, 396

S

Sacramentals, 183–185

Sacraments, seven; meaning and purpose of, 185–190; relation to the bible, 191

Sacrifice, by the Israelites, 56–58; Mass as perfect sacrifice, 221–223; meaning of, 57–58

Saints, "canonization" of, 390; communion of, 389; devotion to today, 391; in our day, 397–398; name of at baptism, 200; our models and intercessors, 389–392; in the liturgy, 247

Salvation, of persons outside Christian Church, 209–212

Sanctifying grace, see "grace"

Savior, see "Jesus Christ"

Schools, Catholic, discussion of, 405–406

Scripture, see "bible"

Septuagint, Greek translation of Hebrew scriptures, 162–163, 167

Sex, and respect for body, 134, 138; premarital and Christian morality, 344–347; use of in true love, 268, 438; within marriage, 349–351

Sick, anointing of 329–332, 444

Sickness, 328–334; Christ's power over, 329; our attitude toward, 333–334

Sign of the Cross, 97, 117, 184

"Signs," of the liturgy, 29, 179–189; sacraments as signs, 185–189

Sin, Christ's death shows us seriousness of, 117–118; discussion of in our lives, 299–301; forgiveness of by Christ through the Church, 316–319; forgiveness of by God, 304, 307–309; God's help in avoiding, 40–41; in humanity from its origin, 34–39; judging seriousness of, 301–305; making up for, 307–309; mortal, 301–302; overcoming of by Jesus Christ, 103–104; overcoming sin, suggestions for, 309–311; serious sins against love, 40; story of "original sin," 35–36; venial, 302–303; why people are sinful, 36–38

Sinai, Mt., covenant at, 49

Single life, vocation to, 386

Social justice, 282–288

Social life, of a Christian, 437–439

"Son of Man," messianic figure, 60, 76

Soul, and evolutionary process, 24; Christ's teaching on immortality of, 25; individuality and uniqueness of, 24–25; the human spirit, 23–24; reality of, 24

Spiritual direction, 272

Sponsor, at confirmation, 295; or godparent at baptism, 199

Stations of the Cross, Catholic devotion, 116–117

Students, attitude of Christian, 437

Suffering, cause of, 118–119; meaning and value of, 119; why God allows us to suffer, 117–119

"Suffering Servant," messianic figure, 60–61

Sunday worship, reason for, 116

Supernatural life, God's grace-presence, 34

Synod of bishops, 146

T

Tabernacle, eucharistic presence of Christ in, 252

Teilhard de Chardin, and the origin of human spirit, 24; and our completion of the universe, 452; and the priesthood, 377

Temperance, in alcohol, drugs, smoking, sex, 98–99; of one united to Christ, 134

Temptation, 309–310

Ten Commandments, 49

Theologians, role of, 146–147

Tradition, continuing today, 171; of Apostles, 168–169; sources of, 169–170

Trinity, see "Blessed Trinity"

Trust, or hope in God, 264–265

Truth, openness to necessary for knowledge of God, 8

U

Unbelievers, faith of, 259; need of Christian cooperation with, 422

Unity, of Christ's Church, 125–127

Universe, Jesus Christ, king of, 113; new universe toward which we work, 451–452; ourselves as "co-creators" of, 26, 451–452

V

Vatican Council II, 21st ecumenical council, 146

Vestments, at Mass, 235–236

Vigil lights, 253

Vocation, to priesthood or religious life, 367–380; to single life, 386

Voting, Christian duty, 437

Vows, of Religious, 375, 378–379

W

War, Christians taking part in, 287; morality of conscientious objection, 288; question of "just war" today, 287, 426–427; unchristian and immoral means of, 287, 427; also see "peace"

Wealth, and morality, 283–284

Women, biblical emphasis on dignity of, 22–23; role of in Church today, 384–387; and priesthood, 385–386

Word, and sacrament, 191, bible as "Word of God," 159; Christ as Word of God, 96

Work, burdensome because of sin, 37; Christian attitude toward, 436–437; natural and necessary, 37

World, Christian presence in, 278–279; end or completion of, 449–450; new world toward which we work, 451–452

Worship, Mass as perfect worship, 216; natural and necessary, 28–30; in the liturgy, 179–183

Y

Yahweh, Israel's God, 44–52